FREE
THINKING

Tom Bergin is an investigative financial journalist for Reuters. His work has prompted parliamentary inquiries and won numerous awards in Britain, the United States and Asia, including a Gerald Loeb Award for Distinguished Business Journalism and the Orwell Prize for Journalism. In 2013 he was named Business Journalist of the Year at the British Press Awards. His previous book, *Spills & Spin: The Inside Story of BP*, was named a *Sunday Times* Politics Book of the Year in 2011.

Before entering journalism twenty years ago, Tom worked in asset management and as an energy broker. He grew up in Ireland and lives in London.

Praise for *Free Lunch Thinking*

'An essential read if you want to know how economics
has erred – and how it can do better.'
Gabriel Zucman, author of *The Hidden Wealth of Nations*

'I couldn't put it down. A thorough and nuanced examination of
the evolution of supply side economics and the debates we had
around how to put the theory into practice. I loved it.'
Arthur Laffer, creator of the Laffer Curve

FREE LUNCH THINKING

8 ECONOMIC MYTHS
AND WHY POLITICIANS
FALL FOR THEM

TOM BERGIN

PENGUIN BOOKS

To my father, who brought me up to appreciate
the value of knowledge.

PENGUIN BOOKS

UK | USA | Canada | Ireland | Australia
India | New Zealand | South Africa

Penguin Books is part of the Penguin Random House group of companies
whose addresses can be found at global.penguinrandomhouse.com

Penguin
Random House
UK

First published in the United Kingdom by Random House Business in 2021
This edition published by Penguin Books in 2022

001

Copyright © Tom Bergin, 2021

The moral right of the author has been asserted

Typeset in 10.12/13.65 pt Minion
by Integra Software Services Pvt. Ltd, Pondicherry

Printed and bound in Great Britain by Clays Ltd, Elcograf S.p.A.

The authorised representative in the EEA is Penguin Random House
Ireland, Morrison Chambers, 32 Nassau Street, Dublin D02 YH68

A CIP catalogue record for this book is available from the British Library

ISBN: 978–1–847–94275–3

www.greenpenguin.co.uk

Contents

INTRODUCTION

The ideas of economists and political philosophers, both when they are right and when they are wrong, are more powerful than is commonly understood. Indeed, the world is ruled by little else. Practical men, who believe themselves to be quite exempt from any intellectual influences, are usually slaves of some defunct economist.

John Maynard Keynes, *The General Theory of Employment, Interest and Money*

In 1661, with the French state's finances in disarray due to mismanagement and the cost of fighting wars, Louis XIV appointed Jean-Baptiste Colbert his foremost finance official, later giving him the title of *contrôleur général des finances* or finance minister. The new minister duly set about reform: he reduced waste and graft and removed many of the tax exemptions that nobles enjoyed. At the same time, he also eased some unfair burdens on the poor. Ultimately, his skilful balancing of fiscal demands allowed him to improve the exchequer's position considerably without alienating the population and threatening the stability of the regime. In explaining his success, he noted that 'the art of taxation consists in so plucking the goose as to obtain the largest possible quantity of feathers with the smallest possible amount of hissing.'[1]

Finance ministers today still cite Colbert's comment. But only to lighten a dry fiscal speech or dull passage in their memoirs. These days, balancing the books without provoking insurrection (or its twenty-first-century equivalent, electoral failure) is only part of the art of taxation, so far as policymakers and their advisers are concerned. Taxation is no longer seen as a zero-sum game of deftly spreading the burden. Skilful taxation now involves combining the raising of revenue with other policy objectives, such as the stimulation of wealth creation or nudging citizens into behaving in a more productive or socially responsible way.

And it's not seen as an art. Taxation today is viewed as a science, underpinned by mathematical models with accurate predictive powers. If a finance minister wants to encourage people to work harder, there is a model to tell him or her how to tailor the income tax rate. If the aim is to encourage businesses to invest and hire more, there's a model that tells the minister how to calibrate corporate taxes. And if a government wants to reduce the consumption of, say, sugary drinks, there's even a model to tell them how much tax should be levied on a can of cola to achieve a given reduction.

The engine powering this mindshift is Economics. It barely existed as a field of serious knowledge in Colbert's time. But in the centuries since, it has evolved from a combination of folk wisdom and intuition into a highly formalised body of study, built on complex mathematics and the exploration of vast data sets. And it's not just the art of taxation that it has revolutionised. How we decide employment protection rules or safety standards on consumer products; how we choose what services governments should provide: how we determine the way different countries interact commercially; all have been transformed by economics. Almost every area of policy that impacts our material welfare is now set with reference to models honed in the great universities of Harvard, Cambridge or

Chicago. These models are all elements of a social science dedicated to showing us how to allocate our limited resources so as to maximise our utility or, in layman's terms, to get the most bang for our bucks.

There is a saying made famous by the Nobel memorial prize-winning economist Milton Friedman that 'There's no such thing as a free lunch' – that we can't magic wealth out of nothing (say, by printing money) or shift costs into the ether. Friedman's view was that if we legislate to reduce a burden on some citizens, or to increase the advantages they may enjoy, there will be repercussions some-where down the line, that will involve a cost for others and might even ultimately mean the measure is counterproductive. So even if a meal is priced at zero, someone, somewhere is paying for it. Modern economics may disparage the concept of free lunches, yet, today, one often gets a sense from key economists and policy-makers that a free lunch isn't that far away. Economics aims to show how we can generate growth by identifying more efficient ways of organising society, thereby making us richer and, hopefully, happier, with the least amount of sacrifice on our part. Such a utopia is achievable, economists believe, because they understand the mechanisms that drive everything from business investment and production decisions to consumer purchase choices, to individual attitudes to saving.

The idea that social scientists can show governments how to boost economies at little or no cost is relatively new. For centuries public finance was something of a one-sided game: when rulers needed to raise taxes to meet such necessary expenses as fighting a war or paying officials, they simply extracted what they needed from the people they ruled and assumed their predations had little or no impact on overall national income.

But, in the eighteenth century, that started to change. A key early figure leading this slow revolution was Robert Walpole, Britain's Chancellor of the Exchequer and first prime minister[2] from 1721 to 1742. Walpole had studied the commercial policies of every government in Europe,[3] and therefore brought an analyst's mind to the problems facing Britain in the 1720s: an exchequer weakened by decades of war with the French, a nascent manufacturing base that needed to expand and a complex and widely-evaded system of taxes.[4]

Conventional thinking would have dictated that the new chancellor should raise tariffs on imports, both to promote a trade surplus and to raise revenues. Walpole didn't. Instead he did precisely the opposite: he cut them. It was a counter-intuitive master stroke. By introducing tariff cuts on such raw materials as dyes and chemicals he reduced manufacturers' costs, thus making exports more competitive.[5] At the same time, the tariff reductions contributed to such a rise in imports of raw materials that government revenues didn't suffer.[6] This was not Walpole's only innovative policy. He also offered subsidies to exporters of manufactured goods, cut export duties and introduced quality controls so that shoddy businesses would not sully the name of Britain as a manufacturer. In addition, he pursued, albeit unsuccessfully, what would today be considered base-broadening tax reform.[7]

It is, however, with the Scottish philosopher Adam Smith and his 1776 work *An Inquiry into the Nature and Causes of the Wealth of Nations* that practical policy making first acquired a fully thought-through and coherent analysis and theory of the workings of a country's economy. Today, many of Smith's insights are so familiar as to seem almost obvious, but at the time he appeared something of a revolutionary – indeed, he was later to refer to his book as a 'very violent attack . . . upon the whole commercial system of Great Britain'.[8]

Smith was openly dismissive of the prevailing mercantilist orthodoxy, which argued that national wealth was increased by exporting more goods than one imported, something governments were supposed to facilitate by levying tariffs on imports and supporting exporters. Instead he argued that maximum prosperity would be achieved if a country allowed its markets to operate unhindered, famously evoking the metaphor of the 'invisible hand' to describe the economic forces that ensured that 'by pursuing his own interest' each person involved in trade 'frequently promotes that of the society'.[9] His notions on everything from international trade to the considerations that governed wages and savings were fresh and often counter-intuitive. The free market ideas he espoused would be adopted and built on by others, including David Ricardo, to become what was known as the Classical School of economics.

Smith's ideas are said to have influenced Prime Minister William Pitt and contributed to his decision to ignore powerful protectionist forces at home and abroad to negotiate a trade liberalisation treaty with France in 1786. But perhaps their earliest significant influence came with Robert Peel's Tory ministry of 1841–6. Peel had a deep understanding of the works of Smith and Ricardo. He cited both men in parliamentary debates in the 1830s and 1840s,[10] and appears to have adopted the classical view of the economy as a mechanism that could be speeded up or slowed down by regulatory adjustments and subtle changes in taxation. He accepted Smith's idea that lower tax rates might actually boost revenues,[11] argued against governments protecting inefficient industries[12] and believed that some taxes were less likely to slow growth than others. It was his repeal of the Corn Laws in 1846, however, that proved to be one of the landmark nineteenth-century examples of economic theory steering policy.

Britain had introduced the Corn Laws in 1815. Drawn up very much in line with the mercantilist thinking that was still influential in the early nineteenth century, they were designed to protect farmers in general and landowners in particular from foreign competition via a sliding scale of tariffs on grain imports. However, over the following decades, as the Industrial Revolution took root and the British population became increasingly urban, the balance of the population began to shift from those who produced grain to those who consumed its derivatives – in particular, bread – and the tariffs came under increasing attack. Some worried that by keeping grain prices artificially high, they made it harder for ordinary people to feed themselves. Others argued that higher bread prices put upward pressure on wages, thereby making British industry less competitive internationally and so threatening Britain's position as the world's pre-eminent industrial power. Matters came to a head in the mid-1840s when Peel made the decision to break with the agricultural interests so key to the Tories and abolish the tariffs, making up the funds forgone through the re-introduction of income tax. The move divided his party. Whether and to what extent it was responsible for the jump in exports that followed has been much debated. Arguably, though, it does signal the moment when economic theory and debate truly started to enter the bloodstream of political life.

The late nineteenth century saw a significant shift in economic theory, thanks to what has been termed the 'marginalist revolution'. Classical economists took the view that the prices of goods or wages were set by the cost of production or sustenance. Now a new generation of thinkers, who came to be known as the Neoclassical School,[13] posited that they were determined by the value or utility attached to them by the purchaser. This world view suggested, among other things, that humans behave in an economically rational way – that their responses to demand, supply and prices follow a predictable course. Its implication was that these responses can therefore be accurately assessed and measured. The French philosopher and mathematician Augustin Cournot was a key early figure in this theoretical revolution. His 1838 book *Research on the Mathematical Principles of the Theory of Wealth* argued that it was possible to calculate human responsiveness to price signals. However, it is Britain's Alfred Marshall who arguably deserves most credit for shaping the modern approach to measuring responsiveness. His 1890 book *Principles of Economics* included, among other things, an outline of the concept of price elasticity of demand, and used what have since become familiar-looking demand and supply curves to describe the mechanisms underpinning human decision-making.

People had always known that raising the price of a good tended to dampen demand for it. People had even previously used the term elasticity to refer to the response to price signals.[14] What was new here was the notion that humans make decisions based on rational preferences that are stable over time; that their price responsiveness can be measured; and that predictions can therefore be made about what individuals or businesses would do if prices of goods, interest rates, tax levels or other economic variables change.

Appropriately enough for an industrial age, this was a view of the economy as a sort of mechanism governed by scientific laws – what one of the founders of Neoclassical Economics, William Stanley Jevons, referred to as 'the mechanics of utility and self-interest'[15] – that could be uncovered, understood and employed to make predictions and set policies that would generate wealth. It had huge practical implications. A business might, for example, use Marshall's concept to establish whether its customers had a high price elasticity (i.e. that they would react to a price increase by sharply reducing demand) or a low price elasticity (i.e. that a price increase would have little or no effect on their buying habits). Equipped with such knowledge, the business could set prices to maximise revenues and profits. The theory had implications for politicians too. They could use estimates of elasticity to set revenue-maximising duties on goods. The US Treasury was among the first government institutions to construct financial forecasts in around 1920 that factored in direct and indirect responses to policy changes,[16] though dynamic economic modelling really only took off in the 1930s with the work of Dutchman Jan Tinbergen and Norwegian Ragnar Frisch. (The two received the inaugural Nobel memorial prize in economics in 1969 for the development of models that described how the economy functions.)[17] That said, the Marshallian world view of rational individuals behaving according to mathematical rules tended not to leave that much room for government involvement.[18] The assumption was that politicians were as likely to hinder progress as to help it – that they introduced inefficiencies into a system that, left alone, would regulate itself.

From Adam Smith to Alfred Marshall, then, economists were mainly concerned with the behaviour of individuals and companies. That, however, changed in the 1930s with the growing influence of the Cambridge-based economist John Maynard Keynes and, in particular, his publication in 1936 of arguably the second most influential book on economics after Smith's *Wealth of Nations*: *The General Theory of Employment, Interest and Money*. Keynes espoused a macroeconomic view of the world. He argued that economic peaks and troughs were endemic to capitalism, that these caused serious economic and social damage, and that it should be the job of government to moderate the impacts of these cycles by intervening as necessary in the nation's economy. Essentially, he believed that governments should increase expenditure or cut taxes in the bad times and do the opposite in the good times. The 1930s economic depression that followed the 1929 Wall Street Crash was, in his view, a function of an absence of demand. Weak demand for goods, he argued, led to weak demand for workers, which led to unemployment, which led to an absence of incomes in the economy, which in turn led to weak demand. Keynes suggested the way out of the depression was for governments to spend money to rekindle demand. That would encourage companies to hire workers and to invest in capacity to generate products to meet this demand. If the spark was successful, it would fire up a virtuous circle that allowed the government to raise taxes to pay back the cost of the jump-start.

While arguments still rage about the causes of the depression and its end, the consensus among economists and most governments in the United States and Britain from the late 1930s on was that the injection of demand by governments – such as Franklin D. Roosevelt's New Deal programme – contributed to the end of the crisis. After

8

the war, Keynesianism became the dominant approach to macro-economics, increasingly supported by sophisticated mathematical models that calibrated the level of demand that needed to be injected or removed. As Walter W. Heller, chair of the Presidential Council of Economic Advisers under John F. Kennedy and Lyndon B. Johnson, noted in 1966, governments were happy to be ruled by these models:

> Economics has come of age in the 1960s. Two Presidents have recognized and drawn on modern economics as a source of national strength and Presidential power. Their willingness to use, for the first time, the full range of modern economic tools underlies the unbroken U.S. expansion since early 1961.[19]

The physics of society

Keynesian demand management finally fell into disfavour in the 1970s, in the midst of new global economic difficulties, but the belief that economists could and should inform government decision-making remained. If anything, it became stronger. As policymakers turned back to the allure of the free market, they seem to have become even more susceptible to expert guidance on how best to make it work. Now, increasingly, economics became an industry in its own right, aided by ever more powerful and affordable computers able to crunch growing quantities of readily available data. Sophisticated models offered answers on everything, from how to control inflation or encourage investment to whether or not a tax rise was advisable. Today, if a country wants to increase women's participation in the labour market, economists can recommend which tax policies or subsidies are most likely to achieve this at the lowest cost to the exchequer. If a government wants to improve the lot of the lower paid, economists will advise on how to calibrate welfare payments so as to provide financial support without deterring self-reliance. In the process they have developed enormous confidence about the reliability of their predictions and the range of issues on which they are qualified to pronounce. As one famous economist, Robert Solow, noted, 'The best and brightest in the profession proceed as if economics is the physics of society.'[20]

The use of the word 'physics' here is telling. The physical sciences are built on immutable rules that allow us to predict outcomes with great precision and certainty – for example, Newton's Laws of Motion and Law of Universal Gravitation will accurately predict physical phenomena, such as how fast an object will move along a track given the application of varying degrees of force, or indeed how much power a rocket needs to break free of the earth's pull.

Governments and the bodies that advise them, like the Organisation for Economic Co-operation and Development (OECD) and International Monetary Fund (IMF), seem to think that economics works in much the same manner. It's assumed that markets allocate resources efficiently, that people respond to particular economic cues in consistent and predictable ways. These days it's also assumed – only slightly more controversially – that government intervention to tackle perceived market failures tends to be inefficient and counter-productive. The result over the past four decades has been remarkable unanimity – in the West, at least – on such policy issues as deregulation, tax cuts for businesses and a weakening of trade unions. These policies have been followed not just by the political right, as one might expect, but also by parties to the left of the political centre. In the UK, the Labour Party cut corporate taxes to boost growth. In Germany, the SDP pursued deregulation to spur employment.

As a recent graduate back in 1995, I felt a similar confidence about economists' ability to plot outcomes. Asked at a job interview with a Dublin-headquartered packaging company why I had elected to study economics, I told the long-serving managing director, who had grown the business from a small local operation into an international enterprise worth hundreds of millions of pounds, that I had done so because I believed it was a discipline that helped one understand how the economy worked. His response rather cut me off at the knees. 'Do you really think so?' he said, in a tone in which irritation, amusement and pity were equally mixed. He did not doubt that markets were good at building wealth, but he said he was sceptical about economists' vaunted ability to understand exactly how the process occurred and their claim to be able to make accurate predictions about the future. I didn't get the job.

The managing director's cynicism has always nagged at me. But what actually prompted me to explore the wisdom or otherwise of governments in recent decades relying heavily on economic models was the events that followed a series of investigations I conducted in 2012 and 2013 into the tax affairs of various multinational companies. To minimise their tax liabilities, I had noticed, a number of high-profile multinationals were channelling profits out of the countries where they earned their money into tax havens. The coffee giant Starbucks was a case in point. On the surface, the largest and most profitable coffee chain appeared to have been operating in the UK for over thirteen years without breaking even. Equally puzzling were the twin facts that it had been informing its investors that the UK was a goldmine and that the executives who ran the supposedly failing UK operation were frequently lauded to investors by Starbucks's chief executive Howard Schultz and promoted within the organisation.[21] My story hit a nerve, and prompted more reaction than I had expected, including boycotts and pickets of stores, and led to the company's chief financial officer being hauled in front of a parliamentary inquiry to explain why, among other things, it was routing coffee beans via Switzerland to ensure that profits derived from sales in Britain were not reported here. In the end, the company agreed to pay an additional £20 million in tax to try to draw a line under the public furore.

I noticed other big organisations used similar practices. The European boss of Google testified at the same parliamentary hearing at which Starbucks' chief financial Officer had received a grilling. Asked by MPs why his company paid almost no tax in Britain either, he explained that because Google Inc. made all its sales to UK clients from Ireland, it didn't actually have a tax residence in Britain, and therefore didn't owe tax there. On scrutinising the OECD Model Tax Convention, I realised that Google's tax advisers had carefully chartered a course through a legal loophole that allowed the company to report its £4 billion a year in advertising sales to UK-based customers as non-taxable exports from Ireland, rather than taxable British sales, even though – according to numerous job advertisements I had seen – Google was regularly recruiting UK-based salespeople and – according to LinkedIn – employed hundreds of staff in London who described themselves as salespeople.[22] The same practices, I found, operated in many other countries too.

At the time I filed my reports, many people in Britain were still experiencing the painful aftermath of the 2007/8 financial crash. Not surprisingly, therefore, there was considerable anger that some of the richest companies in the world appeared not to be paying their way. Politicians swiftly saw which way the wind was blowing. In a dig at Starbucks, Prime Minister David Cameron told the World Economic Forum in Davos that companies needed to 'wake up and smell the coffee' if they thought they could operate in Britain without paying their dues.[23] The G7 launched an anti-corporate tax avoidance effort in conjunction with the OECD.

But the reaction was not universal. As I continued to report on the shenanigans of big businesses, I came across a lot of people who thought the problem wasn't that companies were not paying enough tax, but the exact opposite: that they were being asked to pay too much. There was a view among economists, the British minister then responsible for taxation, David Gauke, told me in 2013, that taxes on corporate profits discouraged businesses from investing and expanding. To that extent they could be regarded as counter-productive. The idea that corporate taxation was a risky financial tool surprised me. I'd never seen any empirical evidence that this might be the case. It seemed a dubious truism.

And it's not the only dubious economic truism to have come my way. I have, for example, frequently encountered highly influential people who bemoan the march of 'health and safety' not only because they distrust government 'interference', but also because they believe such measures are economically damaging. Regulations, the argument goes, impede growth because they distort business decision-making, diverting resources from productive activities to mere compliance. Arguably, too, they can be actively harmful, because they replace the possibility of an agile response by manufac-turers to consumer concerns or demands with slow-moving and heavy-handed bureaucracy. As someone who has investigated fatal disasters at the oil group BP,[24] the sale of dangerous home appli-ances[25] and the appalling Grenfell Tower fire in London, which killed eighty-two people,[26] I have to confess I'm dubious whether such claims hold up. My own researches suggest that they don't.

As I have become more sceptical about such popularly received wisdom in various economic policy areas, I have also become dubi-ous about the ability of many widely accepted economic models to explain the present or predict the future. I recall reading a few years ago that when William Pitt announced his proposal for an income tax in 1798, it was initially predicted that the measure would raise £10 million in the first year; that this figure was reduced to £7.5 mil-lion before the tax was actually introduced in 1799; and that in the event the sum raised was £6 million in the first year and £6.25 mil-lion in the second – not a bad margin of error given the challenges of establishing accurate numbers back then.[27] Yet when, in 2012, the British tax authorities published a lengthy study that examined the consequences of the government's decision in 2009 to increase the top rate of income tax to 50 per cent from 40 per cent, they said that the £3 billion in extra revenue their model originally predicted had actually turned out to be £1 billion.[28] The most sophisticated models they had been able to call on had apparently been proved wrong by a factor of three. It was a performance that compared very unfavourably with a not dissimilar exercise conducted in the Republic of Ireland at much the same time. Here the Department of Finance opted not to use sophisticated estimates of behavioural responses to calculate the likely yield from a new tax – the Universal Social Charge (USC) – introduced in 2011 to help pay for the bail-out of the country's banking sector. Instead it ignored cutting-edge forecasting models and went for what was essentially a back-of-the-envelope calculation that only made some allowance for expected economic growth.[29] Their prediction was that the new tax, levied at 7 per cent on average incomes, would raise 3.2 billion euros in 2011.[30] In the event they got it wrong by just 0.1 billion euros: the actual yield that year was 3.1 billion.[31]

It's not that useful economic thinking must provide us with precise forecasts. As Keynes is supposed to have said (but probably didn't): 'It is better to be roughly right than precisely wrong.' If economic models or theories can point us in the right direction and give us a reasonable estimate of the scale of a force or impact, they're helpful. For example, if consumers are building up levels of personal debt that will require ever-rising house prices and wages to sustain – think the United States in 2006 – economists don't need to tell us exactly how much a drop in GDP this situation will likely result in. If they can simply show the risks are unsustainable and material, this can prompt and inform government action and protect society. The question is whether a model, which may have grown out of theory rather than any observations of the world, provides an answer which is 'roughly right', or is wrong no matter how far back you stand and squint.

In recent decades, economists claimed to have identified copious empirical evidence to justify many of their theories. But empirical evidence in economics is not like empirical evidence in physics. The latter is established by repeatedly running experiments in controlled environments. Economists can't isolate segments of the economy, set up dummy samples and repeat experiments over and over again. As a result, they usually seek proof by studying data sets to identify correlations that are consistent with the theory.

And correlations can be dangerous, as a 2014 paper by Robert Novy-Marx, a professor of finance at the University of Rochester in New York,[32] nicely demonstrates. In it Novy-Marx identified a number of interesting relationships between trends in meteorological and astronomical data and stock market returns – that colder months of the year were typically followed by a strongly performing stock market, for example, and that 'value-driven' investment strategies – that is to say, buying stocks with low price-to-earnings ratios – performed very well during periods of high levels of solar activity. For an investor such findings offered a potential goldmine. But the paper was a joke, intended to highlight the risks of inferring causation from correlations. Interestingly, I first came across it in a research note published in 2018 by analysts at the Swiss bank UBS, where it was included to provide a cautionary story for fund manager clients looking for 'leading indicators' that they hoped might act as signposts to future economic or financial trends.[33] Of course, financial professionals have an incentive not to infer causation from spurious correlations. Doing so will, before long, lead them to make a stupid prediction and thereby put their bonus or job at risk. Economics professors, by contrast, do not face such professional penalties.

Two other considerations have to be taken into account when establishing the discipline's claims to scientific truthfulness. The first is its ideological nature – its tendency, as one author of widely-cited papers on tax and growth told me – to be 'often influenced by the dominating ideology and belief system of the day'.[34] The second, far more fundamental, consideration is that, for a century or more, economics has become a body of study that claims to be able to explain and predict human behaviour, according to the narrowest of criteria: people's supposed responsiveness to price signals. There's no room in the average modern economic model for humans as they actually are, with all their emotions, loyalties, contradictions and irrational impulses.

In the following chapters, I will consider a range of key areas where strongly held but, to my mind, highly questionable economic theories have influenced or shaped the way businesses and governments have behaved. I will seek to demonstrate how a dangerous blend of political ideology, professional self-interest and unwavering adherence to long-held intellectual frameworks has led to policies that have not only failed to help society as a whole but have also actively harmed it. Indeed, I'll explore how a dogmatic approach has at times turned Milton Friedman's 'free lunch' dictum on its head and prompted economists to argue that their theories can provide painless solutions.

1

THE LAFFER CONUNDRUM

Do lower taxes help growth?

On a Friday morning in June 2016, Donald Trump was alerted to a lengthy email that had been sent to a close aide a couple of hours earlier. It was from a journalist, and related to an investigation into the then-presumptive Republican Party presidential candidate's finances. Trump did not like what he read and instructed the aide to get the reporter on the phone.

I was at home in London playing on the sofa with my two young sons when my mobile phone rang and a woman with an American accent asked if I would take a call from Donald Trump. Obviously, my email had touched a nerve. The property developer and reality TV star was campaigning for his country's highest office on his business credentials, saying he could use his commercial acumen to supercharge America's economy. My suggestion that he had lost hundreds of millions of dollars on his golf investments wasn't consistent with that message.[1] Trump wanted to set me straight.

After almost half an hour of being called a 'jerk' and a 'dummy', it was clear to me we had got as far as we were going to on golf, so I decided to change the subject. I asked him about his grand economic plan for the US. As I pointed out, he had been talking about it a lot in speeches and interviews up and down the country, but had not given away much detail. Trump's response was that he wouldn't go

17

into specifics ahead of the plan's official release. He assured me, though, that:

> We're going to have a great economic plan for the country. We're going to make America great again. Just like I have no debt[2] . . . we're going to reduce the debt of the country. We're going to increase jobs.

It struck me as an ambitious plan. Reducing government deficits and increasing employment don't, especially in the short term, necessarily go together. Historically, when governments wanted to reduce their debts, they tried to cut expenditure. This usually involved axing public sector jobs and purchases from suppliers in the private sector, who would then similarly be forced to axe more jobs. In economic language, a fiscal contraction is expected to exert contractionary pressures on employment and the economy generally.

In the weeks after we spoke, Trump went public with a more detailed outline of his plan. The magic ingredient that would square the circle, he said, was a large-scale reduction in taxation. Tax cuts would boost economic activity, which would lead to higher incomes, profits and spending, which in turn would generate higher government revenues, which would allow a reduction in the national debt. It was an attractive message, and it resonated well with US voters. Trump was duly elected. In office he proved true to his word. The signature legislative achievement of the President's term was the sweeping Tax Cuts and Jobs Act 2017. Trump predicted the economy would 'take off like a rocket ship' once his tax cuts kicked in.[3]

His mindset is far from being an international one-off. Over the past decade, the governments of countries from Argentina[4] to Australia[5] have taken office on the back of similar promises. In the UK, Boris Johnson claimed in June 2019 that the government could boost revenue by cutting taxes.[6] He became Prime Minister in July.

Rulers have levied taxes for perhaps 4,000 years,[7] and for most of that time the assumption has been that if you want to increase revenues, you increase tax rates. Now, it would seem, the opposite would appear to be the case. Why? The answer lies partly in the consequences of a decision America made over a century ago about how to pay for a war.

The education of Andrew Mellon

Days after being appointed finance minister of France in March 1917, Joseph Thierry spoke of his fears regarding his 'heavy task.'[8] At the time, France was at one of its lowest points in the war. Few territorial gains had been achieved in the preceding two years, and the strategy of seeking advances by heaping soldiers upon enemy machine guns had so demoralised troops that they would soon mutiny. But Thierry's 'melancholy'[9] was not caused by the challenges at the front. His problems lay in the exchequer. The war had already cost France, he estimated, around $13 billion.[10] This had been raised largely through the issuing of government bonds. But by the third year of the war, the public's appetite for them was showing signs of fatigue. Months later, Thierry would be forced to increase promotional spending to attract buyers for the 1917 issue of government perpetual bonds or *rentes*.[11]

Other fiscal measures the government had been enacting or was planning were similarly problematic. Printing money to fund the war effort had helped, but there was a limit to how far Thierry could go without risking runaway inflation. And the finance minister's ambition to bring more money into the economy by entreating Americans to import more French luxury goods could never do more than make a marginal difference.[12] The fact was that a partially occupied, war-ravaged country was never going to be able to export itself to fiscal sustainability.

Thierry felt the extent of the nation's predicament was perhaps not fully appreciated by his countrymen. He informed members of parliament they were trying to fool themselves about the budgetary position.[13] He told businesses and the public they needed to steel themselves for an arduous financial campaign, in addition to the military campaign.[14] Borrowing and printing money had reached their limits, the pragmatic former commercial lawyer from Marseilles argued. More painful measures would be required to make ends meet. Thierry would have to raid his dispirited fellow citizens' wallets. In the summer of 1917, he announced a hike in income taxes, with a particular focus on top earners. 'We feel confident our new legislation will have the desired results,' he said: 'namely, in throwing the main burden of taxation on our richer classes'.[15]

It wasn't that much of a burden. His measure would lift the marginal rate on the highest earners from 10 per cent to only 12.5 per cent,[16] a fraction of the level now thought appropriate or acceptable in developed nations.

Across the English Channel, the wealthy weren't having it so easy. By the summer of 1917, Britain's top marginal rate of income tax was approaching 50 per cent, enabling the government to fund 28 per cent of the country's war expenditure from taxation, in comparison to France's 18 per cent.[17]

Across the Atlantic, meanwhile, politicians' confidence and ambitions were even greater.

The United States was a relative newcomer to income tax. The Union government had imposed it during the Civil War, but it had subsequently been abolished and was not levied again at a national level until 1913, when the top rate was set at 7 per cent.[18] Within a month of entering the First World War in April 1917, however, Congress began to discuss increasing tax rates to pay for the fighting. Democrats and the so-called 'progressive' or liberal wing of the Republican Party proposed the 'conscription of wealth'[19] – arguing that since the poor were being forced to enlist and give their lives for victory, the rich should, for a time, give up a big chunk of their incomes. Some Republicans, by contrast, preferred the option of funding the fighting through borrowing, arguing it was only fair that future generations contribute to the benefits of the future peace the current generation would be giving its lives to secure.

After months of tortuous debate, in which patriotism was often invoked, the accusation of socialism frequently levied and unintended consequences repeatedly predicted, in October 1917 Congress passed the War Revenue Act.[20] It hiked tax rates to a maximum level of 67 per cent.[21] A year later, further increases would take the top rate to 77 per cent on incomes over $2,000,000 per year.[22]

From 1917 to 1919 the 1917 War Revenue Act raised almost $1.2 billion in income tax annually. This compared to under $200 million being paid in federal income taxes in 1916, and nothing a few years previously.[23] Most of this sum was raised from the great body of people who were paying tax at relatively modest rates. Individuals receiving over $50,000 a year (the top 1 per cent of earners) faced a marginal tax rate – that is to say, the rate on every extra dollar earned above a threshold – of just 16 per cent. One had to be earning $500,000 a year or more (the equivalent of $12 million or more today) before one started to pay over 50 cents in the dollar on additional earnings.[24]

The 1917 tax hikes were introduced as an extraordinary measure and were intended to be temporary. So by the end of the decade, with the war now won and war debts reduced,[25] politicians were beginning to think about a 'Return to Normalcy', as the Republican presidential candidate Warren Harding described it in his campaign speeches. When Harding won the 1920 election, he installed as Treasury Secretary a man with a clear idea about what 'normalcy' should look like in the fiscal sphere.

Andrew Mellon was one of the wealthiest men in America. He had built the banking business founded by his father into a major lender to the nation's industrial tycoons, and had also acquired his own substantial interests in coal, steel and real estate. The grandson of Scots-Irish immigrants who had had to make their way in the world, he believed firmly in the power of personal initiative and the abundance of opportunity afforded by America, which he described as 'a civilisation which offers unprecedented rewards to any man who is willing to work'.[26] Perhaps not surprisingly, therefore, he considered income redistribution by the government as a form of punishment of the industrious, and generally opposed state intervention in the economy (except where it involved restricting actual or potential competitors who posed a challenge to his own commercial interests).[27]

Unsurprisingly, too, he was an admirer of Adam Smith. He was a firm believer in the power of the 'invisible hand'. And when it came to taxes, he held strongly to Smith's view that, if they were pitched too high, they 'may obstruct the industry of the people, and discourage them from applying to certain branches of business which might give maintenance and employment to great multitudes'.[28] Mellon, like Smith, believed that such a financial burden discouraged entrepreneurship, everyday business activity and hard work. Like Smith, he feared that it therefore caused less income to be generated, and taxed, and less demand for goods and services, which in turn meant less tax revenue from those goods and services. As he wrote in his 1924 book *Taxation: The People's Business*: 'It seems difficult for some to understand that high rates of taxation do not necessarily mean large revenue to the Government, and that more revenue may often be obtained by lower rates'.[29]

Mellon's arguments for tax cuts proved persuasive, and in November 1921 Congress approved a Revenue Act that put in place a series of reductions. While it would be unfair to characterise them as 'tax cuts for millionaires', it would probably be accurate to say that they represented cuts that only a millionaire would notice. People earning up to $100,000 a year saw reductions in their marginal rates of 1–2 percentage points.[30] Meanwhile, those on incomes in excess of $300,000 received reductions of up to 15 percentage points.[31] Mellon also introduced a 12.5 per cent capital gains tax rate on assets held for over two years. Previously such assets had been taxed at normal rates, so the move represented a major boost for the better off, who were the most likely members of society to enjoy income from shares or investments in property.

In 1923 President Harding died and was replaced by his Vice President, Calvin Coolidge. The new president turned out to be an even more ardent supporter than his predecessor of Mellon's policies. In 1924 and 1926, the Treasury Secretary was therefore able to step up his tax-cutting efforts. Again, the main beneficiaries of his reforms were high earners. He abolished the highest-earning tax bands, bringing the rate on incomes over $200,000 down to 25 per cent from 58 per cent. He also enacted more modest reductions of 4 to 12 percentage points for those earning under $50,000.

In terms of tax yields, Mellon's policy was seemingly vindicated. Tax return data show that from 1923 income tax revenues began to rise, and that the biggest increases in revenues came from those who received the biggest tax cuts: the wealthy. In 1923, Americans with incomes of in excess of $100,000 paid a total of $320 million in income tax. In 1928, two years after the last of Mellon's swingeing cuts, those in this category paid almost three times as much.[32] It was no wonder, therefore, that with tax rates down, economic growth purring away and the government finances on a healthy trajectory,[33] Mellon's standing politically and with the public should have been rock-solid.

But then came the Wall Street Crash of 1929 and the Great Depression of the 1930s. Almost overnight Mellon's reputation for fiscal acumen was shattered. Not only had he failed to predict the financial collapse, he also failed to grasp just how severe its consequences would prove to be, declaring as late as 1930 that 'I see nothing in the present situation that is either menacing or warrants pessimism.'[34] His popularity nosedived. In 1932 President Hoover gave in to Congressional pressure and removed him from office.

From being acclaimed as a financial genius, he became almost over-night a byword for the callous rich, seeking to entrench their privileges. President Hoover, in his memoirs, described Mellon as actually welcoming some of the cleansing effects of the Great Crash.[35] Some went further, suggesting that not only had Mellon failed to see the crash coming but that he was also largely responsible for it. His tax cuts on the wealthy and, in particular, the cuts on capital gains, they argued, had encouraged stock market speculation and a bubble in share prices.

After the publication of John Maynard Keynes' *The General Theory of Employment, Interest and Money*, Mellon's stock fell further. In the eyes of the macroeconomists of the late 1930s onwards, he had got things completely the wrong way around. When the economy was booming he should have applied the brakes by taking money out of the system. Instead he had overheated it by stimulating demand with tax cuts. When the economy had slowed, he should have injected more stimulus and demand by increasing expenditure. Instead he had cut it. According to the prevailing wisdom of the post-war years, Mellon had exacerbated the peak and trough by applying pro-cyclical, rather than the correct, counter-cyclical policies. By the 1960s, Mellon was largely forgotten.[36] Insofar as his tenure as Treasury Secretary was remembered at all it was usually for mismanagement.[37]

Forty years after Mellon left the Treasury Department, though, events far from Washington would help spark a revival in his reputation.

On 17 October 1973, oil ministers from members of the Organ-isation of the Arab Petroleum-Exporting Countries (OAPEC) met in the Sheraton Hotel in Kuwait City to discuss how best to support Egypt and Syria in the war against Israel they had launched days earlier on the Jewish holy day of Yom Kippur. Their decision was to cut oil production, in the hope that curtailed supply and higher prices would prompt the big oil-consuming nations to pres-sure Israel, which had gained the upper hand in the conflict and counter-attacked, to pull back. Some OAPEC members, including Saudi Arabia, halted all oil exports to the United States and the Netherlands, which were seen as especially supportive of Israel.

Oil prices soared in the following months, adding to lesser increases that oil producers had extracted in the previous few years[38] as part of an effort by the larger Organisation of the Petroleum-Exporting Countries (OPEC) to wrestle control of the international oil market from the 'Seven Sisters' – the big Western oil companies. In March 1974, the oil embargo was lifted without achieving much by way of political advantage for the Arab states.[39] But the economic map had been redrawn between oil producers – mainly developing nations – and the West. As Shah Mohammed Riza Pahlevi of Iran told reporters, 'The industrial world will have to realise that the era of their terrific progress and even more terrific income and wealth based on cheap oil is finished . . . If you want to live as well as now, you'll have to work for it.'[40]

At the beginning of that year, the main concern among Americans and Europeans had been that their economies might be growing too fast. By the end of 1974, it looked as though the Shah's prediction was coming true. And it wasn't just that growth was slowing. In both the United States and Europe, unemployment was rising, while inflation was climbing up into double-digits, a toxic combination which became known as 'Stagflation'.[41] This wasn't supposed to happen. Keynes had held that economic slowdowns were the result of insufficient demand, while inflation was the result of excessive demand brought on by an overheating economy. The solution to the former was to inject demand via additional government spending or reduced taxation, while the answer to the latter was reduced spending or higher taxes. Stagflation, however, left governments struggling to decide whether to hike taxes to cool inflation or to cut taxes and increase spending to tackle unemployment. Confused responses included the US President Gerald Ford's attempts to do one, then the other, within a matter of weeks.[42]

The immediate cause of the problem was the big hikes in oil prices – since Western economies were so reliant on oil, higher crude prices fed through to higher prices for all goods, while shortages hit output. It was an external shock of a type that Keynesianism did not really envision. But the roots of stagflation also went rather deeper. The 1960s economic booms in the United States and Britain had been fuelled, partly at least, by expansionist fiscal policies and low interest rates. These had led to rising inflation[43] and increasing deficits.[44]

In their attempt to manage inflation, the US and UK tried price and wage controls. As most economists predicted, the measures were ineffective, and in the UK helped prompt industrial action.[45] Left with seemingly no cards to play, some experts began to wonder if Keynes had missed something. Perhaps, they thought, the father of macroeconomics had been too focused on demand and had overlooked the importance of the other major force in economic theory: supply. After all, for an economy to function, the supply of goods and services is as important as the demand for them. That left the question, though, whether supply created demand, or demand created supply? It was a classic chicken-and-egg conundrum.

Tackling the supply end of the equation posed a further – practical – problem too. Demand, as Keynesians pointed out when considering how to encourage growth, was something that governments could influence. They could choose to spend public money on, say, building bridges to create demand for workers whose wages would spark higher spending in the shops, or by or paying higher pensions to the retired to directly create higher spending in shops and indirectly create extra demand for workers. Finding a way to influence supply was a far tougher nut to crack, at least in the short term. It was not, therefore, something Keynesians considered very much.

In the years that followed the oil crisis, though, a small group of Keynes sceptics thought they had found the answer.

Voodoo economics

In September 2019 I found myself on the touchline of a football pitch at my children's school in south-west London with another parent. While discussing lift-sharing for the kids, I mentioned that I would soon be travelling to Nashville, Tennessee, a destination unusual enough to prompt my friend to ask why. I thought for a moment about how to describe my research visit, before responding that I was going to meet America's most famous living economist.[46] Although the woman I was talking to had previously worked in finance, she stared at me blankly. 'Arthur Laffer,' I said. She continued to look at me blankly. I decided to resort to a cultural reference I knew she'd recognise.

If you were a teenager in the late 1980s – or perhaps since – a movie moment you'll almost certainly remember will be the classroom scene from *Ferris Bueller's Day Off*. In it, an economics teacher (played by actual economist Ben Stein, a former speech writer for Presidents Nixon and Ford, who became an Emmy-winning comedian and actor) draws an inverted U-shape on a blackboard and proceeds to ask his near-catatonic pupils in a droning voice: 'Anyone know what this is? Class? Anyone? Anyone? Anyone seen this before?'

As with all his questions, the teacher is forced to answer this one himself: 'The Laffer Curve . . . this is very controversial. Does anyone know what Vice President Bush called this in 1980? Anyone? Voodoo Economics.'

The Laffer Curve is that rarest of things: an economic phenomenon. It exploded into the public consciousness in the United States[47] in the late 1970s, and proceeded to become the dominant economic orthodoxy of the US Republican Party. The curve – a visual representation of Dr Laffer's theories – was also widely reported on in the United Kingdom and Australia and adopted by numerous, mainly right-of-centre, politicians in both countries. Many Conservative

Party parliamentarians, including Boris Johnson, still hold faith in the curve.[48]

On the flight to Nashville, a question began to preoccupy me. I wondered why Laffer, who had spent most of his working life in California, should have chosen to move to Nashville. America's most illustrious economists usually live near Ivy League universities on either coast or by the Great Lakes, most notably in Chicago. Tennessee was – and is – an unusual choice.

Shortly after I arrived at Laffer's home – the second-oldest in the upmarket Bellevue neighbourhood west of Nashville – he led me down to a living room with sofas and antique tables and chests on which were crammed stone carvings, cut-glass trinkets, old china and photographs of Laffer with family members and famous politicians.

As his mastiff licked my face and his great Dane nudged my leg, Laffer told me about Nashville's booming economy. Then he told me a joke that answered the question that had been on my mind. 'Did you hear about the man who moved from Tennessee to Illinois?' he asked.

I shook my head.

'No, me neither,' he said, and laughed.

At eighty, Laffer retained the charm, energy, mischievousness and detailed recall of data that made him such an effective marketer of his brand of economics. Illinois, Laffer explained, was a state that levied high income taxes on residents (on top of federal income tax, Americans can also face state and local income taxes). Tennessee, on the other hand, imposed no tax on earned personal income. Laffer said that, a decade earlier, he had grown tired of California's high income taxes. He had therefore looked at the map of the United States to identify those states with no income tax on salaries. Finally he had settled on Tennessee.

'I paid for this house with my first year's tax savings,' he said. And he said he wasn't the only one chasing such savings.

Later, over a dinner of Costco roast chicken, mac 'n' cheese, salad and a little wine and bourbon, he shared a discovery he had made when preparing to leave San Diego. Laffer's large collection of antiques, fine china, paintings and fossils had required a fleet of trucks to move. He had checked the prices of van rental companies like U-Haul and found something that those not initiated into the mysteries of the Laffer Curve might find surprising: the price of renting a truck from Los Angeles to Nashville was twice the price of hiring one from Nashville to Los Angeles.

'What does that tell you?' he asked with a grin.

So Laffer figured he wasn't the only one being lured from California to Tennessee by low taxes or the strong economic growth that these may bring.

The belief that national economies can be manipulated through taxation was, of course, not something Laffer invented. As I have already mentioned, Keynes saw taxes as a tool to manage demand. But Laffer's take on this basic tenet was different. He held, and believed his curve showed, that taxes were also a powerful tool to stimulate or retard *supply*.

What has become known as supply-side economics was first advanced by the Canadian economist Robert Mundell, who in 1999 would be awarded a Nobel memorial prize for economics for his work on currencies and exchange rates. In the 1960s, Mundell had become troubled by the increasing role of the state in the economy. Government spending and tax take as a percentage of total output had risen massively after the Second World War in most Western nations. In the United States, where Mundell spent most of his adult life, the share had risen from around 15 per cent in the 1930s to around 30 per cent in the late 1960s.[49] By the early 1970s, Mundell had become convinced that the increased tax burden in Western nations was weighing heavily on these countries' growth. His reasoning was that taxation acted as a wedge between what one party paid and another party received in commercial transactions. In effect, it reduced the price the selling party received or increased the price the purchasing party had to pay. Neoclassical economic theory holds that people purchase less when prices rise and supply less when prices fall, so to Mundell it logically followed that an increased tax burden inevitably reduced the number of transactions taking place. In short, US tax rates of 50 per cent on salaries, 70 per cent on dividend income and 50 per cent on corporations' income (the levels were higher in Britain at time) were all discouraging people from working, investing, innovating and starting up new businesses. 'The national economy is being choked by taxes,' said Mundell – 'asphyxiated.'[50]

Laffer adopted Mundell's ideas, and joined the offensive against high taxes. As 1970s inflation pushed more and more nominal salary earners, investors and entrepreneurs into the higher income bands, their campaign intensified. They argued that prevailing tax rates were so damaging to the economy as a whole that they were actually producing less revenue than lower tax rates would have done.[51] And they predicted that if the tax boot was taken off the throat of the economy, employment, business start-ups and investment would increase to such an extent that the Treasury would reap higher tax revenues at the lower rates. In his lectures to students, Laffer illustrated the effect via a simple diagram that comprises little more than an X and a Y axis and a curved line.

The curve resembles the nose of a jetliner (unlike the inverted U-curve that appears in *Ferris Bueller* and countless other popular depictions). Tax revenues appear along the horizontal X axis, and tax rates on the Y axis. At the origin, where tax rates are zero, revenues are also zero. As tax rates rise, revenues initially increase. But as tax rates rise beyond a certain point, revenues start to fall, and the line moves back towards the Y axis to the point where, as the tax rate reaches 100 per cent and the curve intersects with the Y axis again, the revenue hits zero again.

Neither Laffer nor Mundell said precisely where they thought the United States or other countries were on the curve, or why they

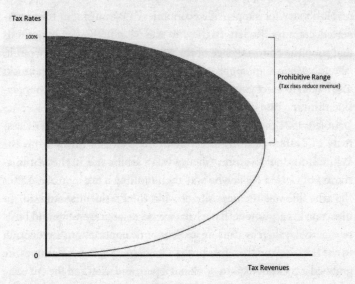

The Laffer Curve

believed the United States was in the prohibitive range on the graph. The curve was a theoretical construct, and not the product of an economic model populated with empirical data.

The response from mainstream economists to Laffer's theories and forecasts was not positive. In 1971, Paul Samuelson, the 'foremost academic economist of the twentieth century', according to the *New York Times*,[52] delivered a lecture at the University of Chicago entitled 'Why They Are Laughing at Laffer'. The attack was perhaps a little cruel, given that Samuelson was America's pre-eminent economist and a Nobel memorial prize winner, while Laffer was still a year off receiving his doctorate. 'It was', as Laffer told me, 'very painful at the time'.

But Laffer persisted. In any case, he was more interested in influencing policy than winning the respect of academic economists. He became friends with Jude Wanniski, an editorial writer at the *Wall Street Journal*, who became, in Laffer's words, 'the crazy, wild revolutionary for supply-side economics'.[53] Wanniski, in turn, converted his boss, Robert Bartley, to the Mundell-Laffer hypothesis and soon the editorial page of the *Journal* became, as Bartley put it, 'the mouthpiece of supply-side economics'.[54] Laffer and Wanniski also began to meet government officials to press them to put supply-side thinking into practice.

In late 1974 the two linked up with Dick Cheney, a former classmate of Laffer's at Yale, at a restaurant a stone's throw from the White House. At the time, Cheney was a senior aide in the administration of Gerald Ford, who was then mulling a tax increase. Laffer thought this was the opposite of what the President should do. To illustrate his argument that a hike would discourage work and business activity, thereby causing an economic contraction, a reduction in the tax base and therefore probably a reduction in tax revenues, he grabbed a cocktail napkin, took out a pen, and sketched the curve he had long used with students. And he explained that, as far as he was concerned, the United States occupied a spot in the upper half of the graph, where higher tax rates produced lower revenues. For Cheney, who was to serve as Defence Secretary to President George H. W. Bush and Vice President to George W. Bush, the napkin scribbles marked 'a significant moment in my own development'.[55]

Months later, Laffer sketched the graph again at a meeting with Ford's Chief of Staff, Donald Rumsfeld, who later said he, too, had found it 'compelling'.[56] But Laffer's ideas didn't get much traction in the White House. Alan Greenspan, Ford's Chief Economic Adviser, who was a traditional balanced-budget fiscal conservative, gave short shrift to Laffer's claims that one could cut taxes and boost revenues at the same time. Ford sided with Greenspan. Years later Ford would remark of supply-side economics that 'I don't believe a word of it.'[57]

But the supply-siders would not give up. Wanniski, later known as 'the hype man' of supply-side economics, set about taking their message to the widest possible audience, penning editorials in the *Journal* and conservative publications like *The Public Interest*. In 1978 he published *The Way the World Works*, a primer and manifesto for supply-side economics that would become a bestseller. In it, he described the 1974 meeting where Laffer drew the curve for Cheney. Laffer reckons he must have drawn fifty curves on fifty napkins, but Wanniski created the folklore of a single momentous dinner, which in later retelling came to include both Cheney and Rumsfeld.[58] The resonance of Wanniski's tale was such that, decades later, the Smithsonian Museum would display a napkin on which Laffer had drawn the curve, claiming it to be the napkin that 'sketched a new direction for the Republican Party'.[59]

The Way the World Works didn't only advance the Laffer Curve. It took on those fiscal conservatives like Greenspan and Ford who believed supply-side thinking to be an economic Ponzi scheme. Echoing Laffer, Wanniski argued that supply-side economics was essentially neoclassical economics and its core principle that people respond in a rational, predictable way to price signals. And taxes on their labour or investments, Wanniski suggested, constitute price signals. He argued, further, that the idea that lower taxes could raise more revenue was not something modern-day supply-siders had dreamt up. The Roman Emperor Augustus, Napoleon, US founding father Alexander Hamilton and Adam Smith were all supply-siders or had been aware of the dangers of high taxes (the fourteenth-century Muslim philosopher Ibn Khaldun and the Anglo-Irish writer Jonathan Swift would also in time be added to the list of historical figures who supply-siders said believed that high taxes could lead to lower tax revenues).

Centuries-old theories, and stories like the napkin anecdote, helped grab the attention of a wide audience, but to convince a sceptical public and a Republican Party historically wedded to balanced budgets, supply-siders needed hard evidence. Fiscal conservatives based their opposition to tax cuts that were not matched by spending cuts on the uncomfortable tendency of such cuts to be followed by inflation and deficits. Wanniski didn't marshal specific data to counter this and support his central hypothesis. But he did believe that the recent past afforded an example of tax cuts leading not just to a Keynsian temporary lift through the stimulation of demand, but to an actual re-engineering of the economy – a booming, low-inflation economy with budgetary surpluses where people worked harder and smarter. The era was the 1920s. And the man responsible – *The Way the World Works*' 'principal political hero', according to a review in *The Public Interest*[60] – was Andrew Mellon.

The rehabilitation of Andrew Mellon

The strong growth and fiscal surpluses the United States enjoyed in the 1920s after Mellon slashed tax rates showed, Wanniski argued, the power of supply-side economics. That left the crash of 1929 to account for, but Wanniski had an explanation for that which absolved Mellon of any blame. According to his thesis, the market collapse and subsequent depression were sparked by a policy that was the antithesis of what Mellon stood for: a tax hike – specifically, the Smoot-Hawley Tariff Act, passed by Congress in 1930, which imposed tariffs on imports. He explained that as the Act made its passage through Congress in 1929, investors and businesses became increasingly alarmed about the potentially damaging impact import tariffs might have on companies and on the economy more generally. Manufacturing prices would rise, they feared, and a trade war might ensue.[61] As their worries grew, the stock market crashed.

It's not, it has to be said, a widely held view. Indeed, the only time I have ever seen a mainstream economist advocate it is in *Ferris Bueller's Day Off*. And lest anyone should think Ben Stein was being serious, he later made it clear that he was ad-libbing. His considered view, expressed in one of his regular *New York Times* columns, was that the idea that Smoot-Hawley caused the Depression was 'almost comical' (given his lone position at the intersection of economics and comedy, he's probably well placed to judge this).[62]

Nevertheless, supply-siders continued to make ground, attracting interest from such politicians as Congressman Jack Kemp, who cited Wanniski's defence of Mellon in Congressional debates, and a potential Republican candidate for the Presidency called Ronald Reagan. Once ensconced in the White House in 1980, Reagan would cite Andrew Mellon's tenure as Treasury Secretary as a high-water mark for the Republican Party's economic stewardship, rather than the embarrassment many Republicans of the previous half-century had perceived it to be. A 1982 Congressional report on fiscal policy stated that 'Secretary of the Treasury Andrew Mellon [is] considered by some the finest public servant to fill that position since Albert Gallatin'[63] (a reference to the longest-serving holder of that office, whose statue today stands outside the Department of the Treasury in Washington, DC, on a pedestal with a plaque describing him as a 'genius of finance'). Mellon ceased to be an instigator of the Great Depression. Instead he became the creator of the 'Roaring' Twenties, cited in political speeches and newspapers all over the world. According to the White House website in 2020, he 'built a thriving business empire before becoming the Secretary of the Treasury, during which time he advocated for economic policies that sparked the tremendous prosperity of the 1920s.'[64]

Wanniski's account of how Andrew Mellon made the 1920s roar helped take supply-side economics from the fringe to the political mainstream, not just in the United States but overseas too. Laffer helped steer Chile's economic restructuring under dictator Augusto Pinochet in the 1970s and 1980s and advised Margaret Thatcher's government on its tax reform in the 1980s. His influence persists to this day. In 2019, Donald Trump (whom Laffer has advised during his candidacy and presidency) awarded the economist the United States' highest civilian honour, the Presidential Medal of Freedom. In Britain, Boris Johnson, who has also long been an advocate of 'supply-side reforms',[65] cited Ibn Khaldun while campaigning for his party's leadership to explain how he could increase revenues by cutting taxes. The idea of tax cuts that pay for themselves is incredibly attractive – a quintessential free lunch; something for nothing.

The day after my dinner with Arthur Laffer I spent several hours with him at his offices in Nashville discussing economics and eating fried baloney sandwiches. In the course of our conversation he listed various examples of the Laffer Curve at work. He also pointed out to me the curious way in which the recipients of the biggest tax cuts in the 1920s – the wealthy – ended up paying a lot more in tax after the reductions than they did before. The implication was clear: if their payments went up, it must have been because Mellon's tax cuts incentivised them to work harder and more productively. If ever there was proof of the Treasury Secretary's genius, this surely was it.

The Roaring Twenties revisited

Laffer's account, however, doesn't tell the full story, not least because it doesn't take it back quite far enough. The fact is that whereas income tax was a known quantity in Britain in the 1910s and 1920s, for countries such as the US and France it was a relatively new experience. By the outbreak of the First World War, the UK had had over seventy years of continuous experience of income tax. The Exchequer knew how to assess incomes and devise anti-avoidance mechanisms. It could therefore impose what even the leader of the Labour Party described as 'bold' tax rates.[66] (Some suggested that Britain should be bolder – the left-wing Fabian Society sought a 70 per cent tax on incomes over £100,000[67] – but concern that such rates would encourage tax dodging beyond what the Revenue Commissioners could counter deterred the government from taking such a step.)[68] For the French authorities, by contrast, such boldness was unthinkable. At

36

the time, all Frenchmen had the vote, while in 1917 only property-owning, which is to say fairly affluent, Britons did, so one might have expected a 'soak the rich' approach in France, not Britain. But Joseph Thierry realised it would be pointless to try to levy high income taxes, because French bureaucrats simply didn't know how to enforce them.[69] His decision to impose a 12.5 per cent rate was a grimly realistic one. It might not raise much, but the chances were that people would find it sufficiently untroubling that they wouldn't try to avoid it. The United States shared France's lack of experience in the field of income tax, but its politicians seemed unaware of the implications of such inexperience. Experts, on the other hand, immediately worried about enforcement. As Edwin Seligman, considered the country's foremost scholar of taxation, noted: 'No machinery has yet been devised to check the returns from individuals engaged in business or occupations.'[70] There were few ways to check whether people were lying in their returns or whether they were exploiting loopholes in the Revenue Act – for example, splitting shares or property between family members to ensure no one individual entered the higher tax brackets, or putting property into companies to avoid tax (technically illegal under the terms of the Act but almost impossible to enforce).[71] So although the US, unlike France, imposed extreme tax hikes, affluent and wealthy Americans had plenty of scope to avoid them.

Their efforts show in the figures. In 1916, when the top income-tax rate was just 15 per cent, 206 Americans reported receiving an income of over $1 million per year. In 1921, when the top rate was 73 per cent,[72] only twenty-one people claimed to have done so. Over the same period, the number of people who said they earned over $300,000 dropped 70 per cent.

There are no reports of the era's millionaires skipping north of the border or to war-damaged Europe's tax havens. Those who appeared in the Richest People in America list featured in *Forbes* magazine for the first time in 1918[73] still lived there in 1923 or had died there. And despite the supposed disappearance of the wealthy, the economy continued to grow in the years after 1917, and incomes overall rose.

So when supply-siders say that the massive tax cuts Mellon introduced in the 1920s were followed by a significant increase in reported taxable incomes and higher tax payments by the richest Americans, they are absolutely correct, but their rationale for this phenomenon is hard to sustain. Congress had made it clear that the high wartime tax rates were temporary. It therefore made sense for the wealthy to hold off declaring income while taxes were high. And when the Democrats attacked the decision to drop the rates to 25 per cent in 1925, it made sense for taxpayers to report income, just in case rates were hiked again under a future government. That the increase in tax yield was greatest in areas such as dividends and capital gains, which can be easily timed, rather than salaried income, further points to a non-supply-side interpretation of the overall statistics.[74]

It's certainly true that there *was* a general economic recovery in the 1920s. It could therefore be theoretically argued that even if tax cuts didn't increase people's productivity as much as the Laffer school would argue, they did have an impact. But even this lesser claim is tendentious. Given that he was appointed in the midst of a deep recession and that the US economy had gone through cyclical phases of growth and recession before his tenure and would do so again afterwards, it's a not unreasonable assumption that Mellon's stewardship would have seen some sort of transition from slump to recovery regardless of what he did. And that other countries with very dissimilar tax regimes experienced similarly strong growth during this period makes it seem even less likely that it was tax cuts in the US that boosted growth. After the war, high levels of debt forced the French government to hike taxes. By 1920, the country's top marginal income tax rates exceeded 60 per cent.[75] Yet France's growth rates in the 1920s exceeded those of the US.[76] Germany, too, which suffered hyperinflation in the early 1920s, experienced higher growth rates than the US in the '*Goldene Zwanziger*' even though it, like France, raised tax levels.[77] The international experience suggests that even if Mellon had not cut taxes in the way he did, the United States would have enjoyed a buoyant decade economically in the 1920s.

Fad economics

If the 1920s are not the proof of concept that supply-siders claim them to be, neither are two other test-case periods they often cite: the early 1960s and the 1980s.

The so-called Kennedy tax cuts, which were signed into law by Lyndon B. Johnson in 1964, cut the top income tax rate from 91 per cent to 71 per cent and the corporate income tax rate from 52 to 48 per cent, as well as introducing a range of other tax breaks.[78] The economy subsequently accelerated, with GDP growth averaging 6.3 per cent between 1964 and 1966, up from the 4.4 per cent average from 1961 to 1963.[79] It is conceivable that the prospect of earning higher post-tax earnings or returns encouraged idle people to take up jobs, businesses to expand and entrepreneurs to launch new ventures. It's much more likely that the tax cuts provided a major Keynesian stimulus, by putting more money back into the economy, albeit at a cost of wider deficits (a topic I will return to in Chapter 8). Overall the reductions were equivalent to about 2.2 per cent of Gross National Product in 1965, according to a Congressional Budget Office estimate.[80] Further demand was created by the Vietnam War and the need to equip a vastly expanded military. That inflation increased significantly during the period suggests additional supply or production in the economy was struggling to keep up with the additional demand, undermining the claim that increased supply was the main growth driver.

The Reagan tax cuts, which were actually inspired by Laffer, also sit uncomfortably as proof of supply-side economics in action. True, average annual GDP growth during the Reagan presidency was a healthy 3.5 per cent, but this was thanks to borrowed money. A massive demand-side stimulus, with deficits averaging over 4 per cent of GDP annually[81] – a level whose only peacetime equivalent was during the Great Depression – left the country saddled with vast debts. Equally embarrassing for the supply-side cause was that Bill Clinton achieved 3.9 per cent annual growth[82] after raising tax rates. Clinton's experience also supported the ancient theory that higher, not lower, taxes helped balance the budget, with federal deficits averaging under 1 per cent of GDP under his watch.

The dearth of hard evidence to support supply-side theory over the past four decades during which politicians have repeatedly put the policies into practice partly explains why the academic community still mostly holds the theory in disdain. Polls of economists since the 1970s – often commissioned when a government announced plans to cut tax rates and boost taxes in the process – have repeatedly shown they reject the idea of self-funding tax cuts. In 2012, for example, Chicago Booth University asked a panel of senior economists whether a cut in US federal income tax rates would raise taxable income sufficiently to ensure that the annual total tax revenue would be higher within five years than without the tax cut. Thirty-three per cent said they disagreed. Thirty-eight per cent said they strongly disagreed. None said they either agreed or strongly agreed.[83] This view seems to be prevalent regardless of the political leaning of the economists involved. The Harvard professor Greg Mankiw, for example, served as Chair of the Council of Economic Advisers to President George W. Bush. Yet in his 1997 textbook, *Principles of Microeconomics*, he discussed supply-side economics in a section titled 'Charlatans and Cranks': 'An example of fad economics occurred in 1980,' he wrote:

when a small group of economists advised presidential candidate Ronald Reagan that an across-the-board cut in income tax rates

would raise tax revenue . . . Almost all professional economists,
including most of those who supported Reagan's proposal to cut
taxes, viewed this outcome as far too optimistic.[84]

The question therefore arises: why has supply-side economics taken
such a hold? Part of the answer has to be Laffer and Wanniski's sales-
manship. Part has to do with the interpretation some have placed on
historical economic data. But it's also important to remember the
circumstances of the decade that gave rise to the theory.

The 1970s are widely remembered as a dismal period economically in Europe and the United States. The previous couple of decades
had witnessed extraordinary growth. In the US GDP had risen by 3
per cent in real terms per capita annually. In some European countries the figure was above 4 per cent. The pre-1973 period also largely
brought full employment on both sides of the Atlantic.[85] Post-1973,
by contrast, growth slowed, and unemployment crept up. In reality,
1970s unemployment was low by pre-Second World War levels, or
modern standards. And if one uses the most widely accepted orthodox measure for long-term economic performance – real GDP
growth per capita – the 1970s rate of around 2 per cent per annum
was about average for the twentieth century.[86] But that was not
people's perception at the time. They felt poorer because they were
witnessing the end of an unprecedented economic boom. They were
also bewildered by the explosion of inflation. Rising prices ate away
at the value of savings and wages, and generally caused huge uncertainty. In Europe inflation contributed to wage disputes, which led to
labour strikes, while in the United States slowing growth and rising
prices contributed to a stagnant stock market that made middle-
class investors feel poorer.

Unsurprisingly, therefore, citizens began to question their
leaders. In the United States, voters 'went from being economic
populists, who thought the system was rigged against them by Wall
Street, to being social and conservative populists, who thought that

government was the problem', according to Karl Rove, a Republican political strategist who was the architect of George W. Bush's White House bid.[87] The result was a seismic political shift. In 1978 Rove himself helped Bill Clements to become the first Republican to win the Texas governorship since 1869.[88] Two years after this, Ronald Reagan swept into the White House, declaring 'In this present crisis, government is not the solution to our problem; government is the problem.'[89] The shift occurred in Britain too. From the late 1940s to the 1970s, the government of the country had been conducted according to the so-called 'Post-war Consensus'. Both major political parties, Labour and the Conservatives, had agreed on policies of high taxes and significant state intervention in the economy. In 1979, the country elected Margaret Thatcher, who promised a fundamental break with these policies. Across developed nations, in fact, 'the view that the growth and financing of the public sector has, on balance, stifled growth' attracted widespread support around the world, the OECD[90] observed in 1985.[91]

A crisis of confidence in the old ways created an opportunity for people to come in and offer new ideas. Supply-side economics fitted the general disillusionment with the effectiveness of government. It also provided answers that seemed easy to execute and that appeared cost-free to governments. True, many experts pooh-poohed its central tenet. But then they were having their own crisis of confidence in the 1970s. And the uncertainty that followed created precisely the right conditions for a fringe idea to take centre stage.

The Chicago School

In the post-Second World War period, many economists implicitly or explicitly subscribed to Wagner's Law, a theory posited in 1883 by the German economist Adolph Wagner.[92] Wagner had mapped how, as a sample of countries had become richer, their public expenditure had increased. He saw this correlation as evidence that rising government expenditure was both a cause and feature of continued growth. The years after 1945 appeared to confirm this. Increased government investment and more detailed stewardship than in the past, it seemed, contributed to robust growth.[93] James Tobin, one of the most celebrated US economists of the twentieth century, who would also be awarded the Nobel memorial prize in economics, summed up the thinking of many of his peers when he said in 1960 that 'Increased taxation is the price of growth.'[94]

Not all economists agreed, though. In 1947 the Austrian economist Friedrich Hayek established the Mont Pelerin Society, a group dedicated to the cause of encouraging free-market, laissez-faire ideas in a period when expanded government involvement in society seemed to be unanimously supported across the political spectrum.[95] Another founder member of this small club was Milton Friedman, who in the second half of the twentieth century would become perhaps the loudest voice raging against Keynesianism. He opposed minimum wage rules and income redistribution and took a poor view of government regulation and government-backed central banks. Friedman and his peers at the University of Chicago argued that government interventions aimed at improving the economy were at best inefficient and at worst counterproductive. The Chicago School, as Friedman and other government sceptics at the university came to be known, held that markets tended towards equilibrium, and that any attempt to steer them led to instability and inefficiency. In practical terms, they argued, governments should resist the temptation to try to smooth out demand in the economy. At its core, this thinking was that of Adam Smith and his intellectual descendants of the Neoclassical School – the belief that human beings respond to price signals in a way that maximises their own welfare; and that this rational and predictable decision-making can only be distorted, and the productive process made less efficient, by government inserting itself in the transactions that power the economy.

Friedman placed enormous faith in the tendency of markets to achieve an economic equilibrium in which employment and productivity are maximised. That such a viewpoint hinged on some assumptions – for example, a belief in perfect competition – that were patently not true didn't trouble him. His view was that the economy was so complex that any theories about it were bound to involve assumptions that might be unrealistic. What mattered was whether these theories allowed one to make accurate predictions. If they did, then whether the assumptions they rested on might or might not be accurate was irrelevant.[96]

Most economists up to the 1970s largely accepted the neoclassical economic thesis that policies that cause market distortions lead to inefficient resource allocation. However, in a context where significant government intervention in the economy, via historically high taxes and spending, didn't appear to be causing any harm, they seemed happy to overlook this contradiction between economic theory and reality. They concluded, for example, that even though higher taxes might make employment less attractive in principle, in reality people were either not influenced by this or felt powerless to respond. Moreover, when they examined data for the period between the end of the Second World War and 1980, they usually found no evidence that the higher taxes and government spending that prevailed then had dampened growth.[97]

But as faith in Keynesianism waned in university economics departments, interest in examining the role of government more critically surged. Academics began building complex models and crunching data sets that related to all kinds of government interventions in the economy. Academic journals in the 1980s became filled with what some described as 'second-generation' analyses of the impact of tax rates and government spending on growth. Their findings offered a stark contrast with those of earlier studies. Now, it seemed, there was indeed a negative relationship between government intervention and economic growth.[98] Higher taxes and government spending did lead to slower growth and, consequently, poorer populations. The dozens of papers that made these points might not have proved the supply-side argument that tax cuts paid for themselves (in any case, otherwise sympathetic figures such as Friedman didn't believe this), but they did suggest both that government was injurious to growth and that taxes shaped people's behaviour. As one of Friedman's colleagues at Chicago University, Robert Lucas, put it, Keynesianism had run out of road. Stimulating the *supply* of labour and investment should now be the focus of economics: 'The potential for welfare gains from better long-run, supply-side policies exceeds by far the potential from further improvements in short-run demand management.'[99]

The pitfalls of correlations

It wasn't long, however, before doubts started to be expressed about both the validity and the methodology of these second-generation studies. In some cases, the problem was that models that looked very convincing on the blackboard didn't hold in the real world. For example, in 1990 the economist Sergio Rebelo used a theoretical model to calculate that a 10-percentage-point increase in taxation would cut a country's growth rate from 2 per cent to 0.37 per cent. 'Taxation can readily lead to development traps and growth miracles,' he concluded in his widely-cited paper.[100] Yet when Rebelo, one of the most prolific authors of peer-reviewed papers on tax economics during the 1990s, and another economist, William Easterly, began to analyse real-world data with a view to proving this definitively, they encountered a problem. 'Many growth models imply a strong negative impact of taxation on growth,' Rebelo told me in late 2019. 'I worked for three years with Bill Easterly on the empirical connection between taxation and growth. We could not find any strong evidence . . . So I had to change my mind and abandon those early models.'[101]

As academics continued to study the links between growth and taxation (usually in the hope of identifying such a link), they repeatedly found a major and systemic flaw: that the claim of a negative relationship between tax levels and growth rates was being made on the basis of selective information and samples. A highly influential 1983 World Bank working paper on the injurious nature of taxes afforded a clear instance. It compared the ratio of total tax revenue to gross domestic product for twenty countries, and concluded from this that low-tax countries enjoyed higher growth rates.[102] However, when the working paper was reappraised, it became apparent that the countries selected for analysis had been chosen almost at random, and that if the model was re-run with a different selection of random countries, the results were not replicated. It was a bit like one study arbitrarily selecting twenty people, finding those who wore dark clothes were taller, and so concluding that it must therefore be the case that all tall people prefer dark clothing; and another study finding that a sample of twenty different people revealed that the tallest wore lighter clothing.

Another study, published in 1991 by the Harvard Professor Robert Barro, which received a lot of attention, found that government spending as a percentage of GDP was inversely correlated with economic growth.[103] But when the study was re-examined it emerged that the results were skewed by the inclusion of countries with different income levels. Developing countries frequently have lower government social spending as a percentage of GDP and higher growth rates than developed countries – the Asian tigers, like Japan and South Korea in the 1970s and 1980s, being an example. But over time, developing countries' growth rates slow and converge with developed countries' rates, and their government spending expands. When Barro's calculations (and those of others

46

who used the same approach) were re-run and the sample adjusted so that only countries with a similar income level were compared, the negative correlation between government spending and growth fell away.[104]

The findings of other studies were distorted by the time period selected. Those, for example, that compared the strong growth of the 1960s, when governments were generally smaller than today, with more modest growth rates in the 1980s, could show a negative correlation between government spending or tax and growth.[105] Those that studied the same assumptions but took a longer view found that the correlation fell away.[106] Poking holes in rivals' findings is, of course, scarcely the unique preserve of economists. What is striking about the whole tax-incentive debate is that it was also the authors of early studies claiming negative correlations between tax levels and growth who found themselves having to report that they couldn't replicate their results if they examined wider data sets.[107]

There was another problem, too, and it's one that has come to dog economic research: calibrating econometric models. Countries differ from one another in endowments, demographics, politics and other ways that can have a big impact on growth. Simple comparisons between GDP rates and tax burdens or spending levels can therefore be highly misleading. For example: Japan's low GDP growth in recent decades has been exacerbated by a falling population.[108] The US growth rate has been supported by a higher birth rate and immigration.[109] If you want to compare the impact of a variable, like tax, on two such countries you have to make adjustments accordingly, perhaps by using GDP per capita. If you don't, you risk concluding that an economy is successful when its population is actually becoming individually poorer, or that it's unsuccessful when in fact its citizens are becoming more prosperous. Longevity is another factor that should be taken into account. Increased longevity is usually seen as an indication of economic and societal success. However, it also reduces GDP per capita growth, since the added years of life are usually non-working years. In the past forty years European longevity has increased far faster than US life expectancy.[110] Not to allow for that when comparing European countries with America can skew a calculation significantly.

When economic studies that posited a link between low tax and high growth were reassessed, this time controlling for age, school enrolment, starting income and various other factors, the earlier published findings often turned out to rest on very shaky foundations, and other factors – such as openness to trade – surfaced as much more likely causal factors. Time and time again, it seemed, second-generation studies adopted models that were questionable, or ones whose results could not be replicated by differently calibrated models.[111] Add to that the inevitable miscalculations[112] – some economists said they couldn't replicate the outcome of their peers using the same data, a common problem in economics[113] – and the new certainties seemed less certain.

But the biggest problem with the second generation of tax research was that, for all the stand-on-one's-head-and-squint-and-you'll-see-them correlations they identified, they could not explain the screaming reality of the previous century. From 1870 to 1912, US tax revenues were just 3 per cent of GDP,[114] and the country experienced average per capita growth of 1.9 per cent per annum.[115] After the Second World War, government spending entered a new, higher level, averaging around 30 per cent of GDP between 1960 and 1997. During this period the United States experienced average per capita growth of 2.2 per cent per annum.[116] The UK experienced a similar trend, growing at its fastest rate ever in the 1950–73 period as the role of government expanded enormously.[117] Longer term, the picture is even more stark. The UK's tax burden and public spending was around 10 per cent of national income in the first decade of the twentieth century and over 40 per cent in the last quarter,[118] yet economic growth averaged just 1 per cent in the first decade and over 2 per cent in the latter period.[119]

Other European countries including France[120] have experienced similar trends, as have Asian countries. Japan experienced average annual GNP per capita growth rates of 1.5 per cent from 1887 to 1917,[121] during which it went through its first great industrialisation, and government spending was just a few percent of the economy.[122] Between 1950 and 1980, growth averaged twice that, despite government expenditure doubling in size to over 30 per cent of GDP.

If public spending and taxation, as a rule, weigh on growth, how could governments expand from 10 per cent to 40 per cent of the economy and their countries not suffer much lower growth rates? Or, if low tax was so good for growth, why weren't the late-nineteenth century and early-twentieth a period of more dynamic expansion? And, by the same token, why do cross-country comparisons show that having a low tax- or government-spending-to-GDP ratio has been a feature common to poor countries, not rich ones? As the renowned tax economist Joel Slemrod wrote in 1995: 'If the cost of government is so large, why is this cost so difficult to discern in time-series or cross-country studies?'[123]

Concerns about big government are not just a feature of the late-twentieth century. In the 1830s Britain elected the Whig Party on the promise of 'retrenchment and reform' of government, after the Napoleonic Wars prompted an expansion of the state. Keynes once suggested that a tax-to-GDP ratio of 25 per cent might be the maximum an economy could bear[124] – well below the 37 per cent level that Britain's 2020 Chancellor of the Exchequer, Rishi Sunak, has identified as his preferred ceiling.[125] But in many respects the focus on government size is often not instructive, not least because the most commonly used metric – tax or spending as a percentage of GDP – is so simplistic as to be misleading. For example, France's spending-to-GDP ratio is inflated by its expenditure on childcare and family support. The US government does not cover all this. However, the United States offers tax deductions for children that the French tax code does not. From a revenue perspective, giving someone money or cutting their tax bill is much the same thing,[126] which is why the technical name for deductions are 'tax expenditures'. Including these in one's calculations can give a very different picture. For example, the Netherlands is often depicted as a quintessential example of a pampering European 'big government', a perception apparently supported by its above-OECD-average tax-to-GDP ratio. In 2010 the OECD estimated the ratio at 36 per cent, compared to 25 per cent in the United States. However, Dutch tax expenditures amounted to just 5 per cent of tax revenue, while Washington gives exemptions worth over 30 per cent of tax revenue.[127]

Leaving aside the problem of assessing precise government size ratios, the fact is that governments can sometimes do things more efficiently than the private sector. The UK spends less than 10 per cent of GDP on its government-run healthcare system. Meanwhile, the United States' largely private system costs 17 per cent of GDP.[128] The UK system provides free universal healthcare, which the US system does not, and, by many metrics, achieves better health outcomes than the US system.[129] Governments have also shown themselves more effective than the private sector at providing roads and bridges (when the private sector does build such infrastructure, it is frequently only when awarded a minimum toll revenue guarantee by government),[130] the provision of security and the administration of justice.[131] And, insofar as a society considers income redistribution desirable, governments have been more effective than the historic private-sector alternative of charity.

None of this means that wasteful government spending is harmless. History shows that big government as a result of profligacy – excessively generous pensions, white elephant projects or exorbitant state employee wages – will as surely lead to unsustainable deficits as a business which loses control of costs will go bankrupt. But failure to find consistent material evidence to show that bigger government leads to slower growth has left us much where we were fifty years ago. Today, economists generally agree that tax cuts can provide short-term boosts to growth, but not nearly enough to make the reductions pay for themselves. Meanwhile, tax-rate rises are seen as likely to curtail growth, but not to such an extent that they will reduce tax revenues, which means that if one does have a budget-deficit problem, taxation almost certainly needs to be part of the solution. The neoclassical theory championed by supply-siders – that we could significantly sharpen incentives to create wealth by reducing the tax burden on society – captured the economics profession's imagination for some time, but more recently has lost its hold, even in traditional free-market bastions like the University of Chicago.[132]

The problem is, though, that claims of a miraculous, welfare-enhancing discovery – such as that magnets can cure cancer or that lower taxes boost growth – invariably attract greater attention than those which offer no easy solutions. For this reason, the constant drip-drip over the past few decades of papers that have echoed the basic supply-sider argument have left their mark on the public consciousness. And they still have a disproportionate and baleful effect on government decision-making.

No free lunch?

After I returned to Britain from Nashville, I got to thinking about U-Haul truck rates, and found myself punching destinations into the online price tool to see if Laffer's theory about truck hire costs being correlated with tax rates was accurate. At first it did indeed seem that the cost of trucks to Nashville from cities in states with high income taxes was higher than the cost of trucks going the other way.

But then I broadened the sample to include other low tax states, and the correlation fell away.[133] What's more, I found that the supposed link between tax rates and internal migration didn't hold up

51

even for Tennessee. Nashville might have been booming, with around 100 people a day moving there, but Tennessee as a whole was losing citizens, despite its low tax rates. Meanwhile, high-tax California was still receiving net inward migration from other states. When I surveyed the literature, I found that economic studies over the years had failed to find a negative correlation between US state tax rates and state-by-state economic growth. On the contrary, the richest states tended to have higher taxes.

It seemed the U-Haul prices were yet another supply-side anecdote that sounded convincing on first hearing but didn't live up to close scrutiny. Supply-side theory failing to predict van rental rates is, however, a relatively harmless shortcoming. Far more serious is the effect of such a theory when it plays out at a national level. In 2016, Donald Trump told me he planned to get the US budget deficit down from its then annual level of $585 billion. Two years into office in 2019, and after his tax cuts, it was $1 trillion.[134]

2

THE FELDSTEIN REVELATION

Do high taxes make us lazy?

The queues tend to build up first on the section of motorway north of Lyon. By noon, the stretch that skirts the Rhône south of the city is also clogging up, and vehicles enter a glacial stop-start rhythm that can involve driving for miles without leaving second gear. The motorway from Paris to Marseille is known as the Route du Soleil ('Road of the Sun'): travel it any Saturday in July or August and you'll find yourself surrounded by barely moving Renault Scenics crammed with bags, board games and beach toys often covered by colourful towels to protect them from the sun. Front-seat passengers rest their bare feet on the dashboard. Up ahead, campervans with bicycles fixed to the back inch past Peugeot SUVs pulling trailers. On the side of the road, electronic signs flash warnings such as '*Véhicule Arrêt –* *Soyez Vigilant*' or tell you that the next service station is closed due to long queues. Occasionally, the traffic begins to clear and cars speed up. That's probably the most dangerous part, because invariably, before long, the cars ahead of you suddenly brake sharply, forcing you to do the same and pray the people behind are doing likewise. To reduce the risk of being tail-ended, motorists activate their emergency lights while slowing, as an additional form of brake light. But the pieces of broken plastic and glass on the side of the road show the system doesn't always work.

For millions of French, the Route du Soleil is synonymous with traffic. It's even earned a place in *Guinness World Records* for the longest ever traffic jam – a 176 km tailback in 1980.[1] In point of fact, that didn't happen in summer. It was in February, and caused by tourists returning from their winter ski break in the Alps.

Why does the road to sunshine, or snow, experience these occasional severe congestion problems? Some (usually foreigners) say bad driving is a factor. The Lyonnais say the passage of the Route through their city centre creates an unnecessary bottleneck. But if you followed the work of US economist Ed Prescott, you might have another answer: taxation.

In 2004, the year he was awarded the Nobel memorial prize for economics, Prescott published a paper entitled 'Why Do Americans Work So Much More Than Europeans?'[2] In it, he sought to explain a large divergence that had emerged over the previous forty years. During the 1960s and early 1970s, Western Europeans and Americans worked a similar number of hours each year – indeed, the French actually worked slightly longer hours than US workers. But by 2000, the situation had changed radically. Now the French were working 15 per cent fewer hours than the Americans. They still do today.[3] A major explanatory factor was an increasing fondness on the part of Europeans in general, and the French in particular, for taking holidays.[4] US workers have no legal entitlement to paid annual leave, although most employers do give some.[5] The French have, alongside the Spanish, the most generous paid vacation entitlement in Europe, with up to 36 days' paid leave each year[6] – longer if one builds up overtime by exceeding the 35-hour working week. Hence the congestion on the Route du Soleil and other autoroutes on '*les jours de grand départ*'.

Europeans' long holidays are a function of government legislation and negotiated agreements between workers and employers. All parties are aware that longer holidays come at a cost: unions generally accept that fewer hours worked means less output, which must result in lower wage increases. This is evident in the macroeconomic data: French workers are just as productive per hour as US workers, but their GDP per capita over the course of a year is lower. So why do Europeans choose, as a group, to forgo income in return for leisure? And why don't Americans?

Some have suggested that varying cultural preferences explain the difference, but Prescott thought the answer lay in the fact that Europeans were rational economic actors. He noticed, when examining labour supply and government revenue data, that 'when European and US tax rates were comparable, European and US labor supplies were comparable'. His conclusion was therefore that the Europeans were simply responding rationally to a price signal. They were working fewer hours, because their governments made working less financially attractive.

Microeconomic mechanisms

In the previous chapter I looked at the arguments that have raged about the economic pros and cons of big government, and showed how, in terms of the overall impact of tax burdens and state spending as a percentage of GDP, there is no convincing correlation between government size and growth or wealth levels. Advocates of small government, though, would argue that this proves very little: modern economies are so large and complex, they say, that even large trends or shifts get buried in the macroeconomic data. What matters far more, and the area where one should be able to more easily spot the impacts of tax policies, is via microeconomic channels such as corporate investment, personal saving decisions and, perhaps most critically, how hard people choose to work. Here one really can measure the extent to which government tax policies affect economic behaviour, because one is looking at individuals and their motivations, not states and their mechanical complexities. And it is in this *micro*economic arena, small government advocates claim, that their arguments for low taxes can be most unambiguously demonstrated and proved.

The notion that lower taxes are an incentive to work is well established in Western societies. Seven of the last twelve UK Chancellors of the Exchequer, going back to Labour's Denis Healey[7] in the 1970s, have cut income tax rates, and done so saying they wished to encourage effort and industriousness (Healey's predecessor, the Conservative Anthony Barber, also reduced income taxes, but his stated aim for the move was a desire to give the economy a Keynesian stimulus).[8] Japanese governments, German chancellors, US and French presidents and prime ministers of Australia,[9] Canada[10] and Ireland have all reduced income taxes in the past forty years citing an intention to stir their populations toward greater effort. Their moves are consistent with the guidance from organisations like the OECD and IMF. Broadsheet newspapers and current affairs magazines around the world regularly state as fact in their editorial and news pages that lower taxes lead to greater effort. Opinion polls from the United States to Latvia have also shown many voters accept this premise.

This idea wasn't created by Arthur Laffer, Ronald Reagan or Margaret Thatcher. It's much more deep-rooted than that. People seem to find it intuitive that if you reduce someone's take-home (post-tax) earnings, they will feel less inclined to work hard. Even when Britain was drifting towards greater egalitarianism in the immediate post-Second World War period, a 1954 poll of 1,429 English and Welsh workers found that 73 per cent of the men questioned said they believed this to be true.[11]

In the post-war period, concerns about the disincentive impacts of taxation had relatively little impact on policy around the world, with top rates of income tax hitting 80 per cent or more in Britain,[12] the United States[13] and Japan.[14] Amid slowing growth in the 1970s, thinking on the matter changed,[15] and between 1981 and 2010 the average top marginal statutory rates of personal tax in OECD members fell from 66.8 per cent to 41.7 per cent.[16] Since then, concerns about growing inequality have prompted much talk about re-imposing higher taxes on the wealthy. And some actions. In 2010, Britain increased its tax rate on top earners to 50 per cent from 40 per cent (later reduced again to 45 per cent). In 2017, the Japanese government approved tax increases for higher earners, helping fund tax reductions for those on lower incomes.[17] Bernie Sanders, a front-running candidate for the Democratic Party's presidential nomination in 2016, launched his 2020 campaign with a proposal to increase the top federal income tax rate to 52 per cent from 37 per cent.[18] The high-profile US Congresswoman Alexandria Ocasio-Cortez even started a campaign for a 70 per cent top income tax rate.[19] And polls show wide support for higher taxes on the wealthy. A 2018 survey conducted for the OECD that asked 22,000 people around the world 'Should the government tax the rich more than they currently do in order to support the poor?' found that, overall, 68 percent said yes (with respondents in the United States more likely to agree than those in France).[20]

But the fact that popular feeling sometimes now inclines towards higher taxes for the ultra-wealthy hasn't destroyed that basic, long-rooted assumption that tax and hard work are uneasy bedfellows. And that assumption is so embedded in the DNA of classical and neoclassical economic theory that it has proved difficult to shift.

To understand why, we need to revisit the development of economics as a science, and rehearse again the basic laws of supply and demand.

The economic law of gravity

As early as the 1690s, the philosopher John Locke stated as axiomatic that 'The price of any commodity rises or falls, by the proportion of the number of buyers and sellers.'[21] Later generations accepted the basic premise, but altered and refined it. For classical economists such as Adam Smith in the eighteenth and David Ricardo in the nineteenth century, prices are ultimately a function of production costs – in other words, goods which are more expensive to create cost more. For economists who created the 'marginal' revolution of the nineteenth century, prices are actually determined by the marginal utility consumers derive from the production – that is to say that a person will be willing to pay for an additional good, such as an extra chocolate bar, a price equivalent to the pleasure they derive from it. If that's £1 for the chocolate bar, then they will pay up to this level even if they find out that the manufacturing cost is only 20 pence. If it's £1, but manufacturing costs take it to £1.50, they won't purchase. Alfred Marshall's model, based on a mechanistic view of human behaviour, whereby people behave in a rational and predictable way in response to price signals,[22] has become familiar anyone who has had even the most basic exposure to economics.

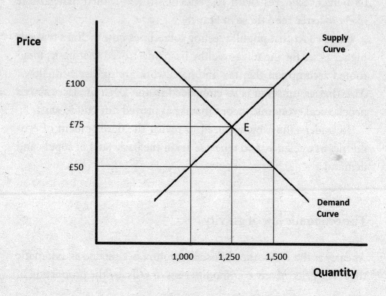

The basic supply-and-demand model holds that the volume of a good or service which suppliers are willing to provide increases with price. This tendency is captured in an upward sloping line called the supply curve. In the example above, suppliers are willing to offer 1,500 units when the price is £100, and just 1,000 when the price is £50. Conversely, the demand curve shows that consumers, in aggregate, will only demand 1,000 units when the good's price is £100, but 1,500 when it's £50. At a price of £50, buyers want more than sellers are willing to supply, while at £100 the sellers will not all be able to find buyers. There is, however, an equilibrium point on the model (E) at which the market 'clears' – that is to say, a point at which the volume demanded and offered will match, and the supply and demand curves intersect. In this particular example, the market equilibrium price is £75.

Key to Marshall's world view was the notion of the elasticity of supply and demand and the ability to quantify it. If someone reduces consumption by 10 per cent when the price rises by 10 per cent, for example, they are said to have a price elasticity of demand of -1 (often expressed without the minus sign). Different people will have different preferences for every product, but even if these are widely dispersed, economists say one can derive an average responsiveness to price for a population that allows useful predictions to be made. High elasticity means a sharp reduction in purchases in response to a price change upwards. In the example below, the shallow curve A shows that a 25 per cent increase in price from £80 to £100 leads to a 75 per cent drop in quantity demanded – the sort of scenario one could imagine with a discretionary purchases of luxury items, such as restaurant meals. The steeper demand curve, B, reflects the preferences of an individual or group with a low price elasticity. Here, even though the price rises tenfold from £10 to £100, the quantity demanded falls just 50 per cent to 125. This could reflect purchases of necessities, like water or medicine.

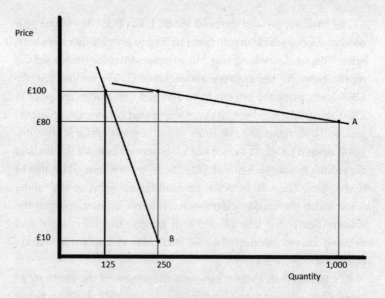

Suppliers are also believed to display price elasticity, although in the opposite direction, with higher prices leading to higher supply, and so displaying a positive elasticity.

Marshall's curves exemplify the neoclassical view of the world. As the Bank of England states on its website in 2020:

> Supply and demand is a bit like an economist's version of the law of gravity. It's the basis which decides how much everything costs: a cup of coffee, a house and even your salary.[23]

Just as physicists believe Newton's laws apply in all circumstances (on this planet at least), so economists believe the laws of supply and demand govern every earthly financial transaction. Some argue the laws even apply to non-pecuniary exchanges. The Nobel prize-winning economist Gary Becker argued that the laws of supply and demand could be applied to the search for love and help

60

explain our choice of spouse. That's something of a niche view, but the founding principle of neoclassical economics is fixed and immoveable: human beings are rational agents exhibiting constant preferences and are eager to maximise their material welfare; their willingness to transact is not guided by whimsical factors such as cloud formations or tarot card readings. Because they are rational, their responsiveness to price changes is predictable and measurable.

Of course, economists know that, just as wind speed and surface temperature may influence the operation of gravity in any given case, so various other external factors may have to be considered when it comes to what determines quantity demanded or supplied. There may, for example, be a 'usual' price for a bottle of water, but if the temperature rises sharply from one day to the next, a beach stall may sell even more bottles of water at £2 each than it did a day earlier at £1 each because buyers are both more numerous and thirstier. Economists therefore qualify their model with the Latin tag *ceteris paribus*: 'all other things being equal'. Inevitably, circumstances never remain constant over time. However, economists also believe that the key factors that influence demand and supply, such as population, the state of technology and, indeed, weather can be factored into models, or assumed to balance out over time. Economists tend to see the factors that cannot be built into models, like changing public mood, as insignificant compared to the importance of price, and consequently the '*ceteris paribus*' qualification is not usually seen as a limitation on the application of the concept of elasticity.

When it comes to income tax, neoclassical theory clearly states that if a worker finds themselves having to hand over some of the money they receive for a good or their work to the government, they will be less inclined to provide that good or their service. It's a mathematical certainty. That much is clear from the upward-sloping labour supply curve. The only detail that has to be ascertained is the gradient of that curve, which will determine at what level the tax rate will start to deter work to the extent that it harms the economy.[24] What, then, is the slope? How elastic is the supply of labour?

Earning more, working less

John Locke never extended his thinking about supply and demand to wage determination.[25] At the time he was writing, the idea that higher prices would stimulate additional supply wasn't one people associated with the labour market. Indeed, many people thought that peoples' inclination to work followed a very different pattern. The English pamphleteer Thomas Manley complained in 1669 that 'nor has the increase in wages amongst us been occasioned by a quickness of trade . . . [people] work so much the fewer days by how much more they exact in their wages.'[26] Mercantilist thinkers of the seventeenth and eighteenth centuries similarly worried that the more workers were paid, the less they worked,[27] dissipating their higher wages in such unhealthy habits as drinking and fornication (perhaps in an attempt to emulate the upper classes of the time), thus in time suffering even worse poverty than before. The gloomy mercantilist view would have been hard to test since in the five centuries to 1800 wages didn't really rise with any consistency.[28] But it was certainly true that, once the Industrial Revolution got under way, wages rose and working hours fell. For example, workers in the carding room of Rhode Island's cotton mills, who in 1840 were toiling fourteen hours a day for $3.28 a week, were by 1884 receiving $5.40 a week for an eleven-hour day.[29] Assuming a six-day week, this means that, even ignoring the modest inflation over the period, per-hour wage rates doubled. It's a picture replicated elsewhere in other developed countries and other industries. In Britain, for example, average real earnings rose 300 per cent between 1860 and 1970, while hours worked dropped by a third.[30]

As with the working hours trends, long-term unemployment data suggested that higher real wages did not stimulate an increase in the labour supply. British unemployment averaged under 5 per cent in the 1870s when wages were relatively low. It averaged over 8 percent in the last quarter of the twentieth century when wages were far higher.[31] US unemployment figures, similarly, were comparatively low in the (lower-paid) nineteenth and early twentieth century, and rose sharply during the (better-paid) twentieth century.[32]

A direct comparison between different countries over this period confirms the pattern of higher pay being correlated with less work. In 1911, for example, among male workers over the age of ten in England and Wales, the employment level stood at 84 per cent. In the better-paid US, by contrast, the employment level was three percentage points lower, despite the fact that, owing to the high level of internal migration of young men, the country had a higher proportion of working-age males and fewer retirees than Britain.[33]

It makes perfect sense. If we can feed, clothe, house and educate ourselves without having to work (or have our children work) fourteen-hour days, why wouldn't we choose to? But this truth also clashes with neoclassical economic principles. If the market rate for an hour's service increases, it follows that a worker should be more, not less, inclined to forgo leisure time and to sell more of their time to employers.

The way economists reconcile the data with theory is to argue that labour isn't like other goods or services. They note that people certainly do respond to higher wages, frequently accepting jobs that involve working longer hours and extra pay (promotions) or doing overtime when their boss offers time-and-a-half. In such situations, what economists call the substitution effect is in play, prompting people to sacrifice leisure time for more money. But at the same time, as they get richer, the 'income effect' comes into play, stimulating them to forgo some of the wages they could have earned if they had elected to work those extra hours in favour of more leisure time.

The substitution and income effects act in opposite directions: one encouraging us to work more, the other to work less. The slope of the labour supply curve, and peoples' responses to wage increases or higher net incomes as a result of tax cuts, hinge upon the relative strengths of the two forces. Two hundred years of working less and less suggests the income effect has historically had the edge, giving a downward-sloping supply curve, or that the elasticity of labour supply is actually negative, not positive, as the laws of demand and supply assume.

This much is apparent from various studies conducted between the 1950s and 1970s. A notable paper from 1968 that sought to establish if there was a link between hours worked and tax-adjusted earnings among male workers conceded that there didn't appear to be one.[34] Others came to a similar conclusion.[35] Research of a more anecdotal nature concurred: at least half a dozen such surveys in Britain, Canada and the United States published in academic journals from 1950 to 1980 indicated that while people might not be happy about a tax hike, they were unlikely to change their working

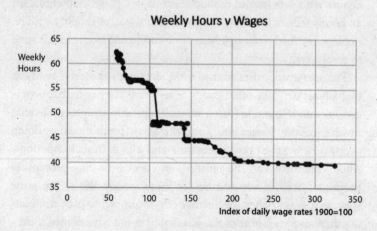

Weekly Hours v Wages

Data source: Bank of England

patterns in response. 'It is generally agreed that the labour supply of all adult males is largely unaffected by changes in marginal tax rates. In most studies, both the substitution and the income effects are very close to zero', stated the Congressional Budget Office in 1978 when Republican Congressman Jack Kemp teamed up with Republican Senator William Roth to pen a Bill that sought to enact big tax cuts.[36]

Economists like Robert Mundell and Arthur Laffer were sceptical of such research. To them, it was simply inconceivable that people did not respond to clear price signals. Perhaps earlier researchers had simply been wrong in failing to find a work-pay link: after all, empirical data analysis was a relatively new field of economic study. Or perhaps the long-term inverse correlation between work and pay no longer held. There were some signs that the century-long downward trend in hours worked had slowed sharply.[37] Perhaps leisure had become less precious now people had more of it and the income effect had lost its potency?

Whatever doubts other economists might have had about Mundell and Laffer's ideas, they proved persuasive with one key group: conservative politicians. And when they took power in 1981, they acted decisively. The Reagan Economic Recovery Tax Act of 1981, with its 25 per cent across-the-board reduction in income tax rates (more for the better off), constituted the biggest tax cut in US history. Here at last was the decisive test for supply-side economics and those seeking to establish how elastic labour supply was to wage and tax cuts. After all, if ever a single piece of legislation gave all Americans reason to work harder, this was it.[38]

Supply-side economics in the dock

So what happened in the US when Reagan adopted his swashbuckling tax cut reforms of 1981? Almost immediately, unemployment jumped upwards, and continued to rise through 1982.[39] It began to fall in 1983, but it wasn't until the end of 1984 that jobless levels fell below the level of early 1981. In 1981 and 1982 hours worked also fell.[40] Far from stimulating people to work harder, it seemed, putting more money in their pockets was making them work less.

One would think that that might have been game over for the supply-siders. Paradoxically, though, Laffer viewed it as a vindication of his views. Later he recalled Ronald Reagan ringing him to celebrate after the Tax Act passed. But Laffer 'wasn't as enthusiastic as he [Reagan] thought I should be'.

The President grew tetchy and pressed him. 'What's the matter, Arthur? Why are you this way?'[41]

In response, Laffer posed a question. 'Sir, how much would you shop at a store a week before that store has a discount sale?'

According to Laffer, the penny dropped for Reagan immediately. 'Oh, my goodness, how bad is it going to be?'

Laffer didn't mince his words: it would be 'terrible', he said; the country was facing 'a barn burner'.

The point Laffer was making was that, while the tax cuts had been enacted in 1981, they were being phased in over three years, from 1982 to 1984. Workers therefore knew that, all other things being equal, their net pay per hour would be higher in 1983 and 1984 than 1981 and 1982. For Laffer, this explained everything: Reagan had effectively created an income effect that made leisure time relatively 'cheaper', in terms of forgone earnings, in 1981 and 1982. Naturally, Laffer argued, it made sense for a rational agent to consume more leisure earlier when it was cheap, rather than in 1983 or 1984 when it would be more expensive. This wasn't contorted, after-the-fact justification either. In December 1981 Laffer wrote an article for *Barron's* magazine in which he argued that the deferral of the tax cuts would encourage people to work less in the near term and that, as a result, 1982 would be a year of weak economic growth.

It's worth mentioning that a lot of other things were going on at the time. In 1981, Europe, where countries had not in the main cut income tax rates, entered a recession. Oil prices spiked, and in the United States the Federal Reserve Chairman Paul Volcker jacked up interest rates to almost 20 per cent in a war against inflation that was inflicting a lot of collateral damage on the economy.

But for Laffer these were minor matters. For him, the recovery of 1983 and rising employment was not cyclical or the result of lower oil prices or monetary policy, but rather the rational response of people to tax cuts. He was, however, if not a lone voice, a rare one. In a 1989 research paper, President Reagan's former chief economic adviser Martin Feldstein examined the precise pattern of the 1983–84 recovery to better understand why it had been stronger than some previous cyclical recoveries, and concluded that there was 'no support for the proposition that the recovery reflected an increase in the supply of labour induced by the reduction in personal marginal tax rates'.[42]

Feldstein was a Harvard professor who had acted as the voice of fiscal caution in the Reagan administration. He had antagonised some in the cabinet and provoked public rebukes from administration officials by giving interviews calling for higher taxes to curb the ballooning deficit. Feldstein thought the Laffer Curve was 'hyperbole',[43] and the two men regularly clashed over advice to Reagan ('I won every battle,' Laffer told me). In his view, the idea that workers had actually chosen unemployment or to reduce hours at the height of the recession, in order to consume more leisure while it was relatively cheaper, was ridiculous. The slashing of interest rates by Volcker in late 1982 offered a far more convincing explanation for the economic revival in 1983.[44] In academic and policy circles, Feldstein's view was widely shared.

True, there were some workers whose behaviour was consistent with Laffer's side of the argument. Surveys over the years have shown that some very low-paid employees in the United States, and Britain, appeared to be highly sensitive to tax changes. But this was because the interplay of the tax and benefit systems was such that in some situations they stood to lose as much in benefits as they gained, post-tax, from working – effectively, they could face marginal tax rates of 100 per cent.[45] Married women, too, according to studies in the United States, UK and Continental Europe,[46] were also sensitive to tax rates. But the calculation in this case was often whether after-tax incomes could cover the costs of working, such as childcare. The more revealing picture, in terms of judging the relative merits of Laffer and Feldstein's competing claims, was that the larger body of workers didn't appear to respond to tax cuts, and even the highest-paid professionals and managers, who received the biggest percentage drops in their average and marginal income tax rates, also failed to work longer hours after the 1980s tax cuts.[47]

None of this would have surprised economists of the 1960s and 1970s, whose consensus the Congressional Budget Office had summarised in 1978. These economists mostly accepted the basic neoclassical theory that individuals should respond to price signals, like higher net wages, but they understood that institutional, social and practical considerations might get in the way. For example, when US corporate executives,[48] Canadian insurance agents and accountants,[49] investment managers[50] and British solicitors[51] told economic researchers doing 1950s, -60s and -70s surveys that tax reductions would not encourage them to work more, they often stated that the reason was that they were already working long hours.

As for the average worker, the median working week in the US in the mid-1980s was forty-two hours.[52] Given other calls on people's time, such as childcare, a large proportion of employees would not have had the spare capacity to work much longer hours even if they had wanted to. Besides, most employees, then as now, were not granted that flexibility. If a business closed at 5 p.m. and was shut at the weekends, its employees couldn't opt to work an extra couple of hours each day or do a shift on a Saturday morning for extra pay. It's possible that some might have elected to secure second jobs or shift to jobs that offered the opportunity to get paid for working more hours, but for the majority such moves were rarely practical.

For entrepreneurs or people investing in new enterprises, theoretical work stretching back to the 1940s holds that taxes actually encourage risk-taking, because, as losses can be set against a tax bill, risk is effectively being shared with the government. Lower tax rates, by contrast, place more of the downside on the entrepreneur or investor.[53] Surveys of entrepreneurs over the years have neither proven nor disproven this belief. What they have shown, though, is that business creators don't consider the tax factor at all when planning new ventures. Entrepreneurs don't decide not to launch a new venture because taxes have gone up. Nor do they rush to register one because a tax cut has just been enacted.

In other words, economists at the time had good reason to assume that the Reagan tax cuts would not boost the economy in the way he hoped. Even those who were more sympathetic to the policy tended to be of the view that tax cuts stimulated demand rather than prompted a big increase in the labour supply. Laffer's confidence notwithstanding, the supply-siders had not yet won the argument.

Working harder, earning more

But if that all makes it seem case closed, a contrary view soon started to circulate, courtesy of a very unlikely expert: 'Marty' Feldstein.

In 1987 Lawrence Lindsey, an Assistant Professor of Economics at Harvard University, published a paper in which he noted that, following the 1981 reduction in the top rates of income tax, the incomes of top earners had increased markedly.[54]

Lindsey's paper didn't offer an explanation for the rise, though in comments later he suggested that it was probably partly connected with tax avoidance, since lower taxes reduce the incentives to hide income from the tax authority. It may also have been connected with the fact that at times when people see a good chance of an imminent cut in taxes (as in 1980 and 1981), they opt for a discretionary delay in reporting income from, for example, the sale of assets such as businesses, shares and property (that much of the increase in high incomes after 1981 came from capital gains supports this view). Lindsey, however, also suggested – without supporting data – that 'perhaps one-quarter to one-third of the increased reporting of income was due to increased effort.'[55]

Lindsey was a protégé of Feldstein at Harvard, had been advised by him on the 1987 paper, and had published it with the National Bureau of Economic Research, of which Feldstein was President. And Feldstein, not surprisingly, was intrigued by the findings.[56] Was it possible, he asked himself, that the rich really had changed their behaviour as a response to tax cuts in a way that wasn't showing up in labour force data? He decided to do some digging, and by 1992 had secured confidential data from the Internal Revenue Service on 4,000 individual taxpayers from the 1980s. This 'panel data' was statistical gold dust. One can observe trends in groups of taxpayers sorted by income group in the published IRS data, but over time the people in those groups change, which means we can't actually see the way specific individuals' behaviour changes. Feldstein's data, by contrast, allowed one to follow actual individuals through time.

Now Feldstein examined the impact of Reagan's second great tax-cutting budget, the Tax Reform Act of 1986, which reduced marginal tax rates for average earners by a few percentage points,[57] but slashed the top marginal income tax rate on wages from 50 per cent to 28 per cent. If ever there was a massive incentive to the better-off to work more, this was it. And what were its consequences? Reported taxable incomes rose. And those of the highest earners – those with the greatest incentive to work more – rose the most. Indeed, the income of the group with average earnings of $479,000 per annum enjoyed a

70 per cent increase in their incomes – and that was excluding capital gains, whose realisation can, of course, be timed to benefit from lower tax rates.[58]

Feldstein's conclusion was that previous studies that had measured labour force responses had 'incorrectly interpreted' the data on hours worked. Hours worked, he argued, don't tell one much about the output of 'higher-income individuals, who have substantial discretion about the intensity with which they work, and for whom variations in effort can substantially affect income even if the number of hours is unchanged'. In other words, if you want to know how hard a high earner has been working, you should look at their pay check, not their time card. Feldstein calculated the elasticity of taxable income, which is to say the supply responsiveness, for the different income categories he examined. In 1978, when the Congressional Budget Office assessed the likely outcomes of the Kemp-Roth bill, which would form the basis for the 1981 tax cuts, it estimated an elasticity of labour supply for average earners to be close to zero, and that low-income groups had slightly higher elasticities.[59] Feldstein found that, including effort as well as hours worked, the average person had an elasticity of over one, while his top income group had an elasticity of taxable income of over three. What this meant was that, for every dollar reduction in the tax bill of those in the $479,000-per-annum category, they generated another $3 in new income. With so much more additional taxable income, as Arthur Laffer had predicted, tax cuts could be self-funding. 'All the arguments I had with Marty, he was on the other side on every one. Until he finally did the research in 1993,' a satisfied Laffer told me in 2019.

Feldstein's reputation, combined with the seemingly high quality of the data he used, helped ensure his research reached a wide audience (not too much emphasis was placed on such shortcomings as the fact that his income-elasticity estimate for top earners was based on the experience of just twenty-two people). In the years after his paper emerged, others did similar research and, working on the basis that incomes rather than hours could be used to measure the productivity of high earners, came to the same conclusion: better-paid employees had much higher responsiveness to tax rates than had previously been observed.[60]

In the early 1980s, Feldstein had branded Laffer and his followers 'extremists'.[61] With Feldstein's help, they had entered the political and academic mainstream.

The great UK elasticity stretch

Before long, the 'new tax responsiveness literature',[62] as it came to be known, was having an impact on state treasuries around the world. They were persuaded by the increasing body of academic work during the 1990s and 2000s that claimed that high-income individuals were responsive to tax rates. They came to believe that the big tax cuts the US and British governments introduced during the 1980s had been the right strategy. True, the research that came after Feldstein usually estimated taxable elasticities as being much lower than three. But they were also a lot higher than zero. Tax cuts for the rich might not always be self-funding, but they still brought in more tax revenue than would have been the case if the elasticity of taxable income was zero. And Feldstein's conclusion that lower tax rates encouraged the rich to work a lot harder also meant cuts made broader economic sense.

If a plumber works an extra hour each day because a tax cut makes this more appealing, this directly boosts the economy to the tune of the approximately £50 he or she charges per hour. If the plumber's clients include other businesses, his or her work may have an indirect benefit on the economy by helping those businesses generate additional revenues. And the plumber's spending of the £50 also boosts the economy. Everyone benefits, albeit by a modest amount.

With a chief executive, not only is the direct impact of working harder and earning more money far greater because their salary is a lot higher than the £50 an hour the plumber earns, but the indirect impact can also be exponentially greater. If a CEO, through additional hours or diligence, sees an opportunity to launch a new division for her or his company, this could well add hundreds of millions of dollars to the economy.

One country where such considerations played out as practical policy was Britain.

In the UK in late 2008, Gordon Brown's government announced a plan to increase the top rate of income tax to 45 per cent from 40 per cent for those earning over £150,000 – the top 1 per cent of earners.[63] Months later, the Labour government announced the rise would actually be to 50 per cent.[64] Conservative-leaning newspapers decried the move as an appeal to 'class war'.[65] Brown and Chancellor of the Exchequer Alistair Darling rejected the accusation that the move reflected a desire to the 'soak the rich'. They argued the move was motivated purely by financial pressures. Britain's economy was in chaos and the exchequer was in crisis as the government struggled to bail out the financial sector. With unemployment soaring, and incomes falling, Labour said the only ones with any money to spare were the better-off.

There's some evidence to support Darling and Brown's defence that they weren't trying to launch a fundamental shift of the tax burden on to the rich. Firstly, the move was intended to be short-term – to last only so long as the country was in crisis.[66] Secondly, at the same time as the 50 per cent rate was announced, the government sneaked in a 60 per cent tax rate for people earning between £100,000 and £115,000. This move, which was expected to raise almost as much as the new 50 per cent rate in its first year,[67] was totally contrary to the principle that the better-off should pay more, as it left British taxpayers facing a rate progression from 20 to 40 per cent to 60 per cent, back to 40 per cent on earnings between £115,000 and £150,000 and 50 per cent thereafter. But it was successful in political terms because this tweak was hidden in the removal of the tax-free allowance, which meant the government raised a lot of money with relatively little bad news coverage.

The Conservative leader David Cameron didn't believe the move to a 50 per cent rate was ideological. But he didn't think it was financially motivated either. He reckoned that high earners were responsive to tax changes, and he suspected Brown and Darling thought so too. His take, therefore, was that the new 50 per cent rate was a political ruse.[68] As the professed party of low taxes, the Conservatives could never support a 50 per cent rate. That meant the party could not deny a desire to cut the rate, which in turn meant Labour could go into the upcoming May 2010 election saying that the Conservative government wanted to give millionaires a tax cut.

The Conservatives did win the election in 2010, and they did want to cut the 50 per cent rate, but they still faced a problem of how to handle a possible public backlash. Fortunately, elasticity of taxable income was on hand to help.

The Labour government had said the 50 per cent rate should raise an additional £7 billion. The question was, would high earners conform to supply-side theory and restrict their efforts and earnings? Alistair Darling believed the temporary nature of the 50 pence rate would mean wealthy people wouldn't find it practical to move abroad or change their behaviour, outside of the predictable income-shifting ahead of the introduction of the rate in April 2010 (i.e. move forward payments to the earlier period). However, when it came to budget forecasts, Marty Feldstein could not be ignored.

By 2009, Her Majesty's Treasury had read a lot of 'new tax responsiveness literature' and was using a vast and complex mathematical equation known as a Computable General Equilibrium (CGE) model to map the impacts of policy changes on the economy. Few people even in policy circles knew how the CGE model worked, or if it worked at all, but tax changes were nevertheless typically fed into the

model to see their impacts. By 2009, this model incorporated an estimate for elasticity of taxable income that was informed by the
work of the mainly US academics who had built on Lindsey and
Feldstein's work.

A Freedom of Information Act request by a think tank in 2009
showed that the Treasury used an elasticity estimate of 0.35 for
people with incomes over £150,000.[69] This suggested that additional
revenue would not amount to £7 billion a year, as the government
had originally intimated, but £3 billion. And it was the £3 billion
figure that therefore duly appeared in the budget projections.

In 2012, as Darling's successor George Osborne prepared for his
third budget, he pressed Cameron hard to allow him to cut the top
rate of tax. The Prime Minister remained concerned that the move
would play badly with the electorate.[70] But the two men had a stroke
of good luck. Shortly before the 2012 budget, HMRC reviewed the
tax data for the first year of the new 50 pence rate and decided an
error had been made by the Treasury under the Labour government.[71] The correct figure for the elasticity of taxable income for
Britain's high earners was, they said, not 0.35 as the Labour government had estimated, but actually 0.48. And possibly higher.[72]

You might not expect 0.13 of a percentage point change in an
arcane calculation would have attracted much interest outside of
tax geeks and local policy wonks. But in the following months,
HMRC's findings were picked up by almost all UK newspapers, the
New York Times,[73] US *National Review*,[74] Breitbart and outlets in
Africa and Asia. It also prompted commentaries from many US
think tanks including the Heritage Foundation,[75] Hoover Institute,[76]
and American Enterprise Institute.[77]

Needless to say, it wasn't the fractional change in an elasticity
number that grabbed peoples' attention, but its overall impact on
the top-line revenue figure. Based on the re-estimation of elasticity,
HMRC had concluded that the 50 pence rate had not raised £7 billion. Nor had it raised the £3 billion that an elasticity figure of 0.35

suggested. At most it had brought in another £1 billion, or possibly nothing, or possibly even a minus sum, as the efforts of the wealthy collapsed under the onerous burden of Labour's tax rise. Osborne was able to declare that the 50 per cent rate had raised 'next to nothing'.[78] Cameron was able to claim that by sending millionaires scurrying from the country, Gordon Brown's 'election gambit cost the country £7 billion'.[79] And the two men were able to make the tax change they had always wanted to. In March 2012, Osborne announced a cut in the rate, to 45 per cent, effective from the 2013–14 tax year.

The result? When the cut came into effect over a year later, reported earnings by high earners immediately soared. Gleeful news stories and editorials from Washington to Sydney proclaimed that Britain had just proved that supply-side economics really did work. In his weekly *Daily Telegraph* column, Boris Johnson noted that Britain 'had seen a classic example of what economists call the Laffer Curve'.[80] Cameron claimed that his political opponents had managed to turn a revenue projection of up to £7 billion into a cash outflow of £7 billion. He had rowed back from their policies, and the beneficial effects were there for everyone to see.

Voodoo accounting

Some years after Osborne abolished the 50 pence rate, I found myself browsing through Table 2.6 of HMRC's income tax data. This, as few people even within HMRC probably know, gives tax liabilities by income source, tax band and marginal rate, and it's not the kind of data set to get many people excited. But my inspection revealed something very interesting: a lot of people paid the 'additional rate', as the 50 and – later – 45 per cent rate was officially known. And at that additional rate they paid a lot of tax. According to my calculations, the move above 40 per cent on top earners had yielded an average of an additional £4.7 billion per year each year between 2010 and 2013. Why then were the government and its advisers claiming the opposite?

It all came down to the very complicated assumptions of what one thought would have happened if taxes had not risen. The Conservative-led government's claim that the introduction of the 50 per cent rate hit revenues, and that the reduction in the rate to 45 per cent in 2013 increased revenues, was based on the fact that reported incomes of high earners were lower in the tax year when the 50 per cent rate was introduced, than in the previous period, and higher in the year the rate was cut to 45 per cent than in the immediately preceding period. HMRC, economists and, outside of political speeches, most politicians knew that a lot of either unrelated or short-term factors impacted these numbers. For example, reported incomes were influenced by the economic cycle and, importantly, what's known as forestalling: the moving forward or delaying of the sales of assets or payment of bonuses or dividends, to ensure gains are reported in a lower tax period. The question in determining how much the tax rates really raised or had the capacity to raise hinged on one's measurement of the change in underlying behaviour, stripping out one-off or short-term avoidance measures.

If there was no underlying change in work effort, then one could simply do as I did with Table 2.6, and apply the 40 per cent rate to the reported income levels to estimate how much additional money the 45 or 50 per cent rates raised (also known as the static revenue impact). But HMRC prefers a costing that factors in behavioural changes, because it believes there are significant behavioural responses or, in other words, that for the wealthy the taxable income elasticities are significantly greater than zero. This means the reported incomes I observed in Table 2.6 were lower than would have been the case if the top tax rate had not been increased.

HMRC came up with its 0.48 elasticity figure, and dynamic costings of the tax changes, by estimating a counterfactual income level in 2010–11 for high earners, assuming there had been no tax change, and comparing this to the actual reported incomes. It came up with its counterfactual outcome by identifying two proxies for the incomes of people earning over £150,000 per year, and using these to calculate escalators that were then applied to the pre-tax-hike reported income levels. It wasn't a bad idea. But HMRC made some key errors with the proxies it identified.

In early 2012 HMRC identified two data sets that were closely correlated with incomes over £150,000, yet not influenced by tax rates on such incomes. First, HMRC observed that incomes of those earning over £150,000 per year had over the previous thirteen years moved in line with the incomes of those in the £115,000 to £150,000 bracket. It then checked some early tax returns for people in this lower category, and found that in 2010–11 their incomes had risen 6 per cent. Secondly, HMRC observed that the incomes of people earning over £150,000 moved almost in lockstep with the stock market – no surprise given that HMRC data showed that around 50 per cent of the people earning over £150,000 were bankers, City of London lawyers, consultants and others who tended to get big bonuses when markets rose, as they did – sharply – in the year the 50 per cent tax rate was introduced.

On the basis of these two proxies, HMRC estimated £150,000-plus incomes should have risen £10 billion in 2010–11, and that the tax change pushed reported incomes £20 billion below where they should have been in that period. Based on capital gains and dividend income returns, HMRC estimated over £12 billion of this was due to one-off shifting of income between periods that didn't reflect any real economic impact, but almost £8 billion was 'attributed to other underlying behaviour' – i.e. wealth forgone due to reduced effort.

But there was a gaping hole in HMRC's elaborate calculations. So keen was it to publish its estimate to coincide with Osborne's March 2012 budget that it did so before it had all the tax returns data of those earning between £115,000 and £150,000 a year. When all the numbers were in, they revealed that incomes in this pay bracket did not rise 6 per cent as the tax experts had assumed. They actually fell 4 per cent.[81] What's more, HMRC's assumption that a recovering stock market signalled a commensurate rise in high earners' incomes was also wrong. In the years after the banking crash, the UK financial sector did not return to its high-paying ways. Accounts for the UK arms of international investment banks, City law firms and accountants[82] all showed it took a decade for even nominal earnings to return to pre-crisis levels. And this wasn't just a London blip. Data for the New York bonus pool also showed average payouts remained below the pre-Lehman collapse highs as late as 2018.[83] The previously observed correlation had simply broken down. Put simply, a clearer examination of both the approaches used by HMRC suggests that even if tax rates had not risen in 2010, higher earners' income would still have fallen. And if HMRC was wrong in assuming that incomes above £150,000 would have risen in the absence of the introduction of the 50 per cent rate, then its estimated £8 billion putative revenue decline disappears, and with it the claim that the elasticity of taxable income is anything like 0.48. Indeed, the actual figure would be more consistent with the labour supply elasticity estimate of 0.063 which the US Congressional Budget Office derived for high earners in 2007.[84] Or possibly even zero. Either way, the £4–£5 billion revenue figure one can see in Table 2.6 remains the best estimate for the exchequer impact of the additional rate.

In what reads like a desperate grasp for the most circumstantial anecdotal evidence to support its elasticity estimate, HMRC cited a news report about London-based hedge fund managers considering moving to Switzerland, and concluded from this that some high earners must have left the UK in the years after the tax rises, so depriving the exchequer of much-needed cash. This wasn't the case. Berne's meticulously maintained records show that the number of financiers moving from London to the Alpine cantons actually shrank from almost none in the mid-2000s to even closer to none in the years after the tax hike.[85]

The decision of one investment firm to move its headquarters to the tax haven of Guernsey grabbed some headlines, but the firm later said that only ten people were hired on the tiny island.[86] In aggregate, Guernsey saw a 90 per cent drop in net inward migration after the financial crisis, suggesting it didn't benefit much from the 50 per cent rate.[87] Neighbouring Jersey reported a similar, if less dramatic drop in net inward migration at this time.[88] The islands do not provide the detailed breakdown that the Swiss do, but when I visited the Channel Islands in early 2020, officials and finance executives I spoke to said they didn't see any impact from the tax change.

Similarly, emigration from Britain to Europe's glitziest fiscal paradise Monaco fell in the eight years after 2008 compared to the previous eight-year period,[89] while reports about potential exoduses to the Caribbean and other tax havens failed to be followed by reports of actual relocations. Perhaps the moves were simply missed because they were so few? After all, how many people are there who have the flexibility to move overseas and continue their current high-paying occupation (financially-motivated emigration is not done for a pay cut), but are also the kind of person who is content to stay put and pay a 40 per cent tax rate but willing to emigrate to avoid paying 50 per cent?

It would be reasonable to assume that HMRC's widely reported belief that tax rises raised no revenues would have caused the Conservative government to move back to the pre-hike levels. After all, George Osborne was keen at one point to cut back to 40 per cent,[90] and Boris Johnson and a raft of other Tory MPs and ministers repeatedly urged for the move. But across four separate Conservative governments, led by prime ministers who had said that the increase of the tax rate to above 40 per cent was economically damaging, no further action was taken to reduce the rate below 45 per cent. Perhaps that was because even at this 5-percentage-point levy on top of the

40 per cent rate, the government was taking in an additional £3 billion to £4 billion per year in revenue.[91] There was no empirical evidence to suggest that Britain's business leaders and wealth creators were even trickling out of the country. And there was no empirical evidence to show that they were working any less hard.

In 2016, Osborne left government and took up a number of roles in the private sector, which, according to parliamentary disclosures and other reports, earned him as much as £1 million per year, a sum that put him squarely in the crosshairs of the 45 per cent rate. But, interestingly, when I spoke to him in 2019, he said he wasn't personally demotivated by the fact he had to give almost half his income to the tax authority. Nor was he worried that this might be a problem more broadly, even though the 45 per cent rate (47 per cent including social insurance charges) represented a 10 per cent increase over the 2010 marginal tax rate – an increase so large it's at the upper end of the range of changes academics use to model elasticities. 'You do get perception tipping points which economic theory wouldn't really pick up,' he told me. 'You can get away with a 49 per cent rate of tax. But a 50 per cent rate of tax, this instantly telegraphs a message around the world that this is half of my income.'

He said he didn't accept the classical view of elasticity. He didn't even think most individuals knew their marginal tax rate, let alone that they would respond to it in a constant, linear fashion when it moved a few points. His view was that people are relatively indifferent until a breaking point is reached – in this case, a breaking point that starts at 50 per cent.

While Osborne's decision to cut the 50 per cent rate cheered conservative thinkers across the world, his rejection of the inner workings of elasticity of taxable income doesn't sit easily with adherents of Martin Feldstein's work. 'His theory is ridiculous,' Stan Veuger, a resident Scholar at the American Enterprise Institute, told me when I visited the think tank's home in Washington, DC, known as the Andrew Mellon Building after its famous former resident. But then, if the calculations behind one of the most celebrated tax cuts of the past twenty years are questionable, and the basic theory under-pinning it is not endorsed by the man who enacted the cut, perhaps the whole basis of the new tax responsiveness literature isn't as rock-solid as groups like the American Enterprise Institute like to believe.

The myths of tax responsiveness

By the turn of the millennium, Americans and Britons had come to realise that their countries were not as equal as they had been in the 1970s. In the United States, the median income had hardly budged in real terms since 1973, while the top 1 per cent of earners had seen their incomes soar. In Britain, the richest 20 per cent saw their incomes rise 50 per cent more between 1977 and 2015 than the low-est quintile.[92] The top 1 per cent of earners saw their share of total pre-tax national income jump from 6.6 per cent in 1981 to 11.7 per cent in 2015.[93] Looking back over that long-term trend, people began to wonder about the basic assumption underpinning the new tax responsiveness literature. Lindsey, Feldstein and others had decided the better-paid must be working harder because they were being paid more. And they were working harder because they got taxed less. But it seemed that the rich also enjoyed income rises when their tax rates didn't change, or even when they rose (as happened after Bill Clinton's 37 per cent hike in the top income tax rate in 1994).[94] Did increases in seven-figure pay slips really reflect a response to tax incentives, or were they just a consequence of an increasingly une-qual world?

In 1999, Austan Goolsbee, who would go on to be Chair of Barack Obama's Council of Economic Advisers, examined tax changes in the United States from the time of Mellon to the late 1960s. His research showed that the strong inverse correlation between tax rates and incomes that Feldstein identified following Reagan's 1986 tax cuts was not part of a broader pattern.[95] In other words, whatever might or might not have happened in the 1980s, it certainly wasn't replicated at other times. For example, the income pattern following the 1970 decision to cut the top tax rate on salaried income from 70 per cent to 50 per cent pointed to an elasticity of taxable income among people earning over $150,000 in 1970 ($1 million in 2020 money) of less than 0.25.

Conversely, Goolsbee noted that when tax rates were increased significantly on high earners in 1935, incomes of 298 of the highest-paid executives in the country (with average incomes of around $840,000 in 1998 dollars) continued to rise, and at a faster pace than for those who were not affected by the tax increases. In aggregate, the implied elasticity of taxable income was actually less than zero, indicating no disincentive impacts on work intensity.

At times, the increase in earnings among the better-off was so steep as to make Feldstein's claim that pay could be seen as a yard-stick of effort seem beyond unlikely. Between 1990 and 2000, for example, the average bonus in the New York Securities Industry rose steadily from $15,540 to $100,530. Bankers may have worked harder over the course of that decade. But is it really possible that they were working six or seven times harder by the end of it? Then there were the earnings differentials among different types of wealthy people to be considered. Between 1979 and 1993, the incomes of arts, media and sports professionals in the top 0.1 per cent of earners enjoyed real growth, excluding capital gains, of 5.2 per cent per annum. Scientists in the top 0.1 percent saw their incomes rise 2.4 per cent annually. Millionaire entrepreneurs outside the arenas of finance, media and real estate enjoyed growth of only 1.3 per cent annually.[96] Super-rich farm and ranch owners saw their incomes fall sharply. Is it really likely that news anchors and top golfers increased their effort materially more than entrepreneurs, scientists and farmers? Did different professions have different elasticities of taxable income? It seems far more plausible that other factors were in play:

deregulation, new technology and globalisation were all enriching some more than others.

A better understanding of tax avoidance has also seen some of the supply-siders' strongest evidence of behavioural responses being increasingly dismissed. Several studies have claimed that the bigger part of observed income elasticities reflects avoidance behaviour such as forestalling.[97] But many of these behaviours are short-term. It is also often argued that seeking to 'over-tax' the rich will fail because they will simply pay tax advisers to find avoidance techniques. But in reality, the biggest tax 'loopholes' are more often than not a deliberate policy decision. When Alistair Darling announced in 2009 that he planned to increase tax rates from April 2010, he was giving those who might be affected by the measure a year to arrange their affairs so as to minimise the hit. Why would he sacrifice revenue like that? Because he was aware that a general rise in income tax was a politically sensitive subject. But when it came to taxing bond traders in the midst of the banking crisis, he didn't have to worry about negative headlines or public opinion, so his late 2009 levy on bank bonuses was made effective immediately.

In much the same way, George Osborne didn't immediately introduce his cut in the 50 per cent rate. He announced it over a year before it became effective.[98] He was signalling to people who were thinking about selling assets or paying themselves dividends from their businesses that they could hold off and realise their profit in a lower income tax environment from 2013. At a single stroke, he saved them money, and gave the government political ammunition against those who said the cut was a sop to the rich, because he could be confident that there would be a big jump in taxable income in 2014 and a resultant increase in exchequer receipts.

Even where income shifting isn't actually encouraged by the government, it's usually a short-term phenomenon. In a world of automatic exchange of information between tax authorities and requirements on taxpayers to disclose tax avoidance structures, other avoidance behaviour, like converting yourself into a company or buying into tax shelters, is not a material challenge to motivated tax collectors and finance ministers. The watertight ways of locking one's money away from the taxman – such as shifting domicile around the sale of assets or use of quirks like Britain's non-domicile rules – represent policy decisions and, to be frank, their uptake remains attractive to the super-rich whether the top rate of tax is 50 per cent or 30 per cent.

So when it comes to measuring elasticity of taxable income, estimates of short-term income responses to previous tax changes (as HMRC attempted in 2012) are of limited relevance in estimating the long-term impacts of a move in tax rates. In 2000, Austan Goolsbee estimated that the short-run elasticity of taxable income exceeded one, but the elasticity after one year 'is at most 0.4 and probably closer to zero'.[99] In other words, almost all of the most widely reported behavioural impacts of tax changes reflect short-term factors or ones that can be tackled by government response, and not increased or reduced effort on the part of the taxpayers in question.

Such findings also suggest that tax-elasticity estimates from the United States, whose tax system offers a wide range of income-tax deductions, giving taxpayers the opportunity to push the envelope in their return, may not be appropriate bases for modelling in other countries. These deductions have been credited with explaining why estimates of US elasticity of taxable income have tended to exceed estimated elasticities in countries such as Canada.[100] Indeed, in Norway, which has strict anti-avoidance rules and a tax authority happy to take avoidance cases to the Supreme Court, economists examining the response to a 1990s tax cut calculated that income elasticity was effectively zero.[101]

The more people have looked at the new tax responsiveness literature, the less it has seemed to describe the real world. In particular, the growing body of research during the 2000s undermined Feldstein and others' conclusions that developed countries' income tax rates were on the wrong side of the Laffer Curve. It was a two-sided debate, but by 2006 even Feldstein had concluded his view was in the minority: 'If you look at the household response to marginal tax rates,' he told an interviewer, 'the typical professional economist's view and also that of most tax policy officials is that people don't seem to respond very much.'[102]

Attempts over the years to tie income tax rates to overall growth have also failed to support the supply-sider case. Certainly, one can find negative correlations between high income tax rates and growth. For example, countries that have lower personal income taxes often grow faster than ones with higher incomes taxes. But that's usually because poorer countries tend to raise relatively little money via income taxes and, in relative terms, they also tend to grow faster than rich ones. High income taxes have been a feature of rich countries, not poor ones. Ironically, even within the United States, high state income taxes are more correlated with affluence than low taxes.

Nor is there evidence that income tax cuts boost growth for any period other than the short term (consistent with a traditional Keynesian stimulus) – and even then they won't be self-funding.[103] This being the case, it follows both that tax cuts now will lead to tax increases later, and that the effect of such measures will be contractionary, because governments will spend that money servicing debt in the future rather than funding stimulative programmes, like road-building or defence spending.

Whose definition of rational?

Taxation, then, doesn't explain why I got stuck between Germany-registered Audis, Dutch campervans and Peugeot estates on the Route du Soleil in July 2019. To be honest, I don't know for sure why the French take more holidays now than they did in the 1970s. I also don't know why the Japanese and Koreans[104] and other nations have begun to behave in the same way. My suspicion is, it's because they can afford to, and because they don't believe that in the long-term you can work a loaves-and-fishes miracle with a tax cut.

As I sat in my hire car listening to raspy-voiced chanteuses on the radio, I wondered about the concept of the rational economic agent. Ed Preston and Martin Feldstein believed a rational person would slack off if they were taxed more. Indeed, Feldstein held that a utility-maximising individual would not be as likely to go to college or accept a promotion if they thought their future net income was going to be reduced by a higher tax rate. His logic was that they would realise the net lifetime return on their efforts would be reduced, and so they would be less inclined to make sacrifices today for future financial gain. He didn't say it but, by implication, this means that people would also ignore the potential that they might benefit in the future from the higher taxes that were being levied (even though almost everyone is either a state employee, employee of a state supplier or uses government services, like roads).

Even if Feldstein's calculations stood up to scrutiny, which they don't, I find it hard to accept his definition of rational behaviour. For one thing, even the most ardent of government critics doesn't operate on the presumption that governments burn all the money they take from taxpayers. A rational person considering all the economic information – Feldstein's premise – would assume they would benefit somewhat from the government spending that higher taxes generate and this should moderate the presumed disincentive to work.

But the more fundamental difficulty I find with his predictions is his assumption that a rational individual would engage and disengage professionally in line with changing estimates of the discounted value of their long-term post-tax income stream.

The best career advice I ever got was to work hard. It's the recurring guidance I have received from the nuns, Christian Brothers and Jesuits who taught me since I was four years of age. I heard it on

Bavarian automobile production lines, in New York restaurants, on Dublin derivative-dealing desks and in London newsrooms. No one ever said to vary your effort and investment in yourself based on changes in your remuneration. No one said take your foot off the pedal if your bonus disappoints, take a longer lunch hour if the raise you wanted doesn't come through, or don't bother doing night courses if the company cuts back on its discounted share purchase plan. Studying hard, getting a job and working hard have been the simple rules that, for a century, have underpinned individuals' financial self-advancement in the developed world.

True, long-term earning potential does influence people to choose some careers over others – say, investment banking over charity work. But that's a question of ranking, rather than a graduated preference. Being motivated primarily by money means going for the best-paying job, not that 10 per cent fewer students on the milk round will apply for the Goldman Sachs trainee programme because a regulatory change means bond trading now pays 10 per cent less than it used to. Do Wall Street or City of London graduate applications really tack up and down with tax rates? Feldstein must have thought so. He'd have us believe that the most financially motivated people accelerate or brake their efforts like a throttleman trying to glide a power boat across choppy waters.

In the real world that's just not practical. The most ambitious people – the ones Feldstein believed were most sensitive to changes in tax – know that behaviour today has long-term consequences. One's career is not like a commodity market where opportunities to transact are replicable and available ad infinitum. Not studying for a degree in finance in the 1980s might have meant a would-be Master of the Universe missed out on the 1990s explosion in banker bonuses that financial markets deregulation facilitated. Bill Gates almost certainly knew in 1975 that the opportunity he had to start a software company would not exist ten years later. A CEO knows that if she reacts to a change in the tax treatment of options by spending more time getting her golf handicap down, she can be sacked and see the stream of options dry up altogether. A few people might be so offended by a tax increase that they do change their behaviour, but that's not enough of a collective response to have an impact on the economy. I suspect the reason the data doesn't show successful people work less when tax rates rise is because it wouldn't be rational for them to behave in this way. As an economics professor, it's likely that Martin Feldstein was regularly asked by his students for career advice. I wonder exactly how many he told: 'Whatever else you do in life, make sure you have a high elasticity of taxable income.'

Yet despite the weight of evidence against tax being a dampener or stimulator of effort, the notion that it is remains remarkably persistent. Perhaps this reflects fear: an irrational worry that if we try to levy high taxes on the wealthy they will skip town or down tools and send the economy into a tailspin. Perhaps it reflects aspiration: ambitious people don't like to think that some of the rewards of ambition might one day be taken from them if they, too, make it to the top. And it may also reflect a tendency to believe what we'd like to be true: that we can pay less tax and at the same time have lower public debt and enjoy better public services. What it doesn't reflect is what we see happening around us in the real world.

3

THE HIRE AND FIRE DEBATE

Is job security economically damaging?

Early one morning in December 2014, thousands of people began to gather in Turin's Piazza Vittorio Veneto, a vast colonnaded neoclassical square overlooking the Po river. Many wore red hats, singlets or coats. Others prominently displayed light-blue scarves and caps. Red was the colour of the CGIL trade union, Italy's largest; blue the colour of those who belonged to the UIL union. Union leaders had predicted 30,000 would turn out for the protest. By some estimates, the number that gathered on the cobblestones at the centre of Italy's industrial capital was over twice as many.[1]

At around 9 a.m., the crowd began to march out of the square, led by Susanna Camusso, the bright-red-coated General Secretary of CGIL. Italy's largest trade union had been affiliated with the left-of-centre Partito Democratico since the party's establishment, so the PD's entry into government in 2013 should have led to comfortable times for trade unionists. But after the PD leader Matteo Renzi became Prime Minister earlier in 2014, the friendship had frayed. Frayed to the point of prompting Camusso and other union leaders to call a general strike. As union members marched north past the old wood-panelled cafés under the porticos along Via Po, they waved red balloons and flags and held up banners that spelt out the source of their anger in large letters – 'Jobs Act' (the English-language name

Renzi gave to the centrepiece of his economic plan) – alongside the slogan '*Cosi Non Va*' – 'It doesn't work this way.' When the marchers reached the Piazza San Carlo, a baroque gem ringed by façades decorated with intricate plasterwork, Camusso took to a stage and laid into the Prime Minister and his signature reform.

The Jobs Act was the first major piece of legislation passed by the Renzi government, and was designed to tackle one of the highest unemployment rates in Europe by relaxing labour-market protections. The logic was simple: if it could be made easier to fire workers for underperformance or when times were tough, employers would be more willing to risk taking on additional staff when new business opportunities presented themselves or when times were good. For Camusso, this represented the threat of a return to the grim working conditions of the 1920s, to redundancies, to the 'blackmailing' of workers and the 'threatening' of unions, and to the continuing flow of unemployed youth overseas.[2] For Renzi, who had worked tirelessly in previous months to overcome opposition to the measure by giving speeches at factories across the country and warming the sofas of night-time talk shows, it was the only way forward.

His view was shared by Professor Giuseppe Bertola, an economist at the University of Turin, and one of the most widely-cited authors on labour market reform in Europe. But, as Bertola explained to me during a break from marking his students' exam papers, it was clear that it would never be an easy sell. The unions were bound to be hostile: 'It was opposition motivated by a fear of going to a situation where the workers are slaves,' he said. 'This was not a true perception, but this was the psychology, the reason to have this vocal opposition.'

Bertola's positive view of the reforms was shared by most labour economists, the International Monetary Fund,[3] the Organisation for Economic Co-operation and Development (OECD)[4] and other organisations who advise governments on economic policy. Their thinking was straight out of the neoclassical economic textbook:

measures like the requirement on companies to consult employees on lay-offs, give notice of redundancies or pay workers compensation when they are dismissed are seen as 'rigidities' that impede the functioning of the labour market. Modern neoclassical economists believe the maximising of national wealth relies on society efficiently allocating the factors of production, such as land, labour and money. They simultaneously hold that in slowing this allocation, market distortions make it harder for markets to clear and, therefore, result in fewer economic transactions and less output overall.

This thinking doesn't mean the state should never intervene to protect workers. Bertola pointed out to me that if, for example, prejudice leads to people of particular religions or races being effectively barred from certain roles or professions, it may be necessary for government to step in. The reason for this, however, is practical rather than socially enlightened. Economic theory dictates that discrimination leads to lost opportunity and a misallocation of labour, resulting in a lower output of goods and services. Anti-discriminatory rules may therefore be required to enhance efficiency. That they might also make society fairer is a side effect rather than a specific goal. As a rule, though, orthodox economic theory assumes that in most cases firms are best able to decide upon their own labour needs and that they are unlikely to discriminate against capable workers, because that would put them at a competitive disadvantage with companies that don't discriminate.

This thinking harks back to the laissez-faire theories of Adam Smith and the other classical economists. However, it was the neoclassical economists in the late nineteenth century who devised the mathematical view of the economy on which the modern model of labour markets is based. This orthodox view holds that if a government passes a law requiring firms to pay severance to laid-off workers, employers will perceive this as increasing the overall, long-term cost of labour (calculated by incorporating into the actual market wage an estimate of the size of a typical redundancy pay-out, adjusted for its probability) – and restrict their purchases of labour accordingly. Hence, to many economists, it is a mathematical certainty that job protection will be damaging to employment.

The high cost of making workers redundant will also slow employers' responses to changing business environments because the expense involved reduces the cash saved by cutting the head count. For this reason the employer may delay lay-offs until workers' productivity drops so low, and therefore the cost of retaining them gets so high, that it's worth incurring the redundancy costs. This additional cost drains firms' coffers further and makes them even less competitive. At a macroeconomic level, economic theory states that, by deterring dismissals, labour protection measures slow the economy's ability to shift workers from less productive activities, such as low-margin manufacturing, into more productive sectors like software production. Moreover, by delaying a rise in unemployment, employment protection delays the downward adjustment in wage rates during a downturn that might help a country to regain its competitiveness.

In recent decades, economists have devised mathematical models that seek to capture all these effects and estimate the precise impacts of specific labour laws. One model designed in 1993 suggested that employment protection rules that require employers to pay severance packages worth one year's wages will reduce employment by roughly 2.5 per cent and decrease average productivity across the economy by over 2 per cent.[5] Other models have claimed to show that job security provisions have prolonged periods of unemployment[6] and slowed firms' adoption of new technology.[7]

Theory also states that those most adversely affected are the unemployed, because job protection deters job creation. To that extent, the concerns of trades unions are therefore self-interested ones: members fear being cast out onto a sclerotic jobs market.

Camusso's lament about Italy's youth being forced to emigrate are, economists would say, a shedding of crocodile tears. Trade unions' defence of labour market protections is, quite simply, selfish.

So wide is the economic consensus on the issue that Italy hasn't been the only country that has sought to push through reform. In the post-banking-crisis period after 2010 several countries either tabled or introduced measures to cut back on employment protections, including Greece, Slovenia, Portugal and Spain.[8] Spain, with one in four workers out of work in 2012, was pressed by the European Union and IMF, which had saved the country from default with large loans, to curtail its generous severance pay regime. Even Britain, the country seen as Europe's least generous in terms of dismissal benefits, came up around this time with a plan to slash employment protections in the hope this would help address a near doubling of unemployment after the 2008 crash.

As the Great Recession cut tax revenues and forced governments to spend more on unemployment benefits, countries didn't have much money to spend on fiscal stimulus programmes. Even if countries had independent control of interest rates – and eurozone members did not – rates were generally so low that additional reductions were unlikely to stoke growth. Labour market reform was seen as one of the few levers EU governments had at their disposal that might jolt their economies back towards growth. And the lever was free – there was no cost to the exchequer, unlike other unemployment-fighting policies often advocated by international organisations, such as training programmes or investment in infrastructure. In Italy, therefore, despite fierce opposition and slipping poll ratings, Renzi pressed ahead in 2015 with implementing the Jobs Act.

That countries should be seeking to roll back labour protection measures that neoclassical theorists had always told them were economically counter-productive raises an inevitable question. If it was all such a bad idea, why did individual countries go for it in the first place?

The sharp rise and gentle fall of labour protection

The connection between workers' rights and the Treaty of Versailles is not perhaps an obvious one. Today, we think of the role of the treaty as bringing the First World War to an end. We may be aware that it also created the precursor to the United Nations, the ill-fated League of Nations. But one of the treaty's most enduring creations is usually overlooked: The International Labour Organisation or ILO. Initially known as the 'International Labour Office', the ILO was established to improve the conditions of workers by helping establish rules governing labour conditions, such as hours worked and maternity benefits.

It may seem odd that a treaty aimed at settling the most barbarous conflict humankind had ever engaged in and preventing future industrial-scale slaughter should concern itself with whether, for example, women could be forced to work night shifts. However, there was a logic to this. The authors of the Versailles Treaty were concerned with all potential causes of future conflict, not simply diplomatic and military ones, and they feared that harsh or unjust labour conditions could well 'produce unrest so great that the peace and harmony of the world are imperilled'.[9] 'Peace can be established,' they argued, 'only if it is based upon social justice.'[10] Labour conditions thus came to be seen internationally as key to the sustainable development of societies.

The ILO has never actually had the power to set regulations that govern countries' labour markets. Its 187 members are free to adopt or ignore its conventions and protocols. However, as a forum for discussing and highlighting the concerns and ambitions of ordinary workers it has proved its worth, helping move such issues up the international political agenda and acting as a bellwether of global views. Almost from the start one of its major preoccupations has been with employment protection rules. As early as the 1930s, when a few countries began legislating for compensation in the event of dismissal, the organisation was proposing that all workers should receive severance pay when laid off.

After the Second World War, when the ILO was reconstituted within the UN, it renewed the struggle for greater worker protection. And in 1963 it brought into being its epoch-defining 'Recommendation 119'. Stating that 'A worker whose employment is to be terminated should be entitled to a reasonable period of notice of compensation in lieu thereof', the recommendation set a benchmark for how advanced economies should behave.

Recommendation 119 reflected what some countries were already beginning to do, and helped prompt others to introduce or enhance employment protections. In the same year it was introduced, Britain's Conservative government, dismissing objections from business groups, passed the Contracts of Employment Act, which barred employers from laying off workers without reasonable notice. In 1965, a Labour government passed the Redundancy Payments Act, which not only made redundancy compensation compulsory, but also dictated that it should rise in step with length of service. Other prosperous countries took similar steps. Japan, for example, had first introduced a system for redundancy payments in 1936.[11] In the decades after the war, it built up a set of rules that offered workers some of the strongest anti-dismissal protections in the world. Elsewhere in Asia, other countries also began to require notice periods and redundancy payments. There was a recognition that there were costs attached to labour protection, but those who championed it argued that it was a justifiable form of redistribution from the haves to the have-nots. As the UK Labour politician Julius Silverman put it in 1963:

> It may be said that such payments would constitute a serious charge on industry and I appreciate that . . . But the circumstances for a man who has spent his life working for a firm, and then finds himself thrown on the scrap heap, may be much more difficult, if he is

expected to manage either with no compensation or with an inadequate amount of compensation.[12]

Silverman suggested that it was possible that protecting employees might even benefit the economy. More humane conditions, he
argued, would improve staff morale and so stimulate productivity.
In an era when the world economy was booming, with developed
countries enjoying full employment, economists were prepared to
waive classical theory and its dislike of market distortions, and
accept that any harm such distortions caused might be countered by
benefits such as improved worker motivation that sat outside the
neoclassical framework.[13]

But amidst the widespread move to some form of labour protection there was a notable outlier: the United States. Although the
biggest financial backer of the ILO, America has always been luke-
warm about its goals. For example, while France has ratified 127 of
the ILO's Conventions and two Protocols and the United Kingdom
has ratified 88 Conventions and two Protocols, the United States has
ratified just fourteen Conventions.[14] Over the decades, some
Democratic Party politicians, backed by labour unions, have tabled
proposals to introduce federal provisions for severance compensation, but the moves have never got far. Even today, there is no federal
obligation on US businesses to recompense people who have been let
go, although one or two states and cities have introduced a degree of
redundancy protection, sometime in the face of federal government
opposition.[15] In 1971, for example, Maine ruled that employees
should be given advance notice of mass redundancies or pay severance.[16] The general feeling, though, even among the unions, seems to
have been that it should be left to individual employers and employees to agree severance deals, not that they should be written into
national law.

In the heady decades that immediately followed the Second World
War, America was something of an ideological outlier. But with the

oil crisis and sharp economic downturn of the 1970s, that started to change. Now Keynesian theory was in the dock. All forms of government intervention in the economy were starting to be perceived as suspect. And worker protection, having been widely embraced, was beginning to look distinctly suspect. Academic economists and multilateral organisations such as the World Bank began to claim that worker protection was among the factors that were making Western economies uncompetitive. It implicitly raised labour costs, they claimed (since employers had to factor potential dismissal costs, into their wage bills), and reduced firms' ability to respond to the economic shock they were experiencing.

Since little research had been done on the impact of severance pay, there was scant empirical evidence for their claims. But by the early 1980s the proof seemed to lie in the relative performance of different economies. Western European nations, which had introduced relatively strict labour protections, had relatively high unemployment, while the US, which had much fewer protections, seemed relatively healthier. During the 1960s and 1970s, the International Monetary Fund and OECD had advised countries that the best way to preserve high employment was to ensure good education systems, ongoing training for workers and moderate wage rises.[17] By the 1980s they were regularly prescribing reductions in labour protections.[18] From 1979, the OECD's annual reviews of the world economy routinely cited 'over-protective legislation' as one of the main impediments to better functioning of labour markets. When the IMF gave countries loans, one of its prerequisites in return was greater labour market flexibility.[19]

European nations generally resisted pressure to change tack. Despite urging from many quarters, European Union White Papers in 1993[20] and 1994[21] stuck to the bloc's mantra of 'High Labour Standards' and resolutely refused to engage with the issue of labour reform. The EU Commissioner responsible for the 1994 paper, Padraig Flynn, argued that 'there is no evidence that a free-for-all in the labour market would create jobs.'[22] Critics responded by becoming increasingly vociferous. Europe's introduction of 'extreme' protections, they argued, had helped create a 'Eurosclerosis' of permanently high unemployment rates. US officials, international organisations and commentators alike increasingly urged European countries to launch wholesale labour market deregulation.[23] Of the 1994 White Paper, the European edition of the *Wall Street Journal* baldly declared that 'the report reflects the thinking of a fading era.'[24]

What finally tipped the balance was another great economic crisis: the collapse of the Lehman Brothers investment bank in 2008 and the international banking crisis that followed. By early 2009, interest rates were at historic lows, governments were injecting hundreds of billions of euros into banks and policymakers were scrambling around for any measure to halt a feared economic collapse.

Suddenly, ideas that had previously been considered anathema or ineffective took on a new lustre. Spain, for example, historically had some of the world's most restrictive rules when it came to sacking permanent workers. These said that if an employer wanted to make large numbers of such staff redundant, it had first to show the authorities that there was a valid commercial reason. If it could do so, it then had to pay permanent staff as much as forty-five days of salary per year of service to sever their employment contract. (In order to avoid these restrictions, companies often employed staff (up to a third overall) on temporary contracts that carried few protections.)[25] Now, with a fully-fledged banking crisis and a collapsing housing market, the government turned its attention to labour law. 'We urgently need labour-market reforms for their short-term impact on hiring,' the Bank of Spain's Governor Miguel Angel Fernandez Ordonez said in February 2009.[26] If protections for permanent contracts could be loosened, economists argued, then rational, profit-maximising firms would both hire more workers and increasingly employ them on permanent rather than temporary contracts.

Steered by this logic, between 2010 and 2012 Spain introduced major changes to the rules governing permanent contracts, slashing the amount of severance pay that had to be paid to long-term employees and removing the need for firms to justify sackings to the authorities. To strengthen the incentive to hire more permanent staff, the government gave workers on temporary contracts enhanced rights. Mariano Rajoy, the Prime Minister who pushed through most of those reforms in the face of staunch opposition from unions, was unapologetic. They were 'fair, good for Spain and necessary'. 'This is the reform that Spain needs to stop it from being the country in Europe that destroys the most jobs,' he told a congress of his Popular Party in Seville in 2012.[27] He didn't predict how many jobs would be created as a result of the added flexibility, but said that if his programme were followed, unemployment would be lower than when he took office.

In many ways Italy's labour rules were even more restrictive than Spain's. Article 18 of the 1970 Statuto dei Lavoratori, for example, allowed workers such a low evidential bar when arguing that dismissals were unfair that an employer wishing to sack a worker might find the only practical way to do so was to offer a big pay-off. Not surprisingly, Italian economists loathed such rules and regulations, and had pressed governments for years to make the changes they regarded as essential. When one, Mario Monti, was appointed as Prime Minister by a divided parliament in the midst of a debt crisis in 2011, it briefly seemed that the experts might have their way. As the unelected head of a cabinet of unelected technocrats, however, Monti lacked both a political mandate or a parliamentary power bloc to make substantial change possible. It wasn't therefore until early 2014, when Matteo Renzi, the media-friendly thirty-nine-year-old Mayor of Florence, was appointed Prime Minister that change finally seemed practicable. The new Prime Minister, Italy's youngest ever, promised to shake Italy out of its stupor with a set of bold reforms. He pledged to smash through the vested interests that he said had caused Italy's stagnation, in the process earning the nickname 'demolition man'.

Like Spain, Italy had a two-tier labour market, whereby some staff were permanent and so protected by law and others were hired on temporary contracts and so lacked labour protections. Renzi said that by easing the restrictions on removing permanent staff, his reform gave companies a greater incentive to hire staff on permanent employment contracts. It would 'unlock the fear'[28] to hire staff, he argued. It would be a 'Copernican revolution'[29] in employment. Renzi estimated that at least 200,000 people on temporary contracts would be moved onto permanent contracts within months,[30] and that ultimately more and better jobs would be created. To encourage this, he offered generous tax breaks to employers taking on extra staff before the end of 2015.

Renzi's reforms may have been opposed by the unions, but the economic community welcomed them. As did the international press, who painted the fresh-faced, energetic Prime Minister as just the kind of leader European countries needed to prod their nations out of their stupor. The *Financial Times*, *Economist* and *Wall Street Journal* all lauded Renzi for his courage. International economic organisations also showered praise on him. The World Bank raised Italy eleven positions in its ranking of competitiveness on the back of his reforms. The IMF 'commended' Renzi, saying the Jobs Act would help 'facilitate the reallocation of workers across jobs'.[31] The OECD said the Jobs Act had 'the potential to drastically improve the labour market'.[32] Secretary General Angel Gurrìa said it could be 'the real engine of change' for Italy's economy.[33]

Given such intellectual consensus, it's hardly surprising that Britain, too, considered pushing through labour reform. According to the OECD, Britain offers permanent workers the least protection against individual and collective dismissals in Europe.[34] In global terms of the G20 group of twenty major economies, it is neck-and-neck with Canada and just ahead of the United States and Saudi Arabia in terms of its generosity toward workers. Nevertheless, many Conservatives felt that what protection existed was excessive, and when the Conservative-Liberal coalition came to power in 2010, the Chancellor of the Exchequer George Osborne promised change. The government's first move was to delay the point at which an employee was entitled to protection under the Unfair Dismissal Act from one year of employment to two years. It also considered seeking opt-outs from European Union employment protection rules for British employers. And in order to come up with a framework for more fundamental reform, Prime Minster David Cameron asked a grandee of the private equity industry, and significant Conservative donor, Adrian Beecroft, to draft a report.

Beecroft's report,[35] which was published in 2012, recommended that the UK adopt measures that would allow employers to dismiss staff they saw as underperforming or surplus to requirements at will for modest payments. He predicted that if his plans were ignored, unemployment would continue to be a major problem, but that if they were adopted, firms would become more efficient and more prepared to take on staff. Within nine years, he suggested, his measures could add 5 per cent to GDP. 'We're in a sort of phase in this country and probably most of the Western world where we're so frightened of injuring people's feelings, we ignore all the people,' he told the *Daily Telegraph*.[36]

Senior Conservative party figures, including former Defence Secretary Liam Fox[37] and future Foreign Secretary and Deputy Prime Minister Dominic Raab,[38] loudly supported the no-fault-dismissal measure. However, the Conservatives' junior coalition partner, the Liberal Democrats, refused to support the move, so it was dropped. It was left to Spain and Italy, therefore, to point a possible future path for Europe.

The jobs boom that wasn't

By the end of 2015, Renzi was claiming that the evidence showed that his measures were working. 'The numbers are stronger than any predictions,' he wrote on his website in December. By early 2016, he was talking of 'The Jobs Act boom'.[39] And at one level he was right. Italy's unemployment rate was indeed lower than it had been – down from 12.8 per cent when Renzi took office to 11.5 per cent in early 2016.[40]

Whether or not this was a sign that the Jobs Act was working, however, was rather more questionable.

Throughout Europe, the banking crisis and the recession that came in its wake led to a spike in unemployment. This was followed by an inevitable improvement as the global economy began to recover, and all European countries experienced stronger demand for their exports, increased tourist visitors and increased foreign investments. The question, therefore, is not whether unemployment fell in Italy after Renzi's reforms, but whether the fall outstripped that of other European countries in the same period. And the fact is that it didn't. Indeed, the fall in Italy's unemployment rate was disappointing. Between 2013, the year before Renzi proposed the Jobs Act, and 2018, Italian unemployment fell 1.5 percentage points. Across the European Union, however, the average was a 4.1 percentage point reduction – despite the fact that Europe as a whole had had lower unemployment than Italy and therefore less slack to take up.[41]

What's more, such improvement in the employment figures as Italy was able to show was demonstrably not down to the Jobs Act pushed through by its Prime Minister. If Renzi's claims had been correct, there should have been an upsurge in new permanent jobs. There wasn't. Thanks to legislation passed in 2011 to restrict early retirement, more over-55-year-olds were remaining in post by 2015. Employment actually fell among under 50s.[42] And more temporary jobs were being created. The removal of supposedly toxic restrictions on permanent employment signally failed to boost this part of the labour market. One early study bluntly concluded that 'the analysis shows that the Jobs Act failed in achieving its main goals'.[43] The European Commission, which had piled pressure on Italy since at least 2009 to introduce the reforms, similarly and embarrassingly had to agree when it produced a detailed assessment in 2017. Instead it made the vague and optimistic promise that 'The impact of the overall reform on productivity is expected to materialise in the longer term.'[44]

Spain's experience was very similar. Again, unemployment fell in the years after the reform, but again at a slower pace than in other European countries. It wasn't that Spain's economy was being left behind. It enjoyed relatively robust economic growth after the labour reforms were introduced. However, this growth wasn't being converted into jobs in the way analysts said it should have.[45] A review by one EU agency in 2015 found that 'The reform has not contributed much to the creation of employment.'[46]

Nor was this a peculiarly European phenomenon. Australia's Productivity Commission, which had been asked to review the country's workplace relations (WR) framework, concluded: 'surmise aside, there is little robust evidence that the different variants of WR systems over the last twenty years have had detectable effects on measured economywide productivity.'[47]

What went wrong?

The failure to establish any statistical link between labour market protections and unemployment levels in Italy and Spain shouldn't have come as any particular surprise. The fact is that a provable link has eluded economists for at least thirty years. A rash of theoretical studies in the 1980s and 1990s that devised models claiming to show employment protection weighed on jobs were rapidly overtaken by empirical studies that rejected their findings.[48] Professor Giuseppe Bertola – who supported labour market deregulation in principle – concluded as early as in 1990 that:

> job security provisions are often cited as a major factor in the high unemployment in European economies. This paper finds that such provisions do not bias labour demand toward lower average employment.[49]

By 2006, even the OECD accepted that the large body of evidence was against the economic orthodoxy that less protection meant more jobs.[50] One review of previously published papers in 2005 summed up the body of knowledge on the subject thus: 'Our results suggest a yawning gap between the confidence with which the case for labour market deregulation has been asserted and the evidence that the regulating institutions are the culprits.'[51]

One gets the sense that this is an area where surmise and wishful thinking tend to trump hard facts. Adrian Beecroft, interviewed by a parliamentary committee shortly after publishing his review for the UK government about the predicted gains from cutting job protections, said: 'I will accept the accusation that my views on whether or not this would improve the efficiency of people working in businesses is [sic] based on conversations, not a statistically valid sample of people.'[52] That no-fault dismissals would boost job creation was 'self-evident', he told members of parliament.[53]

Those like the IMF and the World Bank and financial commentators in the broadsheet press who still claim – or, as the Australians put it, 'surmise' – a link between unemployment and employment protection frequently cite America as a shining beacon of workplace flexibility and job creation. But, again, the evidence is simply not there. It's certainly true that American workers tend to move from job to job more frequently than their European counterparts. Indeed, Professor Bertola concluded in a 2000 study that they do so twice as often.[54] But job turnover rates are not the same as employment rates, and an impression of job dynamism is not the same as job creation.

In 2010, consultants McKinsey tested the theory that the fifteen core, long-standing European Union members (which excludes fast-growing eastern European economies) were laggards on job creation. Its conclusion was unambiguous: 'Between 1995 and 2008, the EU-15 created 23.9 million jobs, of which only 8.7 million were related to its increase in population during this period. In comparison, the United States generated 20.5 million jobs, most of which (18.8 million) accommodated a rising population.'[55] These findings were of a piece with an earlier study that argued: 'There is no evidence that jobs are created and destroyed at a more rapid rate in North America than they are in Europe. However,' it went on, 'workers do appear to circulate faster through the existing jobs in North America.'[56]

Bad for business?

In 2017, James Dyson, inventor of the eponymous vacuum cleaner and Britain's foremost entrepreneur, was asked what it would take to create a manufacturing renaissance in the United Kingdom. 'Easier to hire and fire,' he responded bluntly, acknowledging his answer would be 'controversial'. He said the 'very difficult employment laws' in Britain made it hard to 'flex your workforce' up and down in line with demand so as to remain efficient.[57]

Interestingly, though, when Dyson shifted production of his vacuum cleaners out of Britain in 2002, he chose to move to a part of the world – Malaysia – where redundancy costs were actually higher than in the UK: four weeks' pay per year of service versus 1.5 weeks in Britain.[58] Of course, it could be that he felt the need to defend his decision to move manufacturing from his home country and was looking for a suitable scapegoat. Or it could be that, when he was being interviewed, labour rules happened to be topmost in his mind.[59] But it's a mark of the gap between the accepted wisdom and reality, that even those who say employment protection represents a powerful disincentive to investment don't respond to the supposed disincentive themselves. The fact is that, while employment protection may be a mortal sin against the rules of economics or some peoples' views about how the economy should be structured, its actual impact on firms is far more modest than often depicted. Take Spain, which was seen by economists, before Rajoy's 2010–12 reforms, as being particularly inflexible. For decades the country had been punching above its weight in terms of attracting foreign investment, even in highly mobile sectors like car-making. And whatever dismal picture economists may have been painting, the experience foreign carmakers in Spain had in managing their workforces seems to have been a very positive one. Indeed, Ford long held that its Valencia plant was one of its most efficient and flexible plants in Europe.[60] Besides, when the economic hurricane of 2007 hit the world, the carmaker was able to react flexibly, reducing its Spanish workforce to meet the challenges it faced. That a country has employment rules that prevent flippant workforce churn does not mean that businesses are unable to react to strong headwinds. As it happens, Ford was able to take the same defensive steps in both Spain and Britain, even though one country has strong employment protection, and the other the weakest in Europe.[61]

Besides, fluid labour markets also have downsides. High staff turnover creates upheaval and increased training and recruitment costs. Magnus W. Alexander, the first President of the Conference Board, a US business-backed think tank, and author of possibly the first empirical study of such matters, certainly found this to be the case. His 1916 paper, entitled 'Hiring and Firing: Its Economic Waste and How to Avoid It',[62] argued that two sure ways to boost the economy were to train flagging employees better and select candidates more carefully. Labour rules provide an incentive for employers to take these measures. They also act as a disincentive to employees to move, since they create a hypothetical cost to the employee – in terms of lost severance entitlement – of leaving their current job. As most individuals are risk-averse, they are likely to value the effective insurance benefit severance pay offers above the cost to the firm.

German executives sometimes argue that their country's strict employment protection rules force them to think hard whether candidates will fit before deciding to take them on, resulting in less time wasted on recruitment in the long run. Admittedly, this is a hard thing to quantify, but it's nevertheless suggestive that in one survey conducted in Britain after the introduction of unfair dismissal legislation, around 11 per cent of firms surveyed said they had made changes to improve the quality of their hiring choices.[63] It's similarly hard to prove the truth or otherwise of a claim made by some British politicians when severance pay was introduced in Britain in the 1960s that such protection would inspire employees to work harder, watch the clock less and show more initiative. But it's likewise notable that companies frequently offer severance packages when they don't have to – as happens commonly in the United States – or more generous packages than is required by law. Clearly, they see a benefit to themselves in terms of improved productivity that exceeds the financial cost of giving these commitments.

A related potential benefit of employment protection that has attracted a lot of attention in recent years is 'skills deepening'. The idea is that an employee, if they think they are going to be around for a long time, may invest more energy in improving their skills, and in particular in ways that might only have relevance in that organisation, as opposed to focusing on getting experience in the firm or doing evening classes that would position them for their next role at a different company. They therefore boost their current employer's productivity. At the same time, if the employer believes the employee will be sticking around, he or she may be more willing to invest in training and so, again, boost productivity.[64] One study following Britain's decision in 1999 to increase the number of workers covered by the unfair dismissals act concluded that employers paid greater attention to their employees and that they paid them more.[65] At the other end of the spectrum, easy firing is associated by some with the growth of low-skill, low-productivity and inevitably low-income jobs.[66]

Numerous studies conducted in Europe and the United States also claim that labour rules lead to 'capital deepening': an increased investment in equipment that can boost the productivity of workers.[67] The theory is that if a firm is concerned that employment protection will make it harder to shed workers in a downturn, then it will try to operate with a smaller, more efficient workforce – something that can only be achieved by employing better technology. This, in turn, some have argued, leads to greater innovation[68] and higher growth.[69] While this particular mechanism would have a downward impact on employment at the level of individual firms over the economic cycle, it should simultaneously lift incomes and it should also support employment opportunities across the economy.

The fact remains, though, that no one has found a meaningful positive or negative correlation between productivity and redundancy restrictions.[70] It could be that employment protection brings costs and benefits to firms and that the two balance each other out. Or it could be the positives and negatives are simply not very strong. But what is certainly the case is that if a government cuts employment protection on the promise of high employment, it is a promise that is unlikely to be fulfilled.

And that's not the only downside governments face when they seek to remove employment protections. There's also what economists refer to as opportunity cost. It's not a concept that they themselves devised.[71] Rather it's one of those everyday truisms, like price sensitivity, to which they attach a technical term, thereby creating the impression that they understand the mysterious mechanisms by which we make decisions. Opportunity cost is what ordinary people would call missed opportunity. If we take the less beneficial of two courses of action, we may end up better off than when we started, but still worse off than if we had made the optimum choice. Governments, like individuals, face opportunity costs to actions. In the context of employment rights, the question is whether reforming them is worth the political and social capital and strife involved, given that other reforms might prove far more beneficial.

Italy offers a perfect case history. At the outset of his premiership, Renzi said 'the first thing'[72] he wished to tackle was labour market reform, because he saw unemployment as the country's biggest economic problem. To academics, long-term unemployment is a consequence of a distorted labour market. And Italy's labour market operated under rules that deviated strongly from economic orthodoxy. It seemed logical that the two positions were related and that changing one – the labour market rules – was the solution to the other – a poorly functioning labour market.

Some with more practical experience, however, were sceptical.

'We have never considered Italian labour laws as a problem,' said Sandro De Poli, Chairman of the Italian unit of US giant General Electric (one of Italy's biggest foreign investors), when Mario Monti first attempted to revise Italy's labour rules in 2012.[73] Instead De Poli pointed the finger at Italy's convoluted bureaucracy and byzantine approach to decision-making, whereby, for example, projects require approval from many different authorities. 'This uncertainty on rules is unacceptable,' he argued. 'The fact that at every step you must confront an array of officials, each of them saying something contradictory, does not help and is the biggest hurdle to investment,' he said. 'The next fundamental step is tackling bureaucracy,' he added.

Others have long felt that Italy's focus should be on fixing a courts system that moves so slowly that contracts are often unenforceable.[74] 'A fundamental purpose of government is to create a judicial system that produces efficient, fair, and predictable results,' said John Phillips, the US Ambassador to Italy in 2016, in a speech in Milan. 'Does Italy have this? Many potential investors have told me that, simply put, the answer to that question is "no". And that is the number-one reason,' he added, 'why they decide against investing in Italy.'[75]

Other priorities that have been identified include tackling fraud and corruption. Italy's unusual statute of limitation rules, which Renzi said he wanted to change, give such a narrow window for law enforcement to take action that it is all but impossible to prosecute fraudsters, tax evaders and corruption. Such rules, many have argued, adversely affected governance. According to one 2016 analysis, almost one in ten Italian senators and deputies had either benefitted from the statute of limitations or were then on trial or under investigation for white-collar offences covered by short enforcement windows.[76]

So there were lots of positive reforms Renzi could theoretically have made. But he wasn't in a position to do so. As the political battle to push through and implement the Jobs Act preoccupied him over the course of 2014 and 2015, other planned legislation inevitably stalled or was watered down.

In the event, only one other major reform did work its way through parliament.

In 2016, the legislature approved a bill to remove the existing requirement that both houses of parliament approve all new laws. The reform, which Renzi said would help make governments more stable and allow him to cut the bureaucracy that he argued was strangling Italy, was acknowledged to have enormous and potentially very beneficial significance. However, it required a change in the constitution, and this meant a referendum.

Again, Renzi hit the road and began tirelessly selling a plan to the public that would have done no more than bring Italy in line with its European peers. But things didn't go his way. In Turin, Renzi's Partito Democratico lost the town hall in June 2016, when voters elected a candidate from the populist Five Star movement as mayor. Successive polls and local elections showed support leaching away from the incumbent. It wasn't that voters were particularly wedded to perfect bicameralism. Indeed, it probably wasn't even really an issue for them. As the *Economist* magazine noted at the time: 'Italians will be basing their votes not on the content of the referendum question, but on how they feel about Mr Renzi and a course of labour-market reforms adopted last year.'[77]

In the event, Renzi's proposed constitutional reform was rejected by 59.1 per cent to 40.8.

Looking back on the tumultuous events of 2016 from the vantage point of 2019, Professor Giuseppe Bertola conceded that the Jobs Act was the root of Renzi's failure. 'Prioritising employment protection is in many situations the politically wrong thing to do,' he said, while glancing at a spreadsheet of exam results that showed exposure to economic orthodoxy wasn't having the desired effect in the University of Turin either. 'Politicians, maybe they think it's a free lunch. But maybe firms who can't hire will fire, and those which might hire don't. There's no free lunch.'

Renzi was forced to stand down after he lost the referendum and his planned judicial, education and other reforms were shelved. Italy continued its drift toward populist leaders who offered not so much free lunches as free-for-alls. Just over a year after the referendum, Italy held a general election that returned the Five Star movement, led by the agitator comedian Bepe Grillo, as the largest party. 'Cinco Stelle' agreed to form a government with the far-right 'Lega' or Northern League. Suddenly, economic reform was back on the agenda. But it was reform of an altogether different type from what Renzi and his supporters in the IMF and OECD had had in mind.

Foreign investors dumped Italian assets and government bonds suffered their worst fall in more than twenty-five years as fears grew that the new administration's promises of increased spending and tax cuts would send the public finances into a tailspin.[78]

One of the new government's first moves was to roll back some features of the Jobs Act.

4

THE JENSEN CLAIM

Can money make you a better manager?

In April 1984, around fifty economists gathered in a chapel on the University of Rochester campus, just a few miles from Lake Ontario in upstate New York. They really shouldn't have been there. The donors who had generously sponsored the construction of the interfaith prayer space, a pretty stained glass and concrete structure at the end of the college's main quadrangle and overlooking the banks of the Genesee River, had stipulated that it should be used only for religious events. A gathering of academics exploring the ways of Mammon could hardly claim to fall into that category. But since the Graduate Business School, which was hosting the meeting, was relatively new, and lacked its own conference facilities, its leading lights had had no choice but to go cap in hand to the chapel authorities.

The conference the economists had organised was in honour of William Meckling, the recently-retired Dean of the business school and the key force in its development.[1] His approach had been an unusual one. Most 'B-schools' then, as now, sought to teach students how to tackle business challenges by having them examine specific company case studies and infer dos and don'ts. Meckling, by contrast, believed that the best way to understand businesses and find solutions to the challenges that managers faced was by employing

114

economic theory. The Managerial Economics Research Center, which he and the Business School's first new professor, Michael Jensen, founded in 1977 under the auspices of the business school, was designed, he said at the time, to 'foster the application of economic principles and methods to a range of managerial and organisational problems which have heretofore received little attention from the economics profession'.[2]

Managerial economics at the time was a small but growing field that attempted to use theory to tackle practical tasks, like product pricing, capital structure, cost management and identifying optimal output levels. For example, it would explore how the concept of price elasticity of demand might be used to set the prices a firm charged for their products so that profits were maximised. The 1984 conference was about a subject that had been a concern of Meckling's for at least twenty years, and one that had recently been hitting the headlines for all the wrong reasons: executive pay.

In the early 1980s, many Americans were scandalised by increasingly frequent reports that the biggest publicly-traded US corporations were paying their chief executives annual pay packets that exceeded $1 million. Fat cats, newspaper editorials claimed, were effectively setting their own inflated salaries. Peter Drucker, the country's foremost scholar of management and an adviser to its major corporations, condemned what he saw as a trend of corporate greed and predicted it would demoralise the broader workforce and eat away at the success of US businesses. Some politicians said pay caps should be introduced.

The economists at the symposium, titled 'Management Compensation and the Managerial Labor Market', took a rather different view and approach. They weren't concerned with moral indignation or fuzzy concepts of employee morale. As Jensen and Kevin Murphy, another Rochester economist who helped organise the conference, wrote in a column published in the *New York Times* a few weeks later, 'no one expressed concern that compensation was "too high"'. It was indeed possible, as Professor Jensen suggested in one conference paper, 'that executive compensation is "too low"'.[3] What interested Jensen and like-minded colleagues was the economic effect of remuneration practices, not their ethical justification. Corporate America faced headwinds in the 1970s, with stagnant share prices and millions of good-paying manufacturing jobs lost. Executives had taken to routinely blaming the broader economy for this predicament, but managerial economists such as Jensen wondered whether the fault might not lie within organisations rather than outside them. And one key element, for them, was executive pay.

Jensen, Murphy and their peers were not offended by rising executive pay partly because they understood that, in real terms, there had been no explosion in CEO pay. The rash of seven-figure pay cheques was largely a function of rampant inflation in the 1970s. In fact, in the early 1980s, executive compensation was at the same level relative to average wages that it had been since the late 1940s – that is to say, it had only risen above inflation to the extent that all wages had.[4] What did offend Jensen and Smith, however, was the way in which executives were being paid. For decades, most of the earnings of the top executives of big US and European companies came in the form of a fixed salary. Frequently, and particularly in the United States, bosses also received a bonus, which was typically tied to year-to-year profit performance. In the United States, depending on the prevailing tax treatment of capital gains vis-a-vis regular income, the executives might have received some of this bonus in shares. But the variable element of pay was limited.

For economists such as Jensen and Murphy, this approach was wholly inadequate.[5] An element of incentive was there to coax managers to push their companies vigorously forward, but it simply wasn't powerful enough. If you really wanted dynamic leaders deploying entrepreneurial flair, the economists argued, you needed to offer rich potential rewards. 'On average,' they claimed:

> corporate America pays its most important leaders like bureaucrats. Is it any wonder then that so many CEOs act like bureaucrats rather than the value-maximising entrepreneurs companies need to enhance their standing in world markets?[6]

The problem was not that there were too many fat cats, but rather that there might not be enough.

The Parable of the Talents

Jesus's Parable of the Talents shows (at a literal level, at least) that there is no guarantee that the person you ask to act on your behalf will necessarily reward your trust. Since time immemorial, owners or 'principals' have faced the risk that the managers they hire to oversee their assets may not do so honestly or diligently. The joint-stock companies that became popular in Europe in the seventeenth century were often a byword for incompetence and dishonesty. In *The Wealth of Nations*, Adam Smith wrote of the 'knavery' of their directors, highlighting the many British and European corporate failures they had left in their wake, and arguing that it was inevitable that such managers would be more wasteful and less inclined to seize growth opportunities than owner-managers. Nonetheless, joint-stock companies became more common and, over time, steps were taken to curb their worst excesses. Embezzlement and other forms of fraudulent behaviour were made criminal offences. Companies were required to make public various aspects of their finances, to help mitigate the danger of investors and creditors being wantonly misled about the state of a business's affairs.

It was not until the early twentieth century, however, that attention started to move from curbing the egregious abuses of managers to finding ways to improve their performance. And here, as in so much to do with the corporate world, it was the USA that led the way. Slowly, from the 1910s, more rapidly in the 1920s, some of the country's biggest companies began to supplement standard salaries for their top executives with substantial bonus schemes linked to performance.

The American Tobacco Company affords a classic – and early – instance. The corporate giant had emerged from a monopoly of the same name created by the son of a poor farmer turned tycoon, James B. Duke, which, by the end of the nineteenth century, controlled almost all of the US cigarette market. Forced to see his group split up into several companies as a result of the trust-busting drive pioneered by President Teddy Roosevelt and formulated in the anti-monopoly Sherman Act, Duke had then moved to England to run a sister company called British American Tobacco, that would decades later buy American Tobacco. By the time of his death in 1925, the business he had built with his brother had yielded Duke a personal fortune of over \$100 million.[7]

The new American Tobacco Company that emerged was floated on the New York Stock Exchange in 1912 under the command of Percival Hill, a Harvard man who had served with Duke for twenty years. He faced stiff challenges. Thanks to the Sherman Act, former stablemates had now become rivals, and although the American Tobacco Company boasted strong brands including Bull Durham and Pall Mall, the going proved tough. Cigarette prices had to be cut and promotional efforts intensified.

To galvanise his managers to negotiate this difficult new landscape, Duke decided to introduce an incentive scheme. If profits increased from the then level of \$10 million per year to over \$11.4 million, he declared, his fellow top executives would receive 7.5 per cent of the additional sum. He himself would take 2.5 per cent of the excess. It was a deal that paid off handsomely for managers. In 1918 earnings hit $17 million. In 1925 – the year in which Percival Hill died – they reached a record $22 million.

Hill was succeeded as president by his son, George W. Hill, who had been with the company since 1904 and had been head of the Pall Mall Brand. His genius was advertising. It was under his auspices that what would become America's favourite cigarette brand, Lucky Strike, was launched. According to his adman Albert Lasker, its promotion became 'a religious crusade' for George W. Hill.[8] He would have packets of Lucky Strikes dangled on strings in the windows of his Rolls-Royce, whose tail lights were emblazoned with the brand's logo. Hill even named his pet dachshunds Lucky and Strike.[9]

The spirit of continuity at the top of American Tobacco extended to compensation arrangements. Under Hill junior, the 1912 bonus scheme not only remained in place but also remained steadfastly linked to the 1912 targets. What had once been seen as a reward for extraordinary achievement became a trough at which management could gorge itself. By 1930, Hill was earning around $1 million a year, over 800 times the average industrial wage.[10] And he wasn't the only tycoon to be doing well. By now American Tobacco's former sibling Lorillard had a similar scheme. So did General Motors and Loews,[11] the owner of the Metro-Goldwyn-Mayer film studios. Bethlehem Steel had an even more generous plan, which in 1929 yielded its boss Eugene Grace over $1.6 million.[12] In the past five years the CEOs of British American Tobacco have been paid an average $9.7million per year.[13] Had their pay been calculated on the same basis as George Hill's, they would each have received over $100 million a year.

Nonetheless, Hill and his board didn't feel the 1912 scheme offered them sufficient incentive, and in 1930 they introduced an additional arrangement that allowed all staff to purchase company stock at a quarter of its market value. 'I am certain,' Hill was quoted as saying, 'that modern business practice, conforming with the policies of many large business enterprises, approves the wisdom of offering inducements by way of stock ownership in the company to the men who make the success of that company possible.'[14] What he didn't reveal was that over half of the benefits of the new plan, which were estimated to be worth $30 million in total, would go to the directors.[15] Based on his own expected pay-out, Hill was set to receive $1.2 million in share gains for 1930, on top of his salary and cash bonus of over $1 million.

American Tobacco's lack of candour about management compensation wasn't unusual. Most companies did not disclose their executive incentive schemes, leaving shareholders unaware just how much they were paying to have their companies managed. But all that changed with Hill & Co.'s 1930 share grab. The scheme happened to catch the eye of an enterprising lawyer called Richard Reid Rogers, who smelt a rat. He purchased some American Tobacco stock and then petitioned the courts to block the share plan, on the grounds that shareholders had not been given the information necessary to make an informed decision. Forced to come clean by the courts, in early 1931 American Tobacco disclosed Hill's $1 million salary[16] and bonus, and the $1.2 million he was due from the new share scheme.[17]

Reid Rogers' actions were probably not altruistic. It seems he may have hoped to extract a pay-off from American Tobacco in return for dropping his lawsuits. But whatever his motivation, the investigation he prompted shone a light on practices that would otherwise have gone unnoticed. And in the context of the Great Depression, they struck many people as unacceptable.

One Montana Democrat said the excessive salaries were 'outrageous' and 'unpatriotic', and called for legislation to prohibit them.[18] Senator Thomas Gore of Oklahoma, a member of the Senate Finance Committee and an antecedent of Bill Clinton's Vice President Al Gore, wanted an 80 per cent tax on all salaries over $75,000.[19] Their demands were not met. But in 1934, Congress did pass legislation requiring companies listed on the stock market to publish annually the remuneration of their most senior executives.[20] And by the end of the 1930s all the big listed companies were doing so. Thanks to the Great Depression, many profit-linked bonus schemes were by now yielding nothing, while others had been abandoned. Some executive salaries had risen to help cover the gap, but overall the effect of the new rules was to reduce pay for top bosses. Disclosures in 1935 showed that pay had fallen sharply at most companies for which there was comparable data from 1929.[21] By 1936, George W. Hill was having to make do with a total pay package worth $246,174, including his bonus – around 10 per cent of what he had been slated to receive for 1931 before a judge put a hold on his $1.2 million share bonus. Eugene Grace at Bethlehem Steel had to settle for just $180,000, all of which appeared to be salary (up from a base salary of just $12,000 in 1929).[22]

For forty years, from the mid-1930s onwards, CEO[23] pay largely stabilised in real, inflation-adjusted terms.[24] The pay practices reflected the thinking of the time, shaped by people like Drucker, who saw the organisation as a whole as the prime driver of success and was sceptical of the economic contribution of any one individual or class of individuals.[25] Company bosses were paid at a level that was consistent with having unusual skills, but not with being seen as the overwhelming force behind the corporation's success.

Just after he was named as Dean of the Rochester business school in 1964, William Meckling went on a tour of other US business schools to examine what was being taught in these institutions. At one he encountered a famous senior policy professor leading a discussion about executive compensation at General Motors. The conclusion was that no one was worth the near $750,000 per year that the then-GM CEO was paid.[26] Meckling may have been bemused, but it was a view that at that time would have been shared by most Americans – and economists.

It was a 1976 academic paper that was instrumental in moving executive pay back in a direction American Tobacco's Hill would have found familiar. Entitled 'The Theory of the Firm', it wasn't strictly speaking about manager pay, but rather sought to devise a new explanation for why firms existed. Most people probably see corporations as existing to allow economies of scale to be achieved, but to economists, firms are a theoretical paradox. Mainstream economics perceives the world as being made up of independent economic agents interacting through an infinite number of transactions, each of which allocates resources perfectly efficiently. Attempting to organise and plan these interactions would, theory goes, create inefficiencies. However, that's what corporations do – they organise the production process. A British economist called Ronald Coase had attempted to square the circle by hypothesising in his 1937 paper 'The Nature of the Firm' that the reason that firms existed was because transaction costs sometimes made open-market purchases or sales of goods or services expensive, and that, by effectively internalising transactions, firms avoided such costs. It's an arcane discussion that preoccupies few people outside economics but exercises many within the profession. Coase won a Nobel memorial prize for his ideas on transaction costs.

Not everyone liked Coase's idea, in part because it held that markets were not always efficient. 'The Theory of the Firm' challenged Coase's view, and argued that firms were actually platforms for conducting more, and more complex, market-based transactions. Corporations were, as the paper put it, 'legal fictions which serve as a nexus for a set of contracting relationships among individuals'. This meant that the firm was simply a proxy for its owners, and that its behaviour was defined by the contractual arrangements that existed between it and clients, suppliers and staff. The significance of this for executive remuneration was that it showed managers would behave in a way which fulfilled their employment contracts but could never truly act in the shareholders' interests – because the manager was not a partner or guardian of the shareholder but rather a self-interested seller of their time and efforts to shareholders. The paper presented a new model for understanding what by this time had come to be known as the 'agency problem': the risk that hired managers might not look out for shareholders' best interests. 'The Theory of the Firm' argued that, assuming all parties were rational and sought to maximise their utility, it was a mathematical certainty that managers would indeed behave in a self-serving way: they would seek to avoid tasks they didn't like, such as haggling with unions or making lay-offs, that might be required to preserve the health of the firm. They would seek to soak up perks of the job – attending gala dinners, say – but avoid actually doing the job. The way to minimise the agency problem, the paper argued, lay in improving the contractual relationship between the shareholders and the managers, namely by 'devising and applying an index for compensating the manager which correlates with the owner's (principal's) welfare'.

The paper's authors were two alumni of the University of Chicago who shared the free market ethos of Milton Friedman. They had left Chicago but not gone far, settling at one of the other 'freshwater' belts of free-market-orientated, anti-Keynesian economics departments based near North America's Great Lakes. The lake was Ontario and the university was Rochester. The authors were Michael Jensen and William Meckling.

Jensen had no doubts about the significance of 'The Theory of the Firm'. When he came to the University of Chicago to present the paper, he announced to his host, and former thesis supervisor, Eugene Fama that the paper would 'destroy' key parts of Fama's book *The Theory of Finance*, known as the 'White Bible' because of the regard in which the white-covered tome was held among academics.[27] It was a comment that was typical of Jensen's provocative style:[28] once, in a debate with Warren Buffett, he compared the great investor to a lucky coin-flipper, a comparison Buffett described as 'rude'.[29] But he was right about the impact the paper would have. It

123

was destined to become one of the most widely-cited economics papers in history – with over 88,000 citations as of 2020 – and would make its authors famous in scholarly circles.

Jensen's paper might not have made it beyond such circles had it not been for the context in which it was published. Economists had written about the agency problem since at least 1932,[30] but it was a niche concern among academics and people in the broader world had taken little notice. Why would they? The economy and corporations were doing well, with profits and shares rising at a healthy clip, so it didn't look as though the agency problem, if it existed, was a big one. But in the 1970s things changed. Stock markets stagnated, and they did so as a new theory, spearheaded by Eugene Fama, was taking hold. Efficient Markets Theory, which years later would win Fama a Nobel memorial prize, argued that stock markets were perfectly efficient and rational.[31] This meant that if share prices were languishing, it reflected the fact that investors had carefully considered all the evidence and concluded firms' management was bad. Suddenly, it seemed, the agency problem was bigger than people had realised.

As the 1970s gave way to the 1980s, a new phenomenon arose that further heightened concerns around the agency problem. The years after the appearance of 'The Theory of the Firm' were ones of turmoil for big businesses on either side of the Atlantic. Buccaneering US financiers like T. Boone Pickens, Kirk Kerkorian and Carl Icahn and British knights James Goldsmith, Gordon White and James Hanson ruthlessly discarded the cosy consensus whereby the managers of rival companies might compete aggressively for the same market but not for control of each other's assets, and elected instead to blast their way into boardrooms with uninvited takeover bids that threatened to upturn or even wipe out companies that had stood for generations.

Their tactics were immortalised in movies such as *Wall Street*, *Other People's Money* and *Pretty Woman*, which tarred them as villains but also gave them a veneer of glamour. Labour unions, executives and many politicians may have accused corporate raiders of putting the long-term health of the industrial sector at risk for a quick buck (the Hanson group, for example, was notorious for slashing research budgets after buying companies), but the raider playbook of buying companies with (usually) borrowed money, and then selling off the parts, proved highly lucrative. At least for a while.

For those economists who took a hard-nosed, cynical view of human behaviour, the players in these corporate battles often confirmed the psychology at the heart of the 'agency problem'. Tobacco and food group RJR Nabisco's chief executive officer F. Ross Johnson was a case in point. Immortalised in the book *Barbarians at the Gate*,[32] he was seen as a negligent and profligate manager who was more interested in flying around on the company's fleet of corporate jets and playing golf with sports stars than running his business. For managerial economists, RJR's takeover by private equity firm KKR represented the triumph of an efficient market. Jensen saw the takeover battle as 'the arena in which alternative management teams compete for the rights to manage corporate resources'.[33] If a corporate raider was prepared to pay a higher price for a company than the value its prevailing share price ascribed, then it was because the prospective new owners were able to make more money out of the company's assets. This was to say, they were better managers. Not all chief executives were like Johnson, according to Ron Schmidt, a colleague of Jensen's at Rochester who also presented a paper at the 1984 conference, but there were nevertheless more than a few of them. 'And the takeover people looked for companies like that,' he said.[34] That America's largest corporations lobbied Congress to introduce measures to make it harder to launch hostile takeovers only served to reinforce the views of economists like those at Rochester, that takeovers were a clash between good and at best mediocre management. 'Managers formerly protected from competition for their jobs by antitrust and financing constraints that prevented takeover of the nation's largest corporations are now facing a more demanding environment and a more uncertain future,' Jensen wrote. 'It is not surprising that many executives of large corporations would like relief from this new competition for their jobs.'[35]

Solving the agency problem

Meckling was acutely aware when he and Jensen founded the Managerial Economies Research Center at Rochester in 1977 that 'We know little about how alternative compensation and performance evaluation schemes affect behaviour.'[36]

But in the late 1970s and early 1980s a flock of academics began to examine agency theory, and a consensus of sorts emerged among them as to how one might influence the behaviour of managers to ensure they did act in a way that would best serve investors' interests. The key, so the thinking went, was to make the experience of chief executives and shareholders more similar. As it was, in the early 1980s, the positions of the two parties were very different. Shareholders stood to gain if managers did a good job, but could also lose money or just see their investment stagnate if managers did a bad or mediocre job. Managers, on the other hand, got a fat salary whatever happened, and maybe a bit of a bonus if things went well.

By reframing the employment contract to make a manager's experience reflect that of investors, this new wave of economists argued that managers would, in working for their own benefit, simultaneously and almost incidentally perfectly serve shareholders' interests. The key to everything was to link pay to share prices. As Fama had argued, the stock market prices all relevant information about the performance of a company into its share price immediately.[37] This meant that one didn't have to think about how to measure whether a manager did a good job: if they did, the share price would go up. And at the same time, investors would benefit. It was all very neat and simple.

But the idea that the market was always right was also a bold claim, and at the time one far from universally accepted by other economists. 'The stock market often makes mistakes,' the Director of the Federal Trade Commission's Bureau of Economics, F. M. Scherer stated in evidence to a Congressional hearing into hostile takeovers. 'At any given moment in time, some companies will be undervalued by the market relative to their long-run earnings potential, while others are overvalued.'[38] Robert Shiller, who mapped the relationship between earnings and share prices across many decades and concluded markets were fundamentally irrational, and who, ironically, won the Nobel prize jointly with Eugene Fama in 2013, was scathing of his fellow economist's views. 'I don't know if Fama ever states his theory really clearly,' he said; 'if he did it might sound a little odd.' Not only did he think Fama's ideas were wrong, he didn't even think they were science. Rather, he viewed Fama's efficient market hypothesis as part of a deliberate plan by Milton Friedman and his University of Chicago colleagues to twist economics to advance an anti-government political agenda. 'I shouldn't try to psychoanalyse Eugene Fama,' he said,

> but I know that he is committed . . . to a libertarian philosophy, teaching at the University of Chicago where Milton Friedman once lived. It must affect your thinking somehow that they really believe in markets. I think that maybe he has a cognitive dissonance. His research shows that markets are not efficient. So what do you do if you are living in the University of Chicago? It's like being a Catholic priest and then discovering that God doesn't exist or something, you can't deal with that, you've got to somehow rationalise it.[39]

The Nobel prize committee tried to justify their decision to honour two men with diametrically opposed views by arguing that Fama was talking about the short term and Shiller about the long term, a distinction Shiller didn't entertain.

Despite scepticism among many economists, the notion that a company's share price could serve as a useful measure of the relative success of a manager gained ground. But that still left the question of how to calibrate rewards to ensure maximum success. The principles of risk aversion state that humans won't generally accept a bet unless they believe the odds to be stacked in their favour – or at least that they won't be left worse off than if they hadn't gambled at all. So, for example, a chief executive on a fixed $1 million pay package is unlikely to accept an offer of $2 million if they are told that this is conditional on a significant rise in share price, and that they will receive nothing if the share price flatlines. If one wants to significantly motivate a manager, a significant upside therefore has to be offered. The view taken was that while one way to achieve this was to pay the manager in shares, a better and more efficient mechanism was stock options. By giving a manager the option to buy shares at the current market price, at some time in the future, one created the potential for them to make a profit if the shares appreciated in value, while simultaneously ensuring no cost to the shareholder if the manager's efforts failed to deliver. And, of course, the more the manager drove up the share price, the more they and the investors would receive. Some naysaying economists suggested that if bonuses really were to shift the dial they would have to be on such a generous scale that they might damage the overall profitability of the firm.[40] But such pessimism was rejected by adherents of the idea.

With the economic theory and justification established, firms that advised companies on executive compensation started to come on board. In 1984 their industry body, the American Compensation Association, formed the Task Force on Executive Compensation, on which Rochester's Kevin Murphy sat, to consider how packages should be designed. Investors welcomed the idea, and soon the idea of remuneration that was predominantly share-linked, rather than fixed, took off.

Some worried that to rely on rising shareholder value when evaluating the performance both of a company and those leading it was a dangerous metric. 'Shareholders tended to be short-term in their thinking. We didn't have a lot of recognition of the short-term, long-term debate,' said John Wilcox, who in the early 1990s was chairman of Georgeson & Co., a New York based firm that advised fund managers on how to vote on resolutions at company meetings.[41] Short-termism was seen as a particular problem among professional fund managers. After all, they arguably had a financial incentive to be short-termist. Their investors might predominantly be people saving for retirement on a twenty-year or more time timeframe, but fund managers were judged on year-to-year performance. They benefitted from successful short-term strategies. Whether those short-term strategies proved beneficial in the long term was not their concern. That said, there were plenty of people who warmly embraced the new incentives approach. 'In general, they're one of the best forms of compensation when it comes to aligning the CEO with the shareholder . . . options turn managers into shareholders,' said Cari Christian, executive director of United Shareholders Association, a shareholders' advocacy group, in 1992.[42]

By the early 1990s most big US companies had adopted compensation plans whereby most of a chief executive's pay potentially came in the form of share price-linked awards, and in the years that followed executive pay in the US started to rise sharply. In 1990, the average CEO of a company in the S&P 500 index of major firms earned around $3.7 million in 2018 prices. In 2000, they received $22 million.[43] Over the same period, the median wage for US workers rose just 40 per cent to $41,990.[44] One study calculated that the aggregate compensation paid by public companies to their

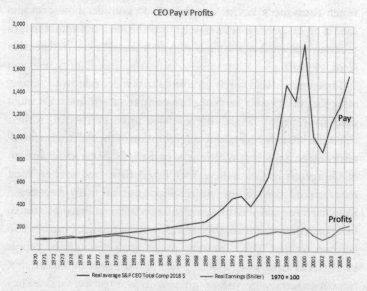

Data source: Economic Policy Institute and Robert Shiller

top-five executives between 2001 and 2003 amounted to 10.3 per cent of the aggregate earnings of these firms during the period.[45] This was a return to levels that had sparked so much outrage in the early 1930s.

Executive pay in the UK: Let our executives grow rich

America wasn't alone. On the other side of the Atlantic, views of corporate pay in Europe were also undergoing a sea change. Up until the late 1980s, surveys consistently showed that UK executives were poorly paid in comparison with their European peers. This was partly due to the fact that many private companies listed on the London Stock Exchange were dominated by large shareholders (often company founders or families of company founders) who kept a tight grip on management pay (though some did pay – relatively small – cash bonuses).[46] And it was to an extent because some of Britain's biggest corporate beasts, like jet-engine maker Rolls-Royce, airline British Airways and carmaker British Leyland, were partly or wholly in public ownership, and so under constant political scrutiny.

But mindsets were starting to change. In 1975, the newly elected leader of the Conservative Party, Margaret Thatcher, made a ground-breaking speech to business leaders at the St Regis hotel in New York, in which she attacked the 'progressive consensus' that she believed elevated an obsession with equality above the ambition for growth and wealth creation. 'The pursuit of equality itself is a mirage,' she said.

> Opportunity means nothing unless it includes the right to be une-
> qual . . . I would say, let our children grow tall and some taller than
> others if they have the ability in them to do so. Because we must
> build a society in which each citizen can develop his full potential,
> both for his own benefit and for the community as a whole, a society
> in which originality, skill, energy and thrift are rewarded.[47]

Her view was clear-cut. Some people were intrinsically more productive than others. They should be encouraged and rewarded. Society as a whole might become more unequal as a result, but society as a whole would also gain. As Thatcher's former Chancellor of the Exchequer Norman Lamont put it many years later, 'Inequality is the natural product of a society which is dynamic.'[48]

Thatcher's world view was and remains controversial. But it played well with voters, tired of rising unemployment, high inflation and seemingly endless industrial unrest. Her vision of a dynamic, upwardly mobile society won her three election victories, and it was, in time, even taken up by the left-of-centre Labour Party. Indeed, the architect of Labour's 1997 election victory, Peter Mandelson, remarked that the party was 'intensely relaxed about people getting filthy rich'.[49]

By the end of the 1980s, the shareholder bases of Britain's biggest companies had become privatised and diversified.[50] Companies thus gained more flexibility in setting manager remuneration and during the 1990s began to adopt the share-linked pay practices that were sending pay soaring in the United States. Typically, this involved bolting option plans onto existing fixed salaries (which also continued to rise at above-inflation levels), so the shift to performance-related pay offered little downside to managers. Initially, the share awards were a small portion of overall compensation, but by the end of the 1990s the share-linked element of compensation came to dominate many pay packages.[51]

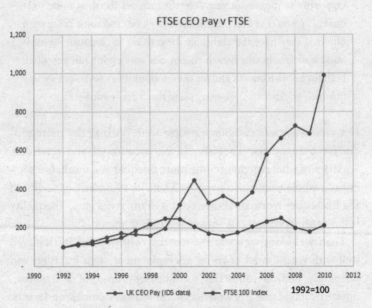

Data source: IDS data and FTSE 100 Index

Between the early and mid-1990s pay for top executives doubled, prompting calls for legislative curbs. The government opted to force companies to publish more clearly the value of share awards, hoping that transparency might exert downward pressure on pay or at least link it more closely to performance. It failed to cool the rise in pay. In 1992 the average boss of a company in the FTSE 100 index of the biggest UK firms earned £450,000. By the turn of the millennium, this had increased to around £1.5 million. By 2010, FTSE CEOs were earning an average £4.5 million.[52] Over this period when CEO pay rose tenfold, and managers took an ever-larger chunk of corporate profits,[53] average pay didn't even double.[54]

Indeed, remuneration consultants and companies argued that government action to increase transparency had encouraged CEOs to demand pay rises to keep up with higher-paid peers[55] – a somewhat disingenuous claim given that large UK-registered companies, both listed and unlisted, had been obliged to publish the pay of their highest paid director – almost always the chief executive – for decades.[56] Their charge, though, was of a piece with that made in the US by academics and consultants like Kevin Murphy, who blamed President Clinton's decision in the 1990s to restrict the tax deductibility of fixed CEO pay above $1 million on the escalation in tax-deductible share-related pay.[57] Essentially, those economists sympathetic to the cause were telling government to keep out of matters that didn't concern them and leave executive remuneration to those who knew best: firms and the economists whose ideas had powered the pay explosion.

In the decade since the 2007 financial crash, CEO pay in the United States and Britain has largely stabilised, at levels somewhat below the all-time peaks in real terms. Nonetheless, compared to ordinary people, top executives get paid on a scale that was unimaginable fifty years ago. The average boss of one of the 350 biggest US companies was paid 278 times what the average worker was in 2018, up from 34 times in 1980 and just 20 times in 1965.[58] In the UK the average FTSE 100 boss earned 117 times average pay in 2018, up from 20 times in 1980.[59] Continental European chief executives have also seen sharp rises in pay and a shift to largely equity-linked remuneration, although the rises have been less extreme.[60]

Performance-related pay in the dock

So is there any empirical evidence to show that the theory works in practice? Do generous bonuses at the top really drive business success?

Initially, there were strong signs that aligning management's financial incentives with those of shareholders was working as intended. By 1990, most big US companies had instituted equity-biased executive remuneration programmes, and in the years that followed the stock market soared.

A local Rochester company provided a case in point. It had endured a tumultuous experience in the 1970s and 1980s, with modest returns for shareholders. Michael Jensen and Kevin Murphy probably would not have been surprised because, until around 1980, Eastman Kodak's managers were indeed paid very much like government employees. That is to say, Kodak was rare among US corporations for not offering its managers incentive pay.[61] Top executives received fixed remuneration and a 'wage dividend': a performance-related bonus that was awarded to all staff on the same basis. This accounted for a small share of an executive's overall compensation. For example, in 1952, the company President, as the top executive was then known, received $162,365 in salary and another $22,898 in wage dividend. The pay practices reflected the ideals of the company's founder.

In April 1880, George Eastman, a Rochester resident who had developed a keen interest in photography, leased the third floor of a building on State Street, where he began to produce a new form of photographic plate he had patented.[62] This part-time venture soon gave rise to another which focused on roll film. Roll film would make photography available to the masses and generate enough wealth to allow Eastman to become one of his era's greatest philanthropists. Rochester University would be one of his biggest beneficiaries, and in recognition named its main quadrangle after him.

By the beginning of the twentieth century, Kodak had become a major multinational. In 1914, it built a skyscraper on State Street to house its burgeoning headquarters. It had a steel structure and a brick façade in what has been described as a 'modified French Renaissance style'. For decades it was the tallest building in Rochester and overlooked a vast site where the company's roll film was produced. To this day, Kodak Tower is still the Eastman Kodak Company's corporate headquarters.

Eastman was generous to his staff, paying them well, and in 1924 personally giving them a third of his shares.[63] However, Eastman Kodak was not an especially generous company when it came to remunerating managers. Around 1930, when its profit was half the level of American Tobacco's, its boss earned under $100,000 compared to the $1 million awarded to American Tobacco's Hill.

During the early 1980s, amid sagging earnings due to increased competitive pressures from overseas rivals like Fujifilm, Kodak began to offer managers modest share option plans.[64] But profits, and the share price, continued to flag. So in 1989, after a collapse in earnings, the company announced a sweeping restructuring plan that included large job cuts. It also decided to tie manager compensation more closely to share price performance, placing up to 40 per cent of the managers' annual pay at risk.[65] Then, in January 1993, as earnings and turnover fell again,[66] Kodak doubled down on the strategy with a plan to require the firm's top forty managers to hold up to four times the amount of their annual salaries in company stock. 'All our senior managers will act and behave like owners of this company,' said the then Chief Executive, Kay Whitmore, 'because they will be substantial owners.'[67]

Whitmore was succeeded that year by George Fisher, who was hired in from technology group Motorola Inc., where he had presided over explosive growth. Fisher galvanised the company, refocusing Kodak on its key money-spinning division – the high-margin camera film business – and selling off some of the businesses, such as digital imaging, which had previously been bought to diversify the company's income streams. He was hailed a hero, and profiled in Forbes magazine in January 1997 under the headline 'How an outsider's vision saved Kodak'. His leadership saw Kodak's share price soar.

Fisher was richly rewarded. In the late 1980s, the long-serving CEO, Colby Chandler, earned around $1 million per year.[68] In the early 1990s, Whitmore had received average annual compensation of around $1.5 million per year. Between 1993 and 2000, Fisher received remuneration valued at $120 million, mostly in options.[69] But with the stock at an all-time high, investors were not complaining.

A raft of studies published during the 1990s showed that executive pay and the return shareholders received had become much more correlated than before:[70] clear evidence, they concluded, that managers were responding as economic theory predicted they would. Given that a shift from paying staff in cash to paying in shares will automatically lead to some sort of correlation between pay and share prices, perhaps the authors of those studies should not have been surprised. Even Murphy acknowledged that the correlation didn't necessarily show 'that the increase in stock-based incentives has led CEOs to work harder'.[71]

Indeed, the closer one looked at the evidence, the harder it proved to sustain the argument. Not every company had dived as fervently into equity-linked pay as Kodak did during the 1990s. The share price performance of those that didn't was no worse or better than that of those that did.[72] And it was apparent in any case that in any organisation there are many forces at work over which executives – brilliant or otherwise – have little control. On top of all that, studies from the 1990s failed to find evidence that companies that richly rewarded their CEOs actually reported higher earnings than those that did not.[73] One found that financial performance accounted for just 4 per cent of the variance in CEO pay levels.[74]

The evidence from the historical record was none too encouraging either. The 1920s was a period of soaring executive pay in the United States, yet real per-share earnings for the S&P Composite Index were lower between 1920 and 1929 than in either of the previous two decades. The period from 1945 to 1970 saw CEOs paid 'like bureaucrats', yet also witnessed the strongest run of US corporate earnings growth in the country's history.[75] Theory states that share prices should reflect the future earnings potential of a company, which makes sense because that represents the cashflow that will be available to investors over time. But by mapping share prices and earnings across over a century, Nobel laureate Robert Shiller found that share prices often have as much if not more to do with vague feelings of market optimism or pessimism as with corporate profitability. In 1921, when the US economy was in a deep recession and people didn't feel very optimistic, the average Price–Earnings Ratio for the S&P 500 Index rose was around 5: a level well below historical averages. By 1929, the average PE Ratio was 30. Similarly, between 1990 and 1999, the average PE across the index rose from around 17 to 44. In other words, while agency theory suggests that the market is always logical and right, history shows it is neither. Companies were rewarding chief executives generously not because of what they had achieved but because of the mood of the market.

In 1997, Kodak's shares hit an all-time high of $94.38 per share, but then began to slide. The CEO refused to accept there was a fundamental problem with the company's business model. Indeed, Fisher was so confident he launched a share buyback programme and declared in April 1999 that, at $77, the shares were 'significantly undervalued in the marketplace' and that the company would re-purchase shares, even if they reached $100.[76] He was wrong. Within a year, the shares were trading at less than half that level. As the new millennium unfolded, and new CEOs took over, earning ever-larger sums, film sales collapsed and Kodak's profits evaporated. The shares fell steadily until, in 2012, the company filed for bankruptcy protection. Fisher's decision to refocus on film, a function of his inability to see how quickly digital photography would destroy this market, had been disastrous.

Today the Kodak Tower casts a sombre shadow on State Street. Some of the Kodak campus has been taken over by a community college, whose yellow school buses sit parked around the entrance to the building. Inside the tower, much of the space lies vacant, Kodak's staff now a tiny fraction of its former level. Not far away is the Xerox Tower, a minimalist charcoal-coloured concrete construction that resembles one of the Twin Towers that formerly stood in Manhattan, and that in 1968 overtook the Kodak tower as Rochester's tallest building. Xerox was another company that bet heavily on share-linked performance pay following operational weaknesses in the 1980s. It, too, experienced a major surge in the share price in the 1990s, before it collapsed when fundamental problems with its business model became evident.

Neither company was run by incompetent slouches. Fisher told an interviewer in mid-1997 that he had not taken a holiday since taking up the leadership of Kodak in 1993.[77] And ultimately both companies fell victim to external vagaries beyond their managers' control. Several CEOs had made crucial errors that helped destroy shareholder value, despite being paid ever-increasing amounts not to.

Performance-related pay: the verdict

Ultimately, the great gaping hole in agency theory is that by taking a simplistic, mathematical view of people it comprehensively ignores basic human psychology. People work for money, it argues, so it follows that the more you pay them the harder they will work. This is undoubtedly true in some situations and under certain conditions: it's been shown, for example, that workers paid piece rates may produce more in the course of an hour than those paid a flat rate, at least in the short term.[78] But it doesn't hold as a universal, unwavering rule.

Stark evidence of this basic truth came my way a while back in a rather unexpected way.

In 2018, the German news magazine *Der Spiegel* came into possession of computer hard drives crammed with terabytes of emails, financial reports and other documents related to European football clubs and organisations. The data dump was too large for any one news outlet to process alone, so *Der Spiegel* invited over a dozen organisations around Europe to help mine the information, including my employer, the Reuters news agency.

As part of our investigation into tax evasion and other unethical behaviour involving footballers and their agents,[79] I examined a great number of football contracts and emails. As I read through them, an intriguing pattern emerged: in most cases players were entitled to bonuses when they won games, scored goals or simply lined up to play, but in all cases the inducement represented a tiny part of the footballer's overall compensation. One widely reported example was the Chilean forward Alexis Sanchez, who in January 2018 signed a contract with Manchester United that paid him a basic salary of over £20 million each year.[80] There was also a bonus element to his package. If he scored a goal, he would receive an additional £75,000. If he assisted another player to score a goal he would get £25,000. Assuming he performed much as he had done the previous season, the chances were that he would net over £2.5 million (though, in a move that would surely have made Michael Jensen choke, Man United had capped the bonus at £2 million). In other words, if the Chilean performed well on pitch, he stood to gain a sum of money that was less than 10 per cent of his total pay package.

When I asked football agents whether such bonus arrangements were standard, they responded that they were. There was no point, they said, in a club offering big performance incentives: they would have no effect. No one seriously believed that a top-flight Premiership footballer would not give his best in a game. Underperformance risked the loss of one's place on the team, would jeopardise future playing opportunities at other teams and possibly cost a player accolades such as championship medals and trophies. It was clear from the emails I read about potential team moves and contract terms that footballers were motivated by money. However, it was equally clear no one believed the lure of more money made them a better player.

If that's true of footballers, does it hold for CEOs? There's certainly no evidence that bonuses push executives to work harder or better than their natural inclinations would prompt them to do. George Fisher didn't become a better leader when Kodak started to pay him over ten times what he had earned previously at Motorola,[81] where he had presided over a period of stellar growth (that continued long after he left). In the more than a hundred economic studies of executive pay I have studied, I have not found one that explains how aligning the interests of shareholders and managers could help the managers make smarter choices. As one former CEO who went on to teach at Harvard Business School said, 'All the financial incentives in the world won't transform CEOs into better decision makers.'[82] Conversely, the notion that a CEO might deliberately make sub-optimal decisions or fall asleep at the wheel because he or she was not sufficiently enthused by their potential bonus seems as likely as Alexis Sanchez not bothering to dodge past a defender and stick one in the back of the net because he had already hit his bonus cap and knew he wouldn't receive any cash for the goal.

This seems to be tacitly accepted by the very community that waves the banner for executive bonuses. In early 2020, I counted sixty CEOs of major listed US and European companies who had stood down abruptly since the beginning of 2017.[83] A third of those departures were linked to sexual or other misconduct, allegations of bullying or presiding over 'toxic' corporate cultures and product scandals like the Boeing 737 Max crashes. I identified around forty cases where the CEO's departure followed a period of operational or share price weakness. These cases are probably representative of what boards and investors might consider to be significant under-performance on the part of a CEO. In a dozen cases, the companies said publicly or briefed reporters that the departure followed a disagreement over strategy – the board did not agree with the direction that the CEO wanted to take the company in, in terms of markets the CEO wanted to focus investments on, or major corporate acquisitions or mergers the CEO wished to engage in. In the other cases, investors usually told journalists that the departures reflected the fact that they had lost faith in the CEO after the boss had failed to articulate or execute a clear turnaround strategy. The one thing I was unable to find was any reference to a CEO being sacked because they were not working hard enough. The closest I could come was a demand by the hedge fund Elliott Management in March 2020 that Jack Dorsey stand down as CEO of Twitter Inc. There was a risk, Elliott Management argued, of him being distracted by occupying a similar role at the payments firm Square Inc.

Of course, some might argue that if an executive is not paid enough, they might opt to take their superior decision-making skills elsewhere. High pay is often justified as the result of market forces. This argument has significant flaws, not least because most CEOs are internal hires and the rapid rise in pay in the 1990s did not coincide with any observable change in the market structure that might have driven it. But it's also not germane here. The adoption of share-linked pay was based on the perceived need, argued by managerial economists like Michael Jensen, to improve the quality of managers by aligning shareholder and manager interests, not to stop executives moving around.

Executive bonuses have come in for much criticism in recent years at a popular level, and proof of the relevance of agency theory remains as elusive as ever. Academics have increasingly found the way in which 'the complexities of organisational life are ignored'[84] by the theory hard to, well, ignore. But neither the bonus culture nor the theory that underpins it has gone away. As recently as 2017, Norges Bank Investment Management, one of the world's largest investors in equities thanks to its stewardship of the $1 trillion Norwegian Oil fund, confidently declared that 'Agency theory remains relevant to executive remuneration in listed companies because CEO incentives do not match those of shareholders. It is therefore in the interest of shareholders to better align the actions of the CEO with their interests.'[85] Amid the novel Coronavirus pandemic in 2020, such logic was used by biotechnology company Novavax to justify awarding top managers tens of millions of dollars worth of share options. Although the managers already had options that would net them millions if their company produced a successful vaccine, the company argued that providing them with additional options would make success more likely.[86]

Ironically, two people who have accepted a basic flaw in the thinking that underpinned the shift to share-based compensation in the 1990s are Jensen and Murphy. In 2004, they published a paper saying that the market was not, after all, always right. They wrote that shares could be overvalued, and that in such situations – as they believe occurred in the 1990s – share-based pay could be value destructive for a company. 'In the presence of significantly overvalued equity,' they wrote, 'such equity-based incentives are like throwing gasoline on a fire.'[87]

But while economics lays claim to scientific attributes, it doesn't necessarily feel bound by scientific rules. In physics, finding that a central plank in your thinking doesn't hold is sufficient to send you back to the drawing board, and diminish your reputation in the eyes of peers. Not so in economics. If it were, the repeated proof that the central thesis of Milton Friedman's career – that inflation could only be controlled via managing the money supply[88] and could not be tamed via increasing interest rates[89] – was wrong would have severely damaged his reputation within the economic community. It hasn't.

And so Jensen is in one way consistent when the acceptance of imperfect markets does not cause him to rethink the conclusions built on this assumption. When I spoke to him in 2019, he said he wasn't aware of anything that made him question the conclusions of his earlier research.

'It absolutely had an effect,' he said, with a hint of either pride or defiance.

And that effect, I asked, was to make businesses more efficient?

'Without a doubt.'

5

THE STIGLER HYPOTHESIS

Does a minimum wage cost jobs?

Dartmouth's narrow medieval streets, with their wood-framed houses, record the centuries of affluence generated by the Devon town's bustling port. The town has played a part in some of the most important chapters in Britain's history – the harbour was a gathering point for fleets that departed for the Crusades and in 1588 provided some of the ships that defended England against the Spanish Armada. Just down the coast is the shingle riverbank from where, in 1620, the *Mayflower* set off across the Atlantic in what would become the origin story of the United States of America.

Dartmouth died as a trading port a long time ago, but the town's rich history means it remains a bustling place. The extravagant former merchants' homes are now tea rooms, hotels and pubs. On summer days, the streets are filled with tourists, stopping regularly to feast on such local delicacies as pasties and fudge, and some of the best battered fish and thick-cut chips in England.[1] But being a tourist destination has proved rather less lucrative than being a port for trade and supplying crusaders, man-o'-wars and pilgrims stopping off on their way to change history. The hospitality industry, like the other main employers in Devon and neighbouring Cornwall – agriculture, retail and social care – brings jobs but not much money.

Official statistics bear this out. In 1998, 27 per cent of employees in Dartmouth and neighbouring Kingsbridge earned less than the official threshold for low pay of £3.50 per hour. As the government's Low Pay Commission pointed out that year, there was a higher percentage of low-paid people in this part of the country than anywhere else in England.[2] So when a Labour government decided the following year to try to tackle the problem of poor wages, by introducing Britain's first ever National Minimum Wage, at a rate of £3.60 per hour, Dartmouth found itself in the front line of an economic argument that had raged for over a century.

Sweat shops and the birth of the minimum wage

Dartmouth is a far cry from the sort of place we popularly or historically associate with low pay. In Britain, at least, poverty wages are more often associated in the public imagination with the emergence of the grim factories and industrial towns that sprang up in the eighteenth and nineteenth centuries. In point of fact, though, the earliest debates about subsistence or below subsistence wages focused on the plight, not of factory workers, but of the 'sweated' labourers who took on subcontracted work in, for example, the clothing industry, and who worked in small workshops or at home on such tasks as sewing and making shirts. Because they were so widely dispersed and often self-employed, they lacked the muscle of the nascent trades union movement, active in factories, and so were particularly open to exploitation by unscrupulous bosses and the manufacturers who outsourced work to them.

So bad had their situation become by the second half of the nineteenth century, that in 1888 a Select Committee of the House of Lords was set up to look at the whole issue of sweated labour. Hearings were held and witnesses called.[3] In 1890, the committee published its fifth and final report, and its chairman, the Irish peer

Windham Wyndham Quin, better known as Lord Dunraven, put forward a parliamentary motion 'That, in the opinion of this House, legislation with a view to the amelioration of the condition of the people suffering under that system is urgently needed.'

Dunraven graphically described the state in which great swathes of the British populace lived. He decried

> the miserable pittance for which these people exchange their almost unremitting toil – the scanty fare, barely enough to keep starvation from the door; the horrible insanitary conditions in which they work, the overcrowding in their dwellings, men, women, and children, often not even members of the same family, sleeping huddled up on the floor of the dilapidated room in which they live and work, and work and die; the children sick of infectious diseases.[4]

He argued that the unorganised status of sweated labour meant employers enjoyed an unfair advantage when it came to agreeing wages, and could therefore set them artificially low.

Although he didn't say so in as many words, Dunraven was essentially making a case for setting a national minimum wage. It was something that had never been done before.[5] But although both his own Conservative Party and the opposition Liberal Party took a laissez-faire approach to business, Dunraven could have argued that there were precedents for the sort of market intervention he was proposing Parliament should make. Trade unions were legally permitted to organise and use the threat of strikes to achieve higher wages. In Ireland, land courts had been established to set 'fair' rents for tenants who felt the 'market' rate demanded by their landlord was excessive. He could also have argued that such interventions had not caused economic damage to the country at large. It was not generally held that unions had dented the success of British industry or that the land courts had damaged Ireland's agricultural productivity. Rather, such policies were seen as purely redistributive – shifting money from the pockets of consumers, employers and landowners to workers or tenants with no or little efficiency losses, and possibly productivity gains as those who had previously been so impoverished became more industrious.

Other parliamentarians agreed the conditions endured by many were grim, but their analysis took a very different form. A chief critic of the minimum wage proposal, Frederick Stanley, the Earl of Derby, saw no misfunctioning of the labour market. Wages were low, he said, because there was an excess of unskilled labour: 'We all know that the real difficulty – the real danger – is the rate at which the poorest class are increasing in London and in our great towns.'[6] His argument was that low wages allowed more people to enter work. His view of a minimum wage (apart from a belief that it would be very difficult to enforce in the informal sweating sector) was that it would force employers to eliminate low-skill, low productivity jobs that could not justify a higher wage. The way to tackle poor pay, he suggested, was either to increase demand for labour through a large public works programme or to encourage emigration. The latter solution, he thought, had its merits; the former would be prohibitively expensive. Ultimately, he thought, the real 'cure' was to convince the poor to abstain from early marriages and stop having children they were unable to provide for.

In the short term Derby's view prevailed, and it was the colonies he was so keen to export 'excess' workers to and which still welcomed them – Australia and New Zealand – that became the first to introduce minimum wage rules. However, the issue of low pay in Britain didn't go away. It remained a niggling sore in the minds of the public and in the press. In 1906 the *Daily News*, a newspaper founded by Charles Dickens, even organised an exhibition devoted to the issue. Finally, in 1909, Winston Churchill, the President of the Board of Trade, steered legislation through Parliament to establish Trade Boards that would set minimum pay levels in certain industries in which workers did not generally enjoy trades union protection. His argument in favour of his Trade Boards Act was one that Dunraven had advanced: 'It was formerly supposed,' Churchill argued,

> that the working of the laws of supply and demand would naturally regulate or eliminate that evil. The first clear division which we make on the question today is between healthy and unhealthy conditions of bargaining. That is the first broad division which we make in the general statement that the laws of supply and demand will ultimately produce a fair price.[7]

In other words, he took the view that the laws of supply and demand were not freely working due to the exceptional power of employers to influence wage rates. His intention was to rebalance the relationship, without otherwise interfering in the day-to-day conduct of business.

The issue of low wages was also being explored in the United States at much the same time, though with a slightly different emphasis. In Britain, a perceived excess of labour meant many politicians feared that a minimum wage would lead to unemployment. The United States' traditionally tighter labour market (which Adam Smith said explained the higher wages in the colonies) meant people there were less concerned on this front – the country's leading economist of the late-nineteenth century, John Bates Clark, argued that any jobs lost by 'unfit' companies going under as a result of a minimum wage would be absorbed by the expansion of 'fit' companies.[8] That left the larger, ideological question as to whether it was appropriate for the state to interfere with workers' and businesses' commercial negotiations. Putting more focus on the matter of fairness than the principle of laissez-faire, individual states (Massachusetts being the first, in 1912) began to introduce minimum wage rules, initially covering just women.[9] Employers challenged the laws in the courts and during the 1920s and 1930s won a raft of victories, including several Supreme Court judgements that ruled that the fixing of a minimum wage was unconstitutional.[10] It was not until 1938 that a federal minimum wage, which would withstand legal challenges, was introduced, during the presidency of Franklin Delano Roosevelt.[11]

The minimum wage's rocky path

Having established the principle of a minimum wage, however, both Britain and the United States gradually retreated from it after the Second World War. Trade unions on both sides of the Atlantic favoured negotiated wage settlements over state-enforced minimums, and worried that the latter would remove the need for workers to join unions. In the absence of strong support for it, the US minimum wage failed to keep up with inflation, making it less and less relevant. In Britain, the government's Trade Boards (later know as Wage Councils) had a decreasing role, as those occupations it covered, like corset-making and working with ostrich and other types of 'fancy feather', became less common.[12]

What ramped up the debate again was the economic turmoil of the 1970s and 1980s. In Britain and America, as traditional unionised industries, such as car-making, shipbuilding and coal-mining, began to decline, and service industries rose, trade union membership started to fall, and the number of people benefiting from negotiated wage agreements fell with it. British unions came to view the notion of a national minimum wage as less of a threat than they had a few years previously and, one by one, dropped their opposition, paving the way for the Labour Party to include the policy in its manifesto for the 1987 general election.[13]

In the United States, meanwhile, reconsideration of the minimum wage was given urgency by the realisation that the well-paying manufacturing jobs lost in the 1970s and 1980s were being replaced by low-skill, low wage-roles. As the Joint Economic Committee of the US Congress reported in 1986 in *The Great American Job Machine*:

> For more than a decade, the United States has produced more new jobs than most other industrialised nations – nearly 20 million new jobs during 1973–84. However . . . compared to the period 1973–79, the net new employment created between 1979 and 1984 has occurred disproportionately at the low end of the wage salary distribution (i.e., below \$7,000 in 1984 dollars). Between 1979 and 1984, the number of workers earning more than the 1973 median (\$14,024 in 1984 dollars) actually declined by 1.8 million.[14]

No increase in the federal minimum wage had been approved since the 1970s, and the prevailing figure of \$3.35 per hour was in 1986 worth less, in inflation-adjusted terms, than in the 1960s. Labour unions urged reform. The US Catholic church, too, pushed for change, arguing that a higher minimum wage constituted 'an essential measure of economic justice'.[15] Many voters seemed to like the plan too. One poll found that 71 per cent of Americans supported Senator Ted Kennedy's plan for a \$4.65-an-hour minimum.[16] Michael Dukakis, the Democratic nominee for President in the 1988 election, also supported an increase.[17]

But the dominant political climate was hostile. In Britain, Margaret Thatcher made clear her total opposition to any idea of a national minimum wage. The prospects of young people would be blighted by Labour's minimum wage policy, she argued, 'because people could not then afford to employ them and give them a start in life. A quarter of a million jobs could be at risk.'[18]

Her US political soulmate, Ronald Reagan, felt the same. He believed the minimum wage was a fundamentally flawed policy and that giving it additional bite would cost more jobs than were already being lost. 'The minimum wage has caused more misery and unemployment,' he said in 1980, 'than anything since the Great Depression.'[19] Business groups agreed. The US Chamber of Commerce argued that a proposed increase to $4.65 an hour over three years would by 1995 cause the loss of 1.9 million jobs.[20] Crucially, many progressives shared this concern. Some Democratic politicians teamed up with Republicans to oppose Ted Kennedy's plans to restore the US minimum wage to its historical levels as a percentage of the average wage.[21] Some in the 'liberal' media, swayed by the arguments of economic theory, backed their opposition. In the 1920s, when the argument had been whether or not to allow government intervention in private contracts to improve the lot of the poor, the *New York Times* editorial page had supported the introduction of a minimum wage. But in the late 1980s, when the paper saw the trade-off as being between higher earnings for some low-paid citizens and fewer jobs for the poorest, it concluded that 'The idea of using a minimum wage to overcome poverty is old, honorable – and fundamentally flawed.'[22]

In late 1988, the US Democrats dropped their congressional effort to raise the minimum wage. In Britain, Labour's support for it was felt to be one of the causes of their narrow 1992 defeat, the Conservatives having made hay with their claim that such a policy would cost two million jobs. In 1993, the Conservative government passed the Trade Union Reform and Employment Rights Act, which abolished the Wages Councils, save for the Agricultural Wages Board.[23] Almost a century on from the first legislative moves to end low pay in Britain and the United States, the debate appeared mired in the mud. Over that period, people had increasingly expected governments to intervene in the economy to make outcomes fairer, but when it came to how society paid those at the lowest rung of the labour market, political thinking appeared to have moved in the opposite direction. The reason for this was the entry of a new party into the debate: economists.

Economists enter the fray

The Committee on the Sweated Trades' investigation was vast in its scope. Interviews were conducted with 291 witnesses on how the low-wage labour market operated.[24] Every possible constituency and category of expert was consulted, from retailers, shoemakers, priests and rabbis to the superbly titled Superintendent of the Nuisance Department, as Manchester's then-chief sanitary inspector was known. Every category of expert, that is, except for one: no economist was asked to offer their thoughts on how the labour market worked or how wage controls would affect employment.[25] This was probably because at the time 'political economy', as the area of study was known, was perceived to reside in a similar category of knowledge to philosophy. It might broadly guide thinking on a few major themes such as trade, but, like philosophy, it was not deemed to be of practical help with everyday problems.

Economists had first given serious thought to the idea of a minimum wage at least as early as the late-eighteenth century, when Jeremy Bentham wrote of it.[26] His unequivocal view was that it was a bad idea: 'a regulation which fixes the minimum of wages, is a regulation of a prohibitory nature, which excludes from the competition all whose labour is not worth the price fixed.' John Stuart Mill argued much the same in his 1848 work *Principles of Political Economy*. He thought such a measure would lead to the elimination of jobs and higher unemployment across the economy, requiring state subsidisation of the unemployed. Marshall's development of supply-and-demand curves allowed a visual expression of how this would work in practice.

The graph shows labour supply and demand – the former sloping upward to reflect the economists' assumption that higher prices stimulate additional supply, and the latter sloping downward.

At equilibrium point E, there is a market-clearing wage, in this case £10 per hour, where the demand for workers and supply are

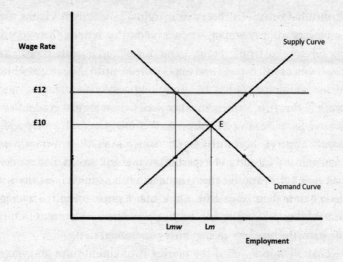

perfectly matched. This gives a total level of employment (conceivably measured in hours or the number of jobs) of Lm. However, if the government imposes a wage floor which is above the market-clearing wage, then the amount of labour which employers will demand falls, to Lmw.

Supply-and-demand curves didn't become part of the popular consciousness until some years after Marshall published his work. It's therefore fair to say that early advocates of the minimum wage, including Winston Churchill, didn't see the labour market precisely in Marshallian terms or as a straightforward matter of supply and demand. Rather they regarded wages as being a product of negotiation. As a result, they felt that employers could afford to pay their workers more and that a government could safely intervene and rebalance things in favour of workers without dampening overall labour demand.

In 1899, the American neoclassical economist John Bates Clark devised a model that, in theory at least, showed that labour markets were not driven by such fuzzy forces as 'bargaining power',[27] but by discernible rules. His theory of marginal productivity claims that employers will pay employees an amount that reflects their contribution to the firm's profits, and therefore, by extension, that employment will expand and wages increase up to the point at which hiring additional staff at the prevailing wage rate offers no more profit to that firm – when, in other words, the marginal productivity is zero. So, for example, a supermarket might opt to employ additional cashiers to deal with long checkout queues, thereby improving customer service and so increasing revenue and profits. But at a certain point, the extra income generated by an additional cashier will drop below their wage cost. Once that happens, and the average profitability per cashier falls to the point where it threatens to turn negative, the retailer will stop hiring additional staff.

That all works well if the market is in equilibrium and wages are set according to the marginal productivity of workers. But, the theory posits, if an increase in wages is imposed via, say, a government-mandated minimum wage, then suddenly the marginal productivity of many workers will not be sufficient to cover their wages. At this point, assuming the firm retains its existing staffing level, it will be losing money.

If you hold the Churchillian view of labour markets as a power play between workers and employers, then it is difficult, if not impossible, to model the mechanisms that determine wages or employment in a way that allow you to make predictions about the outcomes of different policies. However, if you accept Clark's theory and the principle that the demand curve for labour absolutely determines employment and wage levels, then predictions are entirely possible, and the realm of wage-setting attains the authority of a science. It's no surprise, then, that Clarke's analysis should have been welcomed by economists and that it should have become hugely influential. Over the decades that followed, even those economists most at ease with government intervention in the economy argued that minimum wages were synonymous with unemployment.

In a 1930 paper on government-prescribed wage levels, John Maynard Keynes concluded that a minimum wage would be unworkable as it would cause capital flight.[28] Post-war Keynesian economists including Nobel laureates James Tobin[29] and Gunnar Myrdal,[30] a development economist dismissed as a socialist by some conservatives,[31] both argued that a minimum wage would price workers out of employment. In 1988 Paul Samuelson argued that the policy actually hurt the poorest families and favoured middle-class families.[32] A 1976 survey of professional economists found that 90 per cent 'generally agreed' or 'agreed with provisions' that 'a minimum wage increases unemployment among young and unskilled workers'.[33] The most widely sold textbooks of the 1960s, 1970s and 1980s, such as *Economics: Principles and Policy* by William Baumol and Alan Blinder ('minimum wages reduce employment') and – my own university tome – *The Applied Theory of Price* by Donald McCloskey ('the minimum wage causes unemployment') were clear on the point that minimum wages reduced employment.

Through the decades there were a few dissenters in academic circles. In 1946 Richard Lester, an associate professor at Princeton, published the results of a survey he conducted among businesspeople that showed that executives did not base their hiring decisions on such abstruse considerations as the marginal costs of labour.[34] Indeed, they didn't even know what these costs were. His conclusion was that the traditional supply-and-demand model simply didn't apply to employment, and that institutional factors such as community attitudes, the presence of labour unions, etc., were important determinants of employment levels and wages. 'Reasoning about labour markets as though they were commodity markets,' Lester later wrote, 'seems to be an important explanation for erroneous conclusions on such matters as minimum wages.'[35] The response from the mainstream of the profession was scathing. A University of Chicago alumnus who would in time become one of the Chicago School's leading scholars, George Stigler, published a rebuttal in 1946, and called peers to be 'outspoken and singularly agreed' that minimum wages killed jobs.[36] In the decades that followed, Stigler's view would prevail among economists. But it didn't seem to influence policymakers much. In 1949 President Harry Truman approved a near doubling in the minimum wage; countries including France, Japan, the Netherlands and Spain introduced minimum wage rules. True, as stated earlier, the impact of statutory wage floors waned in the UK and United States in the 1950s and 1960s, but only because labour unions preferred collective bargaining as the primary wage-setting mechanism.

But as in so many other arenas, thinking shifted in the 1970s and 1980s, and as politicians looked to free-market forces to tackle economic problems, the voices of those who claimed to understand how markets worked became more influential.

In 1977 Jimmy Carter established an independent Commission to examine the evidence on the minimum wage so that future policy on the issue would be fact-based. Four years and $50 million (in 2020 dollars) later,[37] the Minimum Wage Study Commission published its final report, which encapsulated, in great detail, the sum of academic knowledge on the matter. The voluminous study, and a 1982 summary of it published by three economists who sat on the Commission,[38] led economists to coalesce around the idea that minimum wages had adverse effects on low-skilled employment – the roles which it principally impacted.[39]

Gradually, the accepted wisdom in economics became the public policy orthodoxy, practised by governments, advocated by organisations such as the IMF and OECD and accepted by the mainstream media. It's unclear whether Margaret Thatcher and Ronald Reagan's positions on minimum wages were dictated by economic theory (although Thatcher did cite free-market economists such as Milton Friedman[40] and Friedrich Hayek[41] as strong influences) but the near unanimity among economists in the 1980s, and their rising influence, meant the decision to allow wage floors to wither away seemed like a simple case of following scientific advice.

But, then, a small band of economists had the temerity to test the science.

Fast food economics

In November 1991, the economics departments of Princeton and Cornell University, two Ivy League colleges, held a conference at Cornell's campus in Ithaca in upstate New York. The topic was the minimum wage, and the papers presented at it were deemed noteworthy enough to prompt *Industrial and Labor Relations Review* to feature some of them in a special edition on the minimum wage it issued the following year. Among them were three by the economists Alan Krueger, Lawrence Katz and David Card, which, in time, would turn received wisdom on its head. The three young economists had examined data following recent changes in the federal and state minimum wages and, they claimed, had failed to find any negative employment effects. They had also scrutinised previous research and come to the conclusion that those papers critical of the effects of a minimum wage had made erroneous calculations. One paper by Katz and Krueger, which examined employment at fast food restaurants in Texas after a 1991 increase in the federal minimum wage, even suggested that those firms likely to have been most affected by the increase in the minimum wage had seen a relative increase in employment.[42]

Not surprisingly, their findings ruffled feathers in the economic community. Several researchers, including David Neumark, William Wascher and Finis Welch, whose work was criticised by Card, Katz and Krueger, became particularly active in countering the three men's accusations of bias, while Neumark and Wascher sought to turn the tables further by claiming that there were errors in Card, Katz and Krueger's own work.

The debate became even more frenzied after the publication in 1994 of Card and Kreuger's research paper on the impact of the minimum wage on fast food restaurants in the adjacent states of New Jersey and Pennsylvania. Based on telephone surveys of over 400 outlets, it compared the relative unemployment rates in a state where the minimum wage had been raised in 1992 (New Jersey), with those in a state where there had been no change (Pennsylvania). Its unequivocal conclusion – that the minimum wage increase had had no impact – did not go down well with the fast food sector, which feared legislators might use the research to justify further minimum wage hikes, or with Neumark and Washer, who did their own study, using payroll data from 230 restaurants in the two states, to suggest that Card and Krueger's findings were incorrect and that in fact employment growth in New Jersey had been hampered by the minimum wage. Card and Krueger issued a riposte, criticising Neumark and Wascher's sample size and its source (some of the data had been supplied by an industry group), and defending their own methodology. Things became frosty. Welch told the *Wall Street Journal* in 1996 that the new Jersey-Pennsylvania study was 'generally dismissed by professional economists'; and when some of the protagonists faced off on a panel at an event hosted by the American Economic Association, Card was so infuriated by Welch he refused to even join the debate, and sat glaring at his opponents.[43] It was clear, according to his co-panellist that day, that 'These guys didn't like each other at all.'[44]

It wasn't that Card and Krueger were seeking to overturn neoclassical supply-and-demand theory altogether. They believed that minimum wage rates above 50 per cent of median pay risked killing jobs. 'David and I have said all along,' Krueger said in an interview, 'that there was a tipping point where a great enough increase in the minimum wage would start to reduce employment.'[45]

But the economic establishment saw the claim that an imposed wage increase would not diminish labour demand as a frontal assault on one of the basic pillars of economics. 'The inverse relationship between quantity demanded and price is the core proposition in economic science, which embodies the presupposition that human choice behaviour is sufficiently rational to allow predictions to be made,' the Nobel laureate James M. Buchanan said of the men's work in 1996. 'Fortunately,' he added, 'only a handful of economists are willing to throw over the teaching of two centuries; we have not yet become a bevy of camp-following whores.'[46] The Nobel memorial winner Gary Becker similarly saw Card and Krueger as denying the laws of gravity. 'Even a wizard would have a great deal of difficulty repealing the economic law that higher minimum wages reduce employment,' he said. 'Since politicians are not wizards, they should not try.'[47] Harvard Professor Robert Barro, considered one of America's most influential economists, described Neumark as a 'hero' for pushing back against the Card-Krueger-Katz work.[48]

But the view taken in politically liberal circles was rather different. The new wave of minimum wage research received a wide readership among labour unions and centrist or left-of-centre political parties, which in the 1990s took control in the United States, Britain and France, and helped inform the Clinton administration's decision to increase the minimum wage in 1996 by 21 per cent.[49] In Britain, the Card-Krueger research and a 1994 London School of Economics study, which found that a reduction in the pay levels set by Wages Councils, as a percentage of average wages, had done nothing to increase employment,[50] also allowed Labour to argue that its minimum wage policy would not cost jobs.[51] When Tony Blair and his Chancellor of the Exchequer Gordon Brown were elected in 1997, they faced dire warnings from business organisations, international organisations like the OECD,[52] many financial commentators,[53] and of course mainstream economists. But they nevertheless pressed ahead with their plans. It was a huge political gamble, and made Britain a test bed in one of economics' most heated debates.

Dominant wisdom overturned

In an effort to minimise opposition from business groups, and because, despite arguing that a minimum wage could help the economy, Gordon Brown himself feared a minimum wage could potentially kill jobs, the Labour government chose to introduce the minimum wage at a modest level, with the hope of gradually bringing more people under its protection.[54] The rate of £3.60 per hour represented around 40 per cent of median adult hourly earnings. This was just ahead of the US federal minimum wage, which then averaged 37 per cent of median earnings, but was well below that in the Netherlands (54 per cent), France (60 per cent) and Australia (65 per cent).[55] In a city such as London, where the cost of living has traditionally been high, and wages have had to be pegged accordingly, it had little practical effect and caused little concern among employers.

But in Dartmouth the £3.60-per-hour level prompted alarm. A spokesman for the Federation of Small Businesses based in nearby Paignton predicted the minimum wage would have 'a devastating effect'[56] on local small businesses. At Dartmouth's Royal Castle Hotel, which over the years has hosted Cary Grant, Faye Dunaway and Gregory Peck, it helped drive up wages as a percentage of costs from a historical level of 30 per cent to 40 per cent. Since the owner felt that to cut head count would be to damage the quality of service, he saw no choice but to absorb the additional expense.

Other small businesses in the area pushed up prices where they could, but otherwise resigned themselves to taking a hit on margin.[57] However, when all is said and done, the one thing they didn't do was what orthodox economic thinking said they must inevitably do: cut jobs.[58] In the year after the minimum wage was introduced, the number of people in South Devon recorded as out of work dropped to its lowest since records began thirteen years earlier and the number of job vacancies soared.[59] By 2002, Devon's unemployment rate had dropped from 4.2 per cent in 1998 to 2.5 per cent.[60] In the South-west as a whole (including the rest of Devon and Cornwall), the unemployment rate fell 4.3 per cent in 1999, 8.9 per cent in 2000 and 12.2 per cent in 2001.[61]

Obviously, factors were in play here that had nothing to do with the existence or absence of a minimum wage. Britain overall in these years, like most of the European Union, experienced healthy growth.[62] But what's notable is that, totally contrary to what economic theory predicted, the areas more affected by the minimum wage didn't produce fewer new jobs than the rest of the country. The combined drop in unemployment in the South-west was 23 per cent between 1998 and 2001, compared to a 17 per cent drop in London,[63] where fewer than 5 per cent of employees earned less than £3.50 per hour in 1999 (as compared with 27 per cent in Dartmouth).

In the years that followed, the minimum wage was repeatedly increased at a pace that outstripped the rise in average wages, prompting further dire warnings about hitting a tipping point that would lead to unemployment. But the data continued to confound the economic orthodoxy. The Low Pay Commission, which was set up by the government in 1997 and which was made up of representatives of business groups, trade unions and economists to study the impacts of the National Minimum Wage (NMW) and advise the government on the level of future increases, concluded in 2015: 'Research we have commissioned to inform our decisions – now totalling around 140 projects – has generally shown that the NMW has led to higher than average wage increases for the lowest paid, with little evidence of adverse effects on employment or the economy.'[64] It also established that those on the minimum wage weren't predominantly young people on the first rung of the employment ladder, students working part-time or during summer breaks, or other groups whose modest earnings, opponents of the minimum wage say, should not provoke concern. Most – 68 per cent – were twenty-five years of age or older; many were their family's primary bread winners; some were people of pensionable age.

By the end of 2014, the national minimum wage had put a higher floor than ever on what the lowest paid should earn, relative to median or average earners. However, the slow recovery from the financial crash and great recession meant average wages had not kept up with inflation. And since the Low Pay Commission linked recommended increases in the national minimum wage to changes in median pay, between October 2007 and October 2013 the real value of the wage had fallen 5 per cent.

Given its historical stance on the issue, the Conservative Party should have welcomed the erosion in the absolute value of the minimum wage. After all, in 1999 they fought its introduction to the bitter end, slamming the Confederation of British Industry for dropping its opposition[65] and forcing the House of Lords to sit all night to get the bill through. But as George Osborne, a senior adviser to Conservative ministers in the 1990s before he entered Parliament as an MP in 2001, acknowledged to me in 2019, the predictions of economic theory had 'certainly not proved to be the experience of Britain'. As Chancellor of the Exchequer after 2010, he remained wary, pushing back against trade unionists and others demanding significant hikes in the minimum wage, and feeling in his gut that the basic economic orthodoxy made basic economic sense (after all, as economists in the United States sometimes say, a \$1 million minimum wage would *certainly* kill jobs).[66] But he wasn't happy about Britain's transformation into a lower-wage economy. He also wasn't happy that the government was paying out more and more in top-up benefits for the working poor. And so in 2015 he made a critical decision: to stop listening to the economists.

In July of that year, Osborne announced a step change upwards in the minimum wage, one that alarmed even the Low Pay Commission.[67] He announced that by 2020 the minimum would rise to 60 per cent of the median wage[68] – a level well above the average for OECD members, and one estimated to impact around 2 million workers. The result? In 2019, the Low Pay Commission announced that it had failed to find statistically significant negative employment effects. Back in 1997, in an article in the Institute of Economic Affairs journal, Professor Walter Oi, a labour economist at the University of Rochester, had stated that 'a policy that can raise the wages of those at the bottom of the wage ladder with no job losses is remarkable. It rivals a perpetual motion machine or alchemy.'[69] It appeared that Britain had just become a nation of alchemists.

And it wasn't alone. Looking across the nations of the EU, the European Commission concluded in 2014 that 'minimum wages have only a small negative effect on employment, not usually found to be statistically significant.'[70] Hungary afforded a case in point. In 2001, the country's right-wing government unexpectedly increased its minimum wage by 57 per cent. One study found that this reduced employment in small firms – those usually most affected by the minimum wage – by almost 3 per cent.[71] In 2002, the government followed up with another hike, lifting the wage by a combined 96 per cent over the 2000 level. Another study found that out of 290,000 minimum wage workers in Hungary, around 30,000 lost their jobs.[72] But what was noteworthy here was that while some people clearly and regrettably did lose their jobs, there was no overall increase in unemployment. It would appear that most, if not all, of those workers who were displaced by the hike in the minimum wage went on to find other jobs. And this was in a country where the minimum wage effectively doubled within two years. In 2014, Europe's biggest economy, Germany, adopted a minimum wage. Analysts predicted doom, particularly in the country's poorer East, but, again, no damage could be detected and the country proceeded to experience record low unemployment.[73]

In the face of so much evidence that what didn't work in theory seemed to be performing pretty well in practice – or, at least, not causing actual economic damage – many of those who previously opposed minimum wages changed their tunes. Some big names, like James Tobin, who had previously spoken out against the minimum wage, began to call for it to be raised.[74] Polls of economists showed they were now less convinced that minimum wages cost jobs. Economics textbooks revised their claims that this was its effect.[75] International economic organisations also changed their tune. In 2014, the IMF[76] and OECD[77] called on the US to increase its minimum wage, saying this could be done without killing jobs. In 2017, the OECD also urged Japan to hike its minimum wage in an attempt to help stimulate its economy.[78]

The dominant wisdom was shifting. But this left the question as to why economists got it so wrong in the first place.

Minimum fact studies

The pillars of the economic establishment who slammed Card and Krueger's work didn't dismiss it simply for challenging theory: they said the men ignored the facts. 'During the past several decades, many studies found that raising the minimum wage does reduce the employment of teenagers and others with low skills,' Gary Becker wrote in 1995.

This wasn't a fair characterisation of the state of academic knowledge at that point. It would be more accurate to say that economists had spent decades trying to find convincing empirical evidence that the minimum wage led to unemployment but had failed, and that they had stubbornly insisted that their failure reflected unreliable data or problematic methodology. The report of the commission

Jimmy Carter appointed to study the minimum wage – on which the economic consensus against the minimum wage was based – never concluded that the minimum wage reduced employment of low-skilled workers generally. It just couldn't put its finger on positive proof.

That said, there was one area of the labour market where the Commission identified what it saw as a convincing link between employment and the minimum wage: teenage employment. The number of teenagers in work, it posited, would decline by 1–3 per cent if the minimum wage was increased by 10 per cent.[79] Since the percentage decrease was so modest (even within the 1–3 per cent range it suggested, the Commission tended to the lower end) and the section of the workforce involved such a narrow one, this finding was not sufficient to alter the Commission's overall, very tentative conclusion: 'The direction of the effect on adult employment is uncertain in the empirical work . . . Uncertainty about the effects on adults is a serious gap in the literature.' It was sufficient, however, to give true believers both hope and the evidential ammunition they craved. Sixteen-to-nineteen-year-olds were unskilled workers, they claimed (not uncontroversially). They could therefore be taken as a proxy for unskilled workers more generally. If their employment prospects were damaged by the minimum wage, it followed that other unskilled workers suffered in the same way. It just happened to be that the data the researchers relied on wasn't good enough.

It was a bold extrapolation. It was certainly true that teenagers occupied an area of the US labour market that had experienced a dramatic collapse in employment in the previous decades. But, as ever, correlation doesn't equate to causation. Other factors were in play. Some teachers pointed out that by the 1970s and 1980s teenagers couldn't take on work to the extent they had formerly done, because they had to focus more on getting good grades than earlier generations had. Others argued that teenagers were more likely to engage in volunteer work, because college admission departments were placing more value on this than the experience of, say, waiting tables. Some parents said that safety concerns deterred them from encouraging their kids to get jobs. In 1979, Martin Feldstein, who would go on to be Chairman of President Reagan's Council of Economic Advisers and author of a study that 'proved' the claims of his old sparring partner Arthur Laffer, came up with another answer: teenagers had become work-shy. He conducted a survey of sixteen- to nineteen-year olds, which revealed that the drop in work was not related to a drop in demand for young workers. Rather, he found that:

> Most of this 'out of the labor force' group show relatively little inter-est in finding work . . . For many of them, there is relatively little pressure or incentive to find work.[80]

His findings suggested that almost half of the supposed unem-ployed teens he surveyed 'reported having no work-seeking activity during the previous four weeks, including such things as asking friends or looking in the newspaper'. That teenage employment fell during this period in other countries, like Britain, which didn't even have a minimum wage (but where parents bore similar concerns about their children's work ethic), suggested Feldstein might have been on to something.

In the years after the 1981 Minimum Wage Commission report, Charles Brown, one of its authors and the lead author on the land-mark 1982 review based on it, continued to follow the published research. As he did so, he noticed a worrying trend. 'As researchers extended the sample period through the 1980s,' he wrote, 'even with statistical specification exactly the same, the estimated effects of the minimum wage on teen employment became smaller.' His reaction to this was 'one of puzzlement'.[81]

Years later, Alan Krueger argued that such trends were evidence that earlier data had been manipulated. He said that earlier studies had used the specification of models to give a result that showed the minimum wage had a statistically significant negative impact on employment (which, in any case, only means the impact was most likely not random – not that the impact was large). However, as the data set increased in size with the inclusion of more years, this book-cooking became harder to sustain, and the truth began to shine through.

Looking back in 1996, Brown concluded that, rather than looking at the possible effects of an increase in the minimum wage on employment, researchers would have been better off seeing whether employment levels had changed in those sectors where a minimum wage had been brought in for the first time – or, as he put it, 'The most promising place to look for long-run effects should be in coverage changes, with the expectation that they would be relatively large and easy to find.'[82] In 1950 only 53 per cent of all private non-farm non-supervisory wage and salary workers had been covered by the minimum wage. In 1977 that had risen to 84 per cent. It should have been fairly easy, therefore, to pinpoint correlations, if they existed. But they didn't. No one could find evidence of job losses in industries after they became subject to the minimum wage. As Brown said, 'the time-series data then bites the analyst with a vengeance – evidence that coverage matters is extremely weak.'[83]

If the lack of evidence for the supposedly baleful effect of the minimum wage should have given adherents of John Bates Clark's theory of marginal productivity pause for thought, so should another economic development of the 1970s. In the immediate post-war period, there had been a high degree of correlation between real, inflation-adjusted wage rates and productivity – just as Clark had stated, wages were being driven (or, at least, appeared to be driven) by productivity. But after 1973, median US wage rates stagnated, even as productivity rose in what became known as 'the Great Decoupling'. Yet the views of true believers remained unshaken.

It was partly frustration with the poor quality of research that was being published in the 1980s that motivated Card and Krueger to look deeper into the minimum wage. The two used to jokingly refer to the 1970s and 1980s literature on the subject as 'minimum fact' studies.[84] Card thought the preponderance of papers that supported the existence of a negative employment effect reflected institutional bias, with studies that challenged this orthodoxy being rejected by journals or simply left in the drawer. As time went on, more economists accepted that such a bias existed. One 2009 analysis of sixty-four studies found that when one corrected for publication selection, 'little or no evidence of a negative association between minimum wages and employment remains.'[85]

How the labour market really works

The inevitable answer to the question of why minimum wages can lift wages for millions of workers without killing jobs is that labour markets are far more complex and nuanced than the rigid supply-and-demand graph would suggest. For example, the basic supply-and-demand model assumes that companies cannot simply pass higher wages on to customers – after all, if customers were prepared to pay more for goods or services before a minimum wage, the profit-maximising firm would have already increased prices. However, some of the biggest low-wage employers in North America and Europe – outsourcing service providers like ISS A/S, ABM Industries Inc and Sodexo SA – say they routinely pass on any increased costs as a result of higher or new minimum wages to customers in the short to medium term so that profit margins are not impacted.[86] For businesses that find it hard to pass on higher costs in the form of higher prices, minimum wages do sometimes squeeze profit margins. Again, that's something economic theory doesn't envisage, since the assumption of competitive markets implies the return on capital employed is at any point the lowest level to convince investors to operate in the business, so that any further reduction in margins and returns would prompt people to exit the business.

The other prediction the neoclassical framework puts forward that has been found wanting is that the imposition of a minimum wage prompts capital – hard assets like equipment – to be substituted for labour. Economists view commercial output as a function of combining interchangeable inputs such as land, labour and machinery according to their relative prices. If one element becomes more expensive, less of it is used, and more of the other elements are consumed in the output-generating process. It therefore follows that higher labour costs eliminate jobs because they encourage businesses to invest in automation. Andy Puzder, a fast food executive tapped by Donald Trump in 2016 to be Labor Secretary, referred to the minimum wage as the 'Robot Employment Act'. David Neumark similarly believes that such legislation harms employment,[87] although his co-author on a paper that sought to show this, Grace Lordan, found that 'overall, the empirical analysis suggests that firms may re-assess their production processes following minimum wage increases, but so far endogenous substitution has been limited.'[88] The area where Neumark and Lordan found the strongest evidence that increased minimum wages did lead to a rise in automation (that is to say, the sector where the correlation between the two was strongest) was in automotive manufacturing. But, of course, the increase of automation in this sector in unlikely to be driven by the minimum wage, since car-making wages tend to be well above statutory minimums, and it is well known that increased automation in the industry is a consequence of advances in robotics being especially applicable in industrial production lines.[89] Generally, the uptake of labour-saving devices such as mechanised farm equipment, self-driving trucks or electronic handsets for waiting staff seems to be a function of technical improvements rather than wage costs, which makes sense when one thinks that the basic principle that people are more expensive than machines has held true for centuries, and created an incentive to invent and use new machines.

Ironically, some minimum-wage proponents wish Neumark was right. Low productivity growth in the service sector is sometimes blamed on cheap labour deterring investment in labour-saving equipment. In this sense, if a higher minimum wage encouraged the replacement of, say, checkout workers with automated tills, this might boost labour productivity and support long-term wage growth. But, as Lordan and Neumark found, there's no clear evidence for this.

In another example of reality trumping theory, some employers say that minimum wages spur them to look at efficiencies in working processes. Theory suggests they would have been forced to do this by market pressures even in the absence of a minimum wage.

There is also an area where employers see the minimum wage boosting productivity but which is ignored by the standard economic model of the labour market: staff turnover. Companies such as McDonalds say reduced turnover helps improve the customer experience they offer and reduces training costs. In an industry like fast food, where staff turnover rates can run to far in excess of 100 per cent annually,[90] and where the cost of replacing even waiting and kitchen staff can be high – an average of $2,000 in the United States in 2019[91] – this can have a material impact on a business and offset at least some of the cost of higher wages. (It's perhaps worth noting, too, that it's the high turnover in low-paid jobs that helps to explain why the minimum wage hasn't hit employment numbers in the way that many economists have predicted. The low-wage economy is also a very mobile one: the worker who loses a position in an inefficient company that cannot afford higher wages will probably, provided overall labour demand is not reduced, quickly find another one – unlike a skilled worker who, if thrown out of a job, will typically find it harder to obtain a suitable replacement.)

There is also a possible indirect benefit to firms from minimum wages that might blunt the impact of higher labour costs. Some companies in the UK reported during the 2000s that the minimum wage had put more money into low earners' pockets, giving them more to spend in shops and pubs – though, as the Low Pay Commission has shown, it's hard to make generalisations here as so much depends on the sector in which they are employed.

Taken together, all these various factors and considerations boost the minimum wage case. They also show that standard economic explanations of the labour market fall short when it comes to predicting behaviour and outcomes. Where, then, does that leave economic theory?

A new theory of employment

In recent years, as evidence for the disemployment effects of minimum wages continues to evade economists, even as their uptake internationally broadens and their average level as a percentage of median wages increases, economists have explored a tributary in the standard labour market theory that was previously dismissed as a dead end.

When Lord Dunraven and Winston Churchill proposed introducing a minimum wage, they argued that it was a justified interference with the laws of demand and supply because they believed competition was not functioning properly – in that it was not leading to the outcome that was the most efficient for all of society. They believed that Adam Smith's 'invisible hand' had gone temporarily limp, and the reason for this was that employers had excessive power in wage negotiation. Dunraven and Churchill didn't outline a detailed theoretical model of how all this worked, but what they described in their discussions on the topic could reflect a condition known to economists as Monopsony.

In a perfectly competitive labour market, neoclassical theory says that wages are a function of workers' productivity.[92] If wages are below the value the worker creates, another employer will lure the employee away with a higher wage. Wages are therefore inherently fair, and workers cannot be exploited. When monopsony prevails, companies have a sort of monopoly power. They have a stronger bargaining position than workers and, consequently, can get away with paying them less than the value they create for the business over and above the basic rate of return the company needs to achieve to justify staying in business. Economists have speculated that there are many possible reasons why an employer might have superior bargaining power. Employees might simply be ignorant of alternative, higher-paying opportunities elsewhere. Companies might be able to convince staff to accept below-market wage increases because they can afford to employ specialist wage negotiators, while staff have relatively less negotiating experience. Employees may face high costs of moving job – the employer's premises might be convenient for commuting or dropping children to school.

However, market dominance also creates a problem for the monopsonist, because if it wants to expand, it has to offer higher wages, unlike firms in competitive markets that only have to offer the going rate. The monopsonist thereby sees a rise in wages for its existing staff (the assumption is existing staff will have to be paid the same as new staff). Hence, the marginal cost of taking on new staff is high (shown in the steep curve in the graph).

The monopsonist firm, however, can pay employees at a level (Point A in the graph) below the marginal productivity of these employees (Point B). What this means is that the government could indeed mandate for a minimum wage above what the employer has been paying, and yet not destroy jobs. Indeed, it could conceivably increase employment, because its actions would persuade people previously unprepared to work because of the low wages on offer to enter the labour market now that it was worth their while. The

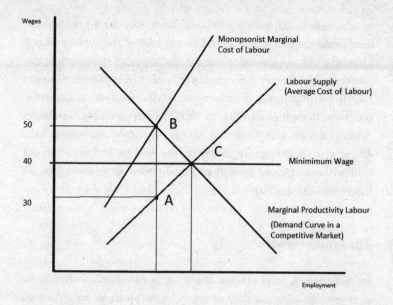

market-clearing point on the labour supply curve – the intersection point – would therefore move from A to C (see diagram).

George Stigler discussed this possibility in his 1946 rebuttal of Richard Lester. However, he dismissed it because he believed that labour markets were competitive. Over the next fifty years, few economists questioned this view. While there were many reasons why an employer might be able to influence wages and push them below the natural market-clearing rate, economists generally took the view that these forces would be balanced out by competitive forces elsewhere, and that the free market would prevail and employees' wages reflect their contribution to profitability.

It's not clear yet whether monopsony can be shoe-horned into a mathematical model able to predict the level of minimum wage that can be applied without hurting an economy. To that extent, academic work has so far not been especially helpful to governments trying to make decisions about minimum wages. Recent studies that have sought to estimate a 'safe' minimum wage have put the ideal level somewhere between 25 and 50 per cent of the average wage.[93] However, that conclusion is not the output of an improved labour market model. Rather, it is simply a reflection of what policy-makers have done (in defiance of economists' advice) without causing obvious harm to their economies. In 2018, statutory minimum wages in developed Asian and Western European economies averaged around 42 per cent of average wages, but several had pushed above 45 per cent without obvious growth or employment slowdowns (the US figure was 23 per cent).[94]

The value of models

In 2016, Alan Krueger talked about the need sometimes to rely on economic models that lacked empirical support in order to find answers or to make predictions. Looking back on his time as chair of Barack Obama's Council of Economic Advisers, he remarked:

> I was struck when I worked in the White House at the range of questions I would get from the President. And you'd want to do the best job answering them. That was your job. And there were some cases where there was very little evidence available and there was some modelling which, if you buy the assumptions of the modelling, could answer a lot of questions. And I think that was probably better than the alternative, which is having a department come in and plead its case based on no evidence or model whatsoever.[95]

It may be reasonable, when one has to make a quick decision and a model is all you have, to act as though that model is correct. But to continue to pretend you have a reliable model when the data doesn't confirm it is perverse.

As early as 1978, one of the high priests of neoclassical economics, the Nobel laureate Robert Solow, had questioned the received wisdom that wages were a function of a competitive market for labour. 'It is plain as the nose on my face that the labour market and many markets for produced goods do not clear in any meaningful sense,' he said then.[96] By the late 1980s, when the economic community had spent decades looking for evidence to support its hypothesis that minimum wages led to joblessness, convincing evidence that they were correct continued to elude them.

Some doubled down. Others followed Solow's lead and questioned the whole neoclassical model of labour supply-and-demand curves.[97] Card and Krueger, for example, did not espouse Richard Lester's view that institutions and societal structures were more likely determinants of wages than demand and supply. They still dedicated their 1995 book *Myth & Measurement: The New Economics of the Minimum Wage* to Lester, however, a sign of their stated desire to question the extent to which the simple supply-and-demand model described how employers and employees operate in the real world.[98] Nonetheless, economists have stuck with the theory of supply-and-demand curves and an equilibrium price where supply and demand clear, or match. Partly this is because, unlike Lester's 'institutionalist' view, the neoclassical view of labour markets allows one to build models that enable the making of precise predictions.[99] And if you can't make predictions, you risk becoming, as Buchanan put it, a 'camp-following whore' or, even worse, a profession that doesn't get consulted on policy decisions.

Was it self-interest that consciously or subconsciously led economists of a conservative and liberal persuasion to stick with the orthodox view of labour markets that dictated that the minimum wage should be economically harmful? That economists could retain fidelity to their models even when they so obviously failed to explain the world was a phenomenon Solow once joked about:

> I remember once reading that it is still not understood how the giraffe manages to pump an adequate blood supply all the way up to its head; but it is hard to imagine that anyone would conclude that giraffes do not have long necks. At least, not anyone who had ever been to a zoo.[100]

Economists like James Buchanan, Walter Oi and countless others who unquestioningly accepted the neoclassical framework were unable to see how a minimum wage could not cost jobs. So, they assumed it did. This approach means that if and when economists do come up with a revised predictive model, they may find policy-makers a bit more sceptical this time.

'You need some attempt to understand how things work and what's going on,' George Osborne told me in the course of an interview in 2019. 'Otherwise you'd be entirely on acting on anecdote. You need economic theory. I think you just need to be conscious of the limits.'[101]

6

THE RUSSELL GRAPH

Do 'sin taxes' work?

Mary shakes her head when she thinks how much her pack-a-day habit cost. 'It was such a waste of money,' she sighs. 'Most of it went to the government, of course.' She reckons that at one point she was spending £1,600 a year on cigarettes, 80 per cent of which was going to the government in tax. But then, in 2004, she finally kicked her dependence on nicotine. And after a year during which she regularly felt terrible, she began to feel physically healthier. She became better-off financially as well, of course. The benefits didn't stop there. Her employer, a large media company, was happy, since non-smokers don't take cigarette breaks and are likely to take less sick leave and time off for smoking breaks. And the government was pleased because Mary was now less likely to contract the smoking-related ailments that would make her a burden on the National Health Service. It was win-win for everyone.

Mary is not alone. In the neighbourhood of Richmond-upon-Thames in London where she lives, half as many people now smoke as did less than a decade ago.[1] That, in turn, is a small fraction of the figure sixty years ago. In 1958, over three-quarters of men smoked.[2]

Various reasons have been given for the massive reduction in smoking in the UK and elsewhere in recent decades: a greater awareness among the public at large of the risks of smoking, effective anti-smoking campaigns, the banning of cigarettes in restaurants, pubs, cinemas and other public spaces. But for economists – and for the policymakers who are guided by their advice – these are minor forces, and the drop is primarily down to basic economic principles: namely the power of price signals and the way in which high and ever-increasing taxes on tobacco products have dampened demand. The experts have even been able to put a number on the 'price elasticity' of cigarettes: after endless number-crunching, the broad conclusion is that, in a developed country like the UK, a 10 per cent increase in the price of cigarettes will lead to a 4 per cent drop in consumption in the short term, and even more in the longer term.[3] The actual numbers echo the economists' argument: between 1970 and 2010, per capita consumption of cigarettes dropped around 70 per cent in the UK[4] as prices rose 121 per cent in real, inflation-adjusted terms. No wonder, then, that price (or, rather, the level of tax imposed) has informed the campaigning efforts of anti-smoking groups and shaped the guidance offered to governments over the past two to three decades by international organisations such as the World Bank. For its part, the World Health Organisation sees tobacco tax increases as 'the single most effective way to decrease tobacco use'.[5]

The drop in the number of people who smoke has helped create the wider belief – pushed by economists[6] – that a whole range of desirable social outcomes, such as increased recycling, more efficient use of oil and gas and healthier eating, can be encouraged through the harnessing of economics. People can be 'nudged' to make better choices through particular financial signals. They can be incentivised or penalised in ways that avoid intrusive bans or paternalistic prescriptions, which may be politically unpopular. Hence the 'fat taxes' introduced in Hungary, India and Denmark, and the taxes on food or drinks high in sugar imposed by Mexico, many US cities and localities, France and a raft of other jurisdictions. Hence, too,

Sweden's tax reductions for repair services, which aim to encourage the re-use of bikes, appliances and other products.[7]

Taxes are not usually popular. But the mainstream media and, increasingly, voters have tended to back them when it comes to some 'sin taxes' and, in particular, tobacco duties. The former Conservative Chancellor of the Exchequer Ken Clarke has gone so far as to say that a hike in the tobacco levy is 'the only popular tax increase'.[8]

But it's not popular with everybody.

'I don't think it's fair,' says Ann, from Hull. She smokes a pack of Lambert & Butler every day and resents the politicians who seem hell-bent on convincing her to give them up. 'I call them the PC [politically correct] brigade,' she says, standing in the rain outside the North Point Shopping Centre in the Bransholme neighbourhood of the city. To her, cigarettes are a source of enjoyment and relaxation. She believes she should be allowed to make up her own mind about the health risks. And she will continue smoking come what may.

And herein lies the problem. Unlike Mary, Ann isn't responding as she should to the financial penalties that cigarettes involve; and she's not doing so even though she is precisely the sort of person who should. Mary is, and was when she quit smoking, in the top 10 per cent of earners in the UK. Ann is in the bottom income decile. Cigarettes accounted for less than 3 per cent of Mary's net income. Ann spends as much as 20 per cent of her earnings on smokes. That someone with relatively little financial incentive to quit would respond to an increase in price, while someone with a very high incentive to kick the habit does not, is not consistent with economic theory. What's more, Ann isn't an anomaly. Over half her neighbours in Bransholme smoke. In Hull overall – one of the nation's most deprived boroughs – 26 per cent of residents smoke, as against 6 per cent in affluent Richmond-upon-Thames.[9] Poor smokers also smoke more cigarettes per day than rich smokers.[10] Nor is this a uniquely British phenomenon. The trend towards non-smoking among the better-off has been apparent for several decades in many countries.[11] Looking across countries, we can also see patterns of smoking that are inconsistent with what theory suggests should happen. We often see that countries where cigarettes are expensive, in term of the minutes of work it takes to buy a packet, such as Bulgaria, Indonesia and Egypt, also have high per capita tobacco consumption. Meanwhile, other countries like the United States and Sweden have below-average consumption and cigarette costs (in minutes worked).[12]

Such inconsistencies highlight the uncertainty around ascribing a trend to a single causal factor when so much else is going on at the same time. How do we know whether 'sin' taxes on tobacco actually have any effect whatsoever, and that economists are not just claiming credit for other people's work and sacrifices? To understand, we need to look into the theory of the rational smoker, and at that word so beloved of economists: elasticity.

Sin taxes and elasticity

The history of governments raising taxes, or offering subsidies, in a way that favours selected groups – often the governing party's supporters – or puts the financial burden on others – such as politically weak constituencies – is a long and substantial one. The history of governments using taxation primarily to discourage particular social practices is rather less so.[13] An early instance arose in 1604 when, months after publishing a diatribe against what he called 'this stinking suffumigation',[14] England's King James I levied swingeing taxes on tobacco in an effort to stamp out the habit. A few decades later, Peter the Great of Russia placed a tax on beards in the hope that, by pressing his subjects to adopt the clean-shaven Western European fashion, they would also become more Westernised in outlook. These were rare pre-nineteenth-century examples of what would now be called 'sin taxes'.

In neither of these cases did the monarchs involved expect taxes alone to achieve their policy goals (which in any case were not achieved). But Alfred Marshall's formulation of the concept of price elasticity of demand in 1890 provided an intellectual framework for how price signals could be effectively harnessed by policymakers to do this.[15] Marshall recognised that total demand for products could be influenced by many factors other than price, including increases in population, changes in incomes, weather and advances in technology (which might create new markets and boost demand for a good or generate substitutes for it); but underlying these, Marshall believed, was a consistent price sensitivity on the part of individuals. Indeed, he saw this as a necessary requirement to allow a person to maximise the utility they could derive from their finite resources. He proposed that one could disentangle all the non-price factors from consumption trends (after all, population and income growth and even weather could be measured), so that one could isolate and measure the impact of price alone on purchase decisions.

The Price Elasticity of Demand reveals to us how much, *ceteris paribus*, all things being equal, a consumer will respond to a change in price. It is expressed as a number and, though it's negative, since price rises usually lead to drops in demand, it is typically written without the minus sign. An elasticity of 1, for example, means a 10 per cent rise in price leads to a 10 per cent drop in demand. Necessities such as life-saving medicine and basic foods are not generally very responsive to price changes, so they are believed to have low elasticities. Luxuries such as restaurant meals or designer clothes are believed to have elasticities above 1.

As I have already pointed out, although elasticity is a widely used concept, it has by no means gone unchallenged. Some people have questioned whether the concept itself, and demand-and-supply curves more generally, are relevant frameworks for understanding the labour market. When it comes to understanding how we make physical purchases, elasticity may also not capture the processes we go through and the decisions we ultimately make. Take a life-saving medicine. If one needed a prescribed dosage to live, one would continue to purchase only this amount even if the price dropped. And if the price rose, one would do the same: indeed, behaving in this way is axiomatic – if one did not, one would die. And if the price rose to a point at which one could no longer afford the drug, one's consumption would drop to zero. Since a half-dose would not sustain a person, one would be dead and buy nothing. In this scenario, there would be no price sensitivity – the elasticity would be zero – and then, at the specific price which is beyond the level the consumer can afford a full, life-saving dose, demand would be nothing: the elasticity would be infinite. In such a situation, describing a consumer as having a price elasticity of zero toward modest price rises and an elasticity of infinity at high prices may sound clever, but it's meaningless.

On the other hand, even if we do have gradated, stable preferences for a good, all other things being equal, the concept may still be useless if the preferences are routinely swamped by changes in factors that cannot be measured and adjusted for, such as mood and fashions or decision-making on the basis of non-rational factors like one's horoscope. So, while the economic 'law of gravity' – the basic supply-and-demand model – says everyone and every product has a price elasticity of demand, in the real world this is not a logical necessity.

Although the term itself wasn't used much at the time, the concept of elasticity became a matter of heated debate, after the Royal College of Physicians published a report in 1962, unequivocally identifying smoking as a causal factor of lung cancer and other ailments,[16] and after the US Surgeon General issued a report with a similar message two years later.[17] Among a raft of measures proposed by British health experts, including an outright ban on tobacco, was the idea of taxes to discourage consumption. This was politically very tricky. Britain already had high tobacco taxes. A meaningful increase in retail price could therefore only be achieved via a significant absolute increase in tax levels. And this raised the question of fairness. As one British MP put it, smoking was 'one of the essentials of life' for many people.[18] Unable to reduce their consumption, they would have no option but to pay the tax. This in turn might further harm their welfare by forcing them to sacrifice other goods or services which were actually beneficial to their well-being, such as healthy foods, healthcare and education.

At the same time, the British government had long relied on tobacco taxes for funds – in the nineteenth century they accounted for 13 per cent of total revenue.[19] Hence, ministers were also concerned that an increase in taxation might reduce demand to such an extent that overall tax receipts fell.[20] What to do depended on one's assumptions about price responsiveness. It was a classic test for the concept of price elasticity. But could economists establish that cigarette consumption followed a rational, predictable and measurable pattern?

Elasticity and the price of tobacco

It was a South African researcher working at the Maudsley Hospital in London, Michael Russell, who came up with one of the first studies of tobacco price elasticity after the 1960s health scares. These days Russell is regarded by many economists on both sides of the Atlantic as 'the father of tobacco control research'. In 1973 he published a comparative study of tobacco price and consumption in the *British Journal of Preventive & Social Medicine*, which included a striking graph that torpedoed any notion that tobacco consumption did not respond to price changes.[21] Rather, he showed a near-perfect inverse relationship between the two.

183

Russell's overall conclusion was that tobacco had a price elasticity of 0.6. That this was below 1 reflected the addictive nature of the product. It was, however, sufficiently large a figure to suggest that price had a material impact on demand – a 10 per cent rise, for example, would reduce demand by 6 per cent. From a government point of view, these percentages were encouraging. They suggested that a rise in tax would not reduce consumption so much that revenue shrank.

A year later, another study, by epidemiologist Julian Peto, showed an even closer correlation between price and demand, with a price elasticity of up to 0.64.[22]

Peto's study also concluded that the health warning issued by the Royal College of Physicians report in 1962 had had little impact – causing perhaps a 5 per cent fall in consumption – and that the 1964 ban on TV advertising of cigarettes had caused only a 3 per cent drop. 'It thus seems likely that systematic tax increases would have an immediate and progressive effect on consumption and recruitment, particularly among young people, who are less wealthy and less addicted,' the report said. 'Although health education has some impact, there seems to be no other way of reducing smoking on the scale demanded by the still mounting evidence of associated morbidity and mortality.'

Tobacco had long been cheap in America, partly because a powerful tobacco-growing lobby prevented the imposition of high federal taxes, so it was harder to spot national trends between prices and demand than it was in Britain. But by building complex models, economists there unpicked the relationship between demand and other factors, and came to much the same conclusion as British researchers. 'Based on 1954–80 data,' one study argued, 'evidence has been presented that the health scare has had little effect on cigarette demand . . . rising costs and taxes on output has had a greater effect on quantity than either the advertising ban or the health scare.'[23]

The federal structure of the United States also created an opportunity for measuring price responsiveness in a different way to Britain. Some US states imposed sales taxes on goods sold at checkouts, while others did not. Some states levied excise taxes on certain classes of goods, such as tobacco, while others, especially tobacco-growing states, did not. Hence, the price of a packet of cigarettes could vary considerably from state to state. By building a 'cross section' of America and matching smoking levels in areas with the price level in those areas, one could construct an estimate of responsiveness to price. In the 1980s a number of influential studies were produced using this method, perhaps most notably two by Gene Lewit, Douglas Coate and Michael Grossman[24] in 1981 and 1982, which found that adults had a price elasticity of 0.45 and – excitingly from a policy-making perspective – teenagers had a price elasticity of 1.44, which meant that for every 10 per cent increase in prices, teenagers cut their consumption by 14 per cent. Since tobacco is highly addictive, and since, therefore, the best way to stop its use is to discourage people from taking it up in the first place, that teenage responsiveness to high prices suggested a promising future policy route.

Elasticity and the policymakers

Lewit and his colleagues' papers did not initially garner a lot of attention, but in 1985 political circumstances dragged them into the limelight. Ronald Reagan's 1981 bumper income tax cuts had been followed by a budget blow-out that had forced the administration and Congress to pass the Tax Equity and Fiscal Responsibility Act of 1982. This had included a temporary doubling of the federal tax on cigarettes from 8 cents a pack to 16 cents. It had been intended as a revenue measure, but by 1985 taxation was garnering more attention as an anti-smoking policy measure, so in April that year, as the expiration date of the excise-tax increase neared, Harvard University's Institute for the Study of Smoking Behavior and Policy hosted a conference that brought together economists and health experts to discuss the issue. The institute issued a report, with Lewit's research at its heart, which was soon after circulated to every member of Congress. The report's stark message was that if the federal excise tax were allowed to fall from 16 cents a pack back to the 8 cents level that had prevailed before 1983, up to 1 million young people would start smoking.[25] After debating the tax, Congress decided to keep it at the higher level, and went on to raise it again in 1992 and 1993.

In Britain, policymakers had also begun to accept that tobacco consumption followed economic principles. By 1984, the Treasury had calculated that the price elasticity for tobacco products was 0.5,[26] and that same year Chancellor of the Exchequer Nigel Lawson levied a big increase in tobacco duty, 'having regard to the representations I have received on health grounds'.[27] Further piecemeal duty increases followed during the 1980s. In the early 1990s there was a step change in policy. In his 1991 budget, Chancellor Norman Lamont increased tobacco excise duty by 15 per cent, leading to an almost 10 per cent increase in the price of a pack of cigarettes. His successor, Ken Clarke, codified the policy of above-inflationary rises, saying that it was 'necessary masochism' which would 'hammer home the message that smoking can seriously damage your health'.[28]

This vigorous position on tobacco taxes stood in contrast to what was otherwise a fairly non-interventionist approach to smoking.[29] Unlike many other developed countries that had imposed statutory bans or curbs on advertising, the UK relied on a voluntary code that set restrictions on the targeting of young smokers and the use of machismo, sexuality or success in advertisements to promote cigarettes.[30] The code was regularly broken by tobacco companies, and it was only when forced by the European Community that the government enacted statutory measures,[31] finally banning television advertising of cigars and pipe tobacco in 1991. Britain also resisted international moves to implement smoking bans on international flights in the early 1990s[32] and the introduction of statutory and stark health warnings on cigarette packs in 1993.[33]

Surprisingly, perhaps, the health lobby proved relatively late devotees to the cause. Some health experts had indeed suggested that taxes should be raised to deter smoking as early as the 1960s, but they'd usually simply tacked this suggestion on at the end of a list of other proposals.[34] The public health community, acutely aware of the addictive nature of smoking, was sceptical that price could be a powerful tool for combatting smoking.[35] When, for example, Gene Lewit and his collaborators applied to a children's health charity for funding for the work that would lead to their ground-breaking 1982 paper on teen smoking, they were turned down, because the charity's psychologists wouldn't believe that child smokers were influenced by price.[36] Public information and education campaigns were the preferred tobacco control strategies.[37] For many years the World Health Organisation's strategy for tackling tobacco excluded a tax element. It was medical and psychological: 'If you have the will power, you'll quit.' 'They thought people don't respond to taxes; that prices matter for other stuff, but smoking was a personal behaviour,' said Prabhat Jha, an epidemiologist who joined the World Bank in 1995.[38]

As experts like Jha reviewed the growing body of economic literature on tobacco price responsiveness, this resistance, however, was gradually overcome. The wide (although not entirely unanimous) consensus among economists who studied the issue helped convey a scientific authority to the studies on elasticity that appealed to medical scientists. Study after study showed that, faced with a price rise, people either cut back on consumption or quit altogether. The price elasticity figures such studies came up with were scattered around the 0.4 level. Economists also honed their framework for understanding the mindset of the smoker. In 1988, the economists Gary Becker and Kevin M. Murphy published their theory of 'Rational Addiction', which stated that the age-old understanding of smoking as an irrational weakness was nonsense. People recognised the addictive nature of smoking, Becker and Murphy argued. The reason they took up smoking cigarettes was because they calculated that the utility they gained from smoking exceeded the long-term costs.[39] If a rational calculation was being made, it followed that increasing the price of tobacco would change that calculation, and that expectations of future price rises would also dampen start rates and demand. 'Rational addiction' would become a common buzzphrase in cigarette consumption models.[40]

Gradually, economists' advice – and jargon – became the stock-in-trade of health officials.[41] The two camps came together when in 1997 the World Bank – where Prabhat Jha had championed the idea of price elasticity and the World Health Organisation teamed up to conduct a global study on the economics of tobacco control and, with the help of a team of over forty economists, epidemiologists and tobacco control experts, to design a framework of policies that countries could follow to reduce smoking.[42] Seventeen thousand copies of their 1999 report entitled 'Curbing the Epidemic – Governments and the Economics of Tobacco Control' were distributed in over twenty languages. The report unequivocally identified taxation as the most effective way to reduce smoking.

If further support were needed for the policy idea, it came from the unlikeliest of sources: the tobacco industry itself. In 1998, as part of a deal between cigarette makers and the Attorneys-General of dozens of US states who had sued the companies for damages to cover the costs of caring for sick smokers, tobacco companies agreed to release millions of secret internal documents. These revealed that the industry had known for years that smoking carried health risks, and that they had suppressed the knowledge. The papers also showed that tobacco companies themselves feared the impact of tax rises.

One memo in particular, written by a Philip Morris employee in 1975, stood out. 'Of all the concerns, there is one – taxation – that alarms us the most,' it read.

> While marketing restrictions and public and passive smoking do depress volume, in our experience taxation depresses it much more severely. Our concern for taxation is, therefore, central to our thinking about smoking, and health. It has historically been the area to which we have devoted most resources and for the foreseeable future, I think things will stay that way almost everywhere.[43]

Today the consensus is that that in developed countries tobacco price elasticity is around 0.4 in the short term and up to 1 in the long term. It is further believed that, in developing countries, short-term elasticity is higher – possibly up to 0.8. This 0.4 to 1.0 range represents a policy-making sweet spot: high enough for tax rises to be effective in reducing demand, but not so high that higher prices hit demand to the point where tax revenues drop. Much lower than that – say 0.1 – and the differential would be so slight that it would be hard to know for sure whether it really was a tax increase that was affecting demand or some other factor such as anti-smoking advertisements. Much higher than that, and a tax increase would result in a significantly lower tax yield.

The economic case seems pretty solid.

Elasticity stretched to breaking point

But things are rarely that clear-cut or straightforward. Consider again Russell's famous 1973 graph mapping male consumption of cigarettes and real prices:

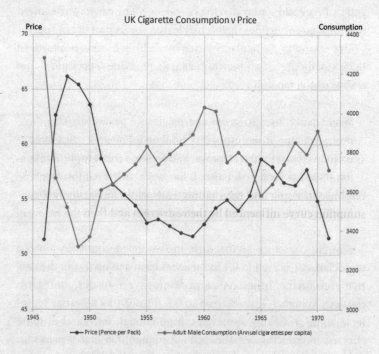

UK Cigarette Consumption v Price

Data source: M. A. Russell

It's a very elegant model of price elasticity that perfectly demonstrates how, when prices soar, demand plummets. It is, in other words, visual proof of what economic theory predicts. But a closer examination reveals some problems. Take, for instance, the most dramatic inverse moves in the inflation-adjusted price and consumption in the immediate post-war years. On the surface, they seem to encapsulate a textbook case of market elasticity. But they also happen to cover a period that was very far from normal.

After the war, Britain faced a currency crisis and, in particular, a shortage of US dollars, which prompted the government to limit the importation of all non-essential goods from the United States, including tobacco. It's true that in an attempt to reduce consumption by 25 per cent,[44] swingeing taxes were introduced that raised the price of cigarettes in 1947 by 23 per cent (had the term elasticity been in vogue then, that would have meant an elasticity of 1), but the real reason why consumption went down was, quite simply, that tobacco was astonishingly hard to come by.[45] Queues formed at tobacconists. A black market in cigarettes flourished.[46] The *New York Times* told Americans of the 'dire shortage' of smokes in England.[47] By 1950, the situation was starting to improve, and tobacco consumption rose as a result. What looks on paper very much like a simple demand response to rising and then falling real prices was actually a consumption curve influenced by the restriction and then the easing of physical supply.

Similarly, the increase in consumption during the 1950s, as real prices fell, doesn't tell the full story of the era. It's perfectly plausible that tobacco consumption rose *partly* in response to increased affordability in the years before the Royal College of Surgeons issued its warning about the health risks of smoking. But to suggest that it rose *wholly* in response to price is to ignore the explosion in television advertising that came with the launch of commercial TV in the 1950s and the five-fold rise (in real terms) in tobacco advertising between 1954 and 1960 that accompanied it.[48] (Those sceptical of the power of advertising might dispute this; American Tobacco President George Hill and his adman Albert Lasker – see Chapter 4 – would doubtless beg to disagree). By focusing on manufactured cigarettes, Russell's elasticity calculation also ignored a major consumer shift during the 1950s and 1960s away from hand-rolled cigarettes and pipes. By the late 1960s, cigarette purchases were up, but tobacco consumption overall was down. Fashions were changing.[49]

Such oversights generated a flawed elasticity estimate, but even they could not conceal the basic truth that both the real price of cigarettes and per capita male consumption at the end of the period

Russell examined were both lower than in 1960 and 1961 when (depending on whose data one uses) UK per capita male cigarette consumption peaked. Total consumption did continue to rise into the 1970s, against a backdrop of falling real prices, but that was due to the social trend of women smoking more. Once that trend ran its course, the data begins to behave in a way that is at odds with economic theory.

True, since 1980, cigarette prices have generally tended to rise and smoking to drop, but what's problematic for the claim that the former has driven the latter is that the period when the UK strongly committed to real price increases – the 1990s – was not a period when smokers either quit[50] or cut consumption at a greater rate than when price rises were less extreme. For example, the price of a 20-pack of cigarettes prices rose 77 per cent in real terms between 1990 and 2000[51] and consumption fell 23 per cent. Prices rose just 14 per cent in the 2000s, but consumption fell almost 40 per cent.[52]

The United States showed a similar pattern. As states loaded up tobacco taxes in the 1990s, real tobacco prices rose 57 per cent, compared to rises of 35 per cent in the 1980s and 45 per cent in the 2000s.[53] However, consumption fell only 25 per cent between 1990 and 2000, the same rate as in the 1980s but far short of the 35 per cent drop in the 2000s.[54]

Other countries also defied the basic economic logic. Finland, for example, experienced sharp drops in consumption in periods when cigarette prices were stable or rose slowly. Sweden and Portugal witnessed periods when prices rose, and consumption did too.[55]

If we take a broader chronological view, the notion of a proportional inverse relationship between price and demand is even harder to sustain. The real price of cigarettes in Britain was lower in 1990 than in 1965,[56] but per capita consumption was 20 per cent lower.[57] In the Britain of 1948, a cigarette cost tuppence (2d)– the same price as a cup of tea purchased in a café.[58] In the Britain of 2020, a cigarette costs, on average, 54 pence,[59] but the price of a cup of tea in most

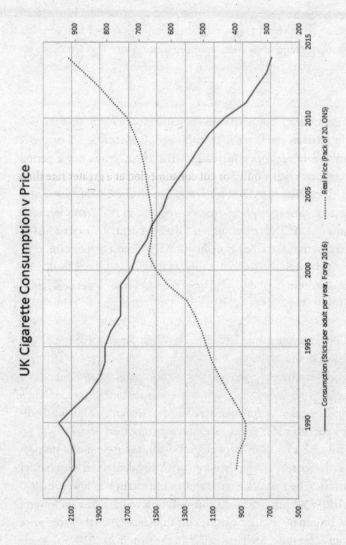

UK Cigarette Consumption v Price

—— Consumption (Sticks per adult per year. Forey 2016) ······· Real Price (Pack of 20, ONS)

Data source: Office for National Statistics and Barbara Forey et al.

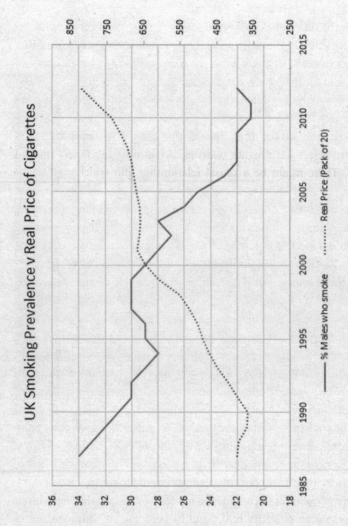

UK Smoking Prevalence v Real Price of Cigarettes

— % Males who smoke .... Real Price (Pack of 20)

Data source: Office for National Statistics

cafés today is at least three times that amount. Over that period the percentage of men who smoke has dropped over 75 per cent.[60]

How could the results of so many econometric studies be at odds with the time-series data – the actual experience of the past several decades? It's not altogether accidental. It's precisely because the time-series data didn't point to a – *ceteris paribus* – price elasticity of demand much above zero that so many economists in the 1980s and 1990s sought out alternative methods to calculate tobacco price elasticity.

Take the studies that showed that people in those US states where prices were higher (usually owing to higher taxes) smoked less. There might be a causal relationship, but which way was it working? Perhaps places where smoking was already less common were simply more likely to adopt such stringent anti-smoking measures as cigarette taxes because they knew that fewer people would express objections? For example, it's certainly the case both that taxes on cigarettes in California are high and that relatively few people there smoke, but it's also the case that the comparatively low incidence of smoking in California predates the draconian tax hikes.[61] Then there's the basic problem of arriving at accurate figures for the number of smokers in individual states. Researchers have usually relied upon government data of tax-paid tobacco sales to establish smoking levels. But that ignores what are often very high levels of tobacco smuggling. The New York State Department of Health estimated that in 2004, for example, 57 per cent of smokers in the state had purchased cigarettes on which taxes were not paid, with 37 per cent doing so regularly.[62] By underestimating New York smoker consumption, a researcher would end up deriving a higher elasticity than true consumption rates would indicate.

Highly complex econometric models of the sort that have often suggested an elasticity of 0.4 and higher pose an additional set of problems.[63] They may claim to be able to strip out all the different factors that might influence cigarette consumption to identify the underlying price responsiveness, and they might be able to do so with numerical factors like price, inflation or average income growth, but how do they measure the impact of, say, an advertising ban? One approach they have come up with is to accept the tobacco industry argument that tobacco advertising doesn't influence over-all demand, but rather only the loyalty of existing customers to particular brands, in order to argue that measures such as the TV ad ban simply increase the costs for companies, who are then forced to use alternative, less effective and therefore more expensive means of advertising to achieve their goal. In other words, rather than influence demand, advertising restrictions push the supply curve upwards by an amount linked to the size of the advertising budget.[64] It's an attractively measurable proposition. The problem with it is that it doesn't make a huge amount of sense.

It's similarly difficult to put a number on the health concerns that have been expressed about smoking. Many economists interpreted the 1960s US and UK reports that for the first time definitively linked smoking to lung cancer and a range of other illnesses as being impacts that could be accurately measured by examining the short-term price response immediately after their release. Julian Peto, for example, ascribed a one-off 5 per cent point drop in demand to the Royal College of Physicians report. This way of thinking about a health warning makes sense if one considers it to be a stark and immediate alert: 'Smoking one cigarette will kill you. Don't do it!' Presented with such an unambiguous message it's reasonable to assume that people will either respond straightaway by dropping the habit or, if they perhaps think the warning is bogus, ignoring it (in which case its repetition won't have any effect on them).

But the people who didn't quit smoking immediately didn't think the Royal College of Physicians and the Surgeon General reports were bogus. They simply thought the warnings were not urgent. And who could blame them? The 1962 Royal College of Physicians report stated that 'most smokers suffer no serious impairment of health or shortening of life as the result of their habit' – not exactly alarmist and not exactly definitive in the context of counter-attacks from the smoking lobby. It would take many years for the stark risks of smoking to become clearer in the public consciousness.

The early UK government response to the report was also restrained[65] and distinctly low-budget.[66] It was not until 1971 that the UK government convinced the cigarette makers (it relied on persuasion, having decided legislation was too heavy-handed) to put a – distinctly muted – health notice on each pack:

Warning by HM Government
Smoking can damage your health

In public statements, the avid smoker and health and finance minister Kenneth Clarke continued to use the 'can' qualification into the mid-1990s. Not surprisingly, most people remained unaware of the full health implications of smoking into the twenty-first century. I remember receiving treatment for a stomach ulcer in 1993 and being very surprised to be repeatedly asked if I smoked. I had no idea the two things could be connected.

Calibrating an econometric model in which health concerns constitute a one-time factor overlooks decades of drip-drip health reports and media coverage of the damage caused by smoking, government warnings and increasingly graphic anti-smoking advertising. Similarly, adjusting a model for the effect of workplace bans in accordance with the immediate short-term response to a statutory workplace ban is an obviously flawed approach. Actual workplace bans happened over time and were, for most people, largely the result of non-statutory, company-by-company or industry-by-industry practices. Economists interpret the effects of such measures as being in the short term. They ignore the fact that they gradually cut demand in the years after they have been announced.

The basic reality is that the elasticity estimates generated by many economic models are a function of assumptions and measurements many people would not consider reasonable. That includes economists. As early as 1981, economists in the tobacco elasticity field were accusing one another of tweaking their specifications to make the data fit their desired conclusions, a practice known as 'over-fitting'.[67]

What about the tobacco industry's anguish about taxation? The famous 1975 Philip Morris memo prioritising taxation concerns over other anti-smoking measures was written at a time when the only serious anti-smoking measure that had been taken was a TV advertisement ban. Workplace bans and smoke-free restaurants were over a decade away. As for what has happened since, the industry's behaviour doesn't suggest a concern that a proportional inverse relationship exists between price and market demand. Cigarette-makers have enjoyed remarkably rude health over the past twenty years, with revenues and profits rising at a healthy clip, helping to make industry shares one of the best-performing sectors over the period. This is partly due to rising demand in developing countries (though in recent years this hasn't kept in step with population increases). And it's partly due to the fact that, even in mature markets, profits have risen. The UK and United States may have heaped inflation-busting tax increases on cigarettes, but manufacturers have managed to increase their own prices faster than inflation.[68] If tobacco companies today believed that a 10 per cent increase in prices leads to a 4 per cent decrease in demand, their annual real price increases of 1 percent would represent a conscious decision to give up 0.4 per cent of their market every year. They themselves would be bringing the sunset a little closer each year, particularly if they accepted the argument that young people – tomorrow's new smokers – are most price-sensitive. There's no evidence, however, that that's what's governing their decision-making.

Sin taxes vs non-price signals

In the short term, especially, economists would concede that many factors have affected cigarette demand. Blips in consumption have been observed around smoking bans, big price increases and the introduction and withdrawal of tobacco alternatives like e-cigarettes. But if you believe that the concept of elasticity correctly captures the cigarette purchase decision and that the magnitude of this effect is 0.4, then you will argue that price increases drove the vast majority of the drop in smoking over the past forty years. If you believe that the long-term elasticity is more like 1 – the level a recent review of literature on UK price elasticity says you arrive at if you employ the four main types of econometric models used in calculating elasticity[69] – then the decline is pretty much all down to the real price rises since 1980.

That's at odds with surveys of those who have actually quit, who consistently place health concerns at the top of their list of reasons. A desire to be healthier was certainly Mary's primary motivation for giving up. After all, smoking wasn't much of a financial strain for her. Economists are suspicious of such surveys. They argue that people often don't accurately report what drives them to behave in the way they do, and that they may not even understand why they have behaved as they have done. There is doubtless some truth to this. Yet, Mary and Ann's reported experiences do seem to hold a clue to the declining popularity of smoking, whether or not one accepts the validity of the surveys of which they formed a part.

On the face of it, the rising cost of tobacco should have encouraged Ann to quit before Mary, because for her cigarettes represent a higher proportion of her weekly budget than they did for Mary. Economists like Prabhat Jha have an explanation for this. They say the relatively weak price responsiveness of less affluent people is due to another economic force that acts in the opposite direction to the price signal: namely, an 'information effect'. Because Ann in relatively deprived Hull is poorer than Mary in relatively wealthy Richmond, the theory goes, she cannot 'afford' to consume as much information as Mary, and so is less aware of the health risks of smoking, and hence is less likely to quit. Ann and Mary are both rational, price-sensitive consumers but they face different resource endowments, all of which directly influence their responses.

That's fine as far as it goes. But it doesn't represent how Ann feels or behaves. She may not be able to afford to read two broadsheet newspapers a day as Mary does, but she watches a lot of TV, where health stories are a staple. Moreover, she sees pictorial health warnings every time she picks up a cigarette packet. Mary stopped smoking four years before these were introduced. Ann also lives in an area with a high incidence of smoking-related illnesses, so she sees the consequences of smoking around her with far greater frequency than Mary. Given all those signals, she should actually be more aware of the risks of smoking than Mary.

Even so, while it's hard to make the case for this particular information effect, and harder still to suggest it explains why people in Bransholme are nine times as likely to smoke as in Richmond, there is a lot to commend the broader argument that the quitting behaviour of different income groups may be linked to differences in their exposure to anti-smoking signals. The fact is that if we look beyond basic health information and price signals, we can see that high earners like Mary have received more prodding than lower-income groups.

When workplace smoking bans were first initiated, they tended to be in white-collar work environments. When Britain first restricted smoking in social environments it went for restaurants (where the affluent are more likely to congregate) rather than pubs. The smoking bans that came into force in the 1990s – on flights, trains and in theatres – similarly affected average and above-average earners the most. Smoking was therefore first 'denormalised', in the sense of

200

being impractical or socially unacceptable, among those on median and higher incomes. And once it became denormalised its decline became self-perpetuating. Affluent people found themselves mixing socially in non-smoking environments. Affluent smokers felt pressure to become ex-smokers. Perhaps, too, the banning of cigarette advertising that had once linked smoking with an aspirational lifestyle had an effect.

Some studies (usually by medical rather than economic experts) have put large numbers on the impact of non-price interventions. And some economic studies have also estimated very low price elasticities for tobacco, quite at odds with the dominant wisdom. But it's questionable how reliable any numerical estimate placed on a single factor can be when many other factors are at play, and when so many of those factors act in a cumulative, long-term fashion. Paradoxically, that perhaps helps to explain why the rational-economic-actor argument has proved so hard to dislodge. If we can't definitively map human decision-making, who is to say that the rational economic actor doesn't exist, even if survey results and the time-series data on consumption trends don't support the idea? Indeed, that's one of the problems with the Rational Addiction Theory. Scientific theories are supposed to be disprovable – it's the key difference between science and faith.[70]

Yet however woolly the detailed workings of non-price interventions may seem to be, the case for them remains a powerful one, not just because they accord so well with the way in which smoking has declined, but because they also help explain patterns of economic behaviour in other spheres of consumption. Beef is a case in point. In the post-war period, as Americans grew richer they gradually consumed more and more of it. But in 1977 the US Senate Select Committee on Nutrition and Human Needs[71] published a report that raised concerns that beef consumption, or at least consumption at the levels then prevailing, could be bad for one's health. Per capita consumption began what has become a steady decline.

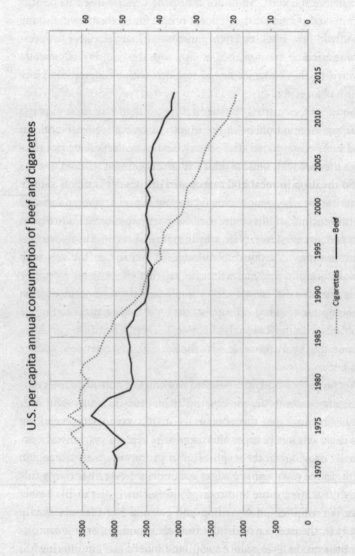

U.S. per capita annual consumption of beef and cigarettes

.... Cigarettes   —— Beef

Data source: Our World in Data

Even though lower production costs caused beef prices to come down,[72] in the thirty years to 2006 consumption declined 28 per cent.[73] It has fallen further since. This compares to around a 60 per cent drop in average cigarette consumption per US adult over the same period.

Sugary soft drinks display a similar pattern. Between 1998 and 2015 – before some cities introduced sugar taxes – per capita US consumption of soft drinks fell over 20 per cent,[74] even though prices during the period did not keep up with inflation.[75] As with beef, the health risks associated with sugary drinks are far less pronounced than they are with tobacco-based products.

So the drop in meat and carbonated drink sales is highly significant. It shows that people can and do respond very strongly to health warnings, and that they can do so without price signals. It also shows that the process doesn't necessarily happen quickly. The fall in beef consumption, for example, has been occurring over the course of four decades, during which time health warnings have been periodically repeated and reinforced. If one applied the concept of price elasticity of demand to beef and cola, one could logically conclude that their elasticity was positive, as consumption fell even as prices fell. That would make economic sense. It just happens to make no other kind of sense.

Some, including the UK government, have claimed that sugar taxes are effective because, whether or not they actually discourage sugar consumption, they encourage drinks manufacturers to use less sugar or employ sugar alternatives.[76] These claims, however, are usually over-stated, the small print of press releases that highlight big headline reductions in sugar use in drinks usually showing that the shift is largely due to increased sales of low-sugar drinks rather than the reduction of sugar in existing drinks like Classic Coke. In any case, the practice of drinks and other food makers reformulating their products to reduce sugar (and indeed salt), or offering less sugary products, long predates sugar taxes. The fact that lower sugar beverages should have experienced stronger sales growth than sugary beverages in the years before (and since) the UK and some US localities introduced sugar taxes, suggests that a desire to cater to shifting consumer tastes was a larger driver for cutting sugar content or introducing sugar-free variants than a wish to avoid sugar taxes. Indeed, industry executives usually cite demand as driving such moves.[77] The difficulty in identifying the extent to which taxes might have spurred reformulation efforts is heightened by the fact that companies may also have been influenced by a desire to avoid other government actions, such as marketing restrictions. Whatever the impact of sugar taxes on corporate behaviour, it doesn't say anything about consumers' responsiveness to price rises.

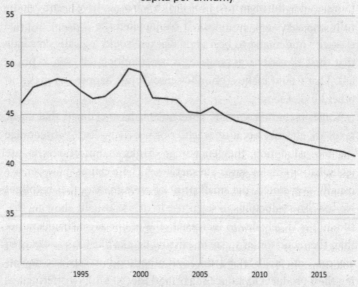

U.S. Carbonated soft drinks Consumption (Gallons per capita per annum)

Data source: IBISWorld

Of course, one could try to argue that even if the rational addiction model isn't entirely accurate and the price elasticity of tobacco is in fact less than 0.4, it was a still good idea to increase prices to dampen smoking demand. After all, it had some effect, if not the full impact that theory dictated. There are, however, two problems with this. First, one can't accept a theory in part unless one is prepared to show how and why the economists who have propounded it for the past fifty years got the rest of it wrong. Secondly, one cannot claim possible benefits unless one is also prepared to explore the possible disadvantages and unintended consequences of having bet so heavily on a policy that appears not to have worked as it should have done. Between 1990 and 2000, the cost of a pack-a-day habit in the UK rose from the equivalent of 11 per cent of the disposable income of those in the lowest earnings quintile to 23 per cent.[78] How was this funded? If beer and fatty foods were sacrificed, perhaps people's health (if not utility) improved. But what if the diversion of income to tobacco led to a shift from healthy to cheaper, less healthy foods or it stopped people from taking family holidays? If people continued to smoke as before, ate less healthily and had less quality time with family, their welfare has clearly not improved. People often argue that such tax burdens are justified due to the added cost of smokers to the NHS. The truth is that the £11 billion a year raised in tobacco taxes[79] covers the £2–3 billion a year additional costs smokers place on the NHS several times over (even before one considers the reduced pension and later life-care cost savings related to smokers' lower life expectancy).[80] Either way, this doesn't impact the economic arguments as to whether tobacco taxation helps improve the health of the smoker.

But the more serious unintended consequence of focusing on tobacco tax is that it can lead us to overlook or underestimate other solutions. In 1988, the UK government's Independent Scientific Committee on Smoking & Health[81] and the British Medical Association[82] called for smoke-free workplaces. Ministers took no action. They prioritised sin taxes. During the 2000s, when Chancellor of the Exchequer Gordon Brown abandoned the automatic price escalator,[83] the government finally focused on restrictions on the distribution and use of cigarettes: imposing work-place smoking bans, prohibiting[84] billboard and print advertising of cigarettes,[85] launching intensified anti-smoking media campaigns and funding NHS initiatives to help people give up cigarettes.[86] Smoking levels now dropped faster than ever before.

Health economists today continue to insist that the best way to help the poorest to quit smoking is to slam taxes on tobacco products.[87] They also argue that because such taxes work they are not regressive. Yet, as the British government imposes above-inflation tax rises on cigarettes, while simultaneously slashing funding of anti-smoking initiatives,[88] smoking remains stubbornly high in many parts of Britain, and is actually increasing in Hull. Usage rates in the city hit 26.1 per cent in 2018, up from a low of 23.1 per cent in 2017.[89] This was despite a 3.8 per cent real rise in cigarette prices over that period.[90]

The American psychologist Abraham Maslow once used the analogy of a hammer to describe the cognitive bias which causes people to see the world through a narrow prism based on their abilities or the resources at their disposal. This bias leads them to create rational justifications for options they are naturally inclined to favour but which may not be the best course of action. 'I suppose it is tempting,' he wrote, 'if the only tool you have is a hammer, to treat everything as if it were a nail.'[91]

Economists view the world as an interconnected set of transactions, to a large part driven by a small number of identifiable factors that can be measured in financial terms. Since the transactions hinge on setting prices, it follows that prices are of prime importance. If you change the price, you change the outcome of the equation. Price is the economists' hammer. But when it comes to tobacco, it's arguable that reliance on this tool delayed the measures that had the greatest impact and put off the search for new, effective measures, leaving large sections of society exposed to the ravages of smoking.

Sin taxes and global warming

This choice between economic and social or political solutions is one policymakers face in an increasing range of areas, as countries seek to tackle problems from obesity to urban congestion. But there is one area that has proved a particular battleground for competing ideologies and theories, and that is climate change.

In January 2009, Barack Obama nominated a new Administrator of the White House Office of Information and Regulatory Affairs. In economic and legal terms, it was a rock-star appointment. The new boss of OIRA, as it's catchily known among the narrow body of policy wonks who follow its workings, was to be Cass Sunstein, one of the pioneers of behavioural economics. Sunstein's 2008 book *Nudge: Improving Decisions about Health, Wealth, and Happiness*, co-authored with the Nobel prize-winning economist Richard Thaler, had been a bestseller, and become almost obligatory reading among policymakers the world over. It even prompted David Cameron to establish the Behavioural Insights Team, better known as the 'nudge unit', at the Cabinet Office in 2010.

A great deal, not always accurate, has appeared in the media about behavioural economics. As a 2014 article in the *Financial Times* noted, behavioural economics has become 'a catch-all term to refer to almost anything that's cool in popular social science'. As if to illustrate the point, the piece appeared under a photograph of a sign in Tonbridge, Kent, which said, 'Take your litter home, other people do.' That's an example of what one psychologist who studies sign design describes as 'emotionally intelligent signage'.[92] In other words, it's psychology, not behavioural or any other kind of economics. As the *FT* noted, behavioural economics is actually based on the traditional 'neoclassical' model of human behaviour. The task of the behavioural economist is to incorporate non-rational but still measurable behavioural tendencies, such as human beings' natural risk aversion (whereby they demand a better than even chance of gain before entering a new transaction), into the neoclassical model, so that better predictions can be made. The key is that behavioural economists, like mainstream economists, believe in the predominant power of price signals, and argue that market solutions are almost always the best ones.[93] Sunstein was excited about taking the job because he knew that Obama subscribed to this perspective. As he said at the time, the president believed in 'doing law in a way that's realistically based on human behaviour . . . he's very attuned to the virtue of free markets.'[94]

From the start of his presidential campaign, Obama had said that he wanted to tackle climate change. And to help tackle climate change, he had said he wanted to make US cars more environmentally friendly by doubling their fuel efficiency over the next eighteen years (despite technological advances, the American penchant for big cars meant that they were no more fuel-efficient in 2008 than in the mid-1980s).[95] Theoretically, that ambition could be met in one of two ways. Obama could tax fuel to discourage consumption. Or he could tighten the Corporate Average Fuel Economy rules (better known as the CAFE standards), which required manufacturers to build vehicles with a specified minimum fuel efficiency.

Sunstein was a long-standing critic of fuel economy standards.[96] Indeed, he was so opposed that he believed in two mutually exclusive reasons for rejecting them. In a 1990 paper, he claimed previous requirements that carmakers increase the mpg of the vehicles they manufactured had 'produced no substantial independent gains in fuel economy'. True, he said, fuel efficiency had improved after Jimmy Carter imposed the CAFE standards amid the 1970s oil crises, but that was because consumers had demanded more fuel-efficient vehicles in response to high oil prices, and not because government regulations to improve efficiency had had an impact.[97] At the same time, Sunstein argued, the regulations 'have led manufacturers to produce smaller, more dangerous cars' that would lead to thousands of additional fatalities.[98] So, on the one hand, car manufacturers were making their cars more fuel-efficient in response to consumer demand in the wake of fuel price rises; and, on the other, they were doing it because the government had told them to do so. Such contradictory reasoning betrayed, if nothing else, economists' traditional disdain for using a regulatory intervention when a pricing solution was available.[99]

Economic theory was clear on this point. Government interference doesn't work because it distorts markets, encouraging wasteful investments, unnecessarily expensive products and lower overall output. It's bureaucratic, costly and time-consuming too: you can't set fuel-efficiency rules unless you're also prepared to employ officials to determine targets and check that they're met. In addition, there's the risk that you might be swayed by special interest groups. A higher levy on fuel, by contrast, simply nudges people to want to buy cars that yield more miles per gallon, and that in turn nudges the carmakers to produce more fuel-efficient vehicles.[100]

Conveniently, by 2009 economists had just witnessed a decade-long natural case study of how motorists responded to fuel prices, so evidence on the matter was there to see. The only problem was that the theory and the experience hadn't actually matched.

In 2000, the average fuel economy of new vehicles in the United States was 19.8 miles per US gallon.[101] In 2009, this had risen to 22.4 mpg – a 13 per cent increase in fuel efficiency. What had driven this improvement? CAFE rules might have helped. The requirements for cars had not changed, but the light trucks standards had tightened 11 per cent. But the likelier candidate seemed to be price. A rapid increase in Chinese oil demand from 1999 had contributed to a massive increase in crude prices, interrupted only briefly by the financial crash. Between 2000 and 2008, pump prices almost doubled in real terms in the United States, before falling back to $2.35 per gallon in 2009, still 27 per cent higher than they had been in 2000, even after adjusting for inflation.[102]

And there's the rub. Even if the potential impacts of other factors are ignored and all the increase in new vehicle fuel economy is ascribed to the oil price increase, it points to a low level of price responsiveness, which is reflected in the fact that, for all the stories about hybrids like the Toyota Prius flying out of showrooms when crude prices hit a peak of almost $150 per barrel, the best-selling vehicles in the United States during this period were actually large pickups like the Ford F Series. In short, motorists had not responded to fuel price rises as they should.

The lessons of the previous decade suggested that if Obama wanted to achieve his goal of doubling fuel economy in eighteen years, he would need to increase prices by over 20 per cent annually[103] – not an easy thing when voters were already complaining about high prices. A glance across the Atlantic, however, would have shown him that there was another way.

The European Union had faced much the same dilemma a decade earlier. In 1997 it had committed to reduce its CO_2 emissions to below 1990 levels by 2008–12.[104] European cars were relatively efficient compared with those in other large markets, but it was clear that if the new targets were to be met further improvements needed to be made. Officials concluded the Union needed to reduce the amount of CO_2 emitted by cars per kilometre driven by 25 per cent to 140 grams.[105] Their hopes were largely realised. Between 2000 and 2009, the average fuel economy of new cars sold in Europe rose 18 per cent to an equivalent of 40 miles per US gallon.[106] In Britain, the improvement in fuel economy was 26 per cent[107] – twice the improvement achieved in the United States.

Did Europe use taxes to accentuate the underlying upswing in crude prices and so provide a sharper price signal than US consumers received? No. Between 2000 and 2009, European pump prices actually fell 10 per cent. And even amid the explosion in crude prices during 2008, the average cost of EU motor fuel only rose to 10 per cent above its 2000 level. Were European consumers more price-elastic than US buyers? No, the EU result had nothing to do with price signals. Rather, in 1998, Brussels agreed with carmakers that they should meet the stringent new 140 grams-per-kilometre efficiency standards by 2009: they simply had to sell more fuel-efficient vehicles.[108]

In 2018, William Nordhaus was awarded the Nobel memorial prize in economics for his work on measures for tackling climate change. He declared at the time that 'there is basically no alternative to the market solution'.[109] But in Europe, the alternative was working pretty well.

Back in the US, Obama realised early on that fuel taxes wouldn't fly in Congress, and so Sunstein didn't get to pursue the option that he, Thaler and everyone else in the economics profession were convinced worked best. Instead, the Administration pushed for an increase in the CAFE standards. Congress supported the move. And over the next decade, the fuel economy of new cars rose by around 12 per cent.[110] It's conceivable the same improvement could have been achieved by tax rises. But, based on the 2000–9 experience, even if the economists were right, it wouldn't have occurred unless there had been an increase in real prices of at least 60 per cent, and probably much more.[111] That would have represented a lot of political pain for legislators for relatively little environmental upside. In the end, the economists' loss seems to have been the planet's gain.

The response of motorists to fuel prices, of smokers to tobacco prices, and of food shoppers to cheaper beef raises questions about how useful the concept of price elasticity is in understanding, predicting and, most importantly, steering human behaviour. The blinkered response of many economists to its failings is a cautionary tale for policymakers. It brings to mind a story one of my university philosophy professors told me.[112] During the Second World War, when Jean-Paul Sartre was working as a teacher in a school outside Paris, he was approached by an older pupil who asked him whether he would advise him to join the Resistance and fight the Germans or, as an only child, stay at home and take care of his widowed mother. Sartre, as a good existentialist, said it was up to the boy to make up his own mind. The boy responded that he was torn, and that if Sartre wasn't prepared to offer advice, he would seek guidance from someone else he trusted, such as his priest or the local community elder, an old communist. Sartre responded that that would still leave him making the choice, because it was clear that the priest would tell him to care for his mother, while the communist would tell him to fight the Nazis.

If you consult an economist, you'll always be told the answer is price.

7

THE PIGOU-COASE
DISAGREEMENT

Does regulation harm economic growth?

In April 2001, hundreds of financial professionals gathered in Washington, DC, to enjoy cocktail parties at the Library of Congress and Smithsonian National Air and Space Museum and – in between times – discuss some of the most arcane aspects of the global banking system. The mood among the delegates at the annual general meeting of the International Swaps & Derivatives Association, better known by its acronym ISDA, was buoyant. And none were more buoyant than those traders, financial engineers and lawyers who worked in one of the newest and perhaps fastest-growing sub-sectors of the derivatives market: credit derivatives.

Credit derivatives, which first emerged around 1995, were based on a simple concept: that the promise to make good another party's debt if that party defaulted could be converted into a tradeable financial instrument. In the past, banks and investors took on credit risk by, for example, making loans to homeowners or buying bonds from businesses and in return receiving interest payments. Credit derivatives allowed a third party to sell credit protection to the lender, but, unlike traditional credit insurance, were standardised so that they could be bought and sold dozens of times before the underlying loan was repaid. They took a little time to get established but, by 1998, the market was worth $100 billion, rising to $1 trillion by 2001. In 2007, contracts worth over $60 trillion would be executed.[1]

Such deals translated into billions of dollars' worth of fees for those who facilitated them. Soon they outshone bonuses in more established areas of finance, such as interest rate swaps and equities sales. It's not surprising, then, that the mood of that 2001 conference should have been so upbeat. 'This was a pretty happy place; a place where people were saying, "We are going to make a lot of money,"' one attendee remembered.[2] This confidence was boosted by the agreement, during the conference, on a new standardised credit derivative contract that would facilitate continued market growth,[3] and a speech by William McDonough, the chairman of the Basel Committee on Banking Supervision, the foremost international regulatory body, in which he said he agreed with ISDA that banks who used credit derivatives should not be required to set aside funds as insurance against the contracts not working as intended.[4]

Back in London, I had recently started reporting on credit derivatives for Reuters. While there had been reports in the financial press about the growth of the market, little had been written about how the tools worked. I therefore sought to plug the gap in my own knowledge by picking the brains of corporate lawyers, credit default swaps traders and financial engineers, and, in the process, trying to get a grip on such mind-bending terms as collateralised debt obligations and synthetic asset-backed securities. And as I came to understand how these financial instruments shifted the risk of parties defaulting on their debts between institutions, I marvelled at how ingenious they were. As I wrote at the time, such credit tools had the potential to 'revolutionise' finance, leading to the transformation of banks from institutions that lent their own money to borrowers in the hope they would be paid back, into 'conduits who simply arrange loans and pass the associated risks on to others'.[5]

But I also spotted two core problems. First, because lending institutions were using credit derivatives to pass loans quickly and easily off their own books onto other investors, those investors who ultimately faced losses if the loan was not repaid could be many links in a long chain away from the original borrowers. They had the most at stake, yet they also had the least information about the underlying borrower or credit risk. Secondly, the complexities of the instruments meant that many investors ended up taking on credit risks they really didn't understand.[6] 'They just see they are getting 2 per cent more yield and go for it,' one fund manager told me, 'and when you have a credit event, the magnitude of the loss will be bigger than expected.'[7] Credit derivatives were great when the sun was shining, it seemed to me. But what would happen if there was a rainy day? Those inside the market seemed to be making too much money to concern themselves with that, while those outside didn't seem to understand the risks.

In the reports I filed, I highlighted some of the potential dangers, and noted that banks were already occasionally being wrongfooted and incurring unexpected losses,[8] but I had neither the data nor, at that time, the experience to tease out all the implications of this shiny new financial instrument. Besides, any reservations that I might have had were more than drowned out by the views of the man whose office was just across town from the Omni Shoreham Hotel where the delegates of the conference were meeting – a man who had all the data in the world and a deeper knowledge of the global financial system than almost anyone else on the planet.

In 2001 Alan Greenspan was in the fourth of his five terms as Chairman of the Board of Governors of the Federal Reserve, a role he had held since 1987. He therefore had ultimate responsibility for supervising the country's banking system and guiding US interest rates. Previously, he had served as Chairman of President Gerald Ford's Council of Economic Advisers from 1974 to 1977; and since the 1950s he had also run a successful Wall Street economics consultancy that had pioneered cutting-edge econometric forecasting models. Not surprisingly, therefore, he had achieved mythic status both at home and internationally, being variously described as 'the second-most powerful man in the United States' and 'the most powerful banker on earth'. In 1998 the *Financial Times* named him its Person of the Year, describing him as 'guardian angel of the financial markets'. When Greenspan spoke about interest rates, growth, the banking system or just how economies should be run, policymakers all over the globe listened carefully.

From the vantage point of his office in the Eccles building, Alan Greenspan wasn't worried about credit derivatives.[9] He believed the instruments helped banks provide cheaper credit to homeowners and businesses, thus helping the economy grow. He also argued that they made banks safer, noting that 'these increasingly complex financial instruments have been especial contributors . . . to the development of a far more flexible, efficient, and resilient financial system.'[10] He saw no reason to disrupt this value-creating innovation by making credit default swaps, which were largely unregulated, subject to greater scrutiny. In this regard, Greenspan felt, banks were best placed to regulate themselves. After all, banks had real-time information about the risks their businesses faced, and the most to lose should they underestimate these risks. Banks would avoid behaviour that threatened their own stability. Moreover, because they wouldn't want to do business with institutions they deemed to be taking unnecessary risks that might end up undermining both parties, they would police each other. Self-interest and the threat of everything blowing up if they got it wrong were seen as more likely to keep the banks honest and cautious than any nosy regulator.

Greenspan's position on credit derivatives reflected his broader view of how economies should work. In his view, governmental regulation distorted the economic signals businesses and consumers received from the market, prompting them to make sub-optimal investment and purchase decisions, which weighed on innovation and productivity and led to slower growth. This was essentially the economics of Adam Smith: faith in the magical force of the 'invisible hand' of the market, and, conversely, suspicion of the cack-hand of government.

Greenspan's views on regulation were long-standing. As a young economist in the 1950s, he had become a follower of the writer and philosopher Ayn Rand, whose books, including *The Fountainhead* and *Atlas Shrugged*, extolled 'rational selfishness' and the virtues of the free market. Rand shared many of the ideas of what was known as the Austrian school of economics, which, led by thinkers Ludwig von Mises and Friedrich Hayek, held that government intervention in the economy was likely to cause instability and weakness, and hence should be kept to an absolute minimum. Rand published a newsletter called the *Objectionist*, to which Greenspan contributed. One 1963 article he wrote on regulation theorised that 'Government regulations do not eliminate potentially dishonest individuals, but merely make their activities harder to detect or easier to hush up.' 'It is precisely the "greed" of the businessman or, more appropriately, his profit-seeking,' he went on, 'which is the unexcelled protector of the consumer . . . Protection of the consumer by regulation is thus illusory.'[11]

Greenspan's perspective would remain reasonably constant over the next forty years. And while his thinking was somewhat controversial in 1963, when people had greater faith that government could intervene efficiently, by 2001 it was more or less mainstream. In the early 2000s, the financial media,[12] regulators[13] and politicians on both sides of the Atlantic, from Gordon Brown[14] to Michael Bloomberg,[15] agreed that a light-touch approach to regulation was the best one for the financial services sector. And also for the economy more broadly. Regulation was seen as 'red tape': often the product of a bureaucrat eager to expand his or her influence; rules that shackled businesses and forced them to waste their time conducting risk assessments, filling out forms on supply-chain sustainability and agonising over memos to ensure no minority group is offended by their wording.

The financial crash of 2007–8 was precipitated in no small part by credit derivatives, which indeed did encourage banks to take on credit risks, especially real-estate loans, that they should not have done, and would not have done if they had believed they would end up holding the loans to maturity. That one of the first victims of the crisis was a German regional bank, which in July 2007 announced it owned €8 billion of bonds crafted from credit derivatives linked to shaky U.S. mortgages[16] – just eleven days after telling investors its exposure was almost non-existent[17] – indicated the instruments' capacity for channelling such risks to unsuitable investors.

This global cataclysm forced a rethink of the view that regulation of the financial sector was unnecessary and economically harmful. Indeed, it caused Greenspan to question his previous assumptions.

'Yes,' he told a panel of lawmakers in 2008, 'I've found a flaw in the model that I perceived as the critical functioning structure that defines how the world works, so to speak.' Earlier in his testimony he admitted that 'Those of us who have looked to the self-interest of lending institutions to protect shareholder's equity – myself especially – are in a state of shocked disbelief.'[18]

Yet the general perception of regulation as a burden on the economy persisted even in the depths of the great recession, and continues today. One policy wonk has compared regulations to pebbles thrown into a stream, which, over time, build up to become a dam that halts commercial activity altogether.[19] Ajit Pai, appointed in 2017 as Chairman of the US Federal Communications Commission, the US communications regulator, articulated this view in 2017 when he outlined the thinking behind the Trump administration's deregulation drive: 'It's basic economics. The more heavily you regulate something, the less of it you're likely to get.'[20]

Polls in the UK and United States over the past twenty years have consistently shown that those who believe there is too much regulation of industry outnumber those who believe there is too little by two to one.[21] The desire to avoid what was seen as stifling regulations on business was a major factor in Britain's decision to leave the European Union. It also generated much of Donald Trump's campaign rhetoric in 2016.

But what is the evidence for this basic and widely accepted economic precept?

The rise of the nanny state

There's long been tension between economists and politicians on regulation. Theory dictates that it's counter-productive to interfere in the day-to-day running of business and commerce. Practice shows that governments – of all political persuasions – find it to difficult not to get involved when the free market generates politically unpopular outcomes. Economists break regulation into two categories: social and economic. Social regulation involves rules that govern firms' approaches to environmental, health and safety issues, the suitability of what they offer consumers, and the measures they take to ensure that any failures on their part don't have catastrophic consequences for the public at large. An early example would be Henry VIII's Apothecaries Wares, Drugs and Stuffs Act, which regulated the quality of medicines.[22] These kinds of rules are of the type usually referred to when commentators complain of 'nanny state' intrusive regulations. Then there is 'Economic Regulation', which refers to rules that control how markets or industries function. Natural monopolies such as railways, utilities and fixed-line telecommunications are frequent targets of such regulations, facing measures such as price caps and minimum service requirements. So fundamental is government rule-setting to this second category of companies' businesses that, even though all industries face some regulations, these industries are referred to by businesspeople and financial analysts as 'regulated industries'.

Economic regulations governing businesses date back at least to Roman times (when, for example, Emperor Diocletian set maximum prices that could be charged for hundreds of goods[23]). Social regulation also has early roots, but really only became a key political remit during the Industrial Revolution. It was then built on during the course of the twentieth century, notably in the decades after the 1930s when faith in laissez-faire policies was at its lowest ebb. Thus, for example, Britain started legislating on air quality in Victorian times, but the most vigorous action was taken in the 1950s when lethal London smogs helped inspire the Clean Air Act of 1956, which set tougher standards and stringent monitoring of these standards. Environmental scandals in the United States around the same time[24] were followed by the Clean Air Acts of 1963 and 1970 and the Clean Water Act of 1972 and the creation of the Environmental Protection Agency in 1970. The thalidomide drugs scandal led to the 1968 Medicines Act in Britain and a beefing-up of the US Food and Drug Administration's role in approving drugs for sale. Workplace safety rules were reinforced by Britain's Factories Acts in 1959 and 1961 and the establishment of the Occupational Safety and Health Administration (OSHA) in the United States in 1971.[25]

In the early days, social regulations were not always quite the enlightened universal moves they might appear. In 1863, for example, the Liberal government in Britain brought in legislation – the Alkali Act – to curb the emission of dangerous gases from the soda factories engaged in the production of soap and detergents. There was a compelling social reason for doing so: one of the by-products of the manufacturing process was hydrogen chloride gas, which caused severe respiratory problems for people living nearby. But it was actually pressure from wealthy landowners concerned about damage to farmland and livestock that prompted the government to act.[26] In an era when laissez-faire views still held sway, it took an influential pressure group to get reform enacted.

Gradually, however, the notion that governments should impose what would today be considered social regulations in the wider interests of the community took root. In Britain, news reports and parliamentary debates from the time show that – certainly before the First World War – there was a growing sense of moral obligation: the country was getting richer and could afford to alleviate harsh conditions. In as much as economics came into it, factory safety rules, working-time restrictions and environmental legislation were largely seen as a justifiable form of redistribution from the richer to the poor. They might, it was accepted, make businesses less efficient, but not to the extent that this would have a severe impact on their profitability.

Interestingly, even those two great political proponents of the free market, Margaret Thatcher and Ronald Reagan, seem to have accepted the role of such rules and regulations. They may have pilloried government meddling in peoples' lives and businesses on the campaign trail, but in office they took far less action against social regulation than their rhetoric implied.[27] Margaret Thatcher's principal achievement in rolling back state control over the economy was in a sustained programme of privatisation of state-owned enterprises. Her best-known deregulation exercise was in the field of economic regulation, with the abolition of (largely private-sector) rules in the City, which had set dealing fees and erected barriers between the roles that different parties could perform (a liberalisation known as 'Big Bang', which facilitated London's emergence as the leading international financial centre). In 1985 her government published a White Paper entitled 'Lifting the Burden', which recommended the reduction of social regulations, such as employment protections and planning rules. But while it aroused furious opposition (Labour warned that the government wanted to remove vital protections for workers and consumers, and a first-term MP by the name of Tony Blair accused Thatcher's government of having an 'ideological obsession with deregulation'),[28] the paper had little practical effect. The 'bonfire of red tape' simply didn't happen. And while it's true that some the new protective regulations introduced during the 1980s were originated in Brussels rather than Westminster, it's also the case that Thatcher's government only occasionally tried to resist them. Ironically, for many thinkers on the right, the Thatcher era is remembered not for pushing back the so-called nanny state but for missed deregulation opportunities.[29]

Across the Atlantic, Ronald Reagan moved into the White House arguing that 'regulatory relief' was one of the cornerstones of his 'economic recovery program'.[30] He duly appointed Vice President Bush to head a new Task Force on Regulatory Relief, which put social regulation in its cross-hairs. Reagan installed James Watt, then-head of a legal foundation that specialised in suing the federal government on behalf of business interests, to run the Department of the Interior, which had responsibility for managing the country's land holdings and waterways. Watt arrived at the department with a promise to 'undo fifty years of bad government',[31] and began by allowing miners access to national parks and opening up previously restricted offshore areas for oil drilling. Carl E. Bagge, president of the National Coal Association, said his organisation was 'deliriously happy' with Watt's arrival at the Interior Department.[32] The Democratic Congressman Morris Udall described the choice of Watt for the role as akin to 'appointing Dracula to head a blood bank'.[33]

Over at the US Environmental Protection Agency, Anne Gorsuch took control, and immediately set to work slashing the agency's budget and staffing, in the belief that its work was hampering economic prosperity. She sought to roll back rules approved by the Carter administration and, where Congressional approval would be required to repeal the rules, pursued a policy of regulatory relief through reduced enforcement. In a similar vein, Reagan's appointee at the Transport Department fought the Carter administration's decision to require auto makers to install airbags or other automatic restraints in vehicles.

Yet the wave of deregulation that looked to be on its way never actually arrived. Faced with considerable opposition from Congress and the public, Reagan felt he had no choice but to ditch Watt and Gorsuch, to cancel plans to lift the ban on lead in petrol, and to allow rules on airbags in cars to go ahead. EPA staffing levels rose again, while the Taskforce on Regulatory Relief was wound down in 1983 (Reagan claimed it had achieved its goals). The administration continued to drag its feet on adopting new environmental protections, such as measures to tackle acid rain, but generally the attack on existing environmental and safety regulations waned.[34]

There is no question that the Reagan era saw substantial regulatory change. Price controls and competition-limiting practices in the airline and railway industries were phased out under his watch, revolutionising the US transport industry in the process (although, to be strictly accurate, the legislation had its origins in the Nixon administration and most of it had been signed into law by Carter). But Reagan's administration could take full credit for abolishing the last price controls on US-produced crude oil and unexpectedly using anti-trust rules to break up the AT&T long-distance phone monopoly that had been blamed for high call prices. Such landmark regulatory changes brought in between 1981 and 1989 were designed to remove anti-competitive practices rather than the kind of red tape that is popularly supposed by its critics to tie businesses in knots. There is general consensus among academics that Reagan's reputation as a slasher of supposedly overzealous environmental and worker and consumer protections – social regulation – is exaggerated.[35] As for Margaret Thatcher, it's worth nothing that her remark (so beloved of conservatives like the former Republican Speaker of the US House of Representatives, Paul Ryan[36]) that 'Every regulation represents a restriction of liberty, every regulation has a cost' was actually published in a book she authored a decade *after* leaving government.[37]

Yet the ambition to cut regulation persisted. In Britain, the future Prime Minister David Cameron promised while in opposition that he would remove one old regulation for every new regulation introduced; that he would invite the public to nominate unpopular regulations that might be scrapped; and that he would include 'sunset' clauses in the charters of organisations set up to police regulation, so that they would cease to exist unless a clear case could be made for their preservation. Once in power in 2010, he promised to 'cut back the health and safety monster',[38] and duly launched a 'red tape challenge', complete with a website that offered the public 'the chance to rip up some of the 21,000 rules and regulations that are getting in your way'.[39] In early 2011, Cameron's director of strategy, Steve Hilton, who would later find fame in America as a Fox News host, suggested that Cameron should abolish maternity leave and suspend the Consumer Protection Act to jump-start the flagging post-crisis economy,[40] an idea some economists termed a 'competitive social deflation'.[41]

In the end, though, the Conservative–Liberal Democrat coalition government's deregulatory drive proved less dramatic. In 2011 the then Business Secretary Vince Cable unveiled plans to remove the requirements for retailers to have an alcohol licence to sell alcoholic liqueur-filled chocolates, to abolish rules governing the safety of pencils and to scrap the war-time Trading with the Enemy Act and its ninety-eight linked regulations, which at last, sixty-six years after the end of the conflict, was finally deemed 'redundant'.[42] (Whether or not any of the rules were actually being enforced is a moot point.) The Chancellor of the Exchequer George Osborne, who had been among those Conservatives who promised to cut red tape to 'unleash' the forces of enterprise,[43] later ruefully told me:

People always want to deregulate in general, but want regulation in the specific. There's a never-ending stream of calls, including from people on the right in politics, for additional regulation when faced with a particular scandal, or some social demand like, to ban plastic cups.[44]

Britain has scarcely been alone in this. The USA has had much the same experience, as have most European countries. An Italian parliamentary hearing in 2014 was told that the apparently impressive axing of 67,872 regulations over recent years had only covered rules that were not being enforced.[45]

Arthur Pigou and public interest

The record of Margaret Thatcher, Ronald Reagan and their successors in the realm of regulation stand in stark contrast to the economic theory that underpinned so much of their thinking. While economists have never agreed on what precisely constitutes regulation (does it, for example, extend to such policy areas as immigration?), most have traditionally been wary of what it usually involves: 'the employment of legal instruments for the implementation of social economic policy objectives', according to one definition.[46] True, government intervention to protect property rights is universally accepted (even by the likes of Ayn Rand and Friedrich Hayek, who, in addition to inspiring Margaret Thatcher, was also cited by many US Conservative politicians including Paul Ryan and Rand Paul as an influence).[47] But even the principle that governments should intervene in markets if a dominant player threatens to stifle competition has not gone wholly uncontested.

Milton Friedman for one argued that worries about market domination were exaggerated, and that all monopolies will ultimately collapse (except where supported by government). That qualification 'ultimately' is a pretty major one: Standard Oil's domination of the US oil market persisted for over four decades until it was broken up by the government; to that extent Friedman's 'ultimately' is reminiscent of Keynes's view that 'in the long run we are all dead.'[48] It perhaps helps explain why Friedman's view should have been a minority one, and why staunch conservatives like George Stigler, who titled his autobiography *Memoirs of an Unregulated Economist*, are generally supportive of anti-trust rules. But it's indicative of the general suspicion with which economists have regarded the whole sphere of regulation.

This scepticism dates back to the early days of classical economics, and figures such as Adam Smith and Jeremy Bentham. Both were clear that the overall wellbeing of the community almost always suffers when the state attempts to impose its own 'artificial' regulations on businessmen.[49] In a situation such as with the soda industry in the 1860s, they would have argued (as factory owners and their supporters did) that a restriction on emissions would have adverse unintended consequences, such as factory closures, rising costs for raw materials and higher prices of soap and detergents for the general public.

At the turn of the twentieth century, however, there was a reaction against this view. Not only did such interventions in the economy not weigh on the national wealth, a new school of economists argued, but rather they could actually increase it. Alfred Marshall is credited with first conceiving of the idea of 'economic externalities', a concept which refers to the side effects of a commercial activity, which, in effect, shift a burden from one party to another. One of Marshall's former students, another Cambridge economist called Arthur Pigou, built on this idea to show how government intervention could not only tackle the injustice of antisocial burden-shifting, but also make a country richer in the process.

The soda industry provides an example of how Pigou's ideas worked in practice. Before the Alkali Act effectively banned the unrestricted emission of hydrogen chloride, a farmer who could prove that crop damage or the death of a calf was the result of a plant emitting noxious gas could seek a Common Law remedy via the courts and so, theoretically, seek to restore the economic balance. But in practice such an approach was fraught with problems. It would involve proving which of possibly many factories was directly responsible, and also involve assessing the true nature of the impact. Was there damage to farm buildings caused by acid rain, for instance? Could it be shown that a spell of illness on the part of, say, a labourer could be attributed to the pollution, and if so how did you put a value on that in terms of sick pay, lost work, and so on? In other words, how did you accurately assess the cost of the damage done?

It so happens that we know one soda manufacturer reported paying out £150 in damages in one year before the Alkali Act,[50] but, given how difficult pursuing a successful case was, it's hard to believe that £150 represented the sum total of the cost of his operation to others. The same manufacturer reported that the cost of installing condensing equipment to remove the toxic gas cost was a one-off sum of £300 (the captured acid could be sold, which meant there was no net operating cost). If the damages claims had run at £150 every year, he would no doubt have installed the equipment unprompted. But it appears to have happened just the once, and therefore he, like his fellow polluters, had no real financial incentive to incur costs to reduce noxious emissions.

In his 1920 work, *The Economics of Welfare*, Pigou identified the divergence between the public cost of particular acts by businesses and the private costs and benefits they incurred. Clearly, in the case of the soda plant, it made sense for society as a whole to incur a one-off cost of £300 to avoid property damage that probably exceeded that level every year,[51] yet the market did not provide sufficient incentive for factory owners to undertake such investment. There was what we would today call a 'market failure'. Pigou's view was

227

that, in such situations, governments could improve overall industrial efficiency and societal welfare by applying 'extraordinary encouragements' or 'extraordinary restraints' to businesses to encourage them to, for example, install anti-pollution equipment. This could take the form of a restraint such as the Alkali Act, which imposed a £100 per offence penalty on polluters, the provision of subsidies to install equipment, or a government tax on emissions. If a tax was in excess of the cost of installing condensers to remove the hydrogen chloride from emissions, it would have the same impact as a ban, as factory owners would be better off by investing in pollution-reducing equipment.

Pigou's views proved influential. In the decades that followed *The Economics of Welfare*, other economists built on his ideas to construct an intellectual framework, known as the Public Interest Theory of Regulation, which argued that market failures may exist in a wide range of areas, and that they may be solved via regulation. For example, in a perfect neoclassical world with fully competitive markets and total transparency regarding product attributes, consumers can make informed decisions on whether they wish to purchase particular goods or not and, having judged their quality, what price to pay for them. In such a world, there is no need for regulation, because people will either decide not to buy something that is inferior or demand that less is charged for it. But in a world governed by Public Interest theories, it's assumed that perfect competition frequently does not exist, and that the producer always has a better idea as to the quality of goods on offer – and the risks they may pose – than the consumer. In such a world a regulator is therefore needed to gather information, bar the sale of shoddy goods, force manufacturers to label their goods accurately – in other words, to ensure market fairness. Such a world blossomed in the US and UK after the Second World War, when there was a significant expansion in levels of regulation. Or as Alan Greenspan told a UK audience in 2004:

Government intervention was increasingly seen as necessary to correct the failures and deficiencies viewed as inherent in market economies. Laissez-faire was rapidly abandoned and a tidal wave of regulation swept over much of the world's business community . . . distortions induced by regulation were more and more disturbing.[52]

But even as Pigou's ideas were catching on in ever more segments of the economy, a new theory on regulation was emerging, promoted – somewhat paradoxically – by an erstwhile socialist.

Ronald Coase and the case against regulation

Ronald Coase was born in 1910 in Willesden, in north-west London, to working-class parents who had left school at around twelve years of age and become staunch Labour supporters.[53] Coase, too, became a socialist.[54] But during his studies at the London School of Economics in the late 1920s and early 1930s, he fell under the influence of the head of the economics department, Lionel Robbins, and abandoned his socialism in favour of Robbin's fervent belief in free markets and his equally fervent antagonism to the liberal ideas then emanating from Cambridge. Robbins was critical of some of Alfred Marshall's work. He was particularly critical of Marshall's former student John Maynard Keynes. Nothing characterises Robbins's thinking and ambitions for the LSE at the time more than his decision in 1931 to hire perhaps the most fervent, or at least longest-serving, anti-Keynesian of the twentieth century, Friedrich Hayek. It's not surprising that some economists see Robbins' LSE as a precursor to the post-war 'Chicago School' of conservative economic thought.

A few years after graduating, Ronald Coase returned to the economics department and became friends with Hayek. Their views did not always align. Coase was nevertheless influenced by the Austrian, and became an early member of his Mont Pelerin Society, which sought, in the post-war years when Keynesianism and expansionist government generally were de rigueur, to promote the values of free markets and highlight the risks of government involvement in the economy. Coase would acknowledge Hayek in his Nobel memorial prize-winning speech in 1991.

Coase began to look at the impact of regulation while still in his twenties, continued with it after he moved to the United States in the 1950s, and in 1960 published his most influential work in this field: 'The Problem of Social Cost'. The paper was a direct retort to Pigou's work, and set out a thinking far from Coase's socialist roots: one he would promote in writings and interviews he would undertake until after his hundredth birthday.

In 'The Problem of Social Cost', Coase posited that, theoretically, whether a factory was permitted or forbidden to emit noxious fumes by law had no impact on overall national wealth because, irrespective of the law, the factory owner and the local residents could come to a financial arrangement whereby a mutually beneficial arrangement was arrived at. If the local residents had the right not to have their properties exposed to fumes, they could sell a right to pollute to the factory owner. If the factory had a right to emit fumes, the locals could pay the factory not to do so (perhaps by financing the installation of smoke-scrubbing equipment). Either way, the outcome would be the same in terms of the total national income. Of course, this rather assumed that no transaction costs (such as legal fees) would be involved, and Coase accepted that these might be significant. But his focus was on the theory of social cost, rather than all its practical implications.

Besides, he argued, government intervention and the bureaucracy it involved was also costly, and one had as well to take account of the economic cost of the market distortions Pigouvian taxes would cause. It probably made more sense to accept transaction costs and conduct private contracts, or even do nothing at all, than incur all the costs that government involvement would give rise to.

Since Coase's work was almost entirely theoretical,[55] he never actually produced evidence to show there really were 'very few good regulations'[56] – in other words, that the benefits of government actions to correct market failures usually exceeded costs. He simply asserted his belief as fact based on his own experience, which included wartime service with the British government. In an era long before people studied data sets to support their ideas, let alone examine the facts behind the data sets, no one actually expected Coase to provide hard evidence of this claim.

Surprisingly, perhaps, Conservative economists were initially sceptical of Coase's ideas. According to George Stigler, around 1960 Coase (then working at the University of Virginia) was invited to a dinner with a group of Chicago luminaries including Mont Pelerin members Milton Friedman and Stigler himself, and got a distinctly chilly reception.[57] The mood soon changed, however. 'In the course of two hours of argument, the vote went from 20 against and one for Coase, to 21 for Coase,' Stigler wrote in his memoir. 'What an exhilarating event! I lamented afterward that we had not had the clairvoyance to tape it.'[58] He would go on to popularise Coase's ideas – or 'the Coase theorem', as he termed it. And over the course of the 1960s Stigler would become perhaps the leading academic critic of government regulation in the United States, arguing, for instance, that government intervention in the electricity and securities sectors had been counterproductive and that racial quotas were a misguided policy.

In time, he and Coase would become perhaps the two most influential economists in the area of regulation,[59] but during the 1960s their position that government attempts to rectify market failures were inefficient and probably ineffectual was outside the mainstream. In part, this may have been because they didn't seem to offer any solutions to the problems people were trying to solve at the time – like pollution, workplaces where people lost limbs, or the sale of dangerously flammable toddler pyjamas. Indeed, they seemed to downplay the problems people faced. Their hypothetical examples of market failure tended to be relatively harmless – such as wandering cows damaging crops (a Coase example that Stigler described as 'picturesque'[60]), or pollution reducing the number of fish in a river, thereby reducing fishermen's incomes, but having no other societal consequence. Graphic instances of non-regulation – for example, the 'phossy mouth' suffered by nineteenth-century match makers that involved excruciating mouth abscesses, facial disfigurement and exposed bones – were not part of their library of examples.

At times, Stigler would simply deny the existence of societal harm. In one debate, he cited the Securities and Exchange Commission's decision to fine stockbrokers for front-running (whereby they bought or sold shares on their own behalf after receiving a large order from a client but before executing it) as an example of regulators' tendency to overreach, and in the process curtail perfectly legitimate commerce.[61] His view was that such insider trading was an acceptable practice, and he was dismissive of objections that the broker's trades distorted the market and caused the client to pay more when buying or receive less when selling their shares. Today, incidentally, front-running is not just a civil but a criminal offence in major financial centres from New York to Singapore, and frequently involves a jail sentence of two years or more.[62]

From around 1970 a growing stream of empirical research, examining data from industries that were faced with new regulations, was produced. Most of this literature focused on US industries,[63] but some examined the UK, and it was all widely read by economists and policymakers in both countries. Not all findings concurred, but the general tenor was that regulation was expensive and harmful. A case in point was a 1973 study by a University of Los Angeles economist Sam Peltzman, that considered the economic impact of the increased powers given to the Food and Drug

Administration in 1962 to limit the sale of ineffective drugs. Peltzman's view was that the compliance costs that government regulation had imposed upon pharmaceutical companies had led to a marked reduction in drug innovation, and that 'benefits forgone on effective new drugs exceed greatly the waste avoided on ineffective drugs.'[64] A further study five years later agreed, and suggested that tighter UK regulation in the wake of the thalidomide scandal had also led to a fall in drug innovation in Britain.[65] Another 1973 study found that there was no evidence that US pharmaceutical rules brought greater safety. Kip Viscusi, a star in regulatory economics, analysed data on accidental child deaths due to aspirin overdoses and concluded that the introduction of safety caps on pill bottles had actually increased child poisonings, because they 'induced increased parental irresponsibility' and prompted grownups to leave pill bottles open.

Peltzman also examined automobile safety regulation in a 1975 paper, which concluded that safety regulations caused additional deaths, since people drove more dangerously when they assumed they were safer.[66] Another study found that OSHA, the Occupational Safety and Health Administration, had little or no effect on accident rates, even in industries where it specifically targeted enforcement efforts. In more general terms, a 1975 study by Murray Weidenbaum, who would go on to be chairman of President Ronald Reagan's Council of Economic Advisors, found that regulations caused inflation and reduced innovation,[67] and other studies found environmental regulations had caused a slowdown in productivity.[68] That inflation had risen and productivity growth had slowed during the 1970s, just as the Clean Air and Clean Water Acts came into force and OSHA was formed, created a correlation between the two trends, which, in the mood of the times, pointed towards a causal link. The general conclusions to be drawn seemed to be that no regulation, from seatbelts to mine safety, was worth the collateral damage it caused, and that, frankly, society as a whole would be much better off if it was left to individuals to decide what risks they might or might not want to take. If you were ill and wished to try a new drug, why shouldn't you carry out such reading about it as you felt necessary, and then make up your own mind whether to take it? If you could earn more by working in an industry that had no safety measures in place than one that had spent considerable sums implementing them, wasn't it for you to make that decision rather than the government?

While such work might have been laughed at twenty years previously, in the 1970s, as the US and European economies slowed and struggled with inflation, the growing scepticism of government created a more receptive audience. Similarly, industry pleading that might previously have been laughed off – like General Motors' chairman Roger Smith claiming that design safety rules had turned car making into a 'regulated industry' like water or gas supply – found a more sympathetic ear from the public and politicians.[69] From the late 1970s, the way to stoke voters' emotions shifted from promising to restrict companies' ability to cause harm to the public to arguing that bureaucrats should be restrained from stopping companies going about their business.

Over recent decades, economists have remained relatively consistent in their views on the subject. One review of the literature on regulation in 2010 summed up the consensus among economists bluntly: 'the mainstream economic literature is implicitly or explicitly critical of the public interest theories of regulation.'[70]

This intellectual consistency pervades the godparents of good economic governance – the World Bank, IMF and OECD – who regularly issue studies that warn of the risks of regulation. Since 2003 the World Bank has issued an annual survey titled 'Doing Business', which ranks countries in terms of how business-friendly they are, features chapters with titles like 'Tackling burdensome regulation' and observations such as 'All too often, however, regulation misses its goal, and one inefficiency replaces another, especially in the form of government overreach in business activity',[71] that could have come from the mouth of Coase or Hayek. The OECD, which produces a Glossary of Economic Terms, gives a definition of 'social regulation' that seems more warning than explanation: 'The economic effects of social regulations may be secondary concerns or even unexpected, but can be substantial. Reform aims to verify that regulation is needed [*sic*]'. (Such qualifications don't appear alongside the OECD's definitions of 'monetary policy instruments' or 'fiscal consolidation'.)

If the experts are clear that regulation is a bad thing, and the public seems to agree, why have governments at least back as far as Harold Wilson failed to deliver on promised 'bonfires' of red tape?

Governments and the case for regulation

In 1980, Milton Friedman made a television series with the US public broadcaster PBS called *Free to Choose*, which introduced his brand of laissez-faire economics to millions of Americans. The series was translated into two dozen languages (and more recently has become a YouTube favourite), playing no small part in popularising internationally the idea that government involvement in the economy restricts growth.

Friedman was an expert communicator, and his skills were on particular display in an episode that dealt with regulation. In this, he stacked copies of the Federal Register, the official record of the rules, proposed rules and notices of government agencies, on the marble floor of the Library of Congress in Washington DC, arranged by year. As he walked along the stacks for 1936 onwards, viewers could see the pile grow taller, and then deeper, creating a powerful visual image that conveyed a sense of government reach into the lives of Americans. In the years since, the annual pile has grown higher still, for 2016 hitting a record of over 96,000 pages. A similar trend has occurred in other countries, and commentators from Sydney to London to Paris regularly echo Friedman in decrying 'mountains of regulations' (or indeed '*montagnes de règles*').[72]

Friedman and his University of Chicago colleague George Stigler saw this propensity to regulate as a natural consequence of the desire of politicians and officials to expand their power and influence. Economic theory stated that everyone sought to advance their own interests. Since rule-setting was how politicians and bureaucrats advanced theirs, this would be the rational thing for them to do. And herein lay part of the problem. Because politicians' primary purpose was not to benefit the public, the public was probably no more protected by their actions than if things had been left to the vagaries of equally self-interested firms whose actions were at least checked by the powers of the marketplace. Friedman and Stigler also argued that regulators were likely to get into bed with the companies they regulated, offering incumbents regulatory frameworks that entrenched their market dominance in return for political support, and thereby sacrifice the public interest to perpetuate their rule-setting powers.

It's a dark view of government. On the other hand, even if one believes people in public service are motivated by a desire to do good, one can see how political pressures may also lead to inefficient rule-making. Special interest groups such as business lobbies, environmental organisations and trade unions can invest considerable time and money arguing for rules about which the general population, whose actions may be restricted by the rules, are ignorant. Each individual rule may impose only a slight burden on the public or businesses, but over time the gradual weight of such regulations may mount up.

Politicians' responses are also inevitably shaped – distorted, some would say – by their fears of the blame that might attach to them if things go wrong: after all, if a bridge collapses, or the cladding on a building fails, or a pandemic exposes frailties in infrastructure and health care systems, it is, understandably, the decision-makers who end up among those in the dock. Such concerns for their own reputation can cause them to take an expensive or ill-thought-through back-covering approach, especially as its full costs may be hard to ascertain by those footing the bill. Even relatively straightforward health and safety measures can prove tricky to price. Back in 1992, I had a summer job at a BMW plant outside Munich, assembling the rear doors of cars in the 7-series saloon range. US safety regulations dictated that cars destined for America (as opposed to those being manufactured for the European, Asian or African markets) had to have side impact bars screwed to the inside of the doors, a requirement that involved extra materials and labour. A decade later, the US National Highway Traffic Safety Administration estimated the cost per vehicle at $129. How they arrived at that figure, I don't know. And since manufacturing costs for the full vehicle were falling in real terms, I doubt anyone really understood or cared. At any rate, it's hard to believe that US consumers would have known how much the slight reduction in overall safety risk was costing them.

But even if one places the most cynical construction on politicians' motives, it has to be recognised that they have good financial reasons for many (if not necessarily all) of the regulatory steps they take. The studies conducted by the likes of Peltzman and Weidenbaum suggested that the collective cost of government regulation had stampeded out of control. Weidenbaum, for example, suggested in 1978 that federal regulation could well be costing businesses $100 billion annually – $400 billion in today's money. But he didn't also attempt to measure the benefits that might be accruing from these regulations, an omission that is not unusual in the academic literature (one 2012 OECD study noted that 'Most quantitative studies deal with the costs of regulation and give little or no attention to quantifying the benefits of regulation.')[73]

And the fact is that reducing harm saves money – potentially a lot of money. Two famous clean-up operations illustrate the point well. The cost of removing the PCBs, or polychlorinated biphenyls, which contaminated the Hudson River from 1947 to 1977, was estimated at $280 million.[74] The cost of tackling the environmental and economic damage caused by the BP oil spill in the Gulf of Mexico in 2010 topped $70 billion.[75] The Hudson River damage would not have happened if the measures in the Clean Water Act had been in place earlier. BP's Deepwater Horizon disaster was linked to the use of a well design that would not have conformed to European regulations.

Such regulations bring other benefits too, some measurable, others less so. Quality regulation has been shown to speed up innovation. Locally or internationally recognised standards facilitate trade. Environmental rules boost productivity and save on healthcare. An early study in 1977 by the US economists Lester Lave and Eugene Seskin estimated that rules that restricted the emissions from fixed sites like power plants were worth $16.1 billion alone (in 1973 prices) in terms of improved employee productivity and lower healthcare costs (that figure excluded a consideration of any improvements there might be in agricultural yields or lessening of damage to property). The overall cost of the measures was estimated at $9.5 billion.[76]

In more recent times, the White House Office of Management and Budget, which produces a regular estimate of regulatory costs and benefits of major federal programmes over the previous ten years, has calculated that benefits have outstripped costs by around 8 to 1.[77] In the run-up to the Brexit referendum in 2016, many commentators touted a £33 billion estimate of the annual cost of the 100 most significant European Union regulations as evidence of the burden of Brussels-originated red tape. Few noted that the same estimate, based on government impact-assessment reports, put the benefit of these regulations at almost twice that figure.[78]

So when on occasion a government announces that it is taking an axe to regulation, as President Trump's administration did when it promised to cut two regulations for every new rule approved, one has to look at both sides of the balance sheet. Take the decision in June 2017 to exempt shipbuilders from a requirement to monitor air quality for beryllium, a carcinogenic element often found in the grit used to blast rust and paint off old ship hulls. Removing the monitoring obligation was estimated to save the repair industry around $12 million a year. The health costs of beryllium poisoning, however, had previously been estimated at $28 million. The repair industry made a saving. But a larger burden was now placed on workers, insurers, medics and others.[79]

This doesn't mean that governments always get the balance right. In early 2020, the Chief Executive of the National Health Service criticised UK planning regulations that had unwittingly made it easier to open a fast food restaurant on a high street than a gym.[80] A 1989 Danish bill intended to promote the expansion of forest cover was blamed by one environmental group for unintentionally encouraging landowners to clear some tracts of untouched woodland.[81] Japan's calculation of vehicle fuel economy obligations based on a vehicle's weight has had the unintended consequence, some researchers have argued, of encouraging manufacturers to make cars heavier.[82]

More frequently, there are value-for-money questions. Arguably, only a very hard-headed economist would suggest that the 2004 study that estimated US vehicle safety rules (like those that forced me to screw tubular supports into BMW doors) saved almost 21,000 lives in 2002, at an average cost of $544,000 per life, simultaneously demonstrated that the regulations didn't justify the cost.[83] In the same way, it might be difficult to reject the rule requiring steering columns to be capable of absorbing energy from impacts on the grounds that it cost $100,000 per life saved.[84] However, one can reasonably ask whether the ban on using the growth-enhancing hormone DES in cattle feed, on the basis it carries a cancer risk, is necessarily justified at a cost of $132 million per life saved (studies suggest the cancer risk is actually very low, and that the ban increases the cost of beef).[85]

In the banking sphere, some observers have argued that the wave of financial regulation that has been drafted since the financial crisis imposes large, unnecessary burdens, in this case restricting access to lending and making it unnecessarily expensive. The so-called Volcker Rule, which effectively bans US lending and deposit-taking banks from engaging in speculative trading with their own money (a rule intended to avoid losses from those activities leading to a collapse in the real economy), is frequently cited as an example. That the European Union decided, after much consideration, not to adopt its own Volcker Rule suggests that the critics might have a point.[86]

But even if many individual regulations do represent inefficient use of societal resources, they don't prove the broader point that we're drowning under red tape, or that the idea of government regulation is flawed. True, some studies have measured a growth cost from the macroeconomic burden of regulations. One 1990 study estimated that environmental regulation alone reduced the level of US gross national product by 2.59 per cent.[87] But it did not consider whether such regulation might not itself stimulate economic activity, such as product innovation, or stem the economic damage caused by pollution. It's also true that environmental regulations can influence business locations. The ship-breaking yards on the beaches north of Chittagong, Bangladesh, where old vessels are run aground before being dismantled by hand, are a phenomenon that emerged in the 1980s after other Asian countries like Taiwan toughened their environmental rules.[88] One 2002 study found US companies in polluting industries were more likely to steer their overseas investment towards countries with less strict environmental protection.[89] But studies have also consistently failed to find evidence that stricter environmental rules weigh more broadly on growth.[90] As one major review of literature on air and water protections put it:

> there is relatively little evidence to support the hypothesis that environmental regulations have had a large adverse effect on competitiveness . . . studies attempting to measure the effect of environmental regulation on net exports, overall trade flows, and plant location decisions have produced estimates that are either small, statistically insignificant, or not robust to model specification.[91]

And as it happens, rich countries tend to have tighter, not weaker, environmental rules.[92]

The case for linking increased regulation to slower growth is also weakened by the historical record, which demonstrably shows that regulation expanded most when US and European economies were growing the fastest, in the 1945-to-1973 period. It's a problem which Alan Greenspan addressed in his 2007 memoir.[93] However, since he wrote it in the days before his world view was severely battered by the financial crash, he didn't see the need to spend much time on an explanation for the discrepancy. His off-the-cuff, slightly flippant suggestion was that the post-war era didn't punish such deviations from good practice because it was a 'less pressing period', and that things were different now that countries faced the pressures of globalisation.

As for the World Bank's 'Doing Business' report and the grumbling tone it adopts when talking about regulation, it's striking that the metrics it looks at don't cover the sort of rules one assumes it to be so against. It considers such factors as the ease of registering a company, dealing with construction permits, getting an electricity connection, registering a property, getting credit, protecting minority investors, ease of paying taxes, restrictions on international trade, legal enforceability of contracts and rules which permit bankruptcy resolution. All fair enough if one is trying to ascertain whether the private sector in a particular country is performing key functions well and whether the state is supporting the private sector, but hardly enlightening on what might be termed 'government overreach' in the area of social regulation. Maybe that's why Denmark and Sweden – countries with strict social protections – typically score well in the World Bank reports. Yet the popular perception is that the World Bank 'Doing Business' Survey seeks to call out growth-constricting red tape – a perception amplified by the way in which it often forms the statistical basis for other studies keen to claim that freedom from the heavy hand of government is correlated with growth.[94]

The more one examines the studies on which the intellectual case against social regulation sits, they shakier they seem. Coase and Stigler's work was purely theoretical, and relied on a narrow definition of a rational person that ignored most of the realities of the economy. Much of the empirical work that 'proved' that regulation was inefficient wasn't empirical in any real scientific sense. Viscusi used regressions of data sets to prove his argument that safety caps on medicine bottles made parents careless. However, he didn't examine individual cases of child poisoning to see if carelessness was the cause. And when another academic re-ran similar regressions years later, he failed to find the trend Viscusi observed.[95] Peltzman sought to show that motorists drove more dangerously as their cars became safer, but again inferred this from strained correlations in the data rather than actually identifying behavioural changes. I was relieved to hear his reassurance, when I spoke to him in 2019, that his own driving hadn't deteriorated as the cars he drove improved.

About a mile away from Greenspan's old office in Washington, DC, stands the home of the *bête noire* of liberals across America, the libertarian Cato Institute, which publishes a quarterly journal called *Regulation*. 'Why do we bother?' might be a better title. The journal's gregarious editor, Peter van Doren, is, like his predecessor Murray

Weidenbaum, a harsh critic of government health and safety rules. He considers it undemocratic for politicians or bureaucrats to restrict individuals' choices about what they buy, where they work, who they should marry and even what recreational substances they should consume, and believes the power of the market would keep us just as safe as any government regulator. Indeed, he holds the view so strongly that he feels he doesn't need shaky secondary arguments to support his position. Van Doren rejects the idea that state involvement slows growth as Greenspan claimed: 'If you look at the rate of economic growth in US, the UK or the whole OECD,' he says,

> you see that it's strikingly constant – 2 per cent per year forever . . . Economic growth seems to purr along and we don't know why. Politics has scrums about this but economic growth shouldn't be part of the discussion.

For Van Doren, regulation is a political and philosophical issue. It's about the restriction of choice and the loss of freedom that goes with it. The large body of economists who claim that regulation dampens growth would not accept their position is similarly ideological. Rather they say their concerns about regulation are based on mathematical models, empirical data and studies like those penned by Kip Viscusi and Sam Peltzman. Perhaps it's partly because I lost my mother in a car accident at a young age, but I struggle to see how reasonable, sceptical people (as economists claim to be) could form a view of human behaviour based on the supposedly 'empirical' evidence presented in Peltzman's works on car safety, or how they could expect that such studies should guide public policy in relation to matters of life and death. The 1970s and 1980s studies that dismissed the effectiveness of auto safety and other safety rules, without actually investigating real-world examples of how people behave, and how lives were lost, seem far too flippant to be useful in helping society to manage risk and reduce harm.

It isn't that regulation is always good – clearly not; rules are created by humans. But each rule must be assessed on its own merits, and amended where a clear case for this exists, rather than discarded because someone presents an arresting image of a stack of rules being too high. The quality of a government cannot be measured in the quantity of laws it passes. Nor in the number of rules it rips up.

8

THE JORGENSON THESIS

Are taxes on business damaging?

In April 2013, Jamie Dimon, Chief Executive of America's biggest bank, JP Morgan Chase, and, according to the *Washington Post*, a man 'rarely without an opinion on . . . well, anything',[1] sat down in his eighth-floor corner office in a modernist skyscraper on Fifth Avenue to write a letter that he felt to be of immense importance to the bank's shareholders. Accustomed to offering public pronouncements on everything from regulatory relief to the need to help ex-convicts re-enter the workforce, he felt no hesitation in laying down the law on his latest bugbear: 'Our corporate tax policies,' he declared, 'are, at the margin, driving capital overseas'.[2] If reform wasn't enacted, he argued, good jobs, the competitiveness of US companies, the very wealth of the nation, would be under threat.

Dimon had also campaigned for changes to personal taxes. In 2009, he had made what was described as an 'angry' phone call to the then Chancellor of the Exchequer Alistair Darling to complain about Britain's plans to put additional taxes on banker bonuses.[3] In 2012, he had joined a chorus of US chief executives arguing for spending cuts and personal tax hikes to help tackle a growing deficit.[4] But 2013 marked a new phase, as Dimon embarked on a five-year forthright assault[5] on the US corporate tax rate. The time, he felt, was ripe for change. Japan had reduced its corporate tax rate the previous year, leaving the United States with the highest headline rate among developed countries. Barack Obama had said during his first term that he supported a reduction in the tax rate on corporate profits,[6] and in 2013 there had been tax rises for the wealthiest in society. All these factors seemed justification to Dimon (and others) for a reduction in corporate taxes over the coming years. In interviews, speeches and editorials he delivered a simple and blunt message: 'Reduce it, become more competitive.'[7] He rejected arguments that such cuts would be a windfall for wealthy Americans, who owned most shares in businesses, and claimed a tax cut would drive up investment and so 'would help the people who need it the most – the people at the bottom of the ladder'.[8]

Reform, however, remained elusive. Many business leaders and Republicans, who controlled Congress,[9] felt Obama's proposed reduction in the headline federal rate to 28 per cent from 35 per cent was not steep enough, and they opposed his plan to keep the overall reform revenue-neutral by eliminating loopholes. Four years after his opening salvo, Dimon felt frustrated that nothing had changed. 'The urgency for tax reform cannot be overstated,' he told reporters in June 2017.[10] A month later, he told investors that 'we should be ringing that alarm bell' about the need to cut taxes.[11]

Dimon's rationale for change was simple. Overseas rivals typically faced statutory tax rates of 25 to 30 per cent while US companies faced headline rates of 35 to 40 per cent (when one included state and local income taxes), and he saw this as making US firms less competitive. As it happened, American companies tended to dominate the industries in which they competed overseas – like technology and banking – and such international companies didn't actually pay effective tax rates anywhere near 35 per cent. They nevertheless argued that, despite this, the higher headline tax rate left them with less leeway to cut prices when bidding against foreign firms for clients, or to increase their offer when bidding against such rivals to buy other companies or assets like land, or to hire the brightest and the best to work for them. What's more, they said, it made it more attractive for them to invest and create jobs overseas, where taxes were lower, rather than at home. One of America's largest companies, Cisco Systems, offered a telling instance of this. In 2015 the CEO of the computer server, telephone equipment and software giant, John Adams, said that, while he wanted to hire in America, he was being driven more and more to hire instead in countries such as Israel, India and France. 'Our tax policy is causing me to make decisions that I don't think is [*sic*] in the interest of our country, or even in our shareholders, long term,' he said.[12] This was the basic laws of supply in operation. If America's tax regime meant that investments abroad produced higher yields, jobs and capital would automatically flow there. As Dimon said pithily, if a little ungrammatically, 'Economics are economics.'[13]

Unconventional grammar, economically orthodox thinking

Dimon was right about the theory. Economists have always been uncomfortable with the distortionary potential of taxation. Corporate taxation has caused them particular discomfort, because they believe it creates a disincentive for investment, which they see as the engine of business activity.[14] As Kevin Hassett, an economist with the Conservative think tank the American Enterprise Institute, who would go on to become Chairman of Trump's Council of Economic Advisers, put it in 2011, corporate taxes were 'the economic equivalent of the ball and chain'.[15] It's a truism accepted by everyone from the OECD to the IMF to the World Economic Forum.[16] The near unanimity among leaders of economic thought has fed through to media coverage, so that articles on business taxes typically contain background paragraphs or asides such as 'Studies have shown that high corporate-tax rates discourage business investment and entrepreneurship',[17] without any suggestion that the contrary could be the case. The economic orthodoxy has prompted countries from Canada to New Zealand to cut their corporate tax rates in the hope of giving their economies a shot in the arm.[18]

Because of the perceived injurious impact of corporate taxes on investment, reductions are also often seen as having modest impacts on exchequer receipts. One UK study suggested that the increased business activity that would result from a corporate tax cut meant that the government would regain half the revenue it was calculated to lose if one had assumed no behavioural response (in other words, the 'dynamic' cost was half the 'static' cost), because after the cut the actual behavioural response of additional activity meant there would be so much more profit being taxed.[19] Another study that examined the 'dynamic' cost of tax cuts – the cost adjusted for the impact of induced growth effects – constructed a model for the United States in which an estimated 70 to 90 per cent of the revenue lost by slicing the rate would be recouped thanks to the increase in the tax base.[20] Hassett, who had been an adviser to the presidential campaigns of George W. Bush, John McCain and Mitt Romney, went further, telling a Congressional inquiry in 2011 that his analysis 'found significant evidence that a reduction of the corporate tax rate in the US would increase corporate tax revenue'.[21]

But there have been powerful dissenting voices. Just as Dimon hit the airwaves and editorial pages, America's two richest men began to voice a counter view. Microsoft co-founder Bill Gates told one interviewer that 'the idea that there's some direct connection, that all these innovators are on strike because tax rates are at 35 per cent on corporations, that's just such nonsense.'[22] The investment legend Warren Buffett said that US companies were exaggerating the extent to which tax put them at a disadvantage in regard to foreign peers. 'Corporate taxes are not strangling American competitiveness,' he stated.[23] Their critics argued that this is just what you would expect from a couple of liberal businessmen. Gates was a self-professed 'fan of progressive taxation',[24] who believed that America's 'greatest assets come from government-supplied investments'.[25] Buffet had long argued that the rich should pay more taxes, and even had a plan for a minimum tax rate on millionaires named after him.[26] Their views chimed with others at the more progressive end of the political spectrum, and also with public opinion: in regular surveys between 2004 and 2019, pollster Gallup has found up to 73 per cent and never less than 62 per cent of Americans believed corporations paid too little tax.[27]

It's not hard to understand why people were sceptical. Dimon might have been arguing for what he believed to be long-term advantages for the whole of society, but it was clear that, in the short term, there would be a shift in resources from the government to the richest in society. A corporate tax cut immediately and automatically increases the net profits of businesses, leaving more money for investors. This can facilitate an increase in dividend payouts and also leads to an immediate jump in share prices. Both benefit shareholders who may own stock directly or indirectly via unit trusts or pension funds. But only around half of Americans do,[28] because millions have no pension or save via bank accounts or government bonds. Of the half with some form of equity ownership, the richest 10 per cent own most of the stock market – 84 per cent of shares by value, according to one 2017 study.[29] The other group of direct beneficiaries of a stock market rise are top executives, since their pay is usually directly tied to share prices and net earnings per share.

In the longer term, economic theory argues that the increased net rates of return will encourage companies to invest more money into the country, which over time should lift profits and thereby help tax revenues recover, while also creating new jobs and putting upward pressure on wages (which can also lead to additional tax receipts).

Whether tax cuts are a good idea depends on how strong the second effect is and how long it takes to kick in. Some adherents of the neoclassical viewpoint predict corporate tax cuts can work their magic in months;[30] others say up to a decade.[31] Of course, people like Buffett say never.

With so many countries cutting their corporate taxes between 2005 and 2015, you might think there would be plenty of case studies to prove the argument definitively one way or the other. However, most of the cuts were small and, since national economies are complex animals, it was often difficult, if not impossible, to tell whether a particular tax change was the true cause of any particular outcome.

There was one nation, however, that enacted such a dramatic series of cuts that it is possible to arrive at a more confident assessment of their consequences. Between 2008 and 2015, Britain moved from a corporate tax rate of 30 per cent to 20 per cent.

The process had commenced at the height of the financial crisis, when the Prime Minister, Gordon Brown, took the decision to move from 30 per cent to 28 per cent, having already as Chancellor in the previous decade cut the rate in 1997 and 1999 in pursuit of an ambition to 'have the lowest corporation tax rate of any of our major competitors – Germany, France, America or Japan'.[32] These were not the traditional moves of a left-of-centre government, and were the result of considerable soul-searching for Labour and a two-year review that had begun while Brown was still in opposition. The Labour old guard had remained unconvinced. But Brown had been persuaded by such experts as Chris Wales, an Arthur Andersen tax accountant who had advised Labour on tax and economic policy since the 1980s and who was well versed in the emerging academic literature on tax economics and their generally critical stance on corporate taxes. 'In the end, politics has to take some account of the underlying economics,' he told me in 2013.[33] Such a view played well with the more pragmatic Labour party of the 1990s.

The Conservative government under David Cameron that replaced Brown in May 2010 went even further. A month after their victory, the new Chancellor of the Exchequer George Osborne unveiled plans to slash the rate by at least 4 percentage points. In the years that followed he gradually went further, taking the rate to 20 per cent in 2015, and indicating a desire to go ultimately to 15 per cent.[34]

According to the Treasury in 2016, the results spoke for themselves. 'These reforms have been central to the UK's economic recovery,' it reported. 'The UK has been one of the fastest growing economies in the G7 and the OECD forecasts the UK to be the fastest-growing G7 economy in 2016. There are 2.3 million more people in employment since 2010.'[35] This was all powered – as a chart in the Treasury report vividly showed – by a 26 per cent rise in business investment since the first quarter of 2010.

But the icing on the cake was the reported price tag for all of this: zero. As Osborne told parliament: 'Not only have our corporation tax cuts given us the lowest corporation tax rate of all the advanced economies of the world, but we have seen a 20 per cent increase in receipts from corporation tax – because businesses are coming to this country, growing their businesses in this country.'[36]

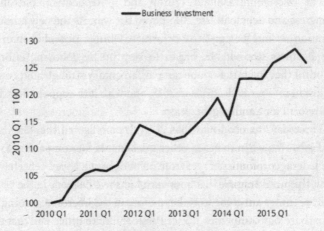

UK business investment since 2010 (indexed)

Graph and data source: HM Treasury

251

Before the Conservatives began the step-change in corporate tax policy, UK companies such as WPP Plc, the world's biggest advertising group,[37] and publisher Informa Plc [38] had shifted their headquarters overseas to escape Britain's tax system. Now, UK ministers noted, they were back again. In addition, businesses that included the Houston-based oil driller Rowan Companies, Chicago-based insurer AON Corp and US car parts manufacturer Delphi Automotive were relocating to Britain.[39] True believers were cock-a-hoop. The *Wall Street Journal* editorial page gushed about 'Britain's Laffer Curve', noting that 'While America dawdles over tax reform, new evidence from Britain shows that cutting corporate tax rates is a tax revenue winner.'[40] 'Good, reasoned, globally-minded economic policy in the United Kingdom', was the judgement of the Business Roundtable, which comprised the chief executives of 200 of the country's biggest corporations and was perhaps the main corporate cheerleader for tax cuts at the time.[41] One scholar at the conservative Cato Institute lauded 'the United Kingdom's smart moves on corporate taxation' and prayed that 'maybe this more sensible approach eventually will spread to the United States.'[42]

The election of Donald Trump and a Republican-controlled Congress and Senate in late 2016 paved the way. As the new administration set out its legislative priorities, Dimon, now chairman of the Business Roundtable, began to step up his lobbying efforts, mindful that the rare Republican parliamentary stranglehold could be lost in mid-term elections in 2018, and with it the opportunity for tax reform for another generation.

Three days before Christmas 2017, Trump signed the Tax Cuts and Jobs Act, which, among other tax benefits for companies, took the federal corporate tax rate from 35 per cent to 21 per cent. In his view, this would ensure that 'more products will be made in the USA. A lot of things are going to be happening in the USA. We're going to bring back our companies.'[43] Vice President Mike Pence said that the changes would 'unleash the boundless potential of the American economy for every American'.[44] Kevin Hassett predicted the US GDP growth rate would jump to between 3 and 5 per cent – around twice its long-term average – while Treasury Secretary Steve Mnuchin predicted a surge in exchequer receipts.

There was early anecdotal evidence that businesses' behaviour would, indeed, conform with economic theory and the administration's expectations. A raft of companies issued announcements saying they intended to pay bonuses to their staff. AT&T said it would give 200,000 employees a $1,000 bonus each and invest an additional $1 billion in the United States.[45] Boeing said the tax cuts would provide 'additional billions of dollars' to invest in training and to expand production of the 737 and Dreamliner jet ranges.[46] One of the biggest announcements came from behind the classic 1960s façade of glass and vertical steel mullions at 270 Park Avenue. JP Morgan issued a press release saying that, following 'recent changes to the US corporate tax system', it planned a five-year $20 billion investment programme.[47] A day later, Dimon appeared at the World Economic Forum in Davos and predicted an acceleration in the US economy.[48] It seemed like a perfect example of economic theory and empirical evidence illuminating the path to good policy.

But there was a problem. Amid all the celebrations and buoyant forecasts, some Americans noticed that the country that had championed low corporate taxes most loudly over the previous two decades was beginning to have second thoughts.

Another sighting of the Laffer Curve?

As the US put its lower tax rate into effect, George Osborne's successor, Philip Hammond, claimed that corporate tax cuts since 2010 had increased revenues by £20 billion[49] – a 56 per cent rise. But by now even people in his own party were losing faith in the policy. They knew the apparently robust receipts were not all they seemed.

For a start, the £19.5 billion increase between the 2009–10 tax year and 2017–18[50] ignored inflation. Adjusted for that, the increase was only £10 billion, or £8 billion if one stripped out receipts from the tax surcharge imposed on banks in 2016.[51] Hammond also ignored the 6 per cent increase in the UK population from 2009 to 2017,[52] and the fact that the cuts in corporation tax had made it more tax-efficient for individuals to pay themselves via dividends rather than through salary. In response, tens of thousands of tradespeople, computer programmers and others had set themselves up as companies rather than sole traders or employees. One OBR estimate was that such tax-motivated incorporations would boost Corporation Tax receipts by almost £3 billion, but in the process reduce income tax and national insurance receipts by over £6 billion.[53]

But more importantly, the earlier claim that the corporation tax cut was self-funding – an example of the Laffer Curve in action – proved to rest on very shaky foundations indeed, since it was shown to rely on a comparison of the receipts from the bottom of the crisis to those of the post-recovery period: the kind of trough-to-peak comparison no sane statistician would make. An altogether different picture emerged when one looked at the companies that were affected by the tax cut. Since 2005, the 100 Group – the collective voice of 100 of the UK's largest companies – has produced an annual assessment of their tax contributions in terms of money paid or gathered from staff and customers. In its first report, the 100 Group estimated that its members paid corporation tax of £9.1 billion. The figure for 2007 was £14.5 billion. In 2017 it stood at just £6.4 billion – half the 2005 level on an inflation-adjusted basis.[54]

Even if corporate tax cuts had not paid for themselves, it might have been possible to justify them if they had led to a clear increase in overall growth. But again the evidence wasn't there. True, as the Treasury said in 2016, the UK had performed more strongly than some other economies in the immediately preceding years, but that was a reflection of the sharper-than-peers' drop in the economy

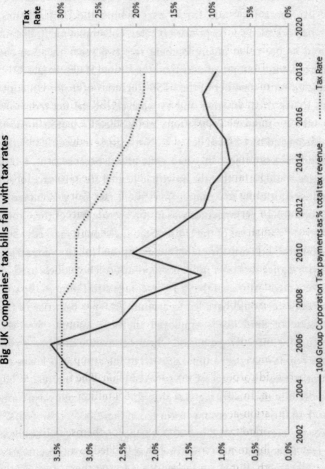

Big UK companies' tax bills fall with tax rates

—— 100 Group Corporation Tax payments as % total tax revenue ········ Tax Rate

Data source: The 100 Group

during the crash due to the country's reliance on financial services. Looking across the cycle, the UK's performance didn't seem unusual. It was 2015 when Britain recovered its 2007 peak GDP per capita level in real, inflation-adjusted terms – on average the same as other EU countries,[55] and three years behind the United States, which had not then cut corporate tax rates. On employment, Britain achieved its pre-crash unemployment rate two years ahead of the European Union, but no quicker than the United States. In late 2012, I contacted every member of the FTSE 100 index of major UK companies to ask them whether and to what extent the tax reduction they and their industry associations had lobbied for had influenced their hiring and investment decision. Not a single one could identify a single business project that had gone ahead because of it. Not a single one could claim that the move had helped create or save jobs.[56]

And when it came to Britain's investment rate as a percentage of GDP, its 2007–15 performance was in the bottom half of the Group of 7 nations: just ahead of the United States, although markedly better than Italy.[57] Looking through time, as opposed to across countries, the performance was even more disappointing. The models used by the government estimated that a 1 percentage point drop in the corporate tax rate should have led to around a 0.2 per cent rise in the total value of hard assets employed in the economy. However, between 2010 and 2017 – a period when the tax rate dropped 9 percentage points – average annual growth in the capital stock was 1.6 per cent, versus an average of 2.2 per cent from 1998 to 2007. What was especially disappointing was that the 2010–17 rate wasn't any better than the 1.6 per cent rate recorded in the 2008–9 crisis years.[58]

Over the course of 2012 and 2013, the government's independent financial forecaster, the Office for Budget Responsibility, whose model assumed tax cuts automatically led to business investment growth, found itself repeatedly revising down its forecasts for investment spending.[59] By the middle of 2015, investment had grown half as much as the OBR had predicted in 2010.[60]

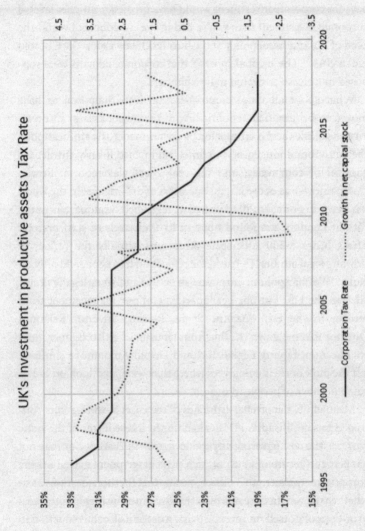

UK's Investment in productive assets v Tax Rate

——— Corporation Tax Rate   .... Growth in net capital stock

Data source: Office for National Statistics

Three years into the strategy, even those who had been canvassing for the cuts accepted things were not going to plan. 'Any model you have for corporate investment would have predicted a higher level of corporate investment than you've had in the last couple of years,' the head of tax and fiscal policy at the business lobby group the CBI told me in 2013.[61] The 'animal spirits'[62] that corporate tax cuts were supposed to unleash appeared to be a chimera.

What about all those companies that were supposed to have moved to Britain? The redomiciling of big corporations captures a lot of headlines and is trumpeted by governments as a vindication of their economic strategies, but in Britain's case it only involved a handful of companies, and the real effect was modest. Rowan Companies – one of the largest operators of drilling rigs in the world – is a case in point. In 2014 I visited its registered headquarters in the City of London, but found none of its thousands of staff present. That's because 160 Aldersgate Street was actually the offices of Rowan's legal adviser. In truth, the relocation had happened only on paper. 'We changed our corporate structure and we're legally domiciled in the UK, but our headquarters and our management team remain in the US,' Suzanne Spera, Rowan's Investor Relations Director told me down the line from Houston.[63] Other banner movers like Aon, Liberty Global Inc. and Delphi Automotive similarly left the bulk of their employees where they were, and took on only a small number of people in Britain.

Meanwhile, the official estimates of the costs of the tax cuts continued to soar. By 2019, HMRC had upped its estimates of the static cost (i.e. the cost ignoring any induced growth that may or may not happen as a result of a cut) of each percentage point shaved off the corporation tax rate to £3 billion, prompting further questions as to whether the return in terms of extra investment was worth the tens of billions of pounds in revenue being foregone. For the reduction to 17 per cent this pointed to an annual cost of £33 billion, and even if one accepted the government's estimate that the 'dynamic' cost was half this, the £1.6 billion additional investment by 2021 that the tax minister David Gauke predicted in late 2015 still seems poor value for the taxpayer.[64]

The weak response to the tax cuts prompted increasing objections to the plans to proceed to a rate of just 17 per cent, even from the most ardent tax cut campaigners. 'I hope [the Chancellor] does rethink,' Bill Dodwell, the head of tax policy at accountants Deloitte told the *Financial Times* in November 2017. 'Business welcomed the drop to 20 per cent. Nobody seems to welcome the cut to 17 per cent.'[65] Finally, in November 2019, Prime Minister Boris Johnson axed the plan to reduce the rate further, arguing he'd rather spend the £6 billion pounds cost of it on the National Health Service.[66]

Tax cuts and job creation

Britain's experience may have been at odds with what theory and policymakers predicted would happen if one cut corporate tax rates, but it should perhaps have served as reassurance to one group: investors in US companies. In the years up to 2017, chief executives had lobbied for tax cuts, saying it would allow them to build more factories, open new entertainment venues and expand office parks. But although shareholders were excited about the extra cash they'd enjoy after tax cuts, they were also aware of the warning issued by analysts that companies might become less choosy about new investments, and might therefore waste money on low-return projects or value-destructive mergers and acquisitions.[67] After the tax act was signed in December 2017, analysts at Morgan Stanley even ranked companies and sectors in terms of 'reinvestment risk' (tobacco fared well due to 'fewer investment options', but the packaged-food sector had potential for earnings-depressing capital expenditure and hiring).[68]

On earnings calls at the end of 2017 and early 2018, chief executives received a barrage of questions about how they planned to spend the additional profit they would enjoy. The word they used again and again was 'discipline'. They might have more cash to play with, but they were anxious to reassure investors that they would spend cautiously, and that they would keep a tight control of wages (so much, then, for the claim that tax cuts benefitted everyone, and for the calculation made by Trump's economic adviser Hassett in 2006 and 2010 that for every 1 per cent drop in the tax rate, wages would rise between 0.5 and 1 per cent).[69] One analysis of transcripts of conference calls S&P 500 companies held with investors in the first quarter of 2018 found that only 22 per cent mentioned planned increases in investment that were linked to the tax cuts.[70] In fact, healthy investment levels were reported for the first half of that year, albeit at levels below 2017, which was a bumper year by many metrics. But as the months passed, it appeared that chief executives were indeed being cautious. Most of the additional cashflow reported was going on higher dividends and share buybacks rather than new equipment, factories and research. As analysts at UBS bank said in November of that year, 'When the tax cuts were enacted, we did not believe they would directly boost investment spending, and that view appears to be consistent with the data. Instead, the tax cuts were used to buy back equity.'[71] The Berkeley tax economist Alan Auerbach, who collaborated with Hassett on several papers, said in October 2018 that 'Investment has been OK, nothing spectacular. If you didn't know there had been a tax bill passed, you wouldn't say, "A-ha, something is going on."' Investment growth rates reverted to pre-2017 levels in the second half of 2018, before turning negative in 2019.[72] A survey of businesses in January 2019 by the National Association of Business Economics found that 'A large majority of respondents – 84 per cent – indicate that, one year after its passage, the 2017 Tax Cuts and Jobs Act has not caused their firms to change hiring or investment plans.'[73]

Nor was there much evidence for the trickle-down effect of tax cuts. An analysis of statements from 150 companies in early 2018 by the investment bank Bank of America Merrill Lynch found that 30 per cent had announced one-time bonuses for staff and that nearly 25 per cent had said they would increase wages.[74] But as time passed there was little concrete evidence for this happening. Indeed, Bureau of Labour data showed a dip in real, inflation-adjusted earnings growth in 2018 before it rose modestly in 2019.[75] Across those two years, the increase averaged 1 per cent – beneath the average for 2015–17 and modest for an economy which had been at full employment for over three years.[76] The result was also well short of the 20 to 40 per cent increase in wages that Hassett's studies said workers could have expected from a 40 per cent cut in the tax rate.

As for those big investment plans announced at the time the tax act was signed, they proved similarly elusive. It's impossible to know what individual companies would have done in the absence of tax cuts – they don't publish their capital expenditure plans in a way that would allow one to judge. However, the announcements that followed the signing of the Tax Cuts and Jobs Act made it clear that the impression given of the act spurring huge new investments didn't quite fit the reality. JP Morgan affords a good example. It had claimed it was putting a $20 billion plan into operation. It was certainly true that it was expanding, but when Marianne Lake, the bank's Chief Financial Officer, was asked to comment, she said:

I wouldn't really put tax reform as being a primary reason for what we're doing on investments. I would say that we have identified the opportunity to accelerate capabilities that are consistent with our clients' strategic long-term goals, and so we've been leaning into that this year.[77]

Some of the $20 billion investments, including an expansion in small business lending, were announced before the tax cut[78] and, like other companies, the bank didn't publish capital expenditure plans in a way that would allow one to compare actual investments with investment plans in the absence of tax cuts. It's also worth noting that, while some new branches did open, a larger number closed as JP Morgan, in line with its competitors, continued to reduce its branch network.[79]

On the tax revenue side, the figures were equally disappointing. In the 2018 fiscal year, corporate tax receipts in the US collapsed to $205 billion from $297 billion, before recovering somewhat in 2019 to $230 billion. In inflation-adjusted terms, receipts were down 26 per cent[80] after two years, despite a growing economy and corporate profits holding steady.[81] By the end of 2019, the official data, independent economic analysis and statements from industry executives all pointed to corporate tax cuts having failed to spur business investment, and blown a hole in the budget.

Which begs large questions about the underlying theory.

Investment theory vs investment practice

Much of the rhetoric that surrounds corporate tax cuts has nothing to do with economic theory, or is actually at odds with it. Economists don't argue that companies are 'unshackled' by tax cuts, that 'corporate confidence' is 'unleashed' in the C-suite or that companies will definitely be buying some more machinery and hiring more machinists just because they find themselves with a few spare million in the bank after paying their tax bill. Neoclassical economics regards commercial transactions as automatic responses to price signals. The predictions it makes are founded on a strictly mechanistic view of human behaviour. Theory states that people save and invest because they expect to receive a return, and that their willingness to invest is influenced by the return they receive: they will invest more if a higher return is offered and less if a lower return is offered. Tax comes into this because it has an impact on the return the investor receives.

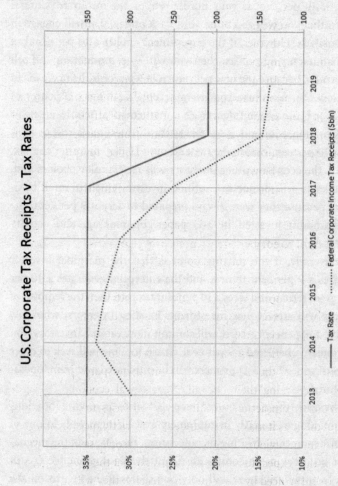

U.S. Corporate Tax Receipts v Tax Rates

— Tax Rate .... Federal Corporate Income Tax Receipts ($bln)

Data source: U.S. Bureau of Economic Analysis

Take a situation where you can achieve a 10 per cent return by engaging in a small manufacturing business – perhaps by purchasing a 3-D printer and hiring someone to operate it to make paper clips. If 10 per cent is your hurdle rate or the minimum annual return that you will accept on your cash outlay, you will engage in the business. However, if the government applies a 10 per cent tax on manufacturing profits, then you will stop production and sell the printer, because the new net return of 9 per cent the tax leads to is below the minimum you deem acceptable. It's not a matter of mood or business confidence: it's a mathematical requirement. In this situation, economists would say the business has a cost of capital of 10 per cent before the tax and over 11 per cent after the tax. Across the economy other investors will face similar choices and, while some will decide to continue investing in their small businesses because they were always prepared to accept 9 per cent, the total amount invested in 3-D paper-clip making, and activity undertaken, will fall.

Conversely, if the starting point is that the marginal investor requires a 9 per cent return, and the enterprise generates a 10 per cent gross return and faces a 10 per cent tax rate, then the removal of the tax will attract new investment. Existing investors, who now receive a 10 per cent return, will commit more capital. Investors who previously considered a 9 per cent return too low will seek to enter the business. More 3-D printers will be purchased and more operators hired.

Obviously when one moves from a situation involving individuals investing personally in equipment and hiring people to one of large corporations making such decisions, the nature of the mechanism becomes more complicated, but the basic principle is still seen to apply. Investors will only buy shares if the return on the investment – the long-term discounted value of dividend flows – matches their desired rate of return, and this determines the return that the business must offer, which in turn determines the hurdle rate, or minimum return, the business must achieve when assessing whether to invest in a new factory or copper mine. A reduction in the corporation tax rate makes it easier for the company to meet its investors' desired rate of return, and projects which did not meet the previous hurdle rate are now capable of delivering a net return that investors find acceptable. In the short term, more money is spent on buying productive assets. It is a simple matter of supply and demand. If the supplier of money for investment is offered a higher price (return) for their money, they will supply more money for investment.

Economists hold that not only is this response certain, but it is also measurable, via what is known as the elasticity of investment, relative to changes in the cost of capital or to changes in tax rates. If the elasticity is high, then a small tax cut can have a big impact on capital expenditure – investment in hard assets by companies. It might even make the cut self-funding, spurring growth and corporate profitability to such an extent that the total tax revenue remains unchanged, even though it's being levied at a lower rate.

Studies done over recent decades have led many economists to see a clear proportional link between tax rates and investment. The UK's Office of Budget Responsibility has said its main forecasting model (the same model that has consistently over-estimated Britain's business investment levels) estimates that every 1 percentage point reduction in the corporate tax rate leads to around a 0.5 per cent rise in business investment.[82] Others have estimated larger impacts.[83]

There's a rather significant problem with this theory, though. It may be in line with Adam Smith's view that entrepreneurs' and financiers' willingness to invest in an enterprise is driven by the return they can expect to receive from the activity.[84] But when economists first actually tried to measure what drove companies' decisions about how much to spend building their operations, they discovered that such expansions and the rate of return did not correlate closely.

In the early 1900s the Americans Thomas Nixon Carver[85] and John Maurice Clark and the Frenchman Albert Aftalion[86] devised what came to be known as the Accelerator Theory of investment.[87] They observed that both in the short and long term, investment by businesses and individuals was closely correlated with demand in the economy, which could be measured via total spending or output (which had to be equal). It followed, they concluded, that firms were adjusting their stock of output-generating physical assets, such as equipment, towards a level that was proportional to the level of output customers would demand. It was a notion that had an intuitive ring to it, and seemed to reflect everyday experience. Quite simply, if consumer demand for products rises, it seems superficially reasonable at least that businesses will expand their facilities to meet this demand. The theory also matches what companies say they do. To this day, when the chief executives of big publicly-traded companies discuss their capital expenditure plans on quarterly conference calls with investors and analysts, my experience is that they almost always tie those plans to expected demand for their own goods or services. Surveys of businesses consistently say much the same thing.

It follows from this that if national income rises, so does investment, and that other factors such as the cost of capital and corporate tax rates have little impact on the outcome. In the real world, the accelerator model provides predictions that, over time, closely mirror actual outcomes, as the graphs on the following page from the April 2015 IMF World Economic Outlook show.

Many mainstream economists have traditionally felt uncomfortable that the accelerator theory doesn't fit with the broader neoclassical economic world view of commercial activity being driven by rational, profit-maximising individuals and firms whose actions are guided by price. In terms of investment in assets, the neoclassical framework lays down that firms should only increase investment in fixed assets if these become cheaper or the return from owning them rises. A hope of future economic growth doesn't

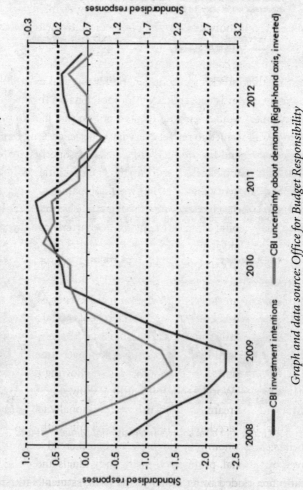

UK Investment Intentions and Demand Uncertainty

CBI investment intentions
CBI uncertainty about demand (Right-hand axis, inverted)

Graph and data source: Office for Budget Responsibility

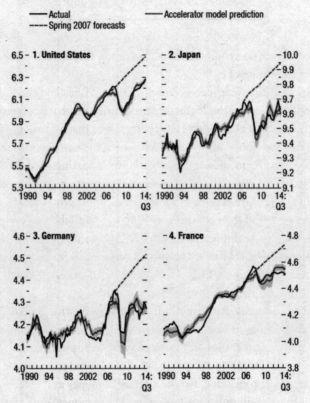

Accelerator Model: Real Business Investment
(Log index)

Actual business investment has been close to the level predicted by the accelerator model since the crisis.

Graph and data source: International Monetary Fund

constitute a clear pricing signal to the firm, since a bigger market size doesn't necessarily mean bigger margins. Other criticisms have been made of the accelerator theory too, not least that it doesn't explain how or why a firm would respond if labour costs rose. The neoclassical framework offers a clear prediction: a rational firm cuts its use of labour and increases investment in equipment as a share of revenue, since equipment has become cheaper and labour relatively more expensive. The accelerator principle also doesn't predict how firms whose investment is apparently driven only by demand react to technological changes. Neoclassical theory accommodates the adoption of new technology by explaining that technological change effectively makes equipment cheaper, prompting a profit-maximiser to employ more of it.

In 1930 the American economist Irving Fisher laid the foundations for an alternative to the accelerator principle that was consistent with neoclassical theory.[88] His argument was that a firm or individual invests money up to the point where the net present value of investment turns neutral – that is to say, investing money only in projects that repay the investment and generate a positive or zero return. Firms are expected to invest in the most profitable opportunities first, and then continue backing less profitable projects up to the point where the expected return of the projects on offer hits zero, and then stop. The theory holds that no one will invest in a project whose net present value – the total value of expected future cash flows, minus the cash invested – is negative.

Fisher also calculated that, whatever happens with demand, total investment has to be equal to total savings, because this represents the money that is used to buy shares and bonds in companies and feed cash through to the purchase of hard, productive assets. And from that he concluded that the amount of money available for such investments will only rise if savers put more money aside, and they will only do this if the rate of return they receive rises.

It was an intellectually coherent idea, but suffered the drawback that saving, investment and rates of return are not actually that well correlated. It may seem logical to argue that individuals spend rather than save when dividend yields or bank or corporate bond interest rates are low, but in reality people don't behave this way. They have other things to think about – for example, the need to build up a sufficient nest egg for retirement (ironically, in this scenario, a high rate of return could actually deter saving, because less cash will need to be put by to achieve the desired nest egg).[89] More importantly, Fisher's principles didn't constitute a mathematical model that would allow one to calculate exactly how higher net rates of return would feed through to investment levels. It was a model that would continue to elude economists for decades.

Whatever the drawbacks of Fisher's theory, however, politicians began to offer tax incentives on the presumption that in the real world the mechanism he described did actually exist. As the economist Otto Eckstein noted in 1962:

> Tax devices to stimulate investment have certainly been the greatest fad in economic policy in the past ten years . . . all sorts of liberalised depreciation schemes, investment allowances and tax exemptions were embraced with enthusiasm all over the non-Communist world.[90]

The problem, though, was that not only was the model propping up such incentives highly questionable, it also didn't fit with observable experience. Survey after survey of business people showed that they displayed a frustrating lack of interest in net rates of return. In one, conducted in Britain in the early 1960s, 181 executives were asked whether, over the previous seven years, any of the tax rises[91] that had been introduced had prompted them to abandon a plan to introduce a new plant or equipment. Not a single one said they had.[92]

This didn't deter fans of neoclassical theory. Perhaps, they thought, appearances were misleading. Perhaps rates of return *were* having a real impact on the supply of investment flows, but the influence was being overshadowed by other economic factors. After all, the world is a complex place.

In 1963, a young economist at the University of California in Berkeley called Dale Jorgenson penned a paper that would spark renewed hope that neoclassical theory and actual investment behaviour could be reconciled.[93] Jorgenson was not impressed by what he regarded as the acute shortcomings of the accelerator theory. To his mind its success in describing and forecasting investment rates might well be just coincidence. 'If a model does not perform satisfactorily by the standards of econometrics, it must be rejected,' he wrote, 'however closely it parallels historical and institutional accounts of the same economic behaviour.' He was also unimpressed by the surveys of executives that appeared to bear out the model, declaring them so scientifically 'defective' that 'no reliance can be placed on conclusions based on them.' Conversely, he was undeterred by neoclassical theory's failure to predict investment behaviour, dismissing earlier attempts as not 'based on a fully rigorous statement of the theory'.[94]

Jorgenson constructed a mathematical model in which investment was a function of the return on assets. To do so he invoked an innovation known as the 'User Cost of Capital', which envisaged the cost of investment in hard assets as being equal to a conceptual rental rate for such assets. Jorgenson's model also factored in taxation, in as much as tax rates impacted investment levels by influencing the user cost of capital.[95]

Critics said that the model was based on unrealistic assumptions (for example, that changes in the level of hard assets employed in a business were costless and happened immediately). But it was nevertheless an ingenious theoretical construct. Through the 1960s, Jorgenson and others worked to gather empirical evidence that his model worked – that it could explain and predict investment behaviour. In a 1967 paper he even claimed to have found decisive proof, using the model to show how 1954 and 1962 corporate tax changes had affected business investment.[96] But when others reviewed Jorgenson's work, they found a troubling feature. The point of using complex calculations rather than simple correlations (which in this case suggested only that demand influenced investment in a material way) is to strip out all other factors that influence investment, to illustrate the impact of the user cost of capital. However, Jorgenson's calculations captured demand effects: he was effectively relying upon the accelerator effect to achieve his impressively accurate results.[97] When others stripped the calculations back to focus purely on the impact of changes in the user cost of capital on investment levels, the results showed little correlation.[98]

Undeterred, and galvanised by the decline in the standing of Keynesianism in the 1970s, those sympathetic to Jorgenson's world view continued to innovate and tweak. Martin Feldstein produced studies that employed models similar to Jorgenson's to claim that the rate of return was materially influencing investment levels.[99] Meanwhile, James Tobin devised an alternative model, the Q Theory, which held that firms invested money when the market placed a higher value on the investments than they cost the firm, and that therefore the net rates of return demanded by the market would influence the level of investment. But the problem remained. However framed or argued, when it came to the acid test of using the cost of capital or rates of return to predict investment levels both the Jorgensonian and Q Theory models fell noticeably short. 'The neoclassical school may have had the theoretical high ground,' Kevin Hassett observed in 2002. '[But] empirical implementations of neoclassical models using time-series data have not been successful.'[100]

And if the net rate of return and investment levels were not correlated, it didn't support the claim that the former (or tax rates, which partly determine the net rate) influenced the latter.

So when politicians and others on both sides of the Atlantic advocated cutting corporate taxes to boost growth, they did so without firm economic evidence for their view. Or as the economists Robert S. Chirinko and Robert Eisner wrote in 1983:

[To institute tax incentives] on the assumption that they will have commensurate effects in increasing investment must . . . rest essentially on faith. Faith is indeed sometimes rewarded. But for our part, in this instance, we remain agnostic.[101]

According to Kevin Hassett, perhaps the loudest voice in America for corporate tax cuts over the past thirty years, 'As the 1990s began, the conventional wisdom – based on a large literature utilising time-series data – was that tax policy had little or no effect on business fixed investment.'[102]

That, however, wasn't the end of the story. In the course of the 1990s, faster computers, more sophisticated modelling software and easier access to data sets facilitated a large expansion in empirical work. Gradually studies started to emerge that reported statistically significant (which isn't to say 'practically significant', or having a meaningful effect) links between investment levels and the cost of capital and corporate tax rates.[103] Hassett and his co-authors produced a whole host of papers that purported to demonstrate this for the United States[104] and twelve of fourteen other countries they examined.[105] In Britain, Michael Devereux, an economist who would later go on to head the Oxford University Centre for Business Taxation, a venture co-founded by Gordon Brown's adviser Chris Wales after he left government, published a number of studies that similarly showed that investment levels and corporate tax rates operated in step. He suggested in one paper that a tax change which led to a 1 to 2 per cent fall in the cost of capital could permanently increase investment by around 5 per cent.[106] Another, of which he was the co-author, found that a rise of $1 in tax would reduce wages by 49 cents.[107] Throughout the 2000s and 2010s, in fact, a whole array of studies seemed to show that corporate taxes influenced investment, jobs and productivity levels. Some produced by the OECD in the mid- to late-2000s proved particularly influential.

By running GDP levels across different countries through complex models, they identified corporate tax as having the greatest dampening effect of all forms of tax on GDP (the studies didn't look at the stimulative effect of the expenditure that taxation supports, but, since the method of gathering revenue doesn't impact how stimulative this expenditure is, this wasn't necessary). Not surprisingly, these studies caught the attention of policymakers around the world. Some supporters of corporate tax cuts conceded that because so many factors shape GDP the OECD research was problematic. But others welcomed it with open arms. David Gauke, then Britain's minister in charge of taxation, even quoted it to me once when I asked him why he had decided to cut corporate taxes.

Once, most of the research in this area had been carried out in the US. Now experts in other countries piled in with national reports and cross-country comparisons. Their findings certainly weren't unanimous[108] or unequivocal. Even Michael Devereux noted in one 1994 paper that 'the apparent irrelevance of tax considerations that appear in principle to establish powerful incentive effects remains perturbing.'[109] In time, he would conclude that the user cost of capital did not have a powerful influence on investment.[110]

But, using models often based on Jorgenson's analysis, economists increasingly came to support his central thesis that net returns and therefore tax rates were key drivers of investment.[111] And, partly influenced by this work, governments cut corporate tax rates with promises to voters that it would prompt companies to build more factories, programming centres and research labs, bringing more and higher-paying jobs. As we've seen, however, the two countries that followed these policies most assiduously failed to see the projected benefits. Somewhere along the line, the world didn't conform to the theory. What went wrong?

Why tax cuts don't boost investment

The cut in the US federal corporate tax rate in 2018 to 21 per cent from 35 per cent[112] gave companies a big, sudden increase in their net return on capital of around 1 to 2 percentage points.[113] Orthodox economic theory holds that this should have led them to drop their targeted rate of return, or 'hurdle' rates, by a similar amount, a change that would have led to a wave of new investment. But that's not what happened.

As Robert Lewis, Chief Financial Officer of Silgan Holdings Inc., which makes the tin cans that hold Campbell's Soup and Del Monte Fruits, told one analyst: 'There's no question that with the lower cash tax rate, your after-tax returns look better, so . . . on the margin, there's opportunity for us to put some good value-creating projects on the list [of projects to pursue].' But, in practice, this didn't happen. Lewis went on to say: 'I think it's incumbent upon us to make sure that we don't open that gap too much so that we're taking on projects that we actually aren't earning the kind of return that we would be accustomed to [previously].'[114] Some companies simply increased the net return they demanded so that they actually ended up screening projects exactly as they did before. JP Morgan, for example, increased its targeted return on tangible common equity[115] – the net return target it focused on —from 15 per cent to 17 per cent.[116] Dimon said that this was necessary to protect against rivals potentially using their tax savings to reduce product prices and, in time, erode his margins. Nor has this been a wholly US phenomenon. A study by the Bank of England in 2018 found that between 2000 and 2015 investment levels in Britain had been relatively unresponsive to changes in the cost of capital. As in the United States in the wake of the tax cuts, the BoE found that British firms over the period had not shifted down their gross hurdle rates in line with drops in the cost of capital.[117] Quite simply, executives' decisions were not influenced by higher net returns in the way theory said they should be.

Insofar as investment levels did come in somewhat higher than previously expected in 2018 (before collapsing in 2019), an IMF study found this was a result of the increased economy-wide demand generated by the tax cuts.[118] One might say that at least this shows the tax cut did have a beneficial impact, even if not in the precise way economists forecasted. But there's a problem with justifying a corporate tax cut for its demand-stoking benefits, rather on the supply-side basis that it will prompt an increase in investment and thereby the supply of goods and services in the economy. If one's aim is to lift demand in the economy through fiscal measures, one should seek the mechanism that generates the most additional spending for any given cost to the exchequer. A government could spend more money – building roads or increasing pensions. Or it could cut some of the hundreds of taxes they typically levy. The question is: which policy tool gives the most bang for one's buck? Certainly not corporate tax cuts. It takes a while for higher net profits to feed through to additional dividends and for people to realise the higher capital gains that higher share prices generate. Besides, such gains accrue mainly (in terms of value) to the better-off, who have a tendency to save rather than to spend such windfalls. On the other hand, low earners typically spend all the money they earn, so giving them additional funds, or taking them away via tax hikes, tends to have an immediate impact on overall consumer spending. The temporary 2 per cent reduction in the payroll tax signed off by President Obama in 2010 shows both sides of the coin.[119] While it was in operation it boosted consumption, with retailers and analysts reporting clear demand effects. Within a month of its expiration on 1 January 2013, the value supermarket chain Wal-Mart was feeling the pain. One of its corporate vice presidents described the drop in sales the company was seeing as 'a total disaster', while another asked 'Where are all the customers? And where's their money?'[120] The company and financial analysts put the impact down to the rising payroll tax,[121] as did economists such as Richard Thaler. 'I wouldn't expect it to have much of an effect on BMW consumption,' he also wryly noted.[122] Such direct cause and effect do not exist in the world of corporate tax cuts.

Even at its most effective, a Keynesian stimulus doesn't create any magical flywheel effect on the economy. In economic terms, it has a limited multiplier effect, which is to say it simply brings consumption forward from a future period to today. That can make sense during a recession, when a dearth of demand risks causing long-term damage to the economy by sending waves of viable businesses to the wall, thereby reducing the economy's ability to bounce back (this is the thinking behind the massive bail-outs prompted by the novel coronavirus pandemic in 2020). Additional demand can also prolong a boom, but there's little sense to bringing forward demand to a period when there is already sufficient demand. No one suggests a Keynesian stimulus creates a magical improvement in the long-term productive capacity of the economy, and times of strong growth are the times governments should be putting money aside for rainy days (such as pandemics), rather than racking up further debt with unfunded tax cuts. Tax cuts today must translate into spending cuts or tax rises later. Unless you accept that lower tax rates encourage more investment due to better rates of return, corporate tax cuts are expensive, and must be paid for by spending cuts or tax rises elsewhere. Britain's forgoing of around £10 billion a year in tax revenue due to corporate tax cuts during the 2010s contributed to cash shortages that required cuts in university tuition, which led to a collapse in part-time students,[123] a drop in school funding,[124] which contributed to rising class sizes,[125] and a reduction in funds available for infrastructure spending. In the 2020s, the cost of Britain's corporate tax cuts will more than double, with an inevitable impact on public investment. There's a social cost here, in terms of what the consequences will be for the less-well-off, although since economists' primary role is to tell us how to become richer as a society rather than how to distribute our wealth, this is not necessarily something for which they may be criticised. What is an indictment of the economic orthodoxy is that, from a purely financial perspective, there will also be an impact on the United Kingdom's long-term productive capacity. In other words, the outcome of a supply-side tax cut, aimed at expanding the factors of production that are actively generating wealth in the economy, may actually be a contraction in the supply of such factors.

The rash of governments that have slashed corporate tax rates in the past twenty years stands as one of the great triumphs of supply-side economics and of neoclassical theory more generally. It represents a strong acceptance on the part of policymakers of the principle that individuals and businesses respond predictably to price incentives. Yet this success has also provided a wide canvas on which the theory's flaws can be clearly seen. In particular, the failure of corporate tax cuts to spur the economy to a higher growth trajectory illustrates how the narrow neoclassical model of firms as simple collections of interchangeable factors, such as labour and equipment, cannot accurately explain or predict corporate behaviour, because it ignores most of the elements that influence investment and production decisions. Perhaps if orthodox economic models could factor in all the key objectives and limitations that individuals and businesses face in everyday life, economists would see that, often, ignoring price signals is the most rational thing for a utility-maximising individual or business to do.

CONCLUSION

The Sveriges Riksbank Prize in Economic Sciences in Memory of
Alfred Nobel is often disparaged as 'not a real Nobel Prize'. True, it
was first awarded sixty-eight years after the original Nobel prizes,
and was sponsored by the Swedish central bank rather than the
estate of the inventor of dynamite, Alfred Nobel. But, like the scientific Nobels, it is awarded by the Swedish Royal Academy of Sciences,
and presumably it and the Nobel Foundation accepted the proposal
of an award for economics because they believed it was consistent
with the general thrust of Nobel's intention: that the prizes he
endorsed should reward and celebrate those who have 'conferred the
greatest benefit to humankind'.[1]

That's probably why we don't have a Nobel prize for Homeopathy,
or indeed for slapstick or for the holding of one's breath under water
(I don't doubt that a sponsor for such awards could be found).
Though these activities may bring joy or relief to many, they don't
meet the threshold of contribution Nobel had in mind when he
decided to establish his awards.[2]

The speech Professor Erik Lundberg of the Royal Academy of
Sciences gave at the inaugural award of the economics prize gives a
sense as to why the Academy felt achievements in economics war-
ranted being put on the same footing as the great discoveries of

279

medicine, chemistry and physics. 'Economic science has developed increasingly in the direction of a mathematical specification and statistical quantification of economic contexts,' he said.

> Scientific analysis along these lines is used to explain such compli-
> cated economic processes as economic growth, cyclical fluctuations,
> and reallocations of economic resources for different purposes . . .
> The attempts of economists to construct mathematical models relat-
> ing to strategic economic relations, and then to specify these
> quantitatively with the help of statistical analysis of time series, have,
> in fact, proved successful.[3]

In the previous chapters I have argued that economists' claims to have explained the 'complicated economic processes' behind every-day life are often false. Does this mean economics ruins the economy? Obviously not always, and it's certainly not the only area where faith rather than fact drives policy decisions. But the profession's ortho-doxies have tarnished economic life for millions of people. There are the low-earners whose only hope of a decent living was an increase in the minimum wage, which never came because economists, with-out evidence, said it would actually make the poor poorer. There are the welfare recipients in places like Bransholme who pay a quarter of their income to the government in tobacco taxes because economists have argued, despite evidence to the contrary, that this is the best way to get them to smoke less. And there are hundreds of millions of workers around the world who have been persuaded that taxing their bosses lightly is in everyone's interests.

In September 2019, on my way back from Nashville, I stopped off at a faux French café in New York's Greenwich Village, where I met a recent recipient of the Nobel memorial prize in economics.[4] Paul Romer, a former University of Chicago scholar, told me he was actu-ally very surprised to have been so honoured. Initially, I assumed this was false modesty. But then I realised that he wasn't saying he wasn't worthy of the prize, but rather that he thought his attacks on the profession had put him beyond the pale. Though a former member of the Chicago School, he had come to the conclusion that its leading lights were 'frauds' and 'pseudo-scientists'.[5] In 2015, he published a paper, 'Mathiness in the Theory of Economic Growth',[6] which accused peers of using complex mathematics not to zero in on truth in a complex reality, but rather to hide flaws in their theories. He followed up a year later with a speech entitled 'The Trouble with Macroeconomics', in which he said he had 'observed more than three decades of intellectual regress' in macroeconomics, and slammed the prevalence of 'post-real models', comparing them to card tricks.[7] His calling out of specific grandees of the economic establishment, including Nobel Laureates, had shocked and irritated many in the profession.

Romer's criticisms were not made thoughtlessly or out of pique. He genuinely felt that a profession that takes itself seriously *should* call out those whose work doesn't stand up to scrutiny, even if they are pillars of the establishment. 'I just gave up on them. I decided to go full-on Voltaire,' he told me. 'It hasn't made me a popular guy.'

I was particularly struck by two general criticisms he made when we met. The first was that, in his view, the Chicago School, which helped set the economic orthodoxy at universities across the world for decades, was a libertarian, anti-government ideological project rather than a scientific endeavour. It was an analysis that reminded me of comments made over the years by such senior figures as Robert Shiller, and by those who felt economics was too inclined to be influenced by the political mood of the time.[8] The second criticism he made took the form of an observation that, as economics began to be taken more seriously, economists came to project themselves as possessing a unique understanding of the invisible forces that drive the world – forces that are hidden from and often counterintuitive to mere mortals. 'Economists actually started to take pride in their scientific credentials and the fact that they would deny things that were obvious to people,' he said.

Romer's comment reminded me of Nobel prize-winner James Buchanan's vitriolic retort to David Card and Alan Krueger's work on the minimum wage. An ex-Chicago alumnus, Buchanan was ideologically opposed to government interventions in the economy, but his anger seemed heightened by the professional implications of the two men's claim that an increase in price, in this case of wages, did not diminish demand (in other words, led to less hiring). 'Such a claim, if seriously advanced, becomes equivalent to a denial that there is even minimal scientific content in economics,' he declared.[9] His worry seemed to be that, without the basic models underpinning economics, the 'dismal science' simply became 'dismal'. To my mind, the danger of such a view is that it gives economists a vested interest in preserving previously accepted frameworks for explaining the world, whether or not they actually work in practice. I wasn't surprised, given the profession's disinclination to question flawed models or call out intellectual dishonesty, that Romer should have taken such a pessimistic view of its future. 'It's not entirely clear to me that we can even save economics at this time,' he said ruefully over his coffee.[10]

Not all agree. David Card cheerfully told me how labour economics is today dominated by people doing empirical work rather than theorists like Stigler, and noted than even the University of Chicago is no longer the bastion of anti-government thinking it used to be. But I think Romer's two criticisms are valid. It's certainly true, in the case of Chicago, for example, that ideology is not as powerful a force as it was in the days of Milton Friedman and George Stigler. But the pushback against its thinking has been only partial. As James Heckman, a Nobel-winning figure in the Chicago School observed in 2010, liberal economists, such as fellow Nobel winners Joseph Stiglitz and Paul Krugman, may have turned the tide against one of the school's two core teachings, namely the efficient markets hypothesis. But the 'claim that people react to incentives, and that incentives are important' has not faced the same challenge.[11] Chicago's Booth Business School regularly surveys a panel of eminent American economists of all political hues from across America about the economic questions of the day. Its polls on everything from taxation[12] to immigration[13] display a strong fealty among these economists to the core – highly questionable – proposition that people respond in a predictable way to price signals.

Behavioural economics is often held up as a solution to the problems that arise from viewing the world through the paradigm of simple Marshallian supply-and-demand curves, in that it allows for the adjustment of economic models to better reflect actual human decision-making. This involves incorporating traits such as 'limited rationality', 'low self-control', or 'a taste for fairness' into models. But are such things possible to measure? And what about the factors that determine economic behaviour that really cannot be quantified or squeezed into economic models? In a eulogy for his late teacher, Alfred Marshall, John Maynard Keynes wrote that 'The master-economist must possess a rare combination of gifts . . . . No part of man's nature or his institutions must be entirely outside his regard.'[14] Yet the economics practised by Marshall, Keynes and even behavioural economists ignores or is simply unable to account for the larger body of factors, including culture, political and judicial institutions, mood and love, that drive human economic behaviour. Orthodox models, of firms as collections of fungible factors like labour and capital, which can be rebalanced with relative ease, ignore most of the real-world challenges in providing goods and services, the overcoming of which is the very essence of wealth creation.

Where does this leave the study of how humanity goes about providing for its material needs?

Perhaps the answer is to resist starting with theory and to start with the world in front of us.

In the later years of his life, Ronald Coase began to muse on the state of economics, lamenting that, though Adam Smith and Alfred Marshall had, respectively, intended classical and neoclassical economics to be studies in real-world wealth creation, the subject had strayed far from considering how businesses actually operated.[15] The problem was what he referred to as 'Blackboard Economics': the focus on theory, mathematical models and the probing of data sets to identify correlations consistent with these. His view was that the profession had, in the twentieth century, gone down the rabbit hole of focusing on price sensitivity, and ignored most of (as Keynes would have said) 'man's nature'. And that in the twenty-first, the slide was continuing.

> At a time when the modern economy is becoming increasingly institutions-intensive, the reduction of economics to price theory is troubling enough. It is suicidal for the field to slide into a hard science of choice, ignoring the influences of society, history, culture, and politics on the working of the economy.[16]

The solution, Coase argued, was to step away from the econometric models. 'I'd like people to go study how people actually work,' he said, 'but by and large this isn't what economist do.'[17]

The 2019 Nobel prize in economics was awarded to three economists who have made names for themselves doing just this. Abhijit Banerjee, Esther Duflo and Michael Kremer's use of randomised controlled trials – essentially surveys – has transformed development economics, helping governments to identify the most cost-effective ways to reduce poverty. This approach seeks to establish how individuals respond to policy measures by observing them directly, rather than by calculating elasticities and estimating proportionate responses to calibrated changes in economic stimulus. The number of randomised trials being conducted in development economics has exploded,[18] and the method is credited with great successes in education and other areas. Some economists are distinctly cool about randomised control trials, noting that the method provides answers of limited application – what works in one country might not work in another, or may not even work in the same country over time (a risk one Nobel prize-winning economist calls the 'transportation problem'[19]). They feel it falls short of the ambition that Robert Solow noted the best and brightest in the profession had for economics back in 1985, namely for it to be 'the physics of society',[20] as does Banerjee and Duflo's view of economists as 'plumbers', whose work can be seen as 'intuition grounded in science'.[21] But the couple (they are married) seem content with devising practical solutions to immediate problems, rather than seeking to formulate hard and fast rules, which, like Newton's Laws, might guide humanity for generations to come.

What this illustrates is that when economists are involved in policy-making, their most valuable contribution often comes when they leave economic theory at the door. Few people believe the world avoided a severe depression after the 2008 financial crash thanks to economies' automatic tendency toward equilibrium. And, significantly, when it came to finding solutions, politicians turned to central bankers (usually economists of considerable repute), who, in the event, opted not to handle things according to any economic playbook, but to act flexibly and pragmatically. As the then Federal Reserve Chairman Ben Bernanke noted in 2014 of one of the central banker's primary tools for staving off depression, quantitative easing (QE), 'The problem with QE is it works in practice but it doesn't work in theory.'[22]

This is not to say that economic theory has no value. Romer's Nobel prize was for his contributions to the theory of 'endogenous growth', namely his analysis that growth comes largely from ideas that often cannot be patented or owned. That's a concept that has implications for how one thinks about wealth creation and income distribution. Coase's observation that the use of market mechanisms to allocate resources incurs potentially significant transaction costs is relevant when, for example, governments consider using internal markets to improve efficiency in the public sector. Commentators on the right[23] and left[24] of the political spectrum in Britain have argued that Conservative[25] and Labour[26] governments failed to appreciate these potential costs of using markets when they advanced NHS reforms in the 1990s and 2000s, and thereby wasted vast sums by creating needless bureaucracy.[27] But such carefully selective and self-critical application of theory is not what the profession as a whole wants. It doesn't see economics as a kind of Philosophy of Money, which offers policymakers loose ideas to consider, any more than it wants to be an improvise-as-you-go-along trade like plumbing.

In a display of arrogance masked as modesty, Keynes once said economists were 'trustees, not of civilisation, but of the possibility of civilisation'.[28] In the twenty-first century many policymakers have come to believe this as an article of faith. In January 2020, for example, the US Treasury Secretary Steven Mnuchin responded to comments by the teenage Swedish climate activist Greta Thunberg about a need to stop using fossil fuels that, if she wanted to find solutions to the climate crisis, she should go and study economics. It's an enormous endorsement for a profession to be asked to provide answers to the world's greatest problems. Would economists retain their influence if they conceded that human behaviour is not guided by the supposedly immutable laws the profession has identified over the recent centuries? The reluctance to make such an admission may explain the frequent reliance by the profession on publishing bias, the over-specification of models, partial use of data, the trumpeting of 'statistically significant' empirical findings without acknowledging their practical insignificance, and other shaky, unscientific practices to support basic neoclassical principles.

An axiom from my undergraduate philosophy studies that has stuck with me over the years, despite it being quite contorted, is a summary of one of Kant's arguments on the nature of the reality, which says that 'Transcendental realism leads to empirical idealism.' It relates to the question of whether we can know if we exist and the world truly exists independently of us – the issue Descartes sought to address with his *'Cogito ergo sum.'* Kant basically says that if you insist that things that you can see and touch – and only those – truly exist, and exist as you experience them, you soon end up having to concede that nothing truly exists: in other words, a staunchly materialistic approach to reality leads to an admission that there is no substance to the world. The observation has stuck with me, not because of any interest I might have in transcendental realism, empirical idealism, transcendental idealism or indeed philosophy at all, but rather because it is an example of the way in which an extreme viewpoint – a position rooted in ideology or emotion rather than in a fair-minded reading of the world around us – can lead one to a position of self-contradiction. We see this around us every day, in the way extreme right-wing views can lead to anarchism or, at the opposite end of the spectrum, an extreme belief in social co-operation can lead one to defend dictatorship.

And so it seems with economics. It is built on the premise that human beings are rational, yet its 'law of gravity' – that humans, if they wish to maximise their utility, should be dictated to by the laws of supply and demand – would lead people to focus narrowly and irrationally on price signals while ignoring much more important forces around us. And in the real world this has helped create a practical contradiction: this body of knowledge that prides itself on telling hard truths, such as that 'There's no such thing as a free lunch', has often led people not to appreciate the need for hard work, sacrifice and carefully thought-through answers, but rather to seek easy answers founded on lazy theory, and find quick fixes via free lunch thinking.

ACKNOWLEDGEMENTS

When I came up with the idea for a book based on the economics of taxation in 2016, I was acutely aware that it might be a hard sell to a publisher targeting a wide, lay audience. Nigel Wilcockson, my editor at Random House, surprised me with his immediate enthusiasm for the idea and recognition of the importance of the topic to a broad readership. Nigel's guidance and persistence have been critical to the crafting of this book.

My agent, Maggie Hanbury, has also been integral to the formulation of this book. Maggie has been a constant encouragement over the years and her advice has been critical to my work.

In researching this book I have benefited from the incredible generosity of time and spirit on the part of many people including economists, businesspeople and politicians including Arthur Laffer, Prabhat Jha, Mike Devereux, Gene Lewit, Nigel Way, Ron Hansen, Paul Romer, George Osborne, Peter Van Doren, David Card and Richard Freeman. I greatly appreciate their assistance. Though I may frequently disagree with them in this book, and may believe their work has at times led to harm, this is a criticism of their views and not of them personally. I don't think that having one's perceptions clouded by ideology or conflicts of interest is the same as lacking integrity or empathy for one's fellow man, or woman.

I have also received considerable assistance from many organisations and government bodies, including the UK's Office for National Statistics, Her Majesty's Revenue and Customs, the staff of the United States Congress Joint Committee on Taxation, the British Library, The Heritage Foundation, American Enterprise Institute and the University of Rochester.

I've been incredibly fortunate to work for Reuters for over 20 years, a role which has given me up-close experience of the matters I write about in this book. For a decade, I have specialised in looking for stories in the areas that others might find too boring to delve into such as complex regulations and accounting practices. I am grateful for Reuters' willingness to afford me the time and resources to do this, and its willingness to robustly resist pressure from parties who seek to use Britain's plaintiff-friendly libel rules to avoid light being shed on their questionable commercial practices. My editors including Simon Robinson, Richard Woods, Alessandra Galloni, Mike Williams and Alix Freedman have been wonderful supports.

It's an incredible privilege to daily meet and talk to the workers, managers, investors and public servants who make our economy tick, to see their workplaces and learn first-hand how the world works in practice. It's also a privilege to be trusted to tell the stories of those who have suffered collateral damage in others' quests to enrich themselves. This book would not have been possible without this experience.

Writing a book involves standing on the shoulders of many people who have gone before you. Parts of this book rely on reporting conducted as far back the nineteenth century, and I am grateful to so many of my professional antecedents who took the time to get the first draft of history right. As part of my research I examined over 1,000 papers and books by professional economists, too many to credit properly, but all of which had some small part in building my understanding of the subjects considered in this book.

ACKNOWLEDGEMENTS

As a boy, my father filled our house with books about international relations, science and the most arcane of historical subjects in a way that wasn't common in Ireland in the 1970s. My mother, who died when I was three, was also an avid reader. Their love of books has influenced my life.

Writing a book is an imposition on those around you. Thank you to my family - my sons Harry and Charlie who fill my every day with joy but most of all to my wife Sophy who has made everything worthwhile possible. I love you.

Tom Bergin
London, November 2020

NOTES

Introduction

1 The origin of this statement is unclear, but it has been widely cited in Britain since at least 1919, when it was referenced in a speech by the President of the Royal Statistical Society reported in *The Times* under the title 'The Burden of Taxes' on 22 January that year.

2 He did not hold the title Prime Minister but is considered by historians as occupying the role during his second term as First Lord of the Treasury and Chancellor of the Exchequer from 1721 to 1742. He also previously held these titles from 1715 to 1717, https://www.gov.uk/government/history/past-prime-ministers/robert-walpole.

3 Ewald, Alex Charles, *Sir Robert Walpole: A Political Biography*, 1878, pp. 113–14, Brisco, Norris A., *The Economic Policy of Robert Walpole*, 1907, p. 125.

4 Innes, A. D., *A History of the British Nation*, 1912.

5 Dowell, Stephen, *A History of Taxation and Taxes in England*, vol. 2, Longmans, Green, 1888, p. 90.

6 Chang, Ha-Joon, *Kicking Away the Ladder*, Anthem Press, 2002.

7 Ewald, Alex Charles, *Sir Robert Walpole: A Political Biography*, 1878, pp. 228–9.

8 Letter to Andreas Holt, Commissioner of the Danish Board of Trade and Economy, October 1780.

9 Smith, Adam, *An Inquiry into the Wealth of Nations*, Book IV, Chapter II, paragraph 9.

10 Peel cited Smith in debates on 14 March 1842 and 15 March 1839. Peel's interest in the writings of Smith and Ricardo is also discussed in Douglas A. Irwin, 'Political Economy and Peel's Repeal of the Corn Laws', *Economics and Politics* 0954–1985, vol. I, no. 1, Spring 1989.

11 Robert Peel, 1842 Budget speech.

12 Irwin, 'Political Economy and Peel's Repeal of the Corn Laws', op. cit. This paper highlights Peel's opposition to the protection of the silk industry.

13 The economist Thorstein Veblen is credited with having coined the term in around 1900, Aspromourgos, T., 'Neoclassical', in Eatwell, J., Milgate, M., and Newman, P. (eds), *The World of Economics,* Palgrave Macmillan, 1991.

14 Robert Peel used the word elasticity to refer to consumption changes following tax changes in his 1842 budget, https://api.parliament.uk/historic-hansard/commons/1842/mar/11/financial-statement-ways-and-means.

15 Jevons, William Stanley, *Theory of Political Economy,* Preface, 1888, p. xvii.

16 Murnane, M. Susan, 'Selling Scientific Taxation: The Treasury Departments Campaign for Tax Reform in the 1920s', *Law & Social Inquiry,* vol. 29, no. 4, 2004, p. 820.

17 https://www.nobelprize.org/prizes/economic-sciences/1969/frisch/facts/; https://www.nobelprize.org/prizes/economic-sciences/1969/tinbergen/facts/.

18 Lefeber, Louis, 'Classical vs. Neoclassical Economic Thought in Historical Perspective: The Interpretation of Processes of Economic Growth and Development' in *History of Political Thought,* vol. 21, no. 3, *States and Societies,* Autumn 2000.

19 Godkin lectures, published in *New Dimensions of Political Economy,* Harvard University Press, 1966, p. 1.

20 Solow, Robert M., 'Economic History and Economics', *American Economic Review,* vol. 75, no. 2, Papers and Proceedings of the Ninety-Seventh Annual Meeting of the American Economic Association, May 1985, pp. 328–31.

21 Bergin, Tom, 'Special Report: How Starbucks avoids UK taxes', Reuters, 15 October 2012, http://www.reuters.com/article/2012/10/15/us-britain-starbucks-tax-idUSBRE89E0EX20121015.

22 Bergin, Tom, 'Special Report: How Google UK clouds its tax liabilities', Reuters,1 May 2013, http://uk.reuters.com/article/2013/05/01/us-tax-uk-google-special report-idUSBRE94005P20130501.

23 Prime Minister David Cameron's speech to the World Economic Forum in Davos, 24 January 2013, https://www.gov.uk/government/speeches/prime-minister-david-camerons-speech-to-the-world-economic-forum-in-davos.

24 Bergin, Tom, *Spills and Spin: The Inside Story of BP,* Random House, 2011.

25 Bergin, Tom, 'The fridges that caught fire', Reuters, 21 October 2011.

26 Bergin, Tom, 'Damages for Grenfell fire victims may total just $5 million', Reuters, 25 October 2017, https://www.reuters.com/article/us-britain-fire-compensation-insight/damages-for-grenfell-fire-victims-may-total-just-5-million-reuters-analysis-idUSKBN1CN1P9; Arconic knowingly supplied flammable panels for use in tower (emails, 24 June 2017: http://www.reuters.com/article/us-britain-fire-arconic-idUSKBN19F05M); silence over whether Grenfell Tower materials passed safety test, 10 July 2017, https://www.reuters.com/article/britainfire-regulations-idUSL8N1K00K4.

27 Dowell, *A History of Taxation and Taxes in England*, op. cit., vol. 3, p. 98. See also, HMRC, 'A Tax to Beat Napoleon', available at http://webarchive.national archives.gov.uk/20130217082231/http://www.hmrc.gov.uk/history/taxhis1.htm.

28 HMRC, 'The Exchequer effect of the 50 per cent additional rate of income tax', March 2012.

29 Irish Department of Finance statement, 2 March 2017.

30 Revenue Commissioners' Annual Report 2011. A slightly larger yield forecast of €3.3 billion was provided by the Minister for Finance in a written answer to a parliamentary question on 25 January 2011.

31 Revenue Commissioners, Total Net Receipts by Taxhead, 2011–18.

32 Novy-Marx, Robert, 'Predicting anomaly performance with politics, the weather, global warming, sunspots, and the stars', *Journal of Financial Economics*, 2014, vol. 112, issue 2, pp. 137–46.

33 'Index Membership, Investor (in)attention to News & Spurious Correlations', UBS, 25 September 2014.

34 Fardmanesh, Mohsen, Associate Professor, Temple University, Philadelphia.

1. The Laffer Conundrum

1 Bergin, Tom, 'Special Report: Is Donald Trump struggling to find the green with his golf investments?', 23 June 2016, http://www.reuters.com/investigates/special-report/trump-golf/.

2 Trump's Office of Government Ethics' financial disclosures highlighted many large debts. This was one of around a dozen easily verifiable falsehoods in the interview.

3 Remarks at Tax Reform Event, Farm Bureau Building, Indianapolis, Indiana, from White House press releases, 27 September 2017.

4 'Argentina tax bill to slash corporate income taxes to 25 per cent', Reuters, 31 October 2017.

5 '$30bn boost for Turnbull's tax reform plan', *Australian*, 8 November 2017, https://www.theaustralian.com.au/nation/30bn-boost-for-turnbulls-tax-reform-plan/news-story/4a0d1c0abd8ad0363548517c00ca3e7a.

6 Boris Johnson repeatedly claimed tax cuts would be self-funding in his columns for the *Daily Telegraph* since at least 2013, most recently in a 10 September 2018 column entitled 'Don't raise taxes, cut them to give the economy the jolt of energy it needs.' During the Conservative Party leadership battle in the summer of 2019, he continued the theme, including in an interview on *Sophy Ridge on Sunday*, Sky News, 30 June 2019.

7 In his 1963 book *The Sumerians: Their History, Culture, and Character*, the archaeologist Samuel Noah Kramer wrote of tablets from around 2000 BC he deciphered which contained many complaints about tax collectors.

8 'Double Aggravation', *Le Temps*, 25 March 1917.

9   Ibid.

10 Interview with United Press news agency, 30 August 1917, cited in *Congressional Record – Senate: The Proceedings and Debates of the First Session of the Sixty-Fifth Congress*, vol. LV, p. 47.

11 Horn, Martin, *Britain, France, and the Financing of the First World War*, McGill-Queen's University Press, 2002, p. 168.

12 Interview with United Press news agency, 30 August 1917, op. cit.

13 'La Chambre Vote', *Le Petit Journal*, 24 March 1917.

14 'Warns French Bankers', *New York Times*, 16 August 1917.

15 Interview with United Press news agency, 30 August 1917, op. cit.

16 Fernald, Charles B., 'French Income Taxes', *American Bar Association Journal*, vol. 3, no. 4, October 1917, p. 700. Thierry also announced schedular taxes that would be introduced in the following years, which could add up to an additional 3.75 per cent on salaried income (from Piketty, Thomas, *Les Hauts Revenus en France au XXe Siècle Inégalités et Redistributions, 1901–98*, p. 651).

17 Brownlee, W. Elliot, Ide, Eisaku, and Fukagai, Yasunori (eds), *The Political Economy of Transnational Tax Reform: The Shoup Mission to France*, Cambridge University Press, 2013.

18 The 1913 legislation provided a 1 per cent normal tax on individuals' taxable income in excess of $3,000, plus a surtax of up to 6 per cent, according to Dubroff, Harold, and Hellwig, Brant J., *The United States Tax Court: An Historical Analysis*, 1979. Similar figures appear in Blakey, Roy G. and Gladys C., 'The Revenue Act of 1918', *American Economic Review*, vol. 9, no. 2, June 1919, pp. 214–43).

19 Senators Robert M. La Follette, Hiram Johnson and Asle Jorgenson Gronna were among those who used the term or a close variant of it. *Congressional Record Senate Sixty-Fifth Congress; First Session*, vol. LV, part 7, 30 August–1 October 1917.

20 *Congressional Record*, op. cit.

21 There is not universal agreement about how the two normal income taxes and two income surtaxes combined to yield marginal tax rates. These results are taken from Blakey, Roy G., 'The War Revenue Act of 1917', *American Economic Review*, vol. 7, no. 4, December 1917, pp. 791–815, and seem to fit with most of the estimates I have reviewed.

22 Haig, Robert Murray, 'The Revenue Act of 1918', *Political Science Quarterly*, vol. 34, no. 3, September 1919, pp. 369–91.

23 Internal Revenue Service Statistics of Income report, 1919.

24 Blakey, R. and G., 'The Revenue Act of 1918', *American Economic Review*, vol. 9, no. 2, June 1919, pp. 214-43.

25 The principal of public debt outstanding peaked at $25.48 billion in 1919 and began to fall in 1920, *Statistics of the United States, Colonial Times to 1957*, series 68–379. Public Debt of the Federal Government: 1791 to 1957.

26 Mellon, Andrew, *Taxation: The People's Business*, Macmillan, 1924, p. 95.

27 Cannadine, David, *Mellon: an American Life*, Alfred A. Knopf, 2006, notes that Mellon used his Republican Party connections to have aluminium added to the list of products that would be protected from overseas competition by import duties in the McKinley Tariff of 1890. The move significantly benefited Mellon's own aluminium company, a precursor to the modern-day Alcoa Corporation.

28 Smith, Adam, *An Inquiry into the Nature and Causes of the Wealth of Nations*, Book V, chapter II, Part II, paragraph 4, 1776.

29 Andrew Mellon, *Taxation: The People's Business*, op. cit., p. 16.

30 The Revenue Act of 1921, https://www.loc.gov/law/help/statutes-at-large/67th-congress/Session%201/c67s1ch136.pdf.

31 The top rate was cut from 73 per cent to 58 per cent. Goolsbee, Austan, 'Evidence on the High-Income Laffer Curve from Six Decades of Tax Reform', 1999, and https://www.taxpolicycenter.org/statistics/historical-highest-marginal-income-tax-rates.

32 Author's calculations based on data in the Internal Revenue Service annual Statistics of Income reports from 1919 to 1934.

33 The White House Office of Management and Budget, Table 1.1: Summary of Receipts, Outlays, and Surpluses or Deficits 1789–2024, https://www.whitehouse.gov/omb/historical-tables/.

34 Statement from Mellon reported under the title 'Mellon Predicts Business Progress', *New York Times*, 1 January 1930.

35 Hoover described Mellon as one of the 'leave it alone liquidationists' who wanted to allow the depression to run its course without government intervening to try to limit the impact. *The Memoirs of Herbert Hoover*, vol. 3, *The Great Depression, 1929–41*, Macmillan Company, 1952.

36 As Nobel prize-winner Robert Shiller notes in his 2017 paper 'Narrative Economics', 'The Mellon name began to fade (outside of Carnegie-Mellon University)'. Indeed, a review of the *New York Times* Archive shows just one reference to Mellon's tenure as Treasury Secretary during the 1960s, but half a dozen in the 1970s.

37 Rader, Benjamin G., 'Federal Taxation in the 1920s: A Re-examination', *Historian*, 33:1, 1970, pp. 415–35.

38 The exact level of increase in international oil prices is unknown. In late 1973, cargoes of crude were reported as selling for as much as $17 per barrel against oil exports from the United States being reported at levels of just $3 a few years previously. The oil prices from the period usually cited today refer to the posted prices agreed between oil companies and governments, but these were primarily used for agreeing tax payments, not buying and selling crude. Oil producers were largely vertically integrated, refining their own crude and selling products in forecourts. It wasn't until a decade later that a liquid international market in crude emerged.

39 The text of the Arab oil ministers' statement issued in Vienna on 19 March 1974 walked back the embargo's aims to being simply to raise the international awareness of the Palestinian plight, and claimed vague statements from the United States and European countries as a kind of victory.

40 'Oil price doubled by big producers on Persian Gulf', *New York Times*, 26 December 1973.

41 The term, a combination of 'stagnation' and 'inflation', seems to have been first used by Ian Macleod, Conservative Shadow Chancellor, during a debate in the House of Commons in 1965, a year when the UK inflation rate hit 5 per cent. This was high by historical standards, but the rate fell and growth rebounded in the following years. In 1975, inflation was over 24 per cent.

42 In October 1974, Ford pressed Congress in his famous 'Whip Inflation Now' speech to increase personal taxes to help curb inflation, which he said was fuelled by expansionary fiscal policies: https://www.fordlibrarymuseum.gov/library/speeches/740121.asp. However, in his State of the Union speech two months later, he advocated a $16 billion tax cut to boost demand in the economy, https://www.fordlibrarymuseum.gov/library/speeches/750028.htm.

43 'Inflation: the value of the pound, 1750–2001', House of Commons Library, Research Paper 02/44, 11 July 2002, https://fred.stlouisfed.org/series/FPCPI TOTLZGUSA.

44 https://www.bankofengland.co.uk/statistics/research-data sets; Table 1.1: Summary of Receipts, Outlays, and Surpluses or Deficits 1789 –2024. Office of Management and Budget, https://www.whitehouse.gov/omb/historical-tables/.

45 *The Times* described economists as being hostile to price controls from 1946 ('Price Controls in US', 22 April 1946) to the late 1970s ('Economists' Prescription for Healthier Industry', 26 September 1977). In a 1964 study, the OECD had argued against price controls (reported in 'World Study Finds Price Curb More Elusive Than Pay Control', *New York Times*, 14 August 1964), and during the 1970s the *New York Times* repeatedly cited economists, including Paul Samuelson ('2 Democratic Economists Support a Larger Deficit', *New York Times* 23 July 1970), as questioning price controls.

46 Whether Arthur Laffer is the most famous living economist is, I accept, debatable. As reviews of Richard Posner's book *Public Intellectuals: A Study of Decline* show, the estimation of the public currency of academics, scientists and other thinkers is a fraught activity. Such people are often better known for the public roles they hold. For example, Alan Greenspan and Mervyn King have had high profiles due to their roles as central bankers, not because of their economic research. Similarly, Paul Krugman is well known as a columnist, but I suspect the public is largely unaware of his contributions to economics. Arthur Laffer is unusual as an economist who is known for his work. Along with the invisible hand, Keynesianism and Ricardo's comparative advantage, 'The Laffer Curve' is one of the few economic concepts that a wide body of people can recognise and link to a single person.

47 Robert Shiller, in a 2017 paper called 'Narrative Economics', calculated newspaper mentions of the curve, noting it 'went viral' in 1978.

48 Johnson professed his faith in the curve in his *Daily Telegraph* columns, including 'Bash the rich and you deprive us of what their taxes pay for', 27 January 2014. Other Members of Parliament who have advocated the curve include the Conservatives John Redwood, David Shaw and Bernard Jenkin.

49 The exact figures are not precisely reliable, since the metrics for measuring economic output have changed so much over the years. The data here is from Piketty, Thomas, *Capital in the 21st Century*, Harvard University Press, 2014, http://piketty.pse.ens.fr/en/capital21c2. Other data sets show a similar trend.

50 Wanniski, Jude, 'It's Time to Cut Taxes', *Wall Street Journal*, 11 December 1974.

51 Wanniski, Jude, 'The Mundell-Laffer Hypothesis: A New View of the World Economy', *The Public Interest*, Spring 1975.

52 'Paul A. Samuelson, Economist, Dies at 94', *New York Times*, 13 December 2009.

53 Dr Laffer comments at the presentation of the Medal of Freedom, 19 June 2019, https://www.whitehouse.gov/briefings-statements/remarks-president-trump-presentation-medal-freedom-dr-arthur-laffer/.

54 Robert Bartley obituary, *Wall Street Journal*, 11 December 2003.

55 'Cheney, Rumsfeld and Laffer Reunite to Talk Taxes – The Dinner Napkin That Changed the US Economy', Bloomberg TV, 4 December 2014.

56 Ibid.

57 Comments to current White House economic adviser Larry Kudlow recorded in Larry Kudlow, 'Cheney, The Supply-Sider', *National Review*, 24 July 2000.

58 Laffer says a 14 October 2017 *New York Times* story, 'A Sketchy Story' by Binyamin Appelbaum, which challenges the Smithsonian claim of a single Laffer-Cheney-Rumsfeld meeting, is accurate.

59 American Enterprise Display at Smithsonian, National Museum of American History, Washington, DC.

60 Reynolds, Alan, 'Reality in One Lesson', Fall Books: A Special Supplement, *The Public Interest*, 1978.

61 Wanniski also outlined his theory in a *Wall Street Journal* column entitled 'The Crash of '29 – A New View', published on 28 October 1977.

62 Stein, Ben, 'The Smoot-Hawley Act Is More Than a Laugh Line', *New York Times*, 9 May 2009, https://www.nytimes.com/2009/05/10/business/10every.html.

63 'The Mellon and Kennedy Tax Cuts: A Review and Analysis: A Staff Study Prepared For The Use Of The Subcommittee On Monetary And Fiscal Policy Of The Joint Economic Committee Congress of The United States', 18 June 1982.

64 Presidential Proclamation on Irish-American Heritage Month, 2019, 1 March 2019, https://www.whitehouse.gov/presidential-actions/presidential-proclamation-irish-american-heritage-month-2019/.

65 In addition to the points made in the earlier footnote on Johnson, he also wrote in a column on 6 July 2015 that 'there are plenty of people who do believe – as I do – in the Laffer Curve.'

66 Arthur Henderson comments during War Budget debate, 19 November 1914: https://api.parliament.uk/historic-hansard/sittings/1914/nov/19.

67 'How to Pay for the War', Fabian Society Research Department, 1916.

68 The Report of the Royal Commission on the Income Tax, presented to Parliament in 1920, showed that the tax rates that were imposed still provided sufficient incentive for Britain's rich to engage in a wide range of creative tax avoidance during the war.

69 Interview with United Press news agency, 30 August 1917, as cited in *Congressional Record – Senate. The Proceedings and Debates of The First Session of The Sixty-Fifth Congress*, vol. LV, p. 47. See also Morgan, K. J., and Prasad, M., 'The origins of tax systems: A French-American comparison', *American Journal of Sociology* 114(5), 2009, pp. 1350–94.

70 Seligman, Edwin R. A., 'The War Revenue Act', *Political Science Quarterly*, vol. 33, no. 1, 1918.

71 The Act said it was illegal to incorporate assets for the purpose of avoiding tax, but the government had to actually prove tax avoidance was the sole motivation in order to be successful in a prosecution, and this requirement rendered the provision useless.

72 The 1918 Revenue Act provided for a normal tax of 12 per cent for 1918 and 8 per cent thereafter, from 1919, plus a surtax of 65 per cent.

73 The 1918 list was republished by *Forbes* in 2017: 'Forbes 1918 list', https://www.forbes.com/sites/chasewithorn/2017/09/19/the-first-forbes-list-see-who-the-richest-americans-were-in-1918/#6c227dc94c0d.

74 In a boom, reported dividend income and capital gains are usually closely correlated with the salaries of high earners. IRS data shows that, in the 1920s, all correlation between paid income and capital income evaporated. Almost all the increase in income reported by people with annual earnings of $1 million or more between 1922 and 1929 came from dividends and capital gains.

75 Estimates vary as to the top tax rate during this period, as the French tax system applied different tax rates based on the source of income, various discounts based on marital and parental status, and average and marginal tax rates on different baskets of income. According to Thomas Piketty (*Les Hauts Revenus en France Au XXe Siècle*, op. cit., p. 262), in 1919 childless bachelors could face a top marginal tax rate of 62.5 per cent. In *Conscription of Wealth: Mass Warfare and the Demand for Progressive Taxation*, Kenneth Scheve and David Stasavage note that, by 1919, the top French tax rate had risen to 50 per cent.

76 France's real GDP per capita grew 46 per cent between 1920 and 1929, while the US's real GDP per capita grew just 12 per cent. Madison Project data: https://

www.rug.nl/ggdc/historicaldevelopment/maddison/releases/maddison-project-database-2018. Industrial production grew 126 per cent in France from 1920 to 1929. US manufacturing output grew 37 per cent: National Bureau of Economic Research, France Index of Industrial Production, Total 1898–1938 and US Index of Manufacturing Production, 1920–39, http://data.nber.org/databases/macro-history/contents/chapter01.html.

77 Germany's real GDP per capita grew 45 per cent between 1920 and 1929, versus 12 per cent for the US, according to the Madison Project database hosted by the University of Groningen: https://www.rug.nl/ggdc/historicaldevelopment/maddison/releases/maddison-project-database-2018. German Industrial Production grew 56 per cent between 1920 and 1929, ahead of the 37 per cent rise in US manufacturing production. NBER data series a01008ad, http://www.nber.org/databases/macrohistory/contents/chapter01.html.

78 'An Analysis of the Roth-Kemp Tax Cut Proposal', Congressional Budget Office, 1978, p. 37.

79 'Real Gross Domestic Product, Per cent Change from Preceding Period, Annual, Not Seasonally Adjusted': https://fred.stlouisfed.org/series/A191RL1A225NBEA. Some academics, including Eric M. Engen and Jonathan Skinner in the 1996 paper 'Taxation and Economic Growth', which claims a negative correlation between tax rates and growth, say that real GDP growth fell slightly after the 1964 cut.

80 'An Analysis of the Roth-Kemp Tax Cut Proposal', op. cit., p. ix.

81 'Federal Deficit as a Percentage of Gross Domestic Product, Annual, Not Seasonally Adjusted', https://fred.stlouisfed.org/series/FYFSGDA188S.

82 Real Gross Domestic Product, Per cent Change from Preceding Period, Annual, Not Seasonally Adjusted, op. cit. Per capita GDP growth shows the same trend.

83 Chicago Booth IGM Panel, 26 June 2012: http://www.igmchicago.org/surveys/laffer-curve.

84 Mankiw, Gregory N., *Principles of Microeconomics*, first edition, Dryden Press, 1997.

85 During the 1950s and 1960s unemployment in Britain averaged 2 per cent (Hatton, T. J., and Boyer, G. R., 'Unemployment and the UK labour market before, during and after the Golden Age', *European Review of Economic History* 9(1), 2005, pp. 35–60). Between 1948 and 1970, US unemployment averaged 4.7 per cent (US Bureau of Labor Statistics Unemployment Rate Series ID: LNS14000000). West German unemployment was below 5 per cent from 1948 to 1973 (Paqué, Karl-Heinz, 'Unemployment in West Germany: A survey of explanations and policy options', Kiel Working Paper 407, Institut für Weltwirtschaft (IfW), Kiel, 1990.

86 Maddison Project long-term GDP data for Europe and North America: Jones, Charles I., 'The Facts of Economic Growth', NBER Working Paper 21142, 2015.

Bank of England, 'A Millennium of Macroeconomic Data for the UK', https://www.bankofengland.co.uk/statistics/research-datasets.

87 *New Yorker*, 10 July 2017, https://www.newyorker.com/magazine/2017/07/10/americas-future-is-texas.

88 The previous Republican governor, Edmund J. Davis, was elected in 1869 and took office on 8 January 1870: https://lrl.texas.gov/legeLeaders/governors/gov Browse.cfm.

89 First Inaugural Address of Ronald Reagan, 20 January 1981: https://www.reaganfoundation.org/ronald-reagan/reagan-quotes-speeches/inaugural-address-1/.

90 The Organisation for Economic Co-operation and Development was formed by developed nations in 1961 to help advise members on economic policy-making, and as a forum for discussing collaboration on matters such as taxation.

91 'Social expenditure 1960–90: Problems of growth and control', OECD, 1985, p. 14.

92 Henrekson, Magnus, 'Wagner's Law – A Spurious Relationship?', *Public Finance*, vol. 46, no. 3, 1993. Available at SSRN: https://ssrn.com/abstract=998269.

93 'Social expenditure 1960-1990', op. cit., p. 11.

94 From Tanzi, Vito, and Schuknecht, Ludger, 'Public Spending in the 20th Century – A Global Perspective', OECD, 2000.

95 https://www.montpelerin.org/about-mps/.

96 Friedman outlined this view in an essay entitled 'The Methodology of Positive Economics', published in *Essays in Positive Economics*, University of Chicago Press, 1966.

97 Tanzi, Vito, and Schuknecht, Ludger, 'Public Spending in the 20th Century', op. cit., p. 15.

98 Examples include Landau, Daniel, 'Government Expenditure and Economic Growth: A Cross-Country Study', 1983; Marlow, Michael, L., 'Private sector shrinkage and the growth of industrialised economies', 1986; Jones, Manuelli, and Rossi, 'On the Optimal Taxation of Capital Income', 1993; Engen, Eric M., and Skinner, Jonathan, 'Taxation and Economic Growth', NBER Working Paper 5826, November 1996.

99 Lucas, Robert E., Jr, 'Macroeconomic Priorities', *American Economic Review*, March 2003.

100 King, Robert C., and Rebelo, Sergio, 'Public Policy and Economic Growth: Developing Neoclassical Implications', 1990.

101 Email exchange with author. Easterly and Rebelo published two papers that illustrated this point in 1993, one entitled 'Marginal income tax rates and economic growth in developing countries', the other 'Fiscal Policy and Economic Growth: An Empirical Investigation'. A 1995 paper Rebelo co-authored with Nancy Stokey, entitled 'Growth Effects of Flat-Rate Taxes', found that 'There is,

as yet, no theoretical presumption or empirical evidence of substantial growth effects from factor taxation.'

102 Marsden, Keith, 'Links between Taxes and Economic Growth – Some Empirical Evidence', World Bank Staff Working Papers 605, 1983.

103 Barro, Robert, 'Economic growth in a cross-section of countries', 1991.

104 Koester, Reinhard, and Kormendi, Roger, 'Taxation, Aggregate Activity and Economic Growth: Cross-Country Evidence on Some Supply-Side Hypotheses', 1989. William Gale and Andrew Samwick note in 'Effects of Income Tax Changes on Economic Growth' that a similar claimed link between tax and growth, reported in Engen, E.M., Skinner J., 'Fiscal Policy and Economic Growth' (NBER Working Paper 4223, National Bureau of Economic Research, 1992), also falls away when one only compares developed countries.

105 Engen and Skinner, 'Taxation and Economic Growth', op. cit.; McGuire, Therese, and Wasylenko, Michael, 'Employment growth and state government fiscal behavior: A report on economic development for states from 1974 to 1984', report prepared for the New Jersey State and Local Expenditure and Revenue Policy Commission, 1987.

106 Stokey, Nancy L., and Rebelo, Sergio, 'Growth Effects of Flat-Rate Taxes', *Journal of Political Economy* 103, June 1995, pp. 519–50.

107 Michael McGuire and Therese Wasylenko's 'Employment growth and state government fiscal behavior: A report on economic development for states from 1974 to 1984' (1987) is an example. In this, the authors failed to replicate the results of their 1985 paper, 'Jobs and taxes: The effect of business climate on states' employment growth rates', *National Tax Journal*, vol. 38, no. 4, December 1985, pp. 497–512.

108 Japan's population was lower in 2018 than in 1999 and 2000 (World Bank data SP.POP.TOTL Population, total).

109 Since 1997, Japan has had net inward migration of around 1 million, while the figure for the United States is 29 million (World Bank, World Development Indicators – Net migration SM.POP.NETM). Births per female were 50 per cent higher in United States than in Japan over the period 1998–2018 – World Bank, SP.DYN.TFRT.IN Fertility rate, total (births per woman).

110 European Union life expectancy rose by more than eight years between 1980 and 2018, whereas US life expectancy rose less than five years (World Bank, 'Life Expectancy At Birth, Total (Years)', SP.DYN.LE00.IN). This has contributed to a situation where the percentage of EU population over sixty-five years of age – the vast majority of whom do not work – rose from 13.1 per cent of the population to 20.2 per cent in 1980, compared to the United States, where over-sixty-fives rose from 11.6 per cent to 15.8 per cent of the population (World Bank, 'Population Ages 65 And Above (% Of Total Population)', SP.POP.65UP.TO.ZS).

111 Michael L. Marlow found a negative tax-growth correlation in his 1986 paper, 'Private sector shrinkage and the growth of industrialized economies', using

estimates of tax to GDP levels calculated by adjusting GDP and government spending data for inflation and then comparing the outcomes. Peter Saunders noted that there was no particular reason given for the inflation adjustment, and that most people just compared the ratio of tax and GDP, an activity which already cancelled out any inflation impact. When he used a simple tax-to-GDP ratio, Saunders did not observe the same trend Marlow identified. Similarly, Folster and Henrekson found a strong growth-tax link in their 2001 paper 'Growth Effects of Government Expenditure and Taxation in Rich Countries', using a 'least squares' regression method. Jonas Agell, Henry Ohlsson and Peter Thoursie argued in their 2006 paper, 'Growth Effects of Government Expenditure and Taxation in Rich Countries: A Comment', that most researchers would routinely use a 'robust cluster estimator', which gave a different result.

112 Agell et al. (2006) reported that they were unable to replicate the results in Folster and Henrekson (2001) using data provided by Folster and Henrekson. In his comment on Michael Marlow's 'Private sector shrinkage and the growth of industrialized economies', Peter Saunders said Marlow had incorrectly stated the level of statistical significance he had identified.

113 One 2016 study (Camerer, Colin F., et al., 'Evaluating replicability of laboratory experiments in economics', *Science*, 25 March 2016) failed to replicate 40 per cent of the economic studies selected.

114 Gale, William G., and Samwick, Andrew A., 'Effects of Income Tax Changes on Economic Growth', Brookings Instution, 1 February 2016.

115 Maddison Project Database, https://www.rug.nl/ggdc/historicaldevelopment/maddison/.

116 Author's calculations. Similar results in Gale and Potter, 'An Economic Evaluation of the Economic Growth and Tax Relief Reconciliation Act of 2001', 2002, p. 32, and Stokey and Rebelo, 'Growth Effects of Flat-Rate Taxes', 1993, p. 30.

117 Crafts, Nicholas, *Forging Ahead, Falling Behind and Fighting Back: British Economic Growth from the Industrial Revolution to the Financial Crisis*, Cambridge University Press, 2018, p. 79.

118 Clark, Tom, and Dilnot, Andrew, 'Long-Term Trends In British Taxation And Spending', Institute for Fiscal Studies, 2002.

119 'GDP(E) growth at market prices', Bank of England, A Millennium of Macroeconomic Data, https://www.bankofengland.co.uk/statistics/research-data sets.

120 Maddison Project Database; Tanzi and Schuknecht, 'Public Spending in the 20th Century', op. cit., chapter 1.

121 Okawa, Kazushi, and Rosovsky, Henry, *Japanese Economic Growth: Trend Acceleration in the Twentieth Century*, p. 28.

122 McKinsey Center for Government, 'Government Productivity: Unlocking The $3.5 Trillion Opportunity', discussion paper, April 2017, p. 3.

123 Slemrod, Joel, 'What Do Cross-Country Studies Teach about Government Involvement, Prosperity, and Economic Growth?', Brookings Papers on Economic Activity 2, 1995.

124 Tanzi and Schuknecht, 'Public Spending in the 20th Century', op. cit., p. 54.

125 House of Commons, 14 July 2015, https://hansard.parliament.uk/Commons/2015-07-14/debates/15071433000001/BudgetResolutionsAndEconomicSituation.

126 The collect-and-spend route may involve a higher processing cost than allowances, but whether there is a material difference is uncertain, since tax allowances involve monitoring costs and compliance costs for taxpayers.

127 'Tax Expenditures in OECD Countries', OECD, 2010, pp. 196 and 217.

128 OECD Data warehouse.

129 The UK has higher life expectancy than the United States, and has been observed to outperform in various studies. A 2017 study that examined the rate at which people die as a result of conditions where successful medical intervention should be able to save their lives found the UK outperformed the United States: https://www.thelancet.com/journals/lancet/article/PIIS0140-6736(17)30818-8/fulltext. A July 2017 report from the US-based Commonwealth Fund listed the UK as first in a Health Care System Performance Ranking of eleven rich nations including the United States, https://interactives.commonwealthfund.org/2017/july/mirror-mirror/.

130 A 2014 report by JP Morgan Asset Management, 'The road not taken: Pitfalls and opportunities in infrastructure investing', reviewed infrastructure over the previous decade and concluded that investors in infrastructure should 'Generally confine investment to established assets supplying essential services, with clear visibility around user demand', and that new assets should only be considered where there were 'adequate protections'. 'Some of these greenfield project risks can be mitigated through partnerships with public entities that allow private investors to earn a predetermined rate of return on invested capital that is backed by a revenue stream not tied to the usage of the new asset (i.e. a sales tax)', it noted.

131 The track record of the private sector in the provision of what might be considered justice services is chequered. For example, the UK's recent experimentation with privatised parole services in recent was abandoned due to poor performance. Another example is private-sector arbitration, which offers an alternative to the law courts as a mechanism for settling commercial disputes, but the courts remain the preferred mechanism to underpin contracts.

132 The argument that tax and growth are negatively correlated has been regularly questioned in papers published in the University of Chicago Press's *Journal of Political Economy* in recent years.

133 A U-Haul spokesman said the company utilises 'a proprietary rates and distribution system, and a management team that considers many factors when determining pricing for equipment rentals', but declined to say exactly how

demand and supply, market affordability and other factors influence rental prices.

134 'US budget deficit passes $1 trillion mark for fiscal 2019', Reuters, 12 September 2019.

2. The Feldstein Revelation

1 *Guinness Book of Records*, 2018, p. 87.

2 Prescott, Edward C., Federal Reserve Bank of Minneapolis, 'Why Do Americans Work So Much More Than Europeans?', *Quarterly Review*, vol. 28, no.1, July 2004.

3 OECD Data set: Average annual hours actually worked per worker.

4 Alessina at al., 'Work and leisure in the US and Europe: Why so different?', 2005, estimated that legally mandated holidays explained 80 per cent of the difference in time worked.

5 https://www.bls.gov/ncs/ebs/benefits/2017/ownership/civilian/table32a.htm.

6 OECD Family Database, PF2.3: Additional leave entitlements for working parents: https://www.oecd.org/els/soc/PF2_3_Additional_leave_entitlements_of_working_parents.pdf. The UK has 28 days paid vacation plus 9 public holidays, given an often-reported figure of 37, but UK employers are allowed to include holidays in the 28-day total and have no obligation to pay workers on bank holidays. Hence, this gives the UK a maximum of just 28 paid days off each year. In France and Spain, the combination of paid annual leave plus paid public holidays gives 36 days in total.

7 Healey is remembered for campaigning ahead of the 1974 election for tax increases, particularly on the rich. However, in his 1978 budget speech, he announced income tax cuts for lower earners, saying he wished to 'increase the incentive for greater effort and to promote social justice'.

8 Barber, Anthony, *Taking the Tide*, 1996, p. 103, and parliamentary debate: https://api.parliament.uk/historic-hansard/commons/1971/may/18/income-tax-charged-at-basic-and-other#S5CV0817P0_19710518_HOC_441.

9 https://www.pm.gov.au/media/delivered-lower-taxes-hard-working-australians.

10 Brian Mulroney's 1991 budget is an example.

11 Survey carried out for the Royal Commission on the Taxation of Profits and Income, cited in Break, George F., 'Income Taxes and Incentives to Work: An Empirical Study', *American Economic Review*, vol. 47, no. 5, September 1957, pp. 529–49.

12 *The Times* estimated in 1967 that the combination of the income tax and surtax gave a marginal rate at £20,000 of 90 per cent ('How taxes cut top people down to size', 15 May 1967). UK rates of income tax and surtax can be found here: https://www.gov.uk/government/statistics/rates-of-surtax-1948-to-1973; https://assets.publishing.service.gov.uk/government/uploads/system/uploads/attachment_data/file/418685/surtaxrates_1948to1973_1_.pdf.

13 US tax rates over 80 per cent: McCombs, J. B., 'An Historical Review and Analysis of Early United States Tax Policy Scholarship: Definition of Income and Progressive Rates', *St John's Law Review*, vol. 64, no. 3, article 2, 1990. Available at: https://scholarship.law.stjohns.edu/lawreview/vol64/iss3/2".

14 Beyer, Vicki L., 'The Legacy of the Shoup Mission: Taxation Inequities and Tax Reform in Japan', *Pacific Basin Law Journal* 10 (2), 1992.

15 See Roed and Stroem, 'Progressive Taxes and the Labour Market – Is there a trade-off between progressivity and efficiency?', 2002.

16 http://oecdobserver.org/news/fullstory.php/aid/3782/How_tax_can_reduce_inequality.html.

17 'High Earners, Smokers and Tourists to See Higher Levies under Planned Fiscal 2018 Tax Reforms', *Japan Times*, 14 December 2017.

18 https://www.bernietax.com/#0;0;s.

19 Website of Alexandria Ocasio-Cortez: https://ocasio-cortez.house.gov/issues/economic-inequality.

20 OECD, 'Risks That Matter' survey, 2018, and 'Risks that Matter: Focus on Latin America: Comparing perceptions of risks and government effectiveness across Europe, Israel and the Americas'.

21 Locke, John, *Some Considerations on the Consequences of the Lowering of Interest and the Raising of the Value of Money*, 1691, p. 16.

22 Alfred Marshall published images of the model in *Principles of Economics*, 1890 (p. 288, 8th edition).

23 https://www.bankofengland.co.uk/knowledgebank/why-are-football-players-paid-so-much?sf98859605=1.

24 The slope of a demand curve does not equate with the price elasticity of demand, but it is an indication of the elasticity.

25 Vaughn, Karen, 'John Locke and the Labor Theory of Value', *Journal of Libertarian Studies*, vol. 2. no. 4, 1978, pp. 311–26.

26 *Usury at Six Per Cent*, 1669.

27 Douglas, Paul, *Theory of Wages*, 1934.

28 Bank of England, 'A Millennium of Macroeconomic Data for the UK'.

29 Laughlin, J. Laurence, abridged version of John Stuart Mill's *Principles of Political Economy with Critical and Explanatory Notes*, 1885.

30 Bank of England, 'A Millennium of Macroeconomic Data for the UK'. Gravelle and Marples, 'Tax Rates and Economic Growth', 2014, highlight a 43 per cent drop in the average workweek in the US between 1856 and 1940.

31 Boyer, G. R., and Hatton, T. J., 'New estimates of British unemployment, 1870–1913 (electronic version), *Journal of Economic History* 62(3), 2002, pp. 643–75, and ONS Unemployment rate (aged 16 and over, seasonally adjusted). Data in the Bank of England's 'A Millennium of Macroeconomic Data for the UK' shows a similar trend.

32 *Historical Data of the United States Colonial Times to 1957*, U.S. Department of Commerce, 1960, Stanley Lebergott, *Manpower in Economic Growth: The*

American Record since 1800, McGraw-Hill, 1964, and Romer, Christine, 'Spurious Volatility in Historical Unemployment Data', *Journal of Political Economy*, vol. 94, no. 1, 1986 for historical data.

33 Data from Douglas, *Theory of Wages*. It's notable that the trend was observable even though the US had no income tax at the time, while Britain did, on high earners.

34 Kosters, Marvin H., 'Effects of an income tax on Labor supply', RAND Corporation paper, 1968.

35 Winston, Gordon, 'An international comparison of income and hours of work', *Review of Economics and Statistics*, February 1966; MaCurdy, Thomas E., 'An empirical model of labor supply in a life-cycle setting', *Journal of Political Economy*, vol. 89, no. 6, 1981; Hausman, Jerry,, 'Labour Supply' in ed. Aaron, Henry J., and Pechman, Joseph A., *How Taxes Affect Economic Behavior*, Brookings Institution, 1981; Hausman, Jerry, 'Taxes & Labour Supply', in *Handbook of Public Economics*, vol. I, 1985; Pencavel, John, 'Labor Supply of Men: A Survey', *Handbook of Labor Economics*, vol. 1, 1986. In the 1980s Thomas MaCurdy, David Green and Harry Paarsch conducted a study using 1970s data and came to the same conclusion ('Assessing Empirical Approaches for Analyzing Taxes and Labor Supply', Special Issue on Taxation and Labor Supply in Industrial Countries, *Journal of Human Resources*, vol. 25, no. 3, Summer 1990, pp. 415–90).

36 Congressional Budget Office, 'An Analysis of the Roth-Kemp Tax Proposal', October 1978.

37 Weekly work hours of full-time production workers in non-agricultural activities rose during the 1970s: Huberman, Michael, and Minns, Chris, 'The times they are not changin': Days and hours of work in Old and New Worlds, 1870–2000', *Explorations in Economic History* 44, 2007, pp. 538–67.

38 The Tax Equity and Fiscal Responsibility Act of 1982 walked back some of the 1981 Act's provisions but, as Briner, 1983, noted, 'Income taxes will only be increased in a limited number of situations.' Briner, Merlin G., 'Tax Equity and Fiscal Responsibility Act of 1982,' *Akron Tax Journal*, vol. 1, article 2, 1983. Available at: https://ideaexchange.uakron.edu/akrontaxjournal/vol1/iss1/2.

39 'Unemployment Rate: Aged 15–64: All Persons for the United States': (LRUN64TTUSQ156S) https://fred.stlouisfed.org/series/LRUN64TTUSQ156S.

40 OECD Data set: Average annual hours actually worked per worker.

41 Interview with author, September 2019.

42 Feldstein, Martin, and Elmendorf, Douglas W., 'Budget deficits, tax incentives and inflation: a surprising lesson from the 1983–84 recovery', 1989.

43 Feldstein, Martin, 'Supply-Side Economics: Old Truths and New Claims', 1986.

44 Interest rate cuts commenced in 1981, but were much larger in 1982. Interest Rates, Discount Rate for United States (INTDSRUSM193N) International Monetary Fund, Interest Rates, Discount Rate for United States [INTDSRUSM193N],

retrieved from FRED, Federal Reserve Bank of St. Louis; https://fred.stlouisfed.org/series/INTDSRUSM193N.

45 Leibfritz, W., Thornton, J., and Bibbee, A., 'Taxation and Economic Performance', OECD Economics Department Working Papers 176, OECD, 1997, publishing. doi: 10.1787/668811115745.

46 Evers, Michiel, and de Mooij, Ruud, 'The wage elasticity of labour supply: a synthesis of empirical estimates', *De Economist*, 2008, and Blundell, Richard, Duncan, Alan, and Meghir, Costas, 'Estimating Labor Supply Responses Using Tax Reforms', 1998.

47 Moffitt, Robert, and Wilhelm, Mark, 'Tax and Labor Supply Decisions of the Affluent', NBER Working Paper, 1998.

48 Holland, Daniel, 'The effect of taxation on effort: some results for business executives', 1969; Morgan, James, et al., 'A Survey Of Investment Management And Working Behavior Among High-Income Individuals', 1965; Sanders, Thomas H., 'Effects of Taxation: On Executives', 1951.

49 Chaterjee and Robinson, 'Effects of personal income tax on work effort: a sample survey', 1969.

50 Barlow, Brazer, and Morgan, 'A Survey Of Investment Management And Working Behavior Among High-Income Individuals', 1966.

51 Break, George, 'Income Taxes and Incentives to Work: An Empirical Study', 1957; Fields and Stanbury, 'Income Taxes and Incentives to Work: Some Additional Empirical Evidence', 1971.

52 Hausman, Jerry, 'Taxes and Labour Supply', *Handbook of Public Economics*, vol. 1, chapter 4, Elsevier, 1985, pp 213–63.

53 Domar, E.D., and Musgrave, R.A., 1944, 'Proportional Income Taxation and Risk-taking', *Quarterly Journal of Economics* 58, pp. 388–422. Other papers include Cowell, F.A., 'Some notes on progression and risk-taking', *Economica*, August 1975; Mossin, Jan, 'Taxation and Risk-Taking: An Expected Utility Approach', *Economica*, February 1968; Tobin, James, 'Liquidity Preference as Behavior Towards Risk', *Review of Economic Studies*, vol. 25, issue 2, 1958.

54 Lindsey, Lawrence B., 'Individual Taxpayer Response to Tax Cuts: 1982–84', 1987.

55 Lindsey, Lawrence B., 'Finance Panel Can Look Back, Carry Forward – Lessons of the 1981 Tax Cut', *Wall Street Journal*, 6 May 1986.

56 'Scholarly Mentor to Bush's Team', *New York Times*, 6 December 2002.

57 Based on Heritage Foundation tax figures, a single filer earning the BLS calculated average wage would have seen their marginal rate drop 2 percentage points. https://files.taxfoundation.org/legacy/docs/fed_individual_rate_history_nominal.pdf.

58 The group whose incomes rose 70 per cent included just twenty-two people, and further research showed this level increase was far above typical for high earners.

59 Congressional Budget Office, 'An Analysis of the Roth-Kemp Tax Cut Proposal', op. cit., p. 15.

60 Navratil, 'Impact of Marginal Tax Rate Reductions on reported income on individual tax returns', 1994; Auten and Carroll, 'Behavior of the affluent and the 1986 Tax Reform Act', 1995; Eissa, Nada, 'Taxation and Labor Supply of Married Women: The Tax Reform Act of 1986 as a Natural Experiment', 1995; Carroll, Robert, 'Do taxpayers really respond to changes in tax rates? Evidence from the 1993 tax act', 1998; Aaronson and French, 'The Effects of Progressive Taxation on Labor Supply When Hours and Wages are Jointly Determined', 2002.

61 Feldstein, 'Supply Side Economics', op. cit., pp. 26–30.

62 Austen Goolsbee coined the phrase, but it became widely used by other academics and bodies like the IMF.

63 Chancellor of the Exchequer Alistair Darling, Pre-Budget Report statement, 24 November 2008.

64 Alistair Darling, Budget speech, 22 April 2009.

65 https://www.telegraph.co.uk/finance/budget/5203642/Budget-2009-Gordon-Brown-declares-class-war-with-tax-on-high-earners.html

66 Alistair Darling, *Back from the Brink,* chapter 9, 2011, electronic version.

67 Budget 2010, 'Securing the recovery', March 2010.

68 David Cameron, *For the Record*, chapter 25, 2019, electronic version.

69 Brewer, Mike, and Browne, James, 'Can more revenue be raised by increasing income tax rates for the very rich?', Institute for Fiscal Studies, 2009.

70 David Cameron, *For the Record*, op. cit.

71 Although not officially under direct control of the Treasury, HMRC tends to conform to the Treasury's policy choices. See Bergin, Tom, 'Special Report: How the UK tax authority got cosy with big business', 27 December 2012, http://www.reuters.com/article/2012/12/27/us-tax-hmrc-idUSBRE8BQ03220121227.

72 HMRC, 'The Exchequer effect of the 50 per cent additional rate of income tax', March 2012.

73 'Britain's Experience in Raising the Top Tax Rate', 27 March 2012.

74 'Britain Abolishes 50 Percent Tax Rate, Lowers Corporation Tax', 21 March 2012.

75 Gardiner, Nile, The Heritage Foundation, 'Britain's Millionaire Exodus is a Wake-up Call to Barack Obama's High tax America', *Daily Telegraph*, 28 November 2012.

76 Cochrane, John, Senior Fellow, Hoover Institute, 'Experimental Evidence on the Effect of Taxes', 28 November 2012.

77 'Why We Can't Go Back to Sky-high, 1950s Tax Rates', American Enterprise Institute, 18 April 2012, https://www.aei.org/economics/public-economics/why-we-cant-go-back-to-sky-high-1950s-tax-rates/.

78 BBC News, 'Budget 2012: George Osborne Cuts 50p Top Tax Rate', 21 March 2012.

79 Prime Minister's Questions, Hansard, 5 December 2012.

80 *Daily Telegraph*, 27 January 2014.

81 Browne, James, and Phillips, David, 'Updating and critiquing HMRC's analysis of the UK's 50 per cent top marginal rate of tax', IFS Working Paper W17/12, 2017.

82 Goldman Sachs International, Freshfields Bruckhaus Deringer LLP and Deloitte LLP are among the firms whose staff or partners saw their average pay remain below peak levels for years after the crash, their accounts lodged at Companies House show.

83 Office of the New York State Comptroller: bonus pool for securities industry employees who work in New York City: https://osc.state.ny.us/press/docs/wall-street-bonuses-2018.pdf.

84 Congressional Budget Office, 'The Effect of Tax Changes on Labor Supply in CBO's Microsimulation Tax Model', April 2007.

85 *Grossbritannien: Einwanderung ständige und nicht ständige ausländische Wohnbevölkerung mit Erwerb*: https://www.bfs.admin.ch/bfs/de/home/statis-tiken/bevoelkerung/migration-integration/auslaendische-bevoelkerung.html.

86 'BlueCrest hedge fund switches from Guernsey to Jersey', BBC News, 14 November 2014, https://www.bbc.com/news/world-europe-jersey-30040235.

87 Guernsey Annual Population Bulletin 2011–13.

88 https://opendata.gov.je/dataset/total-population-annual-change-natural-growth-net-migration-per-year/resource/75c9a5ed-e95e-4052-a7c8-96d5dab8a64a.

89 According to the Institut Monégasque de la Statistique et des Études Économiques, 918 residents arriving from 2008 to 2016 gave the United Kingdom as their previous country of residence, against 982 residents arriving between 2000 and 2008 Census.

90 David Cameron, *For the Record*, op. cit.

91 Author's calculations – excluding any behavioural response – based on table 2.6.

92 Office for National Statistics, 'Average Incomes, Taxes and Benefits by Decile Groups of ALL Households'.

93 World Inequality Database: https://wid.world/country/united-kingdom/.

94 The tax rate increased from 31 per cent to 39.6 per cent, but the lifting of a cap on the Medicare payroll tax meant that, in the view of most commentators includ-ing Martin Feldstein, the actual top rate went from 31 per cent to 42.5 per cent.

95 Goolsbee, Austan, 'Evidence on the High-Income Laffer Curve from Six Decades of Tax Reform', 1999.

96 Bajika, Jon, Cole, Adam, and Heim, Bradley, 'Jobs and Income Growth of Top Earners and the Causes of Changing Income Inequality: Evidence from US Tax Return Data', Working paper, Williams College, 2010.

97 Examples include Long, James, 'The Impact of Marginal Tax Rates on Taxable Income: Evidence from State Income Tax Differentials', 1999; Carroll, Robert, and Hrung, Warren, 'What Does the Taxable Income Elasticity Say About

Dynamic Responses to Tax Changes?', 2005. A wide swathe of other studies have also found that factors other than effort explain a large part of income responsiveness to taxation, including Brewer, M, et al., 'Means-Testing and Tax Rates on Earnings', 2010; Blow and Preston, 'Deadweight Loss and Taxation of Earned Income: Evidence from Tax Records of the UK Self-Employed', IFS Working Paper 02/15 2002.

98 George Osborne announced in his budget speech on 21 March 2012 that the rate reduction would be effective in the 2013–14 tax year.

99 Goolsbee, Austan, 'What Happens When You Tax the Rich? Evidence from Executive Compensation', *Journal of Political Economy*, vol. 108, no. 2, April 2000.

100 Sillamaa, Mary-Anne, and Veall, Michael R., 2001, 'The Effect of Marginal Tax Rates on Taxable Income: A Panel Study of the 1988 Tax Flattening in Canada,' *Journal of Public Economics*, Elsevier, vol. 80(3), pp. 341–56, June 2001.

101 Aarbu and Thoreson, 'Income Responses to Tax Changes: Evidence from the Norwegian Tax Reform', *National Tax Journal*, 2001.

102 Federal Reserve Bank of Minneapolis, *The Region*, September 2006.

103 Barro, Robert, and Furman, Jason, 'Macroeconomic Effects of the 2017 Tax Reform', 2017; Mertens, Karel et al., 'Marginal Tax Rates and Income: New Time Series Evidence', 2018.

104 Data from Feenstra, Robert C., Inklaar, Robert, and Timmer, Marcel P., 'The Next Generation of the Penn World Table', *American Economic Review*, 105(10), 2015, pp. 3150–82, available for download at www.ggdc.net/pwt.

3. The Hire and Fire Debate

1 'Cgil-Uil, Sciopero, *Venerdì corteo per 30.000 a Torino*', *Ansa*, 10 December 2014. A report in *Le Parisien* headlined '*Italie: première grève générale sous le gouvernement Renzi*' said 70,000 turned out in Turin – almost twice the number in Rome.

2 'La Cgil: '*Norme da anni '20. Adesioni oltre il 60%. Scontri a Milano e Torino*', *La Repubblica*, 12 December 2014.

3 'IMF backs Renzi reforms of Italy's labour market', *Financial Times*, 18 September 2014.

4 OECD Economic Surveys, Italy, February 2015.

5 Hopenhayn, Hugo, and Rogerson, Richard, 'Job Turnover and Policy Evaluation: A General Equilibrium Analysis', *Journal of Political Economy* 101:5, 1993, pp. 915–38.

6 Blanchard, Olivier, 'The Economics of Unemployment. Shocks, Institutions, and Interactions', Lionel Robbins Lectures, London School of Economics, 2000.

7 Saint-Paul, G., *The Political Economy of Employment Protection*, Economics Working Papers, University Pompeu Fabra, 1999.

8 OECD Employment Outlook 2013 provides details and a fuller list.

9 *The Peace Treaty*, Part XIII, Section 1, p. 193.

10 Ibid.

11 Holzmann, Robert, et al., 'Severance Pay Programs around the World: History, Rationale, Status and Reforms', IZA Discussion Paper 5731, May 2011.

12 Silverman, Julius (MP), House of Commons, 14 February 1964: https://api. parliament.uk/historic-hansard/commons/1964/feb/14/ redundant-workers-severance-pay-bill.

13 An example is Akerlof, George A., 'Labor Contracts as Partial Gift Exchange', *Quarterly Journal of Economics*, vol. 97, issue 4, November 1982, pp. 543–69.

14 International Labour Organization Ratifications by country, https://www.ilo. org/dyn/normlex/en/f?p=1000:11001.

15 The Reagan administration argued against Maine's severance pay legislation in the Supreme Court when the Fort Halifax Packing Company launched an action against the law: https://supreme.justia.com/cases/federal/us/482/1/.

16 Folbre, Nancy R., Leighton, Julia L., and Roderick, Melissa R., 'Plant Closings and Their Regulation in Maine, 1971–82', *ILR Review*, vol. 37, no. 2, January 1984, pp. 185–96.

17 *OECD Economic Outlook*, 1967 to 1978.

18 *OECD Economic Outlook*, 1979 to 1989.

19 'IMF approves 144.7 million SDR loan for Senegal', Reuters, 22 November 1988.

20 'Growth, competitiveness, employment: The challenges and ways forward into the 21st century', Commission of the European Communities White Paper, 5 December 1993.

21 'European Social Policy – A Way Forward for the Union', White Paper, 27 July 1994.

22 'Deregulation Is No Miracle Cure', Letters to the Editor, *Wall Street Journal Europe*, 29 November 1994.

23 'Leaders Set for Economic Summit', *Seattle Times*, 1 May 1985.

24 'But How About Jobs?', *Wall Street Journal Europe*, 29 July 1994.

25 Dolado, Juan J., Garcia-Serrano, Carlos, and Jimeno, Juan F., 'Drawing Lessons from the Boom Of Temporary Jobs In Spain', *Economic Journal*, Royal Economic Society, vol. 112(721), June 2002, pp. 270–95.

26 'Spain Is Pushed to Cut High Labor Costs', *Wall Street Journal*, 21 February 2009.

27 'Hundreds of thousands protest Spanish labour reforms', Agence France-Presse, 20 February 2012.

28 Renzi, Matteo, '*Berlusconi rispetti i patti, prima l'Italicum poi il Colle. L'Ilva tornerà allo Stato, la salviamo e poi vendiamo*', *La Repubblica*, 30 November 2014.

29 'Renzi says Jobs Act is "Copernican revolution"', ANSA – English Media Service, 24 December 2014.

30 'Italy approves key parts of Renzi's new labour rules', Reuters, 20 February 2015.

31 'IMF Executive Board Concludes 2015 Article IV Consultation with Italy', Press Release 15/321, 7 July 2015.

32 *OECD Economic Outlook*, June 2015, p. 142.

33 'Padoan says Jobs Act will produce "huge" benefits for Italy,' ANSA, 19 February 2015.

34 The OECD indicators on Employment Protection Legislation, https://www.oecd.org/employment/emp/employmentdatabase-labourmarketpoliciesandinstitutions.htm.

35 Beecroft, Adrian, 'Report on Employment Law, October 2011', published May 2012: https://www.gov.uk/government/publications/employment-law-review-report-beecroft.

36 '"Socialist" Vince Cable not fit for office, says Adrian Beecroft', *Daily Telegraph*, 22 May 2012.

37 'Osborne revives divisive plan to let bosses "hire and fire at will"', *Independent*, 23 February 2012.

38 Raab, Dominic (MP), 'Escaping The Strait Jacket', Centre for Policy Studies, November 2011.

39 Renzi declared on his Facebook page on 1 March 2016 that 'The Jobs Act boom isimpressive.'https://www.ansa.it/sito/notizie/topnews/2016/03/01/renzi-impressionante-boom-del-jobs-act_308ba94e-4bfa-4db3-a856-971f27670b64.html.

40 'Renzi's Jobs Act isn't getting Italy to work,' Reuters, 15 December 2015.

41 Eurostat, https://appsso.eurostat.ec.europa.eu/nui/show.do?data set=une_rt_a&lang=en.

42 'Renzi's jobs act isn't getting Italy to work', Reuters, 15 December 2015, and 'Unemployment up as number of 'Inactive' drops', Ansa, 9 January 2017.

43 Fana, Marta, Guarascio, Dario and Cirillo, Valeria, 'Labour market reforms in Italy: evaluating the effects of the Jobs Act', 2015.

44 Pinelli, Dino, Torre, Roberta, Pace, Lucianajulia, Cassio, Laura, and Arpaia, Alfonso, 'The Recent Reform of the Labour Market in Italy: A Review', European Commission Discussion Paper 072, December 2017.

45 Analysts noted that the economy was growing at a rate of close to 3 per cent; history suggested employment should be growing more. See 'Spain's economic turnaround fails to dent jobless rate', Reuters, 3 April 2015.

46 Eurofound, 'Spain: A first assessment of the 2012 labour market reform',, 23 December 2015, https://www.eurofound.europa.eu/publications/article/2015/spain-a-first-assessment-of-the-2012-labour-market-reform.

47 Productivity Commission Inquiry, report overview and recommendations, no. 76, 30 November 2015, p. 9: https://www.pc.gov.au/inquiries/completed/workplace-relations/report/workplace-relations-overview.pdf.

48 Mosley, Hugh, 'Employment Protection in Europe Employment Observatory Policies', *inforMISEP*, no. 44, Winter 1993, pp. 21–27.

49 Bertola, Giuseppe, 'Job security, employment and wages', *European Economic Review*, vol. 34, issue 4, June 1990, pp. 851–79.

50 The 2006 *OECD Employment Outlook* states (p. 209) that 'In line with a number of previous studies, no significant impact of employment protection legislation (EPL) on aggregate unemployment is found.' Also, a 2012 review of academic literature, 'The impact of regulation on growth', prepared by Frontier Economics for the UK's Department of Business, Innovation and Skills, found that 'it is not clear whether labour market regulation has a net positive or negative impact on growth.'

51 Baker, Dean, Glyn, Andrew, Howell, David, and Schmitt, John, 'Labor Market Institutions and Unemployment: A Critical Assessment of the Cross-Country Evidence', Center for European Studies Working Paper, 2003.

52 'Report 'based on conversations'', Press Association, 21 June 2012.

53 Beecroft did not respond to attempts to seek comment.

54 Bertola, Giuseppe, Boeri, Tito, and Cazes, Sandrine, 'Employment protection in industrialised countries: The case for new indicators', *International Labour Review*, vol. 139, no. 1, 2000. This study noted that in the late 1980s the annual rates of labour turnover (sum of separations and new hires during the sample period as a percentage of average employment levels) were respectively 126.4 and 92.6 for the United States and Canada, as against 58 for France, 62 for Germany and 68.1 for Italy.

55 McKinsey Global Institute, 'Beyond austerity: A path to economic growth', https://www.mckinsey.com/~/media/McKinsey/Featured%20Insights/Europe/Beyond%20austerity%20A%20path%20to%20growth%20in%20Europe/MGI_Beyond_austerity_A_path_to_economic_growth_full_report.ashx.

56 Nickell, Stephen, 'Unemployment and Labor Market Rigidities: Europe versus North America', *Journal of Economic Perspectives*, vol. 11, no. 3, Summer 1997, pp. 55–74.

57 James Dyson interview, *The Andrew Marr Show*, BBC1, 12 November 2017.

58 International Labour Organisation, employment protection legislation database – EPLex https://www.ilo.org/dyn/eplex/termmain.home?p_lang=en.

59 Dyson declined requests to elaborate on his comments.

60 'Ford to invest €425 million in Valencia plant', *Automotive World*, 30 August 2007. Ford of Europe president and chief executive officer John Fleming was quoted as saying, 'I have always said it was one of our most efficient and flexible plants in Europe.'

61 Statements from and accounts for Ford's Spanish and UK subsidiaries show jobs were cut at similar rates in both countries.

62 Alexander, Magnus, 'Hiring and Firing: Its Economic Waste and How to Avoid It', *The Annals*, vol. 65, issue 1, May 1916.

63 Mosley, Hugh, 'Employment Protection in Europe', *inforMISEP* 44, Winter 1993.

64 Belot, M., Boone, J., and Van Ours, J., 'Welfare-Improving Employment Protection', *Economica* 74(295), 2007, pp. 381–96.

65 Marinescu, I., 'Shortening the Tenure Clock: The Impact of Strengthened UK Job Security Legislation Job Market', Paper, NBER, Cambridge, MA, January 2006.

66 Damiani, M., and Pompei, F., 'Labour protection and productivity in EU economies: 1995–2005', 2010.

67 Cingano, F., Leonardi, M., Messina, J., and Pica, G. 'Employment Protection Legislation, Productivity and Investment: Evidence from Italy', mimeograph, University of Salerno, 2008; Autor, David H., Kerr, William R., and Kugler, Adriana D., 'Do Employment Protections Reduce Productivity? Evidence from US States', NBER Working Paper 12860, January 2007.

68 Koeniger, W., 'Dismissal Costs and Innovation', *Economics Letters*, vol. 88, 2005, pp. 79–84.

69 Nickell, S., and Layard, R., 'Labor market institutions and economic performance' in Ashenfelter, O.C., and Card, D. (eds), *Handbook of Labor Economics*, 1st ed., 3C, Amsterdam, 1999, pp. 3029–84.

70 'The Distributional Impact of Structural Reforms', OECD, 2016, Table A1, p. 46.

71 A 2005 survey of 192 professional economists by Paul Ferraro and Laura Taylor found that economists don't even understand or agree on what it means.

72 Discussion at Council on Foreign Relations in New York, 24 September 2014: https://www.cfr.org/event/prime-minister-matteo-renzi-growth-and-jobs-italy-0.

73 'ANALYSIS: Italy needs red tape bonfire before labour reform', Reuters, 3 April 2012.

74 A 2014 IMF Working Paper noted that 'the inefficiency of the Italian judicial system has contributed to reduced investments, slow growth, and a difficult business environment.'

75 'Italy's judicial shake-up caught in political conflicts of interest', Reuters, 30 June, 2016, citing website L'incredibile Parlamento Italiano: https://www.reuters.com/investigates/special-report/italy-justice/.

76 Ibid.

77 'If Matteo Renzi's proposals lose, insufficient economic reform could be to blame', *Economist*, 3 December 2016.

78 'Italian bonds suffer worst day in more than 25 years', Reuters, 29 May 2018.

4. The Jensen Claim

1 Conference programme.

2 Managerial Economics Research Center Annual Report, 1978.

3 Jensen, Michael C., and Zimmerman, Jerold L., 'Management Compensation and the Managerial Labor Market', *Journal of Accounting and Economics* Vol. 7, 1985.

4 Frydman, Carola, and Saks, Raven E., 2005 'Historical Trends in Executive Compensation 1936–2003', p. 57.

5 Jensen, Michael C., and Murphy, Kevin J., 'Performance Pay and Top-Management Incentives,' *Journal of Political Economy*, April 1990.

6 Jensen, Michael C., and Murphy, Kevin J., 'CEO Incentives – It's Not How Much You Pay, But How,' *Harvard Business Review*, May–June 1990.

7 'James B. Duke Wills Bulk of $100 million to Widow and Child', *New York Times*, 24 October 1925.

8 Albert Lasker, interviews with Professor Allan Nevins and Dean Albertson, *American Heritage*, December 1954.

9 Brandt, Allan M., *The Cigarette Century: The Rise, Fall and Deadly Persistence of the Product that Defined America*, Basic Books, 2007.

10 Rogers v. Guaranty Trust Co. of New York et al., No. 227. Argued: 15, 16 December 1932, https://www.law.cornell.edu/supremecourt/text/288/123.

11 'Bonuses Cause Tilt at Lowes Meeting', *New York Times*, 16 December 1932.

12 'Grace's 1929 Bonus reached $1,623,753', *New York Times*, 22 July 1930.

13 British American Tobacco Plc Annual Reports.

14 'American Tobacco Would Split Stock', *New York Times*, 26 June 1930.

15 Rogers v. Guaranty Trust Co. of New York et al., op. cit.

16 Rogers v. Guaranty Trust Co. of New York, June 13, 1932.

17 'G. W. Hill's pay twice exceeded $1 million', *New York Times*, 6 April 1932; 'G. W. Hill's income put at $2,200,000', *New York Times*, 14 March 1931.

18 Senator Burton K. Wheeler, Montana, quoted in 'Big Salaries Bring Demand for Curbs', *New York Times*, 5 March 1934.

19 'Gore Proposes Tax on Excessive Pay', *New York Times*, 1 March 1934.

20 Securities Exchange Act of 1934: https://legcounsel.house.gov/Comps/Securities%20Exchange%20Act%20Of%201934.pdf.

21 'Big salaries lag below 1929 level', Associated Press, 7 December 1935.

22 'Salaries and Fees Listed by the SEC', *New York Times*, 4 May 1937.

23 In the mid-century top executives in the United States more frequently carried the title President, while in the UK the term Managing Director was common. Here I have used the modern term Chief Executive for easier comparisons.

24 Data from Frydman, Carola, and Saks, Raven E., 'Historical Trends in Executive Compensation 1936–2003'.

25 *Forbes Magazine* interview, 10 March 1997: https://www.forbes.com/forbes/1997/0310/5905122a.html#5e9f716324b9.

26 Meckling, William, speech, 'Three Reflections on Performance Rewards and Higher Education', delivered University of Rochester, 18 April 1984. Published in *Journal of Accounting and Economics* 7, 1985, pp. 247–51.

27 Fama, Eugene F., 'My Life in Finance', *Annual Review of Financial Economics*, 2010.

28 Lemann, Nicholas, *Transaction Man: The Rise of the Deal and the Decline of the American Dream*, Farrar, Straus and Giroux, 2019, outlines other examples of Jensen's provocative style.

29 Lowenstein, Roger, *Buffett: The Making of an American Capitalist*, Doubleday, 1995.

30 Berle, Adolf, and Means, Gardiner, 'The Modern Corporation and Private Property', 1932, is seen as a seminal work that initiated research on agency theory.

31 https://www.nobelprize.org/prizes/economic-sciences/2013/fama/facts/.

32 Burrough, Bryan, and Helyar, John, *Barbarians at the Gate: The Fall of RJR Nabisco*, HarperCollins, 1990.

33 Jensen, Michael C., 'The Takeover Controversy', *Executive Speeches*, vol. 2, no. 10, May 1988. Available at SSRN: https://ssrn.com/abstract=568385.

34 Interview with author, 2019.

35 Jensen, 'The Takeover Controversy, op. cit. Jensen made similar comments on in testimony to a 1 April 1987 hearing held by the House Committee on Energy and Commerce, Subcommittee on Telecommunications and Finance entitled 'Impact of Mergers and Acquisitions'.

36 1978 Managerial Economies Research Center Annual Report.

37 Fama, Eugene, 'Efficient Capital Markets: A Review of Theory and Empirical Work', 1970.

38 Scherer, F. M., testimony to Hearings Before the Committee on Banking, Housing, and Urban Affairs, United States Senate, Ninety-fourth Congress, Second Session, on Regulations Under Federal Banking and Securities Laws of Persons Involved in Corporate Takeovers, 16 February 1976.

39 'Nobel prize-winning economists take disagreement to whole new level', *Guardian*, 10 December 2013:https://www.theguardian.com/business/2013/dec/10/nobel-prize-economists-robert-shiller-eugene-fama.

40 Eaton, Jonathan, and Rosen, Harvey, 'Agency, Delayed Compensation and The Structure of Executive Remuneration', NBER Working Paper no. w0777, 1981.

41 Telephone interview with John Wilcox, June 2019.

42 'Cashing in on Options', *Dallas Morning News*, 1 November 1992.

43 https://www.epi.org/publication/ceo-compensation-2018/.

44 https://www.census.gov/data/tables/time-series/demo/income-poverty/historical-income-households.html.

45 Bebchuk et al., Harvard study on executive pay, 2005.

46 Associated Industrial Consultants survey, reported in *The Times*, 17 January 1969.

47 Margaret Thatcher, 'Let Our Children Grow Tall', speech to the Institute of SocioEconomic Studies, 15 September 1975, Margaret Thatcher Foundation, https://www.margaretthatcher.org/document/102769.

48 *Thatcher: A Very British Revolution*, episode, 'Making Margaret', BBC, 2019.

49 Mandelson, Peter, speech to Silicon Valley Executives in October 1998 while serving as Secretary of State for Trade and Industry.

50 Moyle, John, *The Pattern of Ordinary Share Ownership*, Cambridge University Press, 1971, and Briston, Richard J., and Dobbins, Richard, 'Financial Institutions and the Stock Market', *Managerial Finance*, January 1979, showed that institutional shareholders significantly increased their ownership share of UK quoted companies between the 1950s and 1975.

51 Pay surveys from MPR, Incomes Data Services, MM&K/Manifest.

52 Surveys by Incomes Data Services.

53 Bergin, Tom, 'Bosses take bigger share of top British firms' profits', Reuters, 6 May 2016.

54 Office for National Statistics Table 9: Mean equivalised disposable household income, 1977-2015/16, UK (2015/16 prices).

55 Sir Nigel Rudd outlined this argument in a *Financial Times* interview in 2016. Many others have voiced the same arguments.

56 The 1967 Companies Act extended the disclosure requirements for directors' salaries, fees, and taxable benefits.

57 Jensen, Michael C., and Murphy, Kevin J., 'Remuneration: Where we've been, how we got to here, what are the problems, and how to fix them', Finance Working Paper 44/2004, July 2004. Murphy, Kevin J., 'The Politics of Pay: A Legislative History of Executive Compensation', Marshall School of Business Working Paper FBE 01.11, August 2011.

58 Economic Policy Institute data: https://www.epi.org/publication/ceo-compensation-2018/. Similar figures appear in Murphy, Kevin 'Executive Compensation', chapter 38, figure 15, *Handbook of Labour Economics*, 1999.

59 High Pay Centre data.

60 Société Générale, 'CEO Value' report, May 2012.

61 Proxy statements 1943 to 1980. Former compensation adviser Graef Crystal also gave an account of Kodak's polices in 'Incentives fail to improve Kodak's picture', *Pensions & Investments*, 8 February 1993.

62 Eastman Kodak Co. website: https://www.kodak.com/GB/en/corp/aboutus/heritage/georgeeastman/default.htm.

63 https://www.kodak.com/en/company/page/george-eastman-history.

64 Eastman Kodak Proxy statements, 1980 to 1987.

65 'Kodak unveils restructuring plan, including job cuts,' Reuters, 23 August 1989.

66 Kodak 1993 quarterly earnings statements and 10-K filing for 1993.

67 Crystal, 'Incentives fail to improve Kodak's picture', op. cit.

68 Eastman Kodak Proxy 1986 statement and 'Highest-Paid Public Co. Executives', *Rochester Business Journal*, 6 August 1990.

69 Kodak Proxies. Fisher received around $70 million of this in options, with the value representing the reported grant date present value of the option. Fisher generally held his shares and options even after he was allowed to sell, which meant the share drop after his departure is likely to have meant his final receipts

were less than $120 million. The case is unusual, and Economic Policy Institute data shows that usually realised pay is closely aligned but exceeds the reported value of options granted.

70 Kaplan, Steven, 'Top Executive Rewards and Firm Performance: A Comparison of Japan and the United States', 1994; Boschen, John, and Smith, Kimberly, 'You Can Pay Me Now and You Can Pay Me Later: The Dynamic Response of Executive Compensation to Firm Performance', 1995; Hall, Brian, and Liebman, Jeffrey, 'Are CEOs Really Paid Like Bureaucrats?', 1998.

71 Murphy, 'Executive Compensation', op. cit.

72 Hogan, Chris, and Lewis, Craig, 'The Long-Run Performance of Firms Adopting Compensation Plans Based on Economic Profits', 2000; Cooper, Michael J., Gulen, Huseyin, and Raghavendra, Rau P., 'Performance for pay? The relation between CEO incentive compensation and future stock price performance', 2010; Marshall, Ric, 'Out of Whack: US CEO Pay and Long-term Investment Returns', MSCI, October 2017.

73 Defina, A., Harris, T. C., and Ramsay, I. M., 'What is Reasonable Remuneration for Corporate Officers? An Empirical Investigation into the Relationship between Pay and Performance in the Largest Australian Companies', *Company and Securities Law Journal* 12: 6, September 1994, pp. 341–56; Dalton, D. R., Daily, C. M., Certo, S. T., and Roengpitya, R., 'Meta-analyses of Financial Performance and Equity: Fusion or Confusion?', *Academy of Management Journal* 46, 2003, pp. 13–26; Hogan and Lewis, 'The Long-Run Performance of Firms', op. cit.

74 Tosi, Henry, Werner, Steve, Katz, Jeffrey and Gomez-Mejia, Luis, 'How Much Does Performance Matter? A Meta-Analysis of CEO Pay Studies,' *Journal of Management*, vol. 26, no. 2, 2000, JOI-339.

75 Data from Yale University Professor Robert Shiller's S&P series, http://www.econ.yale.edu/~shiller/data.htm.

76 'Kodak to buy its shares even at $100/share', Reuters, 27 April 1999.

77 'The Forever-Working Vacation', *Wall Street Journal*, 28 July 1997.

78 Some studies claim to have identified this phenomenon, including Lazear, Edward P., 'Performance Pay and Productivity', *American Economic Review,* vol. 90, no. 5, December 2000, pp. 1346–61, which examined the Safelite Glass Corporation. However, other academics argue that the impact is less evident long-term, and can lead to problems with the quality of products produced or services delivered.

79 Bergin, Tom, and Bryan-Low, Cassell, 'Double agents – how soccer clubs, players and advisers play the tax game', Reuters, 9 November 2018: https://www.reuters.com/investigates/special-report/soccer-files-fees/.

80 Buschmann, Rafael, and Wulzinger, Michael, *Football Leaks: Uncovering the Dirty Deals Behind The Beautiful Game*, Guardian Faber Publishing, 2018.

81 Motorola Proxy, 1994, Kodak Proxies, 1994–2001.

82 Kaufman, Stephen P., 'Evaluating the CEO', First Person, *Harvard Business Review* 86, no. 10 (October 2008).

83 I was unable to find a definitive list of CEO departures, so I compiled this list from news reports and company stock market announcements.

84 Davis, J. H., Schoorman, F. D., and Donaldson, L., 'Toward a stewardship theory of management', *Academy of Management Review*, 22, 1997, pp. 20–47.

85 Norges Bank Investment Management, 'Remuneration of the CEO', *Asset Manager Perspective*, April, 2017.

86 Novavax, Inc. Form 10-K/A, 29 April 2020.

87 Jensen and Murphy, 'Remuneration', op. cit.

88 Friedman, Milton, 'Monetary Correction: A Proposal for Escalator Clauses to Reduce the Costs of Ending Inflation', Institute of Economic Affairs, Occasional Paper 41, 1974.

89 'The Role of Monetary Policy', *American Economic Review*, vol. LVIII, March 1968. The vanquishing of high US inflation by Paul Volcker in the early 1980s through swingeing interest rates hikes, after control of the money supply had failed to achieve this, showed decisively that Friedman was flat wrong. The twelve years of central banks keeping interest rates at ultra-low levels after 2008 also show that Friedman's claim that central bankers could not influence interest rates for periods beyond twelve months was nonsense.

5. The Stigler Hypothesis

1 According to my ten- and twelve-year-old sons.

2 First Report of the Low Pay Commission, presented to Parliament June 1998.

3 First Report of the Committee, August 1888.

4 Hansard, 9 June 1890.

5 During the Middle Ages there were efforts to regulate labourers' wages, usually with a view to keeping them down, but nothing that could be considered a national minimum wage.

6 Debate on the Sweating System, Hansard, 9 June 1890: https://api.parliament.uk/historic-hansard/lords/1890/jun/09/the-sweating-system.

7 Debate on the Trade Boards Bill, Hansard, 28 April 1909.

8 Clarke, John Bates, editorial in the *Atlantic*, September 1913, as reported in the *New York Times*, 3 September 1919.

9 Brown, H. LaRue, 'Massachusetts and the Minimum Wage', *Annals of the American Academy of Political and Social Science*, vol. 48, 'The Cost of Living', July 1913, pp. 13–21. There were earlier, unsuccessful attempts at such legislation, including a 1901 Indiana minimum wage law, later overruled by the state Supreme Court ('Minimum Wage Law Void', *New York Times*, 2 April 1903), that set a minimum wage for those working on state contracts. According to Kelley, Florence, 'Minimum-Wage Laws', *Journal of Political Economy*, vol. 20,

no. 10, December 1912, pp. 999–1010, Minnesota and Wisconsin considered minimum wage bills in 1910. In 1912, Ohioans voted in favour of a minimum wage: http://guides.law.csuohio.edu/c.php?g=190570&p=1258419).

10 Adkins v. Children's Hospital, 1923: https://www.law.cornell.edu/supreme-court/text/261/525.) Murphy v. Sardell, https://casetext.com/case/murphy-v-sardell and 'Minimum wage law is declared illegal', *New York Times*, 20 October 1925. Donham v. West Nelson Manufacturing, 1927.

11 In United States v. Darby Lumber Company, the Supreme Court in 1941 dismissed a lower courts ruling that the 1938 Fair Labor Standards Act FLSA was unconstitutional: https://www.oyez.org/cases/1940-1955/312us100.

12 'A Minimum Wage', House of Commons Library Research Paper 95/7, 17 January 1995. Department of Labour, 'Fair Labor Standards Act of 1938: Maximum Struggle for a Minimum Wage', *Monthly Labor Review*, June 1978: https://www.dol.gov/general/aboutdol/history/flsa1938.

13 *Labour Manifesto – Britain will win*, 1987 Page 4.

14 'The Great American Job Machine: The Proliferation of Low Wage Employment in the US Economy', sponsored by the Joint Economic Committee, December 1986.

15 The US Catholic Conference annual Labor Day message, as reported in 'Catholic leadership calls for minimum wage hike', *Houston Chronicle*, 26 August 1988.

16 'Poll finds many favor increasing minimum wage', Associated Press, 26 June 1987.

17 'Dukakis Sounds Economic Revitalization Theme', Associated Press, 9 May 1987.

18 Speech to Conservative Party Conference, October 1986.

19 Cited by President Jimmy Carter in address to members of the Polish community in Philadelphia, 30 October 1980. Weekly Compilation of Presidential Documents, vol. 16, issues 41–52.

20 'Job Losses Possible, Study Says', *Sunday Oklahoman*, 6 September 1987.

21 'Labor's Push to Boost Minimum Wage Draws Unexpected Opposition From Some Democrats', *Wall Street Journal*, 3 June 1988.

22 'The right minimum wage: $0.00', *New York Times* Editorial, 14 January 1987.

23 Pyper, Doug, 'The National Minimum Wage: historical background', House of Commons Library Standard Note SN06897, May 2014.

24 Page iii, fifth report.

25 Robert Giffen, a statistical expert and writer on economic matters, testified, in his capacity as Assistant Secretary at the Board of Trade, on the subject of how the government recorded immigration. He did not discuss economic theory. Giffen is remembered as the conceiver of the idea of a 'Giffen good' – a product for which demand rises as its price rises, perhaps because it is such an efficient source of sustenance that other, less efficient sources of sustenance must be

abandoned as the Giffen good becomes harder to afford. Ireland and the case of potatoes in the nineteenth century was seen as a possible example, but the theory was never proven.

26 Bentham, Jeremy, *Manual of Political Economy*, 1843. Like much of Bentham's work, this was published after his death in the mid-nineteenth century, but the writings that became the *Manual* are believed to have been written between 1786 and 1795.

27 Clark, John Bates, 'The Distribution of Wealth: A Theory of Wages, Interest and Profits', 1899.

28 Keynes, J. M., 'The Question of High Wages', *Political Quarterly*, 1930.

29 Tobin, James, 'Improving the Economic Status of the Negro', 1965; Baily, Martin Neil, and Tobin, James, 'Macroeconomic Effects of Selective Public Employment and Wage Subsidies', 1977.

30 Myrdal, Gunnar, *An American Dilemma*, Harper & Brothers, New York, 1944.

31 https://fee.org/articles/hayeks-rejuvenating-event/. Jackson, Walter A., *Gunnar Myrdal and America's Conscience*, Chapel Hill: The University of North Carolina Press, 1990, p. 330. See also Eliæson, Sven, 'Gunnar Myrdal: A Theorist of Modernity', *Acta Sociologica* 43 (4), pp 331–41, 2000.

32 Samuelson, Robert, 'The Myth of the Minimum Wage', *Washington Post*, 6 July 1988.

33 Kearl, J. R., Pope, Clayne, Whiting, Gordon, and Wimmer, Larry, 'A Confusion of Economists', 1979.

34 Lester, Richard A., 'Shortcomings of Marginal Analysis for Wage-Employment Problems', *American Economic Review*, vol. 36, no. 1, March 1946.

35 Lester, Richard A., 'Marginalism, Minimum Wages, and Labor Markets', *American Economic Review*, vol. 37, no. 1, March 1947, pp. 135–48, as cited in Neumark, David and Wascher, William, 'Minimum Wages and Employment', IZA Institute for the Study of Labor, January 2007.

36 Stigler, George, 'The Economics of Minimum Wage Legislation', *American Economic Review*, vol. 36, no. 3, June 1946, p. 358.

37 Eccles, Mary, and Freeman, Richard B., 'What! Another Minimum Wage Study', NBER Working Paper No. 878, April 1982, put the cost at $17 million at prevailing prices.

38 Brown, Charles, Gilroy, Curtis, and Kohen, Andrew, 'The Effect of The Minimum Wage on Employment and Unemployment: A Survey', NBER Working Paper 846, 1982.

39 Neumark, David, Salas, J.M. Ian, and Wascher, William, 'Revisiting the Minimum Wage-Employment Debate: Throwing Out the Baby With the Bathwater?', NBER Working Paper 18681, January 2013.

40 'Thatcher praises Friedman, her freedom fighter', *Daily Telegraph*, 17 November 2006: https://www.telegraph.co.uk/news/uknews/1534387/Thatcher-praises-Friedman-her-freedom-fighter.html.

41 Margaret Thatcher letter to Hayek, 17 February 1982: https://www.margaret thatcher.org/document/117179. Thatcher is also reputed to have pulled a copy of one of Hayek's books out of her bag once and declared to a Conservative party researcher that 'This is what we believe', but the story seems to be a myth.

42 'The effect of the minimum wage on the fast food industry', ILRR, 1992.

43 Telephone interview with David Card, December 2019.

44 Telephone interview with Richard Freeman, October 2019. Card told the author in December 2019 he just didn't see much point in debating with Welch. Welch made his poor view of Card and Krueger clear in interviews and comments.

45 'Minimum wage at a maximum? even some supporters of the new bill express concerns that raising the wage to $6.15 an hour could lose jobs', *Portland Press Herald*, New York Times Service, 22 March 1998.

46 'Minimum Wage vs. Supply and Demand', *The Wall Street Journal*, 24 April 1996.

47 Becker, Gary S., 'It's Simple: Hike The Minimum Wage, And You Put People Out Of Work', *Businessweek*, 5 March 1995.

48 Barro, Robert J., 'Higher Minimum Wage, Higher Dropout Rate', *Wall Street Journal*, 11 January 1996.

49 Bill Clinton cites the work in chapter 42 of his autobiography, *My Life*, as influencing his decision to increase the minimum wage.

50 'Machin, Stephen, and Manning, Alan, 'The Effects of Minimum Wages on Wage Dispersion and Employment: Evidence from the U.K. Wages Councils', *ILR Review*, 1994, vol. 47, issue 2.

51 'Battle lines are drawn in the struggle for minimum wage', *The Times*, 6 July 1995; 'Labour unveils its economic blueprint', *Independent*, 28 June 1995; *A New Economic Future for Britain*, Labour Party, 1995.

52 The influential 1994 OECD Jobs Study urged members to water down minimum wage rules.

53 *The Times* called the plan 'a homage to the ghosts of old Labour past' – leading article, 'Ghosts of Labour past – The minimum wage will benefit no one, least of all the poor', 28 November 1997.

54 Brown, Gordon, *My Life, Our Times,* Vintage, 2017.

55 OECD Data set: Minimum relative to average wages of full-time workers.

56 'Minimum wage could ruin small businesses', *FSB Western Morning News*, 22 March 1999.

57 Interviews with local businesses and accounts lodged at Companies House.

58 'No job losses from wage increase', *Herald Express*, 16 February 2000.

59 'Jobless hits all time low,' *Herald Express*, 30 August 2000.

60 'Unemployment rates show negligible fall', *Western Morning News*, 18 April 2002.

61 ILO unemployment rate: South-west, Labour market statistics time series, Office for National Statistics

62 World Bank Annual percentage growth rate of GDP per capita based on constant local currency.

63 ILO unemployment rate: London, Labour market statistics time series, Office for National Statistics.

64 Low Pay Commission Report, 2015.

65 'Norman attacks CBI for silence on regulation', *The Times*, 4 November 1998.

66 'George Osborne cautious over 50p minimum wage increase', Press Association, 9 January 2014.

67 'Osborne catches the Low Pay Commission off guard', *Financial Times*, 9 July 2015, https://www.ft.com/content/cc13a008-264c-11e5-bd83-71cb60e8f08c.

68 Low Pay Commission Remit, July 2015.

69 'Warning on minimum wage', *Independent*, 23 June 1997.

70 European Commission, DG Employment, Social Affairs and Inclusion, 'Maximising the minimum: a review of minimum wage approaches and trends in European Member States', Thematic Paper, April 2014. Dolado et al., 'The Economic Impact of Minimum Wages in Europe', 1996, and Machin, Stephen and Manning, Alan, 1997, 'Minimum wages and economic outcomes in Europe', had similar findings.

71 Kertesi, Gabor, and Kollo, Janos, 'The Employment Effects of Nearly Doubling the Minimum Wage – The Case of Hungary', Budapest Working Papers on the Labour Market BWP – 2003/6, 2003, Hungarian Academy of Sciences, Institute of Economics, Labour Research Department, Budapest.

72 Harasztosi, Peter, and Lindner, Attila, 'Who Pays for the Minimum Wage?' *American Economic Review*, vol. 109, no. 8, August 2019.

73 'German jobless rate falls to new record low in March', Reuters, 29 March 2019

74 James Tobin interview, *Region*, 1 December 1996, https://www.minneapolisfed.org/publications/the-region/interview-with-james-tobin.

75 Among the long-running textbooks whose editions published from the mid-1990s omitted earlier bald claims that minimum wage rules killed jobs were William J. Baumol and Alan S. Blinder's *Economics: Principles and Policy* (Eleventh Edition, South-Western Publishing, 2009) and Paul Samuelson and William Nordhaus's *Economics* (Nineteenth Edition, McGraw Hill, 2010).

76 IMF Article IV Consultation, Country Report United States, 2015.

77 OECD Economic Surveys United States, June 2014.

78 Japan Economic Survey, OECD, April 2017.

79 Brown, Gilroy and Kohen, 'The Effect of The Minimum Wage on Employment and Unemployment', op. cit.

80 Brown, Charles C., 'The Old Minimum-Wage Literature and Its Lessons for the New', Chapter 5, *The Effects of the Minimum Wage on Employment*, AEI Press, 1996.

81 Ibid.

82 Ibid.

83 Ibid.

84 Interview with David Card, December 2019.

85 Doucouliagos, Hristos, and Stanley, T. D., 'Publication Selection Bias in Minimum-Wage Research? A Meta-Regression Analysis', *British Journal of Industrial Relations*, Vol. 47, Issue 2, May 2009.

86 ISS A/S, one of the world's largest suppliers of outsourced cleaning, janitorial, catering and security services, has said repeatedly over the years that it usually manages to pass the cost of increased wages on to clients, and that in the short to medium term margins are not impacted. Examples of this include page 58 of the company's 2002 Annual Report, and comments from CEO Jeff Gravenhorst on investor calls on 12 March 2015 (on Germany) and 4 May 2016 (regarding Turkey and the UK). Michel Landel, CEO of French outsourcer Sodexo SA, responded to a question about minimum wage increases on a results call on 14 April 2016 by saying that 'We of course pass these increases to our clients most of the time.' David Telling, chairman of MITIE, owner of pest control firm Rentokil, said in July 1999 that the minimum wage 'caused us no difficulty; we passed it all on.'

87 Adam Smith Lecture, June 2018.

88 Lordan, Grace, 'Minimum wage and the propensity to automate or offshore', 31 October 2017: https://assets.publishing.service.gov.uk/government/uploads/system/uploads/attachment_data/file/661853/LordanMWandpropenstitytoautomateoroffshore_FINAL_2017_Report.pdf.

89 Lordan and Neumark identified the automobile sector as an example but, as Jonathan Tilley noted in *McKinsey Insights*, September 2017, over the past thirty years the average robot price has fallen by half in real terms, helping the manufacturing sector: a prime driver of the results in the Lordan-Nuemark study.

90 Dave Deno, Chief Financial Officer, Yum! Brands Inc., told investors on a results call on 7 December 2004 that the KFC owner had turnover of 100 per cent, below the US fast-food industry average of 180 per cent, and that the company's figure for Mexico was 172 per cent. Panera bread CFO Michael Bufano said in 2019 at CNBC's @Work Human Capital + Finance conference that this company's 100 per cent turnover was below the industry's then average of 130 per cent. The turnover rate in the US restaurants and accommodations sector more broadly was 74.9 per cent in 2018, according to data from the Bureau of Labor Statistics' Job Openings and Labor Turnover (JOLTS) program. ISS CEO Jeff Gravenhorst said in a 17 September 2015 call with investors that his company had a worldwide turnover level of 40 per cent.

91 US National Restaurant Association press release, 20 May 2019: https://restaurant.org/News/Pressroom/Press-Releases/National-Restaurant-Association-intros-ServSuccess.

92 Clark, 'The Distribution of Wealth', op. cit.

93 IMF, 'Finance & Development', March 2019.

94 OECD Data set: Minimum relative to average wages of full-time workers.

95 April 2016 interview with the Washington Center for Equitable Growth.

96 Solow, Robert, 'After the Phillips Curve: Persistence of High Inflation and High Unemployment', Proceedings of a Federal Reserve Bank of Boston Conference Held at Edgartown, Massachusetts, June 1978, cited in Seidman, Laurence S., 'The New Classical Counter-Revolution: A False Path for Macroeconomics', *Eastern Economic Journal*, 1 January, 2005.

97 See Fleetwood, Steve, 'Re-thinking Labour Markets: A Critical Realist-Socioeconomic Perspective', *Capital and Class* 89, 2006, and 'Do Labour Supply and Demand Curves Exist?', *Cambridge Journal of Economics*, August 2014.

98 David Card, interview, *Region*, journal of the Minneapolis Fed, 1 December 2006: https://www.minneapolisfed.org/publications/the-region/interview-with-david-card.

99 Telephone interview with Prof. Richard B. Freeman, November 2019.

100 Solow, Robert, Presidential Address to the American Economic Association, 1980, cited by Mankiw, Gregory N., 'The Macroeconomist As Scientist And Engineer', NBER Working Paper 12349, June 2006.

101 Interview with George Osborne, September 2019.

6. The Russell Graph

1 ONS, The proportion of current smokers among adults aged eighteen years and above by local authority, Great Britain, 2012 to 2018: https://www.ons.gov.uk/peoplepopulationandcommunity/healthandsocialcare/healthandlifeexpectancies/bulletins/adultsmokinghabitsingreatbritain/2018.

2 Royal College of Physicians, 'Smoking and Health', 1962, p. 9.

3 Examples of where this claim has been made include Cancer Council Victoria, https://www.tobaccoinaustralia.org.au/chapter-13-taxation/13-1-price-elasticity-of-demand-for-tobacco-products); UK Treasury, 'Tobacco levy: response to the consultation', September 2015 (https://assets.publishing.service.gov.uk/government/uploads/system/uploads/attachment_data/file/464795/PU1814_Tobacco_Levy_final_v3.pdf); US non-profit Campaign for Tobacco-Free Kids in a 2018 publication, https://www.tobaccofreekids.org/assets/factsheets/0146.pdf.

4 Official data sources like statistical offices often lack complete data sets on consumption and prices, and so industry data and other sources are often relied upon by researchers and the government. Occasionally these sources do not match, so to avoid errors I have tried to use multiple sources when illustrating key trends. Consumption data here is from Nguyen, Lien, Rosenqvist, Gunnar, and Pekurinen, Markku, 'Demand for Tobacco in Europe: An Econometric Analysis of 11 Countries for the PPACTE Project', Report 6, 2012, which gives a figure of 70 per cent drop. Forey, Barbara, Hamling, Jan, Hamling, John, Thornton, Alison, and Lee, Peter, 'International Smoking

Statistics: A collection of worldwide historical data – United Kingdom', 2016, gave a figure of a 66 per cent fall.

5 WHO Report on the Global Tobacco Epidemic, 2019.

6 The economist Jonathan Gruber, who has published extensively on tobacco taxes, is among those who have advocated for the wider application of such measures to other social problems. See 'Value-Added Tax and Excises: Commentary Prepared for the Report of a Commission on Reforming the Tax System for the 21st Century, Chaired by Sir James Mirrlees', 2007, and 'Taxing Sin to Modify Behavior and Raise Revenue', NIHCM Expert Voices, April 2010.

7 Swedish Tax Agency, https://www.skatteverket.se/privat/fastigheterochbostad/rotochrutarbete.4.2e56d4ba1202f95012080002966.html.

8 Ken Clarke, *Kind of Blue*, Macmillan, 2016.

9 http://www.hullcc.gov.uk/pls/hullpublichealth/assets/Smoking2pages2014.pdf.

10 According to the ONS, in 2014 individuals with a personal income of less than £20,000 smoked on average between 11.6 and 11.8 cigarettes per day, and those with an income of £40,000 or more smoked 10.0 cigarettes per day, https://www.ons.gov.uk/peoplepopulationandcommunity/healthandsocialcare/healthandlifeexpectancies/bulletins/adultsmokinghabitsingreatbritain/2014.

11 Various, including WHO, 'Poverty and Health – Evidence and action in the WHO's European Region', 2001; Centers for Disease Control and Prevention (CDC), 'Response to increases in cigarette prices by race/ethnicity, income, and age groups – United States, 1976–93', *MMR Weekly*, 31 July 1998; Townsend, J. L., Cooper, Roderick P., 'Cigarette smoking by socioeconomic group, sex, and age: effects of price, income, and health publicity', *British Medical Journal*, October 1994.

12 'Back to Basics, European Tobacco', research note by UBS, January 2020.

13 Taxation has a long history as a tool in encouraging religious conversion, namely via the Jizya tax that Muslim rulers imposed on non-believers in the Middle Ages, and King George's eighteenth century Penal Laws on Catholics, but such measures may be seen as having a political rather than a social aim.

14 James I, *A Counterblaste to Tobacco*, 1604.

15 Marshall, Alfred, *Principles of Economics*, Macmillan & Co., 1890.

16 Royal College of Physicians, 'Smoking and Health', 1962.

17 US Surgeon General, 'Smoking and Health', 1964.

18 Duffy, Patrick (MP), Finance Bill Debate, 9 May 1972, https://api.parliament.uk/historic-hansard/commons/1972/may/09/finance-bill.

19 Dowell, Stephen, *History of Taxation and Taxes in England*, Longmans Green and Co., 1888.

20 No reliable calculations were done at the time as to the cost of smoking to the National Health Service – indeed, this was not possible since no one realised the full range of ailments and extent of damage caused by smoking. However, in recent decades it has been clear that the around £11 billion a year in tobacco

duty and VAT comfortably exceeds the additional £2–3 billion cost to the NHS of providing care to ill smokers. Including the cost savings from reduced pension payments and elderly care due to reduced life expectancy would make the extent to which smokers are net contributors to the exchequer even greater.

21 Russell, M.A., 'Changes in cigarette price and consumption by men in Britain, 1946-71: a preliminary analysis', *British Journal of Preventative and Social Medicine* 27 (1), February 1973, p. 1–7.

22 Peto, Julian, 'Price and consumption of cigarettes: a case for intervention?', *British Journal of Preventive & Social Medicine*, 2.8, 1974, pp. 241–5.

23 Bishop, John, and Yoo, Jang, '"Health Scare": Excise Taxes and Advertising Ban in the Cigarette Demand and Supply', *Southern Economic Journal*, vol. 52, no. 2, October 1985.

24 Lewit, E. M., Coate, D., and Grossman, M., 'The effects of government regulation on teenage smoking', *Journal of Law and Economics*, 16, 1981.; Lewit and Coate, 'The potential for using excise taxes to reduce smoking', *Journal of Law and Economics*, 1, 1982.

25 Warner, Kenneth E., and Tam, Jamie, 'The impact of tobacco control research on policy: 20 years of progress', *Tobacco Control*, 21, 2012.

26 Written response to question from Harvey Proctor MP, 14 December 1984.

27 Nigel Lawson, Budget speech, 13 March 1984.

28 Kenneth Clarke, Budget speech, 26 November 1995, https://hansard.parliament. uk/Commons/1996-11-26/debates/847bba5d-b410-4d06-85a0-cba67b89f187/ WaysAndMeans.

29 Calnan, Michael, 'The Politics of Health: The Case of Smoking Control', *Journal of Social Policy*, July 1984.

30 Mindell, J. S., 'The UK voluntary agreement on tobacco advertising: a comatose policy?', *Tobacco Control*, 2, 1993.

31 'Clarke isolated as EC votes for smoking law', *The Times*, 17 May 1989. 'Proposed EEC cigarette pack rule leaves Britain's Thatcher fuming,' *Boston Globe*, 17 May 1989.

32 'Smoking Ban on All Flights Near', *New York Times*, 6 December 1992.

33 'EC must stop meddling, says Tory', *The Times*, 18 May 1989; 'Britain to oppose tough EC warning on cigarette packs', *Independent*, 13 November 1989. European Council Directive 89/622/EEC of 13 November 1989 required all cigarette packs sold after 31 December 2012 to carry warnings.

34 Resolutions from World Health Assembly meetings during the 1970s usually listed taxation after 'educational, restrictive and legislative measures'.

35 Reubi, David, 'Health economists, tobacco control and international development: On the economisation of global health beyond neoliberal structural adjustment policies', *BioSocieties*, vol. 8, 2, pp. 205–28, 2013.

36 Telephone interview with Gene Lewit, November 2009.

37 Warner and Tam, 'The Impact of tobacco control research on policy', op. cit.

38 Telephone interview with Prabhat Jha, September 2019.

39 Becker, Gary, and Murphy, Kevin, 'The Theory of Rational Addictions', *Journal of Political Economy*, vol. 96, no. 41, 1988.

40 Gruber, Jonathan, 'Value-Added Tax and Excises: Commentary Prepared for the Report of a Commission on Reforming the Tax System for the 21st Century, Chaired by Sir James Mirrlees', 2007.

41 'Health chief wages war on government tobacco', *The Times*, 23 June 1987.

42 Jha, Chaloupka, 'The economics of global tobacco control', British Medical Journal, vol. 321, 5 August 2000.

43 Philip Morris International, 'The Perspective of PM International on Smoking and Health Issues'. Memo Title, Ness Motley Law Firm Documents (https://www.industrydocuments.ucsf.edu/).

44 Statement of the President of the Board of Trade, Sir Stafford Cripps, to Parliament, 12 June 1947: https://hansard.parliament.uk/Commons/1947-06-12/debates/a66d9bff-a3b1-45da-abb5-35f74b9c0522/Tobacco(Consumption).

45 'Cuts in Supply of Cigarettes', *The Times*, 3 July 1947, and 'Dollar Limit on Cigarettes', *The Times*, 21 August 1948.

46 'Tobacco shortage', *The Times*, 20 August 1948.

47 'British Seek Way to End Dire Cigarette Shortage', *New York Times*, 18 August 1948.

48 Royal College of Physicians, 'Smoking and Health', op. cit., p. 13.

49 Forey, Hamling, Hamling, Thornton and Lee, 'International Smoking Statistics', op. cit., p. 21.

50 As Cancer Research UK noted, 'During the 1990s there were periods when smoking rates stopped declining': https://scienceblog.cancerresearchuk.org/2017/05/19/this-is-the-end-of-tobacco-advertising/.

51 ONS RPI: Average price of cigarettes (20 king-size filter), adjusted using BoE Inflation Calculator.

52 Consumption data from Forey et al., 2016. Consumption data from the Tobacco Manufacturers Association gives a drop in consumption of 21 per cent from 1990 to 2000 and 41 per cent from 2000 to 2010. Data from Nguyen, Rosenqvist and Pekurinen in 'Demand for Tobacco in Europe An Econometric Analysis of 11 Countries for the PPACTE Project Report 6/2012', Finnish National Institute for Health and Welfare, 2012, arrives at very different figures, giving a drop of 44 per cent in the 1990s and a drop of 25 per cent 2000–10, which is consistent with the theory. However, Nguyen et al. use only duty-paid cigarette sales, ignoring the explosion in tobacco smuggling in the 1990s. According to the anti-smoking charity Ash, which supports tobacco taxation, the connivance of tobacco companies in smuggling helped it rise from accounting for less than 5 per cent of the market in 1990 to around 20 per cent in 2000 (https://ash.org.uk/media-and-news/press-releases-media-and-news/tobacco-industry-myths-shattered-as-smuggling-rates-fall-again/).

53 Orzechowski and Walker, 'The Tax Burden on Tobacco 1970–2018', Centers for Disease Control and Prevention, https://chronicdata.cdc.gov/Policy/The-Tax-Burden-on-Tobacco-1970-2018/7nwe-3aj9. Adjusted using the Federal Reserve Bank of Minneapolis Inflation Calculator.

54 Consumption data from *The Tax Burden on Tobacco, Historical Compilation*, vol. 49, 2014. Data from Hoffman et al., 2019, and *Our World in Data* (https://ourworldindata.org/smoking) gives similar results.

55 Nguyen, Rosenqvist and Pekurinen, 'Demand for Tobacco in Europe: An Econometric Analysis', op. cit.

56 Nguyen et al., 2012.

57 Nguyen et al., 2012, and Forey et al., 2016.

58 'Tea for Tuppence', *The Times*, 2 January 1948.

59 Based on ONS RPI: Ave price – Cigarettes (20 king-size filter), https://www.ons.gov.uk/economy/inflationandpriceindices/timeseries/czmp.

60 Forey et al., figures for all tobacco. In 1948 male prevalence for all tobacco was put at 82 per cent, and 21 per cent for 2014. ONS estimates UK cigarette consumption dropped 3.4 per centage points between 2014 and 2018. If this rate of drop continued to 2020 and was followed across all forms of tobacco the total drop in smoking would be to 16 per cent in 2020, a drop of 80.5 per cent.

61 'The Tax Burden on Tobacco', op. cit.

62 New York State Department of Health, 'Cigarette Purchasing Patterns among New York Smokers: Implications for Health, Price, and Revenue', https://www.health.ny.gov/prevention/tobacco_control/docs/cigarette_purchasing_patterns.pdf.

63 For example, one of the potential pitfalls with regression analysis, a commonly used tool in economics, is omitted variables. Before one begins an investigation into the impact of a factor like price on behaviour, one has to decide what factors might influence an outcome and then set about measuring their impact while holding everything else steady. However, the more complex the situation being studied, the harder it is to know whether every causal factor has been accounted for.

64 Harris, Jeffrey, 'The 1983 Increase in the Federal Cigarette Excise Tax', from *Tax Policy and the Economy*, Volume 1, MIT Press, 1987.

65 Berridge, Virginia, 'The policy response to the smoking and lung cancer connection in the 1950s and 1960s', *The Historical Journal*, 49, 4, pp. 1185–1209, 2006.

66 'John Bull Goes Right on Smoking', *New York Times*, 19 January 1964.

67 Schneider, Lynne, Klein, Benjamin, and Murphy, Kevin M., 'Governmental Regulation of Cigarette Health Information', *Journal of Law & Economics*, December 1981.

68 Comments from company annual reports and analyst calls for British American Tobacco Plc, Philip Morris International and Altria Group Inc.

69 Nguyen et al., 'Demand for Tobacco in Europe', op. cit., p. 84.

70 Rogebergyz, Ole, 'Taking Absurd Theories Seriously: Economics and the Case of Rational Addiction Theories', *Philosophy of Science*, July 2004.

71 'Dietary goals for the United States', Select Committee on Nutrition and Human Needs, United States Senate, 1977.

72 *Choices* magazine, fourth quarter of 2003, reported that 'from 1970 to 1998, real slaughter steer and hog prices declined by 50 per cent and 66 per cent, respectively, while real beef and pork farm-wholesale (FW) marketing margins declined by 57 per cent and 65 per cent, respectively'. In 2019, ground chuck steak beef prices averaged $3.94 per pound, according to USDA cuts data. This compares to $1.10 in February 1976, which equates to $4.94 in 2019 dollars.

73 https://ourworldindata.org/meat-production.

74 Ibisworld.com.

75 'The Cost of Healthy Eating', *New York Times*, May 2009, citing BLS statistics. https://archive.nytimes.com/www.nytimes.com/imagepages/2009/05/20/business/20leonhardt.graf01.ready.html?src=tp and 'Why tech stocks deserve to be cheaper than industrials', Reuters, July 2011, blogs.reuters.com/felix-salmon/2011/07/25/why-tech-stocks-deserve-to-be-cheaper-than-industrials/.

76 HM Treasury,' Soft Drinks Industry Levy Comes into Rffect: The "Sugar Tax" Will Help to Reduce Sugar in Soft Drinks and Tackle Childhood Obesity', 5 April 2018.

77 'Irn-Bru Keeps Drinkers Sweet After Sugar Cut', *The Times*, 28 March 2018. 'Reformulated: The Soft Drinks That Have Slashed Sugar and Boosted Sales', *The Grocer*, 26 April 2019.

78 Calculations based on ONS Household income survey 1977–2016 and ONS RPI: 'Ave price – Cigarettes 20 king size filter'. The actual cost increase would have been less than the calculated doubling if low-income smokers also reduced their tobacco consumption. Average cigarette consumption per smoker did fall by 2 sticks a day, according to the Forey et al. data, 1990–2000. However, the ONS has also observed that low-income smokers smoke more cigarettes per day than smokers on average incomes.

79 The Office for Budget Responsibility estimated in March 2019 that revenues from tobacco duties would be £9.1 billion in 2019–20. On top of this, value-added tax of 20 per cent is due on the underlying tobacco cost, plus the duty. https://obr.uk/forecasts-in-depth/tax-by-tax-spend-by-spend/tobacco-duties/.

80 In 2010, Think Tank Policy Exchange put the cost of treating smokers on the NHS at £2.7 billion. In 2019, Action on Smoking and Health put the cost at £2.4 billion. The drop may reflect the fact that today's costs reflect the higher smoking rates of the past, rather than the burden that current smokers will in the future place on the NHS.

81 *Fourth report of the Independent Scientific Committee on Smoking and Health*, Her Majesty's Stationery Office, London, 1988.

82 'Doctors demand a law to forbid all smoking at work', *The Times*, 24 March 1988.

83 Brown said in his Pre-Budget Report in November 1999 that he planned to shift to making duty decisions 'Budget by Budget'.

84 Health Act, 2006.

85 Tobacco Advertising and Promotion Act, 2002.

86 'NHS will pay for nicotine patches', *Guardian*, 14 March 2001.

87 Prabhat Jha told the *Sun* in 2019 that 'Our study debunks the current narrative that higher cigarette prices would negatively impact the poorest among us . . . a higher price would encourage cessation, lead to better health, and save money much more strongly for the poor than the rich', https://www.thesun.co.uk/news/6037310/cigarette-price-increase-a-pack-cost-uk/.

88 'Stop smoking services: *BMJ* analysis shows how councils are stubbing them out', *British Medical Journal*, 24 August 2018. 'Stop smoking campaign in England axed after health budget cuts', *Guardian*, 27 December 2019.

89 ONS, The proportion of current smokers among adults aged eighteen years and above by local authority, Great Britain, 2012 to 2018: https://www.ons.gov.uk/peoplepopulationandcommunity/healthandsocialcare/healthandlifeexpectancies/bulletins/adultsmokinghabitsingreatbritain/2018.

90 ONS, 'Average prices for Cigarettes, 20 king-size filter', series code CZMP, adjusted using Bank of England inflation calculator.

91 Maslow, Abraham, *The Psychology of Science,* Harper & Row, 1966, pp. 15–16.

92 Pink, Daniel H., 'Emotionally intelligent signage', https://www.danpink.com/2012/04/textbook-example-of-emotionally-intelligent-signage/.

93 See, for example, Thaler, Richard, 'Behavioral Economics: Past, Present, and Future', *American Economic Review,* 2016, Hattwick, Richard E., 'Behavioral Economics: An Overview', *Journal of Business and Psychology,* vol. 4,1989, and Pope, Devin G., and Sydnor, Justin R., 'Behavioral Economics: Economics as a Psychological Discipline' from *Handbook of Judgment and Decision Making,* Wiley Blackwell, 2015.

94 'Obama's Regulatory Czar Likely to Set a New Tone', *Wall Street Journal*, 8 January 2009.

95 Environmental Protection Agency, '2017 Carbon Dioxide Emissions and Fuel Economy Trends Report', Table 2.1, shows average new vehicle was 21.0 mpg in 2008 compared to 22.0. in 1987.

96 Sunstein's *Nudge* co-author Richard Thaler told the *Financial Times* in 2014 that Sunstein didn't want to increase CAFE standards in 2009 because 'We all know that's not as efficient as raising the tax on petrol': 'Behavioural economics and public policy', *Financial Times*, 21 March 2014.

97 Sunstein makes this claim in *Paradoxes of the Regulatory State*, 1990, citing Crandall, Gruenspecht, Keeler and Lave, *Regulating the Automobile*, pp. 157–8.

98 Sunstein, Cass, *Paradoxes of the Regulatory State*, citing Crandall, Robert W., and Graham, John D., 'The Effect of Fuel Economy Standards on Automobile Safety', *Journal of Law and Economics,* 1989.

99 A poll in Alston, Richard, Kearl, J. R., and Vaughan, Michael, 'Is there a global economic consensus? Is there a consensus among economists in the 1990s?', *AEA Papers and Proceedings,* May 1992, asked a cohort of economists to comment on the statement 'Effluent taxes or marketable pollution permits represent a better approach to pollution control than imposition of pollution ceilings'. Of them 23 per cent agreed with provisos, and 56 per cent said they generally agreed. Only 21 per cent said they disagreed.

100 Economists tend to ignore or underestimate the administration costs of sin taxes. When Denmark ditched its 'fat tax' in 2012, it cited these costs. 'Denmark scraps its infamous fat tax after only one year', https://www.euractiv.com/section/agriculture-food/news/denmark-scraps-its-infamous-fat-tax-after-only-one-year/.

101 Environmental Protection Agency, '2017 Carbon Dioxide Emissions and Fuel Economy Trends Report', Section 2 tables.

102 US Energy Information Administration (EIA), Weekly US Regular All Formulations Retail Gasoline Prices (Dollars per Gallon), adjusted using Federal Reserve Bank of Minneapolis Inflation Calculator. The years from 2000 on are chosen for comparability as the European Union's European Environment Agency published data only runs from 2000.

103 In nominal terms.

104 The commitment came with the signing of the Kyoto Protocol, which was adopted at the third Conference of the Parties to the UNFCCC (COP 3) in Kyoto, Japan, on 11 December 1997.

105 The discussions at the time worked off a 186g/km CO_2 level for 1995.

106 Yang, Zifei, and Bandivadekar, Anup, '2017 Global Update Light-Duty Vehicle Greenhouse Gas and Fuel Economy Standards', International Council on Clean Transportation, 2017.

107 Department of Transport Table TSGB0303 (ENV0103): figures in miles per imperial gallon (calculated under laboratory conditions that are not comparable with USEPA figures) for new petrol and diesel cars, weighted using SMMT Motor Industry Facts, 2010.

108 European carmakers had until 2008 to meet the target, while a 1999 agreement with Korean and Japanese companies gave them until 2009. In the following years the voluntary targets were replaced by binding limits.

109 '2018 Nobel in Economics Is Awarded to William Nordhaus and Paul Romer', 8 October 2018, https://www.nytimes.com/2018/10/08/business/economic-science-nobel-prize.html.

110 US Environmental Protection Agency 'EPA Automotive Trends Report 2019' found that in the model year 2018 a new vehicle's estimated fuel economy was

25.1mpg, https://www.epa.gov/automotive-trends/download-automotive-trends-report#Summary.

111 Based on the fact that the 1999–2009 result included the impact of tighter fuel efficiency standards on light trucks. Since the fuel efficiency improvement of light trucks exceeded the improvement in fuel efficiency of passenger cars, it suggests the standards did have an impact on fleet MPG figures – see Bureau of Transportation Statistics, Table 4-23: 'Average Fuel Efficiency of US Light Duty Vehicles'. www.bts.gov/archive/publications/national_transportation_statistics/table_04_23.

112 I never discovered whether the story was accurate or legend, but either way it illustrates the existentialist perspective.

7. The Pigou-Coase Disagreement

1 'Outstanding notional amounts of credit default swap (CDS) contracts fell markedly, from $61.2 trillion at end 2007 to $9.4 trillion 10 years later', *Bank for International Settlements Quarterly Review*, June 2018: https://www.bis.org/publ/qtrpdf/r_qt1806b.pdf and https://www.theice.com/publicdocs/globalmarketfacts/docs/factsheets/ICE_CDS_White_Paper.pdf.

2 Interview with Tom Burroughes, September 2019.

3 Burroughes, Tom, 'ISDA contract change cheers investors', Reuters, 5 April 2001.

4 'Fed's McDonough: Basel Mulls Change To Credit Derivatives Charge', Dow Jones, 4 April 2001, and 'Fed's McDonough hints at change to Basel derivative charge', Reuters, 4 April 2001.

5 Bergin, Tom, 'Credit tools seen revolutionising banking', Reuters, 2 August 2001.

6 Bergin, Tom, 'Credit derivatives reach a retail audience', Reuters, 6 July 2001, and 'Insurance companies may shoulder Enron loan losses', Reuters, 6 December 2001.

7 Bergin Tom, 'New emerging market debt tools help hedge but add risk', Reuters, 10 August 2001.

8 Bergin, Tom, 'Banks struggle to manage risks of new derivatives', Reuters, 20 August 2001.

9 'Greenspan Says Regulators Should "Harness" Technology', Dow Jones News Service, 2 May 1996.

10 Remarks at the annual convention of the American Bankers Association, Phoenix, Arizona (via satellite), 7 October 2002, https://www.federalreserve.gov/boarddocs/speeches/2002/20021007/default.htm. Almost identical comments made at HM Treasury Enterprise Conference, London (via satellite), 26 January 2004, https://www.federalreserve.gov/boarddocs/speeches/2004/20040126/default.htm.

11 Greenspan, Alan, 'The Assault on Integrity', *Objectionist*, August 1963.

12 Examples include 'Down on the street', *Economist*, 23 November 2006.

13 UK Government Actuary Chris Daykin, quoted in 'Blame culture's rise laid at FSA's door', *Daily Telegraph*, 28 June 2004.

14 Gordon Brown, speech to the CBI annual conference, 28 November 2005 and Mansion House speech, 21 June 2006.

15 'US group urges relaxing oversight rules on firms', *Wall Street Journal*, 1 December 2006. See also 'Sustaining New York's and the US's Global Financial Services Leadership', http://www.nyc.gov/html/om/pdf/ny_report_final.pdf.

16 'German IKB reveals 8 bn euros subprime crunch', Reuters, 31 July 2007. In November that year, the state-owned KFW Group, which bailed out IKB, estimated losses on the investments would be 4.8 billion euros.

17 'IKB dispels subprime fears with its results',(German: *'IKB zerstreut mit Ergebnis Subprime-Befürchtungen'*), Dow Jones, 20 July 2007.

18 Testimony to the House of Representatives Committee on Oversight and Government Reform, 12 October 2008.

19 Michael Mandel, chief economic strategist at the Progressive Policy Institute, a Washington-based think tank founded by centrist Democrats, has often referred to the 'pebbles in the stream' effect in columns, reports and Congressional testimony.

20 Remarks of FCC Chairman Ajit Pai at 'The Future of Internet Freedom', the Newseum, 26 April 2017.

21 'Americans' Views on Government Regulation Remain Steady', 11 October 2017,https://news.gallup.com/poll/220400/americans-views-government-regulation-remain-steady.aspx; https://news.gallup.com/poll/27286/government.aspx; https://www.comresglobal.com/polls/october-eu-referendum-poll/.

22 Griffin, J. P., 'Venetian treacle and the foundation of medicines regulation', *British Journal of Clinical Pharmacology* 58(3), September 2004, pp. 317–25; Rägo, Lembit, and Santoso, Budiono, 'Drug Regulation: History, Present and Future', in *Drug Benefits and Risks; International Textbook of Clinical Pharmacology*, Wiley, 2001.

23 Joskow, Paul L., 'Regulation of Natural Monopolies', 2006, from Polinsky, A. Mitchell, and Shavell, Steven (eds), *Handbook of Law and Economics*, 2007.

24 For example, during the 1950s and 1960s the Cuyahoga River caught fire on numerous occasions. This was seen as a key factor in the creation of the Occupational Safety and Health Administration (OSHA).

25 OSHA was a product of the Occupational Safety and Health Act signed in December 1970.

26 MacLeod, Roy M., 'The Alkali Acts Administration, 1863–84: The Emergence of the Civil Scientist', *Victorian Studies*, vol. 9, no. 2, December 1965. The transcripts of parliamentary debates from the time also give a clue to the background

to the Act, Hansard, vol. 9, no. 2, December 1965, pp. 85–112; https://hansard. parliament.uk/Commons/1863-06-19/debates/8376c3d1-268f-41a3-803e-d9453 6925f39/AlkaliWorksRegulationBill(Lords)%E2%80%94Bill135.

27 In speeches during the 1970s, including to the Conservative Party Conference in October 1976 and a May 1978 speech to the Bow Group, Margaret Thatcher warned against excessive regulation under the Labour government. In the 28 October 1980 presidential debate with Jimmy Carter, Ronald Reagan declared that 'are literally thousands of unnecessary regulations that invade every facet of business, and indeed, very much of our personal lives', and he also indicated separately that he wished to abolish the OSHA.

28 https://api.parliament.uk/historic-hansard/commons/1985/jul/16/lifting-the-burden.

29 Booth, Philip, 'Thatcher: The Myth of Deregulation', Institute of Economic Affairs Discussion Paper, 2015.

30 Statement by the President on Regulatory Relief, 5 June 1981.

31 'In the Nation; Mr. Watt's Coastline', *New York Times*, 10 July 1981.

32 'The Watt Controversy', *Washington Post*, 30 June 1981.

33 Jefferson, Decker, *The Other Rights Revolution: Conservative Lawyers and the Remaking of American Government*, Oxford University Press, 2016.

34 'Reagan's goal of easing environmental laws elusive', *Wall Street Journal*, 18 February 1983; McGarity, Thomas O., 'Regulatory Reform in the Reagan Era', *Maryland Law Review*, vol. 45, 1986; Jefferson, Decker, 'Deregulation, Reagan-Style', *Regulatory Review*, 13 March 2019; Peltzman, Sam, 'The Economic Theory of Regulation After a Decade of Deregulation', Brookings Papers on Economic Activity, Microeconomics, 1989; Meiners, Roger E., and Yandle, Bruce (eds), *Regulation and the Reagan Era: Politics, Bureaucracy and the Public Interest*, Independent Institute, 1989.

35 Taylor, John B., 'Changes in American Economic Policy in the 1980s: Watershed or Pendulum Swing?', American Economic Association, vol. 33(2), 1995.

36 Ryan, Paul, *The Way Forward: Renewing the American Idea*, Twelve, 2015.

37 Margaret Thatcher, *Statecraft: Strategies for a Changing World*, Haprer Perennial, 2003.

38 'David Cameron vows to cut back health and safety "monster"', *Daily Telegraph*, 5 January 2012.

39 Department for Business, Innovation and Skills and the Rt Hon. Dr Vince Cable, 'Red tape challenge kicks off', 7 April 2011, https://www.gov.uk/government/news/red-tape-challenge-kicks-off.

40 'David Cameron's senior adviser Steve Hilton suggests UK should abolish maternity leave', *Daily Telegraph*, 28 July 2011. Hilton's former colleague, Giles Wilkes, confirmed the details of the story in a series of messages on Twitter in 2015. Hilton declined to comment when approached by the author.

41 Fitoussi, Jean-Paul, 'The Problem of Social Deflation', from Hemerijck, Anton, Knapen, Ben, and Van Doorne, Ellen (eds), *Aftershocks: Economic Crisis and Institutional Choice,* Amsterdam University Press, 2009.

42 Department for Business, Innovation and Skills and the Rt Hon. Dr Vince Cable, 'Government axes retail red tape', op. cit., https://www.gov.uk/government/news/government-axes-retail-red-tape—2.

43 George Osborne, speech at the Conservative Spring Forum in Brighton, 1 March 2010.

44 Interview with George Osborne, September 2019.

45 http://www.senato.it/japp/bgt/showdoc/17/DOSSIER/0/979262/index.html?part=dossier_dossier1.

46 Hertog, Johan den, 'Review of Economic Theories of Regulation', Tjalling C. Koopmans Research Institute, Discussion Paper Series 10–18, December 2010.

47 https://www.margaretthatcher.org/archive/Hayek.asp.

48 Keynes, John Maynard, 'A Tract on Monetary Reform', p. 80, 1923.

49 Marshall, Alfred, *Principles of Economics*, pp. 628 and 629. See also Bentham, Jeremy, *Manual of Political Economy.*

50 House of Lords, 22 May 1865: https://api.parliament.uk/historic-hansard/lords/1865/may/22/alkali-act-inspectors-report#S3V0179P0_18650522_HOL_36.

51 The system also involved administration costs, but the costs were not material: one inspector at an annual income of £700 and four sub-inspectors each paid £350, against an industry turnover of £2.5 million annually (https://hansard.parliament.uk/Commons/1863-06-19/debates/8376c3d1-268f-41a3-803e-d94536925f39/AlkaliWorksRegulationBill(Lords)%E2%80%94Bill135).

52 Speech to HM Treasury Enterprise Conference, London (via satellite), 26 January 2004, https://www.federalreserve.gov/boarddocs/speeches/2004/20040126/default.htm.

53 Ronald Coase, interview, the Library of Economics and Liberty, *Econlib,* 21 May 2012: https://www.econtalk.org/coase-on-externalities-the-firm-and-the-state-of-economics/.

54 In a 2012 interview, Ronald Coase said of himself in the early 1930s that 'I was a socialist at that time.' EconTalk podcast, the Library of Economics and Liberty, 21 May 2012: https://www.econtalk.org/coase-on-externalities-the-firm-and-the-state-of-economics/.

55 Coase referred in his Nobel lecture to 'economists like myself, who write in prose', as opposed to those who conduct empirical studies.

56 Interview with Ronald Coase, Inaugural Conference International Society for New Institutional Economics, St Louis, Missouri, USA, 17 September 1997: https://www.coase.org/coaseinterview.htm.

57 *Memoirs of an Unregulated Economist,* University of Chicago Press, 1985, p. 75.

58 Ibid., p. 76.

59 Coase was listed number 3 and Stigler number 5 in numbers of citations in law journals, behind Adam Smith and John Stuart Mill. Henderson, M. Todd, *The*

NOTES TO PAGES 231–238

Influence of F.A. Hayek on Law: An Empirical Analysis, NYU Journal of Law and Liberty, vol. 1, no. 0, 2005. Stigler was listed number 1 in a 2011 Australian Government paper listing the 50 most important authors on regulation.

60 *Memoirs of an Unregulated Economist*, op. cit., p. 74.

61 Cohen, Manuel F., and Stigler, George J., 'Can Regulatory Agencies Protect Consumers?', American Enterprise Institute, September 1971.

62 https://www.fnlondon.com/articles/former-hsbc-executive-sentenced-to-two-years-following-front-running-conviction-20180427.https://www.straitstimes.com/singapore/courts-crime/3-singaporeans-jailed-for-front-running-in-land mark-share-trading-case.

63 Joskow, Paul, and Noll, Roger, 'Regulation in Theory and Practice: An Overview', in Fromm, Gary (ed.), *Studies in Public Regulation*, MIT Press, Cambridge, MA, 1981, pp. 1–66.

64 Peltzman, Sam, 'An Evaluation of Consumer Protection Legislation: The 1962 Drug Amendments', 1973.

65 Grabowski, H., Vernon J., and Thomas, L., 'Estimating the Effects of Regulation on Innovation: An International Comparative Analysis of the Pharmaceutical Industry', *The Journal of Law and Economics*, February 1978.

66 Peltzman, Sam, 'Effects of Automobile Safety Regulation', *Journal of Political Economy*, August 1975.

67 Weidenbaum, Murray, *Government-mandated Price Increases: A Neglected Aspect of Inflation*, AEI Press, 1975.

68 Gray, Wayne, and Shadbegian, Ronald, 'Environmental Regulation and Manufacturing Productivity at the Plant Level', NBER Working Paper no. 4321, 1993, found that a \$1 increase in compliance costs appears to reduce Total Factor Productivity by the equivalent of \$3 to \$4. See also Haveman, Robert H., and Christainsen, Gregory B., 'Environmental Regulations and Productivity Growth', *Natural Resources Journal*, vol. 21, no. 3, July 1981, pp. 489–509.

69 Crandall, R., Gruenspecht, H., Keeler, T., and Lave, L., *Regulating the Automobile*, Brookings Institution Press, 1986.

70 Hertog, Johan den, 'Review of Economic Theories of Regulation', op. cit.

71 2019 World Bank, 'Doing Business', 2020.

72 'Fintech : une régulation à ne pas manquer', *Decideurs*, 17 October 2018, https://www.magazine-decideurs.com/news/fintechs-une-regulation-a-ne-pas-man-quer? locale=fr, and 'Dossier des pesticides: On est né pour un petit pain!', *La Vie Agricole*, 16 April 2019.

73 Parker, David, and Kirkpatrick, Colin, 'The economic impact of regulatory pol-icy: a literature review of quantitative evidence', Expert Paper no. 3, August 2012, https://www.oecd.org/gov/regulatory-policy/3_Kirkpatrick%20Parker%20 web.pdf.

74 Meyer, Nicole M., 'The economic impacts of PCBs in the Hudson River: a cost-benefit analysis', City of New York University, 1991.

75 Bergin, Tom, *Spills & Spin: The Inside Story of BP*, Random House Business, 2011, gives an early accounting of the costs, which rose sharply over the following decade. BP's 2018 annual report put the total cost, net of contributions from other firms, who had paid BP $5.7 billion, at $67 billion. In 2019 it announced additional costs of $319 million and said it expected no further costs. On top of this, BP had to pay $4 billion in penalties under the Clean Water Act and a SEC civil penalty of $525 million.

76 Lave and Seskin, *Air Pollution and Human Health*, Resources for the Future Press 1977.

77 OMB Office of Information and Regulatory Affairs, '2016 Draft Report to Congress on the Benefits and Costs of Federal Regulations and Agency Compliance with The Unfunded Mandates Reform Act', found that 'The estimated annual benefits of major Federal regulations reviewed by OMB from October 1, 2005, to September 30, 2015, for which agencies estimated and monetized both benefits and costs, are in the aggregate between $208 billion and $672 billion, while the estimated annual costs are in the aggregate between $57 billion and $85 billion, reported in 2001 dollars. In 2014 dollars, aggregate annual benefits are estimated to be between $269 and $872 billion and costs between $74 and $110 billion.' (https://obamawhitehouse.archives.gov/sites/default/files/omb/assets/legislative_reports/draft_2016_cost_benefit_report_12_14_2016_2.pdf)

78 Open Europe, *The Top 100 costliest EU-derived regulations in force in the UK*, 2015. The discrepancy is actually even greater, since there is often one-sided counting by the analysts, for example, whereby a cash cost to an employer of giving parental leave to a staff member is counted, but no cash benefit is recorded for the staff member who receives the leave.

79 'Special Report: The political battle behind the dismantling of a worker safety rule', Reuters, 24 January 2019: https://uk.reuters.com/article/us-usa-beryllium-rule-specialreport/special-report-the-political-battle-behind-the-dismantling-of-a-worker-safety-rule-idUKKCN1PG1CQ.

80 'NHS chief has warned that "perverse" planning rules restricting gyms from opening are undermining efforts to solve the obesity epidemic', *Daily Telegraph*, 5 January 2020. https://www.telegraph.co.uk/news/2020/01./05/nhs-chief-has-warned-perverse-planning-rules-restricting-gyms/.

81 Convention on Biological Diversity: https://www.cbd.int/doc/case-studies/inc/cs-inc-denmark-technical-en.pdf.

82 Ito, Koichiro, and Sallee, James M., 'The Economics of Attribute-Based Regulation: Theory and Evidence from Fuel-Economy Standards', NBER Working Paper, September 2014.

83 Kahane, Charles J., 'Lives Saved by the Federal Motor Vehicle Safety Standards', Report No. DOT HS 809 833, National Highway Traffic Safety Administration, October 2004.

84 Morrall I, John F., III, 'Saving Lives: A Review of the Record', Office of Management and Budget Working Paper 03-6, AEI-Brookings Joint Center for Regulatory Studies, July 2003.

85 Office of Management and Budget Regulatory Program of the US Government, June 1987. There may be reasons other than the cancer risk to ban hormones, but the ban is not based on these.

86 'EU scraps its answer to US Volcker Rule for banks', Reuters, 24 October 2017.

87 Jorgenson, Dale W., and Wilcoxen, Peter J., 'Environmental Regulation and Growth', *RAND Journal of Economics*, vol. 21, no. 2, Summer, 1990, pp. 314–40. This omission was not unusual – one OECD study noted: 'Most quantitative studies deal with the costs of regulation and give little or no attention to quantifying the benefits of regulation', https://www.oecd.org/gov/regulatory-policy/3_Kirkpatrick%20Parker%20web.pdf.

88 'Taiwan ship-breakers ask to delay closure of yard', Reuters, 3 August 1988.

89 Xing, Yuquing, and Kolstad, Charles D., 'Do Lax Environmental Regulations Attract Foreign Investment?', *Environmental and Resource Economics*, vol. 21, 2002, pp. 1–22.

90 Antoine Dechezleprêtre and Misato Sato's review of the literature in 'The impacts of environmental regulations on competitiveness', 2014, found no impact. In their 2002 paper 'Do Lax Environmental Regulations Attract Foreign Investment?' Yuquing Xing and Charles D. Kolstad said that 'empirical papers have failed to find an effect on industrial location of weaker or stricter environmental regulations.'

91 Jaffe, Adam B., Peterson, Steven R., Portney, Paul R., and Stavins, Robert N., 'Environmental Regulation and the Competitiveness of US Manufacturing: What Does the Evidence Tell Us?', *Journal of Economic Literature*, vol. 33, no.1, March, 1995, 132–63.

92 Grossman, Gene M., and Krueger, Alan B., 'Economic growth and the environment', *The Quarterly Journal of Economics*, vol. 110, issue 2, 1995.

93 Greenspan, Alan, *The Age of Turbulence: Adventures in a New World*, Penguin, 2007.

94 Djankov, S., McLeish, C., and Ramalho, R., 'Regulation and Growth', World Bank Working Paper, 2006; Haidar, Jamal Ibrahim, 'The impact of business regulatory reforms on economic growth', *Journal of the Japanese and International Economies*, 2012; Hanusch, Marek, 'The Doing Business Indicators, Economic Growth and Regulatory Reform Policy', World Bank Research Working Paper 6176, August 2012; Loayza Norman V., Oviedo Ana María and Servén Luis, 'Regulation and Macroeconomic Performance', World Bank, September 2004.

95 Rodgers, Gregory B., 'The Effectiveness of Child-Resistant Packaging for Aspirin', *Archives of Pediatrics and Adolescent Medicine*, September 2002.

8. The Jorgenson Thesis

1 https://www.washingtonpost.com/business/economy/jamie-dimon-speaks-the-financial-gospel-according-to-jpmorgan-chase-ceo/2012/10/10/e6cb0a86-130c-11e2-a16b-2c110031514a_story.html.

2 JP Morgan Chase, Annual Report, 2012.

3 'JP Morgan CEO calls Chancellor over bonus tax,' *Daily Telegraph*, 29 December 2009.

4 'CEOs Call for Deficit Action', *Wall Street Journal*, 25 October 2012.

5 https://www.businessroundtable.org/archive/media/news-releases/jpmorgan-chase-chairman-and-ceo-jamie-dimon-named-chairman-business-roundtable.

6 Budget for Fiscal Year, 2012 and 2013.

7 Fox Business interview, 13 January 2015.

8 Interview on CNBC's *Squawk Box*, 12 May 2016.

9 https://history.house.gov/Institution/Session-Dates/All/.

10 Business Roundtable press call, 6 June 2017.

11 Second Quarter JP Morgan Chase & Co Earnings Call, 14 July 2017.

12 Bloomberg TV Interview, 20 February 2015: https://www.bloomberg.com/news/articles/2015-03-04/u-s-companies-are-stashing-2-1-trillion-overseas-to-avoid-taxes.

13 Letter from New York, *Financial News*, 28 July 2014.

14 Examples include Vartia, 2008, who finds that corporate tax rates negatively affect TFP by reducing company profitability. Similarly, Arnold and Schwellnus, 2008, find a negative effect of corporate taxation on both firm-level productivity and investment levels.

15 Hassett, Kevin, Testimony to House Committee on Ways and Means, 20 January 2011.

16 The OECD's 2010 report 'Tax Policy Reform and Economic Growth' declared that 'Corporate income taxes are the most harmful for growth as they discourage the activities of firms that are most important for growth: investment in capital and productivity improvements' (page 22). The IMF said in its 2015 report 'Fiscal Policy and Long-Term Growth' that 'corporate income taxes have the most negative effect on growth', while The World Economic Forum's Competitiveness report 2015–16 said that 'It is well established that taxation in general affects productivity by reducing investment'.

17 https://www.economist.com/special-report/2014/02/20/plucking-the-geese.

18 https://www.oecd.org/tax/beps/corporate-tax-statistics-database.htm.

19 Analysis of the dynamic effects of Corporation Tax reductions, HMRC and HM Treasury, December 2013.

20 Strulik, Holger, and Trimborn, Timo, 'Laffer strikes again: Dynamic scoring of capital taxes', *European Economic Review*, vol. 56 (6), 2012.

21 Hassett, Kevin A., testimony before the House Ways and Means Committee, 20 January 2011.

22 Interview on CNN's *Fareed Zakaria GPS,* 17 May 2015.

23 Andrew Ross Sorkin interview on CNBC, 27 February 2012.

24 Gates letter to Arthur Laffer, 17 April 2008.

25 Gates letter to Arthur Laffer, 5 December 2006.

26 https://obamawhitehouse.archives.gov/blog/2012/04/10/white-house-report-buffett-rule-basic-principle-tax-fairness.

27 'More Americans Say Low-Income Earners Pay Too Much in Taxes', 15 April 2015, https://news.gallup.com/poll/182426/americans-say-low-income-earners-pay-taxes.aspx and https://news.gallup.com/poll/248681/tax-day-update-americans-not-seeing-tax-cut-benefit.aspx. Gallup appears to be the most consistent in the questions it asks voters, but the regular polls conducted by the Pew Research Center also point to a similar position on the part of the public, as do the occasional polls conducted by news organisations such as ABC News and the *Washington Post* (https://abcnews.go.com/Politics/thirds-large-corporations-pay-federal-taxes-poll/story?id=50082215) and non-governmental bodies (https://americansfortaxfairness.org/issue/new-poll-shows-americans-strongly-want-to-close-tax-loopholes-benefiting-the-rich-and-corporations-in-next-budget-deal/).

28 Pollster's Gallup's Annual Stock Ownership surveys give figures of between 52 and 59 per cent, https://news.gallup.com/poll/233747/stock-ownership-among-americans-trends.aspx. A 2013 Pew Research Center survey put the figure at 47 per cent, https://www.pewresearch.org/fact-tank/2013/05/31/stocks-and-the-recovery-majority-of-americans-not-invested-in-the-market/.

29 Wolff, Edward N., 'Household Wealth Trends in the United States, 1962 to 2016: Has Middle Class Wealth Recovered?', NBER Working Paper 24085, November 2017.

30 The then Chairman of the President's Council of Economic Advisers, Kevin Hassett, told reporters at a press briefing on 10 September 2018 that 'the notion that the corporate tax side has about paid for itself is clearly in the data.' https://www.whitehouse.gov/briefings-statements/press-briefing-press-secretary-sarah-sanders-cea-chairman-kevin-hassett-091018/.

31 Brill, Alex and Hassett, Kevin A., 'Maximizing Corporate Income Taxes: The Laffer Curve in OECD Countries', *American Enterprise Institute*, 2007: according to this the Revenue modelled a payback period of several years. Another paper by the Tax Foundation, 'The Economic Effects of Adopting the Corporate Tax Rates of the OECD, the UK, and Canada', 2015, indicates that most of the costs were recouped by the tenth year after a cut.

32 Gordon Brown, Budget speech, 2 July 1997.

33 Bergin, Tom, 'Scrap corporate tax and benefit long term, some conservatives say', Reuters, 6 June 2013.

34   Osborne announced the reduction to 18 per cent in July 2015 and the 17 per cent goal in March 2016. In July 2016, he told the *Financial Times* he wished to take the rate to under 15 per cent.

35   Source: HM Treasury, 'Business tax road map', March 2016.

36   https://hansard.parliament.uk/Commons/2016-07-04/debates/E5406AB8-380A-4B1D-AF82-C71DD7A26661/SurplusTargetAndCorporationTax.

37   'WPP ups pressure on TNS, moves tax base to Ireland', Reuters, 29 September 2008.

38   'Publishing firm Informa blames budget for Swiss tax switch', *Guardian*, 1 May 2009.

39   The Exchequer Secretary to the Treasury David Gauke to HMRC Annual Conference for Stakeholders, July 2013, and speech to British-American Business Council at Beverly Wiltshire, California, 10 April 2013.

40   'Britain's Laffer Curve', 5 December 2013, https://www.wsj.com/articles/george-osborne-and-the-laffer-curve-1386274223?tesla=y.

41   'Britain to lower corporate tax rate, proving BRT's point', 21 March 2012, https://www.businessroundtable.org/archive/media/blog/britain-to-lower-corporate-tax-rate-proving-brts-point.

42   https://www.cato.org/blog/progress-laffer-curve.

43   https://www.whitehouse.gov/briefings-statements/remarks-president-trump-signing-h-r-1-tax-cuts-jobs-bill-act-h-r-1370/.

44   Pence, Mike, speech made by the Vice President at the American Enterprise Institute, 24 October 2017.

45   Company statement, 20 December 2017, https://about.att.com/story/att_tax_reform.html.

46   Boeing CEO Dennis Muilenburg, interview on CNBC, 15 February 2018.

47   Company statement, 23 January 2018, https://www.jpmorganchase.com/corporate/news/pr/multi-billion-investment-employees-local-economies.htm.

48   CNBC interview, 24 January 2018, https://www.cnbc.com/2018/01/24/jp-morgan-ceo-jamie-dimon-says-tax-cut-will-lead-to-higher-wages-inflation.html.

49   Budget speech, November 2017, https://www.gov.uk/government/speeches/autumn-budget-2017-philip-hammonds-speech.

50   HMRC, Corporation Tax Statistics, 2018: https://www.gov.uk/government/statistics/analyses-of-corporation-tax-receipts-and-liabilities-document-august-2015.

51   From 1 January 2016, banks became liable to the 'Bank Surcharge', defined as a 'Corporation Tax measure', which poses an extra 8 per cent tax rate on top of the standard CT liability.

52   The UK's population rose from 62.3 million in 2009 to 66 million in 2017: https://www.ons.gov.uk/peoplepopulationandcommunity/populationandmigration/populationestimates/timeseries/ukpop/pop.

53   OBR Economic and fiscal outlook, November 2016, Box: 4.1, p. 121.

54 The 2019 estimate was £6.5 billion: https://www.pwc.co.uk/services/tax/total-tax-contribution-100-group.html.

55 Eurostat, Real GDP per capita, chain-linked volumes (2010), euro per capita, https://ec.europa.eu/eurostat/databrowser/view/sdg_08_10/default/table?lang=en.

56 Bergin, Tom, 'Analysis: UK record challenges link between corporate tax cuts and jobs', Reuters, 17 October 2012, http://uk.reuters.com/article/2012/10/17/uk-britain-tax-jobs-idUKBRE89G0UD20121017.

57 ONS Gross fixed capital formation as a percentage of gross domestic product between G7 nations, fourth quarter of 2007 to Q4 2015, used to avoid the collapse in investment linked to the Brexit vote.

58 Average annual growth in the gross capital stock. The figures for net capital stock show 2010–17 at 1.3 per cent versus 1.2 per cent in 2008–9 and 2.0 in 1998–2007. https://www.ons.gov.uk/economy/nationalaccounts/uksectoraccounts/bulletins/capitalstocksconsumptionoffixedcapital/2018.

59 OBR Forecast evaluation, October 2015, Chart 2.23.

60 Ibid.

61 Bergin, Tom, 'Scrap corporate tax', op. cit.

62 John Maynard Keynes coined the phrase 'animal spirits' to refer to forces of the marketplace, and various parties from US hedge fund manager Ray Dalio to Indian billionaire Harsh Goenka have used the phrase in relation to corporate tax cuts.

63 Bergin, Tom, 'INSIGHT: Britain becomes haven for U.S. companies keen to cut tax bills', Reuters, 9 June 2014.

64 Financial Secretary to the Treasury David Gauke, speech to the American Enterprise Institute in Washington, DC, 29 September 2015. The OBR estimates a higher long-term investment impact for the cuts, but it still falls far short of the budgetary cost.

65 'Tax experts call for "rethink" of UK corporation tax in Budget', *Financial Times*, 19 November, 2017.

66 'UK's Johnson drops corporate tax cut plan in bid to woo voters', Reuters, 18 November 2019.

67 For example, analysts at UBS observed in a note to clients entitled 'How might Trump corporate tax reform and repatriation impact Equities, the USD and Rates?' in November 2016 that 'The liquidity could be used to execute additional reinvestment, share buybacks, additional dividends and M&A sponsorship. These corporate actions have the ability to generate as well as destroy value.'

68 'Who Is Getting The Biggest Tax "Refund"?', Morgan Stanley, 7 December 2017.

69 Hassett, Kevin A., and Mathur, Aparna, 'Taxes and Wages', AEI Working Paper 128, June. 2006; Hassett and Mathur, 'A Spatial Model of Corporate Tax Incidence', AEI Working Paper, 2010.

70 Hanlon, Michelle, Hoopes, Jeffrey L., and Slemrod, Joel, 'Tax Reform Made Me Do It!', NBER Working Paper 25283, November 2018.

71 UBS Economics team, US Economic Forecast Annual Update, 8 November 2018.

72 US Bureau of Economic Analysis, 'Real Private Nonresidential Fixed Investment [PNFIC1]', retrieved from FRED, Federal Reserve Bank of St. Louis; https://fred.stlouisfed.org/series/PNFIC1, 29 December, 2019; 'BEA Real Nonresidential Fixed Investment', https://www.richmondfed.org/~/media/richmondfedorg/research/national_economy/national_economic_indicators/pdf/all_charts.pdf.

73 '$1.5 trillion US tax cut has no major impact on business capex plans: survey', Reuters, 28 January 2019.

74 Bank of America Merrill Lynch, 'Earnings Preview', 27 March 2018.

75 Bureau of Labor Statistics: Average hourly earnings of production and nonsupervisory employees, 1982–4, dollars. Series CES0500000032.

76 Unemployment fell below 5 per cent, the level traditionally considered to reflect full employment, in early 2016, based on Unemployment Rate: Aged 15-64: All Persons for the United States, Per cent, Quarterly, Seasonally Adjusted, LRUN64TTUSQ156S.

77 Third Quarter 2018, JP Morgan Chase & Co Earnings Call, 12 October 2018.

78 'Chase eyeing branch expansion in "certain other states", consumer chief says', *American Banker*, 13 June 2017.

79 JP Morgan Chase, 2018 10-K Annual Report.

80 Author's calculations based on US Treasury data, https://fiscal.treasury.gov/reports-statements/combined-statement/current.html.

81 https://www.bea.gov/news/2019/gross-domestic-product-third-quarter-2019-third-estimate-corporate-profits-third-quarter.

82 OBR Economic and Fiscal Outlook, March 2013.

83 Jonathan Gruber and Joshua Rauh found in 'How Elastic is the Corporate Income Tax Base?', 2005, that a 10 per cent increase in the effective corporate tax rate reduces aggregate investment to GDP ratio by 2 per centage points. In their 1992 paper 'The Effects of Taxation on Investment: New Evidence from Firm Level Panel Data', (*National Tax Journal*, 45, 243–51) Jason Cummins and Kevin Hassett arrived at an estimate for the elasticity of investment to the cost of capital of -1.1 for equipment and -1.2 for structures. However, not everyone agrees. Schaller, H. (2003), 'Estimating the Long-run User Cost Elasticity', MIT WP 02-31, found the elasticity of both equipment and structures capital with respect to tax parameters close to zero.

84 In *The Wealth of Nations*, Book 1, Chapter IX, 'Of the Profits of Stock', Smith notes that 'It may be laid down as a maxim, that wherever a great deal can be made by the use of money, a great deal will commonly be given for the use of it; and that wherever little can be made by it, less will commonly be given for it.'

85 Carver, Thomas Nixon, 'A Suggestion for a Theory of Industrial Depressions', *Quarterly Journal of Economics*, 1903.

86 Aftalion, Albert, '*La Réalité des Surproductions Générales: Essai d'une théorie des crises générales et périodiques: première partie: possibilité théorique et réalité des crises de surproduction générale, Revue d'économie politique*', vol. 23, 1909.

87 John Maurice Clark, son of John Bates Clark, perhaps America's foremost economist of the nineteenth century, is credited with first using the term 'acceleration' in this context in his 1917 paper 'Business acceleration and the law of demand: a technical factor in economic cycles' (*Journal of Political Economy*, vol. 25, no. 3, March 1917). He expanded on the idea in his 1923 book *Studies in the Economics of Overhead Costs*.

88 Irving Fisher, *The Theory of Interest, As Determined by Impatience to Spend Income and Opportunity to Invest it*, Macmillan, 1930.

89 In Britain no link is evident between Household saving ratio (ONS NRJS) and the Bank of England base rate, and the same applies to US savings rates and the Fed rates. Robert H. Defina's 1984 paper 'The link between savings and interest rates' (*Federal Reserve Bank of Philadelphia Business Review*, 1984) gives an overview of this problem, https://www.philadelphiafed.org/-/media/research-and-data/publications/business-review/1984/brnd84rd.pdf?la=en.

90 From 'Discussion' featuring George F. Break, Otto Eckstein and Melvin I. White, *American Economic Review*, vol. 52, no. 2 (Papers and Proceedings of the Seventy-Fourth Annual Meeting of the American Economic Association), May 1962, pp. 349-55.

91 Corporation tax was introduced in 1965. Before this Britain applied a profits tax, and its burden was mitigated by investment allowances. Changes in both the rates and allowances occurred during the 1950s, creating changes in effective rates.

92 Corner, D. C., and Williams, Alan, 'The Sensitivity of Businesses to Initial and Investment Allowances', *Economica*, February 1965, pp. 32-47. Cited in Engen, Eric M., and Skinner, Jonathan, 'Taxation and Economic Growth', NBER Working Paper 5826, November 1996.

93 Jorgenson, Dale W., 'Capital Theory and Investment Behavior', *American Economic Review* 53, May 1963, pp. 247-59.

94 Jorgenson, Dale, 'The Theory of Investment Behavior', from Ferber, Robert (ed.), *Determinants of Investment Behavior*, NBER Books, 1967.

95 Jorgenson gave a summary of the key innovations in the 1963 paper 'This Week's Citation Classic', *Commentary in Current Contents* 40, 4 October 1982, p. 20, http://garfield.library.upenn.edu/classics1982/A1982PH16700001.pdf.

96 Hall, R. E., and Jorgenson, D. W., 'Tax Policy and Investment Behaviour', *American Economic Review*, vol. 50, no. 3, 1967, pp. 391-414.

97 See Vartia, Laura, 'How do Taxes Affect Investment and Productivity? An Industry-Level Analysis of OECD Countries', OECD Economics Department Working Papers 656, December 2008, https://www.oecd-ilibrary.org/

345

docserver/230022721067.pdf?expires=1585739563&id=id&accname=guest&ch
ecksum=6790CE88E392027C21BEC87A21E29AB7, and Coen, Robert M., 'Tax
Policy and Investment Behavior: Comment', *American Economic Review*, vol.
59, no. 3, June 1969, pp. 370–79.

98 Hassett, Kevin A., and Hubbard, R. Glenn, 'Tax Policy and Business Investment',
Chapter 20 of *Handbook of Public Economics*, 2002, vol. 3, pp. 1293–1343, list
several studies which 'found the user cost effect to be negligible'.

99 Feldstein, Martin, 'Inflation, Tax Rules and Investment: Some Econometric
Evidence', *Econometrica*, vol. 50, no. 4, July 1982, pp. 825–62.

100 Hassett and Hubbard, 'Tax Policy and Business Investment', op. cit.

101 Chirinko, Robert S., and Eisner, Robert, 'Tax policy and investment in major US
macroeconomic econometric models', *Journal of Public Economics*, vol. 20, issue
2, March 1983, pp. 139–66.

102 Auerbach, Alan J., and Hassett, Kevin A., 'Taxes and Business Investment:
Lessons from the Past Decade', Chapter 11 in *Tax Policy Lessons from the 2000s*.
Peter K. Clark noted in 'Tax Incentives and Equipment Investment', 1993, that
'Most empirical analyses relating tax policy to equipment investment have
failed to find strong, independent effects that are as large as those imbedded in
many macroeconometric models.' Jason Cummins, Kevin Hassett and R. Glenn
Hubbard noted in 'Tax reforms and investment: A cross-country comparison'
that 'Economists have long argued that significant reforms of company taxation
can have large effects on firms' investment decisions . . . while extensive studies
of the effects of various tax parameters on firms' user costs of capital have been
prepared and then compared across countries [for the first such study see King
and Fullerton 1984; most recently see OECD, 1991], empirical evidence has not
been overwhelmingly supportive of significant effects of tax policy on investment (see, e.g., the review in Chirinko, 1993) . . . The weight of the existing
evidence appears to lean toward the interpretation that tax variables have little
effect upon firm investment.', *Journal of Public Economics*, vol. 62, issues 1–2,
October 1996, pp. 237–73.

103 One example is Caballero, R. J., Engel, E., and Haltiwanger, J. C., 'Plant-level
Adjustment and Aggregate Investment Dynamics', Brookings Papers on
Economic Activity, vol.2, 1995, pp. 1–54.

104 Cummins, J. G., Hassett, K. A., and Hubbard, G., 'A Reconsideration of
Investment Behaviour Using Tax Reforms as Natural Experiments', Brookings
Papers on Economic Activity, vol. 25, no. 2, 1994, pp. 1–74.

105 Cummins, J. G., Hassett, K. A., and Hubbard, G., 'Tax Reforms and Investment:
A Cross-Country Comparison', *Journal of Public Economics*, vol. 62, no. 2, 1996,
pp. 237–73.

106 Bond, S., Denny K., and Devereux, M., 'Capital Allowances and the Impact of
Corporation Tax on Investment in the UK', *Fiscal Studies*, May 1993.

107 Arulampalam, Wiji, Devereux, Michael P., and Maffini, Giorgia, 'The Direct Incidence of Corporate Income Tax on Wages', *European Economic Review*, vol. 56 (6), 2012.

108 Some papers found little or no responsiveness of investment to costs of capital or tax rates, including Schaller, H., 'Estimating the Long-run User Cost Elasticity', MIT WP 02-31, 2003. Simon Gilchrist and Egon Zakrajsek noted in 'Investment and the Cost of Capital: New Evidence from the Corporate Bond Market' (2007) that 'With the exception of Cummins, Hassett, and Hubbard . . . researchers have had a difficult time identifying the relationship between capital formation and changes in corporate tax policy.'

109 Devereux, Michael, Keen, Michael, and Schiantarelli, Fabio, 'Corporation Tax Asymmetries and Investment: Evidence from UK Panel Data', *Journal of Public Economics*, vol. 53, issue 3, March 1994.

110 Interview with Michael Devereux, April 2020.

111 Chirinko, Robert S., Fazzari, Steven M., and Meyer, Andrew P., 'That Elusive Elasticity: A Long-Panel Approach To Estimating The Price Sensitivity Of Business Capital', Unpublished paper, Researchgate, June 2002; Ellis, C., and Price, S., 'UK Business Investment and the User Cost of Capital', *The Manchester School*, August 2004; Barnes, S., Price, S., and Sebastia-Barriel, M., 'The elasticity of substitution: evidence from a UK firm level data set', Bank of England Working Paper 348, 2008; Smith, J., 'That elusive elasticity and the ubiquitous bias: is panel data a panacea?', Bank of England Working Paper 342, 2008.

112 The Tax Cuts and Jobs Act of 2017 was signed in December 2017 but effective for the year beginning 1 January 2018.

113 For example, the equipment hire group United Rentals Inc. said in its Fourth Quarter and Full Year 2018 Results that its return on invested capital was 8.8 per cent in 2017, but would have been 10.6 per cent if calculated at the lower 21 per cent federal tax rate.

114 Silgan Holdings, Inc., fourth quarter 2017 earnings call, 31 January 2018.

115 The bank calculates this as net income divided by average tangible common equity (TCE). TCE is total stockholders' equity less preferred stock. Source: 2018 Annual Report.

116 JP Morgan Chase & Co, Investor Day, 27 February 2018.

117 Melolinna, Marko, Miller, Helen, and Tatomir, Srdan, 'Business investment, cost of capital and uncertainty in the United Kingdom – evidence from firm-level analysis', Staff Working Paper 717, March 2018.

118 Kopp, Emanuel, Leigh, Daniel, Mursula, Susanna, and Tambunlertchai, Suchanan, 'US Investment Since the Tax Cuts and Jobs Act of 2017', IMF Working Paper, May 2019. UK Weighted Average Cost of Capital trends are illustrated in 'The financial system and productive investment: new survey evidence' by Jumana Saleheen and Iren Levina of the Bank's Financial Stability

Directorate and Marko Melolinna and Srdan Tatomir, *Bank of England Quarterly Bulletin*, 2017, Q1.

119 Tax Relief, Unemployment Insurance Reauthorization, and Job Creation Act of 2010.

120 'Wal-Mart Executives Sweat Slow February Start in E-Mails', Bloomberg, 16 February 2013, https://www.bloomberg.com/news/articles/2013-02-15/wal-mart-executives-sweat-slow-february-start-in-e-mails.

121 'Why is Wal-Mart worried? Payroll tax could cut consumer spending,' *Christian Science Monitor*, February 2013, https://www.csmonitor.com/Business/2013/0222/Why-is-Wal-Mart-worried-Payroll-tax-could-cut-consumer-spending.

122 'Restored Payroll Tax Pinches Those Who Earn the Least', *New York Times*, 7 February 2013, https://www.nytimes.com/2013/02/08/business/restored-payroll-tax-pinches-those-with-the-smallest-checks.html.

123 https://www.theguardian.com/education/2017/may/02/part-time-student-numbers-collapse-universities and https://www.hesa.ac.uk/data-and-analysis/students.

124 Institute for Fiscal Studies, 2018 Annual Report on Education Spending in England, https://www.ifs.org.uk/publications/13306.

125 Department of Education, 'Schools, pupils and their characteristics: January 2019'.

Conclusion

1 Excerpt from the will of Alfred Nobel, https://www.nobelprize.org/alfred-nobel/alfred-nobels-will/.

2 A 2010 House of Commons Science and Technology Committee report, 'Evidence Check 2: Homeopathy', stated that the principles on which homeopathy is based were 'scientifically implausible'.

3 Speech made by Professor Erik Lundberg of the Royal Academy of Sciences at the inaugural awarding of the Prize in Economic Sciences in Memory of Alfred Nobel, 1969.

4 In 2018, Paul Romer was jointly awarded the Nobel memorial prize 'for integrating technological innovations into long-run macroeconomic analysis'. He shared the prize with William Nordhaus, who received his award 'for integrating climate change into long-run macroeconomic analysis'.

5 Interview with Paul Romer, September 2019.

6 Romer, Paul M., 'Mathiness in the Theory of Economic Growth', *American Economic Review*, vol. 105, no. 5, May 2015, pp. 89–93.

7 Romer, Paul M., 'The Trouble with Macroeconomics', delivered 5 January 2016 as the Commons Memorial Lecture of the Omicron Delta Epsilon Society.

8 In the days before his ideology became the orthodoxy, George Stigler also remarked on the way 'fashion' drove thinking and research in economics: cited

in Leeson, R. (ed.), *Essays in the History of Economics,* University of Chicago Press, 2000. 'The Chicago counter-revolution and the sociology of economic knowledge', in Leeson, R. (ed.), *The Eclipse of Keynesianism: The political economy of the Chicago counter revolution*, Palgrave Macmillan, 2000.

9   'Minimum Wage vs. Supply and Demand', *Wall Street Journal,* on 25 April 1996.

10   Interview with Paul Romer, September 2019. I should note that Paul Romer's writings make clear he retains faith in many of the mechanisms and remedies, such as carbon taxes, that I criticise in this book.

11   James Heckman, interview with the *New Yorker,* January 2010.

12   When asked in January 2019 if raising the top federal marginal tax on earned personal income to 70 per cent would raise substantially more revenue without lowering economic activity, a large majority of those who expressed a view disagreed, http://www.igmchicago.org/surveys/top-marginal-tax-rates/.

13   In a range of surveys since 2013, the experts have said immigration will raise economic growth, innovation and tax revenues, http://www.igmchicago.org/surveys/immigration/, http://www.igmchicago.org/surveys/high-skilled-immigrant-visas/ and http://www.igmchicago.org/surveys/low-skilled-immigrants/.

14   Keynes, J. M., 'Alfred Marshall, 1842–1924', *Economic Journal*, vol. 34, no. 135, September 1924, pp. 311–72, Blackwell Publishing for the Royal Economic Society Stable, URL: http://www.jstor.org/stable/2222645, Accessed: 29/06/2010 20:06.

15   Coase, Ronald, 'Saving Economics from the Economists', *Harvard Business Review*, December 2012.

16   Ibid.

17   Ronald and Coase interview, EconTalk podcast, Library of Economics and Liberty,21May2012,https://www.econtalk.org/coase-on-externalities-the-firm-and-the-state-of-economics/.

18   Ravallion, Martin, 'Should the Randomistas (Continue to) Rule?', Center for Global Development, August 2018.

19   Deaton, Angus, and Cartwright, Nancy, 'The limitations of randomised controlled trials',Voxeu.orgblog,9November2016,https://voxeu.org/article/limitations-randomised-controlled-trials.

20   Solow, Robert M., 'Economic History and Economics', *American Economic Review*, vol. 75, no. 2, Papers and Proceedings of the Ninety-Seventh Annual Meeting of the American Economic Association, May 1985, pp. 328–31.

21   Banerjee, Abhijit V., and Duflo, Esther, *Good Economics for Hard Times*, p. 7. See also Duflo, Esther, 'The Economist as Plumber', NBER Working Paper No. 23213, March 2017.

22   Ben Bernanke comments as part of panel discussion at the Brookings Institution, 16 January 2014, https://www.brookings.edu/wp-content/uploads/2014/01/20140116_bernanke_remarks_transcript.pdf.

23   See, for example, 'Wasting Away', *Spectator*, 24 February 2018, https://www.spectator.co.uk/article/wasting-away.

24 'NHS competition could waste millions says Labour, after Care UK complains', *Guardian*, 23 August 2015.
25 The 1990 National Health Service and Community Care Act gave individual NHS local health authorities control over their own budgets, with the view that they would procure services from outside the NHS where this was cheaper.
26 After claiming to have abolished the NHS internal market in the late 1990s, Tony Blair went on to propose an increase in the use of market mechanisms whereby doctors and health authorities could procure operations and other procedures from the public or private hospitals which offered the cheapest prices.
27 'Scrap NHS competition rules, BMA says', *British Medical Journal*, 25 June 2018: BMJ 2018;361:k279.
28 Harrod, R. F., *The Life of John Maynard Keynes*, Macmillan, 1951, p. 193.

BIBLIOGRAPHY

Adams, Thomas S., 'Fundamental Problems of Federal Income Taxation', *Quarterly Journal of Economics* 35 (4), 1921, pp. 527–56.

Agell, Jonas, et al., 'Growth effects of government expenditure and taxation in rich countries: a comment', Stockholm University, 2003.

Aaron, Henry J., and Pechman, Joseph A. (eds), *How Taxes Affect Economic Behavior*, Washington, DC, Brookings Institution.

Andersson, Krister, et al., 'Corporate Tax Policy in the Nordic Countries', from *Tax Policy in the Nordic Countries*, Palgrave Macmillan, 1998.

Alesina, Alberto F., Glaeser, Edward L., and Sacerdote, Bruce, 'Work and Leisure in the US and Europe: Why So Different?', Harvard Institute of Economic Research Discussion Paper 2068, April 2005.

Arnold, Jens, and Schwellnus, Cyrille, 'Do Corporate Taxes Reduce Productivity and Investment at the Firm Level? Cross-Country Evidence from the Amadeus Dataset', 2008.

Arnold, Jens, 'Do Tax Structures Affect Aggregate Economic Growth?' OECD Working Papers 643, October 2008.

Arpaia, Alfonso, et al., 'Labour Market Institutions and Labour Market Performance: A Survey of the Literature', European Commission Directorate-General for Economic and Financial Affairs, 2005.

Atkinson, A. B., 'Top Incomes in the United Kingdom over the Twentieth Century', University of Oxford Discussion Papers in Economic and Social History 43, January 2002.

Auerbach, Alan J., 'Measuring the Effects of Corporate Tax Cuts', *Journal of Economic Perspectives*, vol. 32, no. 4, Fall 2018, pp. 97–120.

Auerbach, Alan, 'Taxation and Capital Spending': paper prepared for the Academic Consultants' Meeting of the Board of Governors of the Federal Reserve System, 7 October 2005.

Auten, Gerald, et al., 'Reactions of High-Income Taxpayers to Major Tax Legislation', *National Tax Journal* 69 (4), December 2016, pp. 935–64.

Auten, Gerald, and Carroll, Robert, 'Effect of Income Tax on Household Income',*Review of Economics and Statistics*, vol. 81, no. 4, November 1999.

Barber, Anthony, *Taking the Tide: A Memoir*, Michael Russell, 1996.

Barro, Robert, and Furman, Jason, 'Macroeconomic Effects of the 2017 Tax Reform', Brookings Papers on Economic Activity, Spring 2018.

Bassanini, Andrea, and Duval, Romain, 'Employment Patterns in OECD Countries: Reassessing the Role of Policies and Institutions', OECD, June 2006.

Bassanini, Andrea, 'Job Protection Legislation and Productivity Growth in OECD Countries', IZA Institute for the Study of Labor Discussion Paper, June 2008.

Baumol, William, and Blinder, Alan, *Economics: principles and policy*, 1st ed. 1979, 12th ed. 2011.

Bentham, Jeremy, *Manual of Political Economy*, from *The Works of Jeremy Bentham*, vol. 3, edited by John Bowring, 1843.

Bergh, Andreas, and Karlsson, Martin, 'Government Size and Growth: Accounting for Economic Freedom and Globalisation', *Public Choice* 142 (1–2), March 2009.

Bergin, Tom, *Spills and Spin: The Inside Story of BP*, Random House Business, 2011.

Berle, Adolf A., Jr and Means, Gardiner C., *The Modern Corporation and Private Property*, Macmillan, 1933 (1st ed. 1932).

Berridge, Virginia, 'The Policy Response to the Smoking and Lung Cancer Connection in the 1950s and 1960s', *Historical Journal*, December 2006.

Bhargava, Sandeep, and Jenkinson, Tim, 'Explicit versus Implicit Profit Sharing and the Determination of Wages', March 1995.

Blair, Tony, *A Journey*, Hutchinson, 2010.

Blanchard, Olivier, and Perotti, Roberto, 'An empirical characterisation of the dynamic effects of changes in government spending and taxes on output', NBER Working Paper 7269.

Blundell, Richard, et al., 'Estimating labour supply responses using tax reforms', *Econometrica*, vol. 66, no. 4, July 1998.

Blundell, Richard, 'Tax Policy Reform: Why We Need Microeconomics', *Fiscal Studies*, August 1995.

Blundell, Richard, and Macurdy, Thomas, 'Labor Supply – Review of Alternative Approaches', 1999.

Bordo, Michael D., and White, Eugene N., 'British and French Finance during the Napoleonic Wars', NBER Working Paper, 1990.

Borjas, George J., 'The Relationship between Wages and Weekly Hours of Work: The Role of Division Bias', *Journal of Human Resources*, vol. 15, no. 3, Summer 1980, pp. 409–23.

Boskin, Michael J., 'Taxation, Saving and the Rate of Interest', *Journal of Political Economy*, April 1978.

Bourne, Ryan, and Shackleton, J. R., 'The Minimum Wage: Silver Bullet or Poisoned Chalice?', Institute of Economic Affairs, 2014.

Brisco, Norris A., *The Economic Policy of Robert Walpole*, Columbia University Press/Macmillan, 1907.

Brown, Gordon, *My Life, Our Times*, Bodley Head, 2017.

Brown, Charles, et al., 'The Effect of the Minimum Wage on Employment and Unemployment: A Survey', *Journal of Economic Literature*, June 1982.

Brown, Charles, et al., 'Time-Series Evidence of the Effect of the Minimum Wage on Youth Employment and Unemployment', *Journal of Human Resources*, vol. 18, no. 1, Winter, 1983.

Brownlee, W. Elliot, et al., eds, *The Political Economy of Transnational Tax Reform*, Cambridge University Press, 2013.

Brummer, Alex, *Hanson: A Biography*, Fourth Estate, 1994.

Burg, David F., *A World History of Tax Rebellions*, Routledge, 2004.

Bush, George W., *Decision Points*, Crown, 2010.

Canto, Victor A., 'The Revenue Effects of the Kennedy and Reagan Tax Cuts: Some Time Series Estimates', *Journal of Business & Economic Statistics*, vol. 4, no. 3, July 1986.

Cameron David, *For the Record*, Collins, 2019.

Carey, Maeve P., 'Methods of Estimating the Total Cost of Federal Regulations', Congressional Research Service report, January 2016.

Carlstrom, Charles T., and Gokhale, Jagadeesh, 'Government consumption, taxation and economic activity', *Federal Reserve Bank of Cleveland Economic Review*, February 1991.

Chetty, Raj, 'Is the Taxable Income Elasticity Sufficient to Calculate Deadweight Loss? The Implications of Evasion and Avoidance', *American Economic Journal: Economic Policy*, vol. 1, no. 2, August 2009.

Cherian, Samuel, 'The Investment Decision: A Re-Examination of Competing Theories Using Panel Data', World Bank Working Paper, 1996.

Cingano, Federico, et al., 'The Effect of Employment Protection Legislation and Financial Market Imperfections on Investment: Evidence from a Firm-Level Panel of EU Countries', IZA Institute for the Study of Labor Discussion Paper 4158, April 2009.

Clark, John Bates, *The Distribution of Wealth: A Theory of Wages, Interest and Profits*, Macmillan, 1899.

Clark, Peter, 'Tax Incentives and Equipment Investment', Brookings Papers on Economic Activity 1, 1993.

Clarke, Ken, *Kind of Blue: A Political Memoir*, Macmillan, 2016.

Clinton, Bill, *My Life*, Knopf, 2004.

Cole, Charles Woolsey, *Colbert and a Century of French Mercantilism*, vol. 2, Columbia University Press, 1939.

Congdon, William, et al., 'Behavioral Economics and Tax Policy', NBER Working Paper 15328, September 2009.

Congressional Budget Office, 'Labor Supply and Taxes', CBO Memorandum, January 1996.

Conyon, Martin, et al., 'Taking Care of Business: Executive Compensation in the United Kingdom', *Economic Journal*, vol. 105, no. 430, May 1995, pp. 704–14.

Cooper, Michael J., et al., 'Performance for pay? The relation between CEO incentive compensation and future stock price performance', SSRN, 2016.

Cournot, Augustin, *Recherches sur les Principes Mathématiques de la Théorie des Richesses*, Hachette, Paris, 1838.

Crandall, Robert, et al., *Regulating the Automobile*, Brookings Institution, Washington DC, 1986.

Crotty, James R., 'Neoclassical and Keynesian Approaches to the Theory of Investment', *Journal of Post-Keynesian Economics* 14:4 (1992), pp. 483–96.

Dalton, D.R., et al., 'Meta-analyses of Financial Performance and Equity: Fusion or Confusion?', *Academy of Management Journal*, 46, 2003, pp. 13–26.

Darling, Alistair, *Back from the Brink*, Atlantic, 2011.

Daunton, Martin, *Just Taxes: The Politics of Taxation in Britain, 1914-1979*, Cambridge University Press, 2002.

Davidmann, M., *Work, Remuneration and Motivation of Directors*, Social Organisation Ltd., 1970.

DeBacker, Jason, et al., 'Macroeconomic effects of a 10% cut in statutory marginal income tax rates on ordinary income', AEI Economics Working Papers, 2015.

De Mooij, Ruud, and Ederveen, Sjef, 'Corporate tax elasticities: a reader's guide to empirical findings', *Oxford Review of Economic Policy*, vol. 24, issue 4, 2008, 680–97.

Decker, Jefferson, *The Other Rights Revolution: Conservative Lawyers and the Remaking of American Government*, Oxford University Press, 2016.

Defina, A., et al., 'What is Reasonable Remuneration for Corporate Officers? An Empirical Investigation into the Relationship between Pay and Performance in the Largest Australian Companies', Company and Securities Law Journal, 12:6, September 1994, pp. 341–56.

Desai, Mihir A., and Goolsbee, Austan D., 'Investment, Overhang, and Tax Policy', Brookings Papers on Economic Activity 2, 2004, pp. 285–355.

Devereux, Michael P., and Griffith, Rachel, 'Taxes and the location of production: evidence from a panel of US multinationals', *Institute for Fiscal Studies*, 1998.

Devereux, Michael, 'Tax Asymmetries, the Cost of Capital and Investment: Some Evidence from United Kingdom Panel Data', *Economic Journal*, vol. 99, issue 395, April 1989.

Diamond, Peter, and Saez, Emmanuel, 'The Case for a Progressive Tax: From Basic Research to Policy Recommendations', *Journal of Economic Perspectives*, vol. 25, no. 4, Fall 2011.

Dickens, Richard, et al., 'The Effects of Minimum Wages on Employment: Theory and Evidence from the UK', NBER Working Paper, May 1994.

Djankov, Simeon, et al., 'The Effect of Corporate Taxes on Investment and Entrepreneurship', *American Economic Journal: Macroeconomics*, vol. 2, no. 3, July 2010, pp. 31–64.

Djankov, Simeon, et al., 'Regulation and Growth', World Bank, March 2006.

Domitrovic, Brian, *Econoclasts: The Rebels Who Sparked the Supply-Side Movement and Restored American Prosperity*, ISI Books, 2009.

Doorne van, Ellen, Hemerijck, Anton, and Knapen, Ben (eds), *Aftershocks: Economic Crisis and Institutional Choice*, Amsterdam University Press, 2009.

Douglas, Paul H., *The Theory of Wages*, Macmillan, 1934.

Dowell, Stephen, *History of Taxation and Taxes in England*, vols 1–4, Longmans Green, 1884–88.

Dube, Arindrajit, et al., 'Minimum Wage Effects Across State Borders: Estimates Using Contiguous Counties', *Review of Economics and Statistics*, vol. 92, no. 4, November 2010.

Dubroff, Harold, and Hellwig, Brant J., *The United States Tax Court: An Historical Analysis*, 2nd ed., US Government Printing Office, 1979.

Eads, George C., and Fix, Michael (eds), *The Reagan Regulatory Strategy: An Assessment*, Urban Institute Press, 1984.

Easterly, William, et al., 'How Do National Policies Affect Long-run Growth?', World Bank Discussion Papers, 1992.

Eccles, Mary, and Freeman, Richard B., 'What! Another Minimum Wage Study?', NBER Working Paper 878, 1982.

Edmans, Alex, et al., 'Executive Compensation: A Survey of Theory and Evidence', NBER Working Paper 23596, July 2017.

Engen, Eric M., and Skinner, Jonathan, 'Fiscal Policy and Economic Growth', NBER Working Paper, 1992.

European Commission DG Employment, Social Affairs and Inclusion Thematic Paper, 'Maximising the minimum: a review of minimum wage approaches and trends in European Member States', 2014.

Evers, Michiel, et al., 'The Wage Elasticity of Labour Supply: A Synthesis of Empirical Estimates', *De Economist* 156, no. 1, 2008.

Ezzamel, Mahmoud, and Watson, Kevin, 'Market comparison earnings and the bidding-up of executive cash compensation: Evidence from the United Kingdom', *Academy of Management Journal*, vol. 41, no. 2, Special Research Forum on Managerial Compensation and Firm Performance, April 1998.

Fabian Society, *Sweating: Its Cause and Remedy*, Fabian Tract 50, 1894.

Feenberg, Daniel, and Poterba, James, 'Income Inequality and the Incomes of Very High-Income Taxpayers: Evidence from Tax Returns', chapter in *Tax Policy and the Economy*, vol. 7, National Bureau of Economic Research, 1993.

Feldstein, Martin, and Elmendorf, Douglas W., 'Budget Deficits, Tax Incentives and Inflation: A Surprising Lesson from the 1983–4 Recovery', NBER Working Paper 2819, 1989.

Feldstein, Martin, and Feenberg, Daniel, 'The Effect of Increased Tax Rates on Taxable Income and Economic Efficiency: A Preliminary Analysis of the 1993 Tax Rate Increases', NBER Working Paper 5370, November 1995.

Fields, D. B., and Stanbury, W. T., 'Income Taxes and Incentives to Work: Some Additional Empirical Evidence', *American Economic Review*, vol. 61, issue 3, 1971, pp. 435–43.

Fisher, Irving, *The Theory of Interest, as Determined by Impatience to Spend Income and Opportunity to Invest it*, Macmillan, 1930.

Forte, Francesco, et al. (eds), *A Handbook of Alternative Theories of Public Economics*, Edward Elgar, 2015.

Foertsch, Tracy, 'Macroeconomic Impacts of Stylised Tax Cuts in an Intertemporal Computable General Equilibrium Model', Congressional Budget Office Technical Paper Series, August 2004.

Fölster, Stefan, and Henrekson, Magnus, 'Growth Effects of Government Expenditure and Taxation in Rich Countries', *European Economic Review*, vol. 45, no. 8, January 2001.

Frank, Robert H., and Cook, Philip J., *The Winner-Take-All Society: Why the Few at the Top Get So Much More Than the Rest of Us*, 1996.

Franke, George R., 'US cigarette demand, 1961–90', 'Econometric issues, evidence and implications', *Journal of Business Research*, vol. 30, issue 1, May 1994, pp. 33–41.

Freeman, Alida Castillo, and Freeman, Richard B., 'Minimum Wages in Puerto Rico: Textbook Case of a Wage Floor?', 1991.

Freeman, Richard B., 'Minimum Wages – Again!', *International Journal of Manpower*, vol. 15, nos 2–3, 1994.

Frydman, Carola, 'Rising through the ranks: the evolution of the market for corporate executives, 1936–2003', *Journal of Economic History*, January 2005.

Frydman, Carola, and Jenter, Dirk, 'CEO compensation', National Bureau of Economic Research, 2010.

Fuchs, Alan, et al., 'Is tobacco taxation regressive? Evidence on public health, domestic resource mobilisation, and equity improvements', World Bank Working Paper, 2019.

Fuchs, Victor R., Krueger, Alan B., and Poterba, James M., 'Why Do Economists Disagree About Policy? The Roles of Beliefs About Parameters and Values', Princeton University, Department of Economics, Industrial Relations Working Papers 768.

Gale, William, et al., 'Would a significant increase in the top income tax rate substantially alter income inequality?', *Economic Studies*, September 2015.

Gale, William, G., and Samwick, Andrew A., 'Effects of Income Tax Changes on Economic Growth', Economic Studies, Brookings Institution, September 2014.

Giertz, Seth H., Congressional Budget Office, 'The Elasticity of Taxable Income over the 1980s and 1990s', *National Tax Journal*, vol. LX, no. 4, December 2007.

Girardi, Daniele, 'Old and New Formulations of the Neoclassical Theory of Aggregate Investment: A Critical Review', Economics Department Working Paper Series 219, 2017.

Godfrey, L. G., *Theoretical and Empirical Aspects of the Effects of Taxation on the Supply of Labour*, OECD, 1975.

Godfrey, C., and Maynard, A., 'Economic aspects of tobacco use and taxation policy', *British Medical Journal*, July 1988.

Goolsbee, Austan, 'Evidence on the High-Income Laffer Curve from Six Decades of Tax Reform', Brookings Papers on Economic Activity 2, 1999.

Goolsbee, Austan, 'What Happens When You Tax the Rich? Evidence from Executive Compensation', Journal of Political Economy, vol. 108, no. 2, April 2000.

Gordon, M. J., 'The Neoclassical and a Post Keynesian Theory of Investment', *Journal of Post-Keynesian Economics*, 14:4, 1992, pp. 425–43.

Gravelle, Jennifer, 'Corporate Tax Incidence: Review of General Equilibrium Estimates', *National Tax Journal*, March 2013.

Gravelle, Jennifer, and Marples, Donald J., 'Tax Rates and Economic Growth', Congressional Research Service, January 2014.

Gravelle, Jane G., 'Behavioral feedback effects and the revenue-estimating process (A New Agenda – Old Constraints)', *National Tax Journal*, 1 September 1995.

Greenspan, Alan, *The Age of Turbulence*, Penguin, 2007.

Grossman, Philip J., 'Government and growth: Cross-sectional evidence', *Public Choice* 65, 1990, pp. 217–27.

Gruber, Jonathan, and Rauh, Joshua, 'How Elastic is the Corporate Income Tax Base?', June 2005.

Gruber, Jonathan, and Saez, Emmanuel, 'Elasticity of Taxable Income – Evidence and Implications', *Journal of Public Economics*, 84, 2002, pp. 1–32.

Gwartney, James, and Stroup, Richard, 'Labor Supply and Tax Rates: A Correction of the Record', *American Economic Review*, vol. 73, no. 3, June 1983, pp. 446–51.

Hanlon, Michelle, and Heitzman, Shane, 'A review of tax research', *Journal of Accounting and Economics*, September 2010.

Hansson, Par, and Henrekson, Magnus, 'A New Framework for Testing the Effect of Government Spending on Growth and Productivity', *Public Choice* 81, 1994.

Hantke-Domas, Michael, 'The Public Interest Theory of Regulation: Non-Existence or Misinterpretation?' *European Journal of Law and Economics*, 15, 2003, pp. 165–94.

Hausman, Jerry, 'Taxes and Labor supply', chapter 4 of *Handbook of Public Economics*, 1985.

Hausman, Jerry, 'Labor supply', in: Aaron, H. and Pechman, J. (eds), *How taxes effect economic activity*, Brookings Institution, Washington DC, 1981.

Hausman, Daniel M. (ed.), *The Philosophy of Economics: An Anthology*, 3rd ed., Cambridge University Press, 2008.

Harberger, Arnold C., 'Taxation, Resource Allocation, and Welfare'.

Hartwell, Ronald Max, 'Taxation in England During the Industrial Revolution', *Cato Journal*, vol. 1, no. 1, Spring 1981.

Hayo, Bernd, and Uhl, Matthias, 'The macroeconomic effects of legislated tax changes in Germany', *Oxford Economic Papers* 66, 2014, pp. 397–418.

Heath, Edward, *The Course of My Life: The Autobiography of Edward Heath*, Hodder & Stoughton, 1998.

Heckman, James, 'What Has Been Learned about Labor Supply in the Past Twenty Years?' Papers and Proceedings of the Hundred and Fifth Annual Meeting of the American Economic Association, *American Economic Review*, vol. 83, no. 2, May 1993), pp. 116–21.

Hill, Brian W., *Sir Robert Walpole*, Hamish Hamilton, 1989.

Hoffman, Steven J., et al., 'Cigarette consumption estimates for 71 countries from 1970 to 2015: systematic collection of comparable data to facilitate quasi-experimental evaluations of national and global tobacco control interventions', *British Medical Journal*, 19 June 2019.

Holland, Daniel M., 'The effect of taxation on effort: some results for business executives', *Tax impacts on compensation*, National Tax Association, 1969.

Holzmann, Robert, et al., 'Severance Pay Programs around the World: History, Rationale, Status, and Reforms', IZA Institute for the Study of Labor Discussion Paper 5731, May 2011.

Hoover, Herbert, *The Memoirs of Herbert Hoover*, vols II & III, Macmillan, 1951–2.

Horn, Martin, *Britain, France, and the Financing of the First World War*, McGill-Queen's University Press, 2002.

Howe, Geoffrey, *Conflict of Loyalty*, Pan, London, 1995.

Hungerford, Thomas, 'Taxes and the Economy: An Economic Analysis of the Top Tax Rates Since 1945', 2012.

Hungerford, Thomas, 'Changes in Income Inequality Among US Tax Filers between 1991 and 2006: The Role of Wages, Capital Income, and Taxes'.

Innes, A. D., *A History of the British Nation*, T. C .Jack & E. C. Jack, London, 1912.

Irwin, Douglas A., 'Political Economy and Peel's Repeal of The Corn Laws', *Economics and Politics* 0954-1985, vol. I, no. 1, Spring 1989.

Jackson, Walter A., *Gunnar Myrdal and America's Conscience*, University of North Carolina University Press, Chapel Hill, 1990.

James, Simon, and Nobes, Christopher, *Economics of Taxation*, 2nd ed., Philip Allan, 1983.

Jevons, W. Stanley, *The Coal Question*, Macmillan, 1865.

Jevons, W. Stanley, *Theory of Political Economy*, Macmillan, 1888.

Johansson, Asa, 'Tax and Economic Growth', OECD Working Paper 620, 2008.

Kahn, Alfred Edward, *The Economics of Regulation: Principles and Institutions*, John Wiley, New York, 1970.

Keane, Michael, and Rogerson, Richard, 'Micro and Macro Labor Supply Elasticities: A Reassessment of Conventional Wisdom', *Journal of Economic Literature* 50:2, 2012, pp. 464–76.

Keynes, John Maynard, *The General Theory of Employment, Interest, and Money*, Macmillan, 1936.

Killingsworth, Mark R., *Labour Supply*, Cambridge University Press, 1983.

Kimball, Miles, 'Labor Supply: Are the Income and Substitution Effects Both Large or Both Small?' NBER Working Paper, August 2008.

King, Mervyn A., and Fullerton, Don, 'The Taxation of Income from Capital: A Comparative Study of the United States, the United Kingdom, Sweden, and Germany', NBER Working Paper, 1983.

King Robert G., and Rebelo, Sergio, 'Public Policy and Economic Growth; Developing Neoclassical Implications', NBER Working Paper, 1990.

Kormendi, Roger, and Koester, Reinhard, 'Taxation, Aggregate Activity and Economic Growth: Cross-Country Evidence on Some Supply-Side Hypotheses', *Economic Inquiry*, July 1989.

Kosters, Marvin H., *The Effects of the Minimum Wage on Employment*, American Enterprise Institute Press, 1996.

Kramer, Samuel Noah, *The Sumerians: Their History, Culture, and Character*, University of Chicago Press, 1963.

Kruger, Alan, and Card, David, *Myth and Measurement*, Princeton University Press, 1995.

Lamont, Norman, *In Office*, Little, Brown, 1989.

Lawson, Nigel, *The View from No. 11: Memoirs of a Tory Radical*, Bantam Press, 1992.

Lefeber, Louis, 'Classical vs Neoclassical Economic Thought in Historical Perspective: The Interpretation of Processes of Economic Growth and

Development', 'STATES AND SOCIETIES: Essays presented to Neal Wood', *History of Political Thought*, vol. 21, no. 3, Autumn 2000, pp. 525–42.

Leman, Nicholas, *Transaction Man*, Farrar, Straus and Giroux, 2019.

Leonard, Thomas C., 'The Very Idea of Applying Economics: The Modern Minimum-Wage Controversy and Its Antecedents', *History of Political Economy*, 2000.

LeRoy, Greg, *The Great American Jobs Scam: Corporate Tax Dodging and the Myth of Job Creation*, Berrett-Koehler, 2005.

Lewis, Alan, 'Social Psychology of Taxation', *British Journal of Social Psychology*, 1982.

Lester, Richard A., 'Employment Effects of Minimum Wages', *Industrial and Labour Relations Review*, January 1960.

Levine, Ross, and Renelt, David, 'Cross-Country Studies of Growth and Policy: Methodological, Conceptual, and Statistical Problems', World Bank Working Paper, March 1991.

Levine, Ross, and Renelt, David, 'A Sensitivity Analysis of Cross-Country Growth Regressions', 1992.

Lewis, Russell, 'Wages need no councils', Centre for Policy Studies, 1984.

Lindbeck, Assar, 'Tax Effect Versus Budget Effects on Labor Supply', *Economic Inquiry*, October 1982.

Lindsey, Lawrence B., 'Taxpayer Behavior and the Distribution of the 1982 Tax Cut', NBER Working Paper 1760, October 1985.

Lindsey, Lawrence B., 'Individual Taxpayer Response to Tax Cuts: 1982–84 with Implications for the Revenue-Maximizing Tax Rate', *Journal of Public Economics* 33, 1987.

Litan, Robert E., and Nordhaus, William D., *Reforming Federal Regulation*, Yale University Press, 1983.

Locke, John, *Some Considerations of the Consequences of the Lowering of Interest and the Raising the Value of Money*, from *The Works of John Locke*, 1824 edition (first published 1691).

Lowenstein, Roger, *Buffett: The Making of an American Capitalist*, Random House, 1995.

Lyon, Andrew, and Schwab, Robert M., 'Consumption Taxes in a Life-Cycle Framework: Are Sin Taxes Regressive?', NBER Working Paper 3932, 1991.

Machin, Stephen, and Manning, Alan, 'The Effects of Minimum Wages on Wage Dispersion and Employment: Evidence from the UK Wages Councils', *ILR Review*, vol. 47, issue 2, 1994.

MaCurdy, Thomas, et al., 'Assessing Empirical Approaches for Analyzing Taxes and Labor Supply', *Journal of Human Resources*, vol. 25, no. 3, Summer 1990.

Machlup, Fritz, 'Marginal Analysis and Empirical Research', *American Economic Review*, vol. 36, no. 4, September 1946, pp. 519–54.

Mackenzie, Donald, *An Engine, Not a Camera: How Financial Models Shape Markets*, MIT Press, 2006.

Major, John, *John Major: The Autobiography*, HarperCollins, 1999.

Mankiw, N. Gregory, *Principles of Microeconomics*, 5th ed., South-Western Cengage Learning, 2008.

Manley, Thomas, *Usury at Six Per Cent*, 1669.

Manning, Alan, 'Top rate of income tax', Centre for Economic Performance, London School of Economics and Political Science, 2015.

Marlow, Michael L., 'Private sector shrinkage and the growth of industrialised economies: Reply', *Public Choice*, vol. 58, 1988.

Marshall, Alfred, *Principles of Economics*, 8th ed., Palgrave Macmillan, 1920 (first published 1890).

McCloskey, Donald N., *The Applied Theory of Price*, Macmillan, 1985.

McClelland, Robert, and Mok, Shannon, 'A Review of Recent Research on Labor Supply Elasticities', Congressional Budget Office Working Paper, October 2012.

Meghir, C., and Phillips, D., 'Labour Supply and Taxes', in 'Tax by Design', *Mirrlees Review*, Institute for Fiscal Studies, 2010.

Mellon, Andrew W., *Taxation: The People's Business*, Macmillan, 1924.

Mertens, Karel, and Ravn, Morten O., 'The Dynamic Effects of Personal and Corporate Income Tax Changes in the United States', *American Economic Review*, vol. 103, no. 4, June 2013.

Mill, John Stuart, *Principles of Political Economy*, Longmans Green & Co, 1920 (originally published 1848).

Miller, Helen, and Pope, Thomas, 'Corporate Tax Changes under the UK Coalition Government (2010–15)', *Fiscal Studies*, September 2015.

Miller, Roger LeRoy, *Economics Today*, 16th ed., Addison-Wesley, 2012.

'Report of the Minimum Wage Study Commission', Washington, DC, 1981.

Mitchell, Daniel J., 'A Victory for the Laffer Curve, a Defeat for England's Economy', Cato Institute blog, April 2011.

Monks Partnership Ltd, *Incentives for management 1993: A guide to incentive practice for directors and snr managers*, Saffron Walden Monks Partnership Ltd, 1993.

Morgan, James N., et al., 'A Survey of the Investment Management and Working Behavior among High-Income Individuals', *American Economic Review*, vol. 55, no. 1-2, 1 March 1965.

Morley, John, *Walpole*, Macmillan, 1913 (originally published 1890).

Mossin, Jan, 'Taxation and Risk-Taking: An Expected Utility Approach', *Economica*, New Series, vol. 35, no. 137, February 1968.

Mundell, Robert, 'A Reconsideration of the Twentieth Century', *American Economic Review*, vol. 90, no. 3, p 333.

Murnane, M. Susan, 'Selling Scientific Taxation: The Treasury Department's Campaign for Tax Reform in the 1920s', *Law and Social Inquiry*, vol. 29, no. 4, 2004, pp. 819–56.

Murphy, Kevin J., 'Executive compensation', from *Handbook of Labor Economics*, vol. 3, chapter 38, Elsevier, 1999.

Myles, Gareth D., 'Economic Growth and the Role of Taxation Theory,' OECD Economics Department Working Papers 713, OECD Publishing, 2009.

Myrdal, Gunnar, *An American Dilemma*, Harper, 1944.

Nelson, Robert H., *Economics as Religion from Samuelson to Chicago and Beyond*, Pennsylvania State University Press, 2001.

Neumark, David, and Wascher, William L., *Minimum Wages*, MIT Press, 2008.

Neumark, David, 'Employment effects of minimum wages', IZA, 2015.

Nickell, S. J., 'Fixed Costs, Employment and Labour Demand over the Cycle', *Economica*, New Series, vol. 45, no. 180, November 1978.

Padovano, Fabio, and Galli, Emma, 'Tax rates and economic growth in the OECD countries (1950–90)', *Economic Inquiry*, vol. 39, issue 1, January 2001.

Pearce, Edward, *The Great Man: Sir Robert Walpole: Scoundrel, Genius and Britain's First Prime Minister*, Jonathan Cape, 2007.

Peltzman, Sam, *Regulation of Automobile Safety*, Washington American Enterprise Institute for Public Policy Research, 1975.

Peltzman, Sam, 'The Effects of Automobile Safety Regulation', *Journal of Political Economy*, vol. 83, no. 4, August 1975.

Pencavel, John, 'Labor Supply of Men: A Survey', in Ashenfelter, O., and Layard, R. (eds), *Handbook of Labor Economics*, vol. I, Elsevier Science Publishers BV, 1986.

Picot, Georg, and Tassinari, Arianna, 'All of one kind? Labour market reforms under austerity in Italy and Spain', *Socio-Economic Review*, vol. 15, issue 2, April 2017.

Posner, Richard A., *Public intellectuals*, Harvard University Press, 2003.

Poterba, James M., and Summers, Lawrence H., 'A CEO Survey of US Companies' Time Horizons and Hurdle Rates', *Sloan Management Review*, vol. 37, no. 1, Fall 1995, pp. 43–53.

'Workplace Relations Framework', Productivity Commission (Australia), 2015.

Rand, Ayn, *Ayn Rand's Marginalia*, Second Renaissance Books, 1995.

Rees, J. F., *A Short Fiscal and Financial History of England 1815–1918*, Routledge, 2017.

Ricardo, David, *On the Principles of Political Economy and Taxation*, John Murray, 1819.

Radcliffe, Cyril, *The Committee on the Working of the Monetary System Report*, 1959.

Raworth, Kate, *Doughnut Economics*, Random House, 2017.

Rebelo, Sergio, 'Long-Run Policy Analysis and Long-Run Growth', NBER Working Paper 3325, April 1990.

Richardson, Joseph, *A Complete Investigation of Mr Eden's Treaty, as It May Affect the Commerce, the Revenue, or the General Policy of Great Britain*, J. Debrett, 1787.

Roed, Knut, and Strom, Steinar, 'Progressive taxes and the labour market: is the trade-off between equality and efficiency inevitable?', *Journal of Economic Surveys*, vol. 16, no.1, 2002.

Romer, Christina, and Romer, David, 'Do Tax Cuts Starve the Beast? The Effect of Tax Changes on Government Spending', Brookings Papers on Economic Activity, Spring 2009.

Rubin, Robert, and Weisberg, Jacob, *In an Uncertain World: Tough Choices from Wall Street to Washington*, Random House, 2003.

Rudd, Kevin, *Not for the Faint-hearted: A Personal Reflection on Life, Politics and Purpose 1957–*, Pan Macmillan, 2017.

Saez, Emmanuel, and Zucman, Gabriel, *The Triumph of Injustice – How the Rich Dodge Taxes and How to Make Them Pay*, W. W. Norton, 2019.

Saez, Emmanuel, 'Using Elasticities to Derive Optimal Income Tax Rates', *Review of Economic Studies*, 2001.

Saez, Emmanuel, et al., 'The Elasticity of Taxable Income with Respect to Marginal Tax Rates: A Critical Review', *Journal of Economic Literature*, 2012.

Samuelson, Paul A., and Nordhaus, William D., *Economics*, 19th ed., McGraw-Hill, 2009.

Sargeant, Arthur John, *The Economic Policy of Colbert*, Batoche Books, 2004.

Saunders, Peter, 'Private sector shrinkage and the growth of industrialised economies: Comment', *Public Choice*, vol. 58, issue 3, September 1988, pp 277–84.

Sergeant, Lewis, *William Pitt*, William Isbister, 1882.

Scheve, Kenneth, and Stasavage, David, 'The Conscription of Wealth: Mass Warfare and the Demand for Progressive Taxation', *International Organization* 64, Fall 2010, pp 529–61.

Schmiechen, James A., *Sweated Industries and Sweated Labor: The London Clothing Trade 1860-1914*, Croom Helm, 1984.

Schmitt, John, 'Why Does the Minimum Wage Have No Discernible Effect on Employment?' Center for Economic and Policy Research, Washington DC, 2013.

Schwellnus, Cyrille, and Arnold, Jens, 'Do corporate taxes produce productivity and investment at the firm level? Cross-country evidence from the Amadeus dataset', OECD Economics Department Working Paper 641, September 2008.

Simpson, R. David, 'Do regulators overestimate the costs of regulation?', *Journal of Benefit Cost Analysis* 5(2), 2014, pp. 315–32.

Sinclair, Barbara, *Party Wars: Polarization and the Politics of National Policy-Making*, University of Oklahoma Press, 2006.

Slemrod, Joel, 'Do Taxes Matter? Lessons from the 1980s', Papers and Proceedings of the Hundred and Fourth Annual Meeting of the American Economic Association, *American Economic Review*, vol. 82, no. 2, May 1992.

Slemrod, Joel, 'What Do Cross-Country Studies Teach about Government Involvement, Prosperity, and Economic Growth?' 1995.

Slemrod, Joel (ed.), *Does Atlas Shrug? The economic consequences of taxing the rich*, Russell Sage Foundation, 2000.

Slemrod, Joel (ed), *Taxing Corporate Income in the 21st Century*, Cambridge University Press, 2007.

Smith, Adam, *An Inquiry into the Nature and Causes of the Wealth of Nations*, 1776.

Smith, David, et al., *Plucking the Goose-Tax from Great War to the Digital Age*, LexisNexis UK, 2016.

Smith, J., 'That elusive elasticity and the ubiquitous bias: is panel data a panacea?', Bank of England Working Paper 342, 2008.

Sorensen, Peter Birch, 'Changing Views of the Corporate Income Tax', *National Tax Journal* 48, no. 2, June 1995, pp. 279–94.

'Work and Remuneration of Directors', Social Research Development Ltd, 1968.

Stasavage, David, and Scheve, Kenneth F., *Taxing the Rich: A History of Fiscal Fairness in the United States and Europe*, Princeton University Press, 2016.

Stigler, George J., *The Theory of Price*, Macmillan, 1947, 1952 and 1966.

Stigler, George J., *Memoirs of an Unregulated Economist*, University of Chicago Press, 2003.

Tanzi, Vito, and Schuknecht, Ludger, *Public Spending in the 20th Century – A Global Perspective*, Cambridge University Press, 2000.

Stiglitz, J. E., 'The Effects of Income, Wealth, and Capital Gains Taxation on Risk-Taking', *Quarterly Journal of Economics*, vol. 83, issue 2, May 1969.

Tansel, Aysit, 'Cigarette demand, health scares and education in Turkey', *Applied Economics*, 1993, pp. 521–9.

Tempalski, Jerry, 'Revenue Effects of Major US Tax Bills', US Department of Treasury, 2006.

Tenreyro, Silvana, External MPC Member, Bank of England, 'Models in macroeconomics', speech given at the University of Surrey, Guildford, 4 June 2018.

Thaler, Richard H., and Sunstein, Cass R., *Nudge: Improving Decisions About Health, Wealth and Happiness*, Penguin, 2009.

Thatcher, Margaret, *Margaret Thatcher: The Autobiography,* Harper Press, 2013.

Thies, Clifford F., 'The First Minimum Wage Laws', *Cato Journal*, Winter 1991.

Thorndike, Joseph J., *Their Fair Share: Taxing the Rich in the Age of FDR*, Urban Institute Press, 2013.

Tosi, Henry, et al., 'How Much Does Performance Matter? A Meta-Analysis of CEO Pay Studies', *Journal of Management*, vol. 26, no 2, 2000.

Townsend, Joy, 'Price and consumption of tobacco', *British Medical Bulletin*, 1996.

Trabandt, Mathias, and Uhlig, Harald, 'The Laffer Curve revisited', *Journal of Monetary Economics*, vol. 58, issue 4, pp. 305–27.

Trabandt, Mathias, and Uhlig, Harald, 'How Do Laffer Curves Differ Across Countries?', Board of Governors of the Federal Reserve System International Finance Discussion Papers 1048, May 2012.

Triest, Robert K., 'The Effect of Income Taxation on Labor Supply in the United States', Special Issue on Taxation and Labor Supply in Industrial Countries, *Journal of Human Resources*, vol. 25, no. 3, Summer 1990.

Trollope, Anthony, *Lord Palmerston*, William Isbister, 1882.

Trudeau, Pierre Elliott, *Memoirs*, McClelland & Stewart, 1993.

Tucker, Garland S., *Conservative Heroes*, Wilmington ISI Books, 2015.

UK Department for Environment, Food & Rural Affairs, 'Emerging Findings from Defra's Regulation Assessment: First update covering 2012', February 2015.

Ulrich, Alexander, 'The easy fire and easy hire', Adam Smith Institute, 24 December 2009.

Underhill, H. Fabian, 'The Incidence of Payroll Taxes', *Quarterly Journal of Economics*, vol. 57, no. 1, November 1942).

US Dept of Treasury, 'A Dynamic Analysis of Permanent Extension of the President's Tax Relief', Office of Tax Analysis, US Department of the Treasury, 2006.

Vernon-Harcourt, Tony, *Rewarding Top Management*, Gower, 1980.

Vernon-Harcourt, Tony, *Director's Remuneration*, Charterhouse Study, Monks Publications, 1983.

Wanniski, Jude, 'The Mundell-Laffer Hypothesis – a new view of the world economy', *The Public Interest*, Spring 1975.

Wanniski, Jude, *The Way the World Works: How Economies Fail – and Succeed*, Basic Books, 1978.

Weidenbaum, Murray, *Government-mandated Price Increases: A Neglected Aspect of Inflation*, AEI Press, 1975.

Welch, Finis, *Minimum Wage Legislation in the United States*, Rand Corporation, 1973.

Whibley, Charles, *William Pitt*, William Blackwood & Sons, 1906.

Zelizer Julian, E., *Taxing America: Wilbur D. Mills, Congress, and the State, 1945-1975*, Cambridge University Press, 1999.

Zimring, Franklin E., and Nelson, William, 'Cigarette taxes as cigarette policy', *British Medical Journal* Tobacco Control, 1995.

INDEX